Practicing Intertextuality

Practicing Intertextuality

Ancient Jewish and Greco-Roman Exegetical
Techniques in the New Testament

EDITED BY
Max J. Lee and B. J. Oropeza

CASCADE *Books* · Eugene, Oregon

PRACTICING INTERTEXTUALITY
Ancient Jewish and Greco-Roman Exegetical Techniques in the New Testament

Copyright © 2021 Wipf and Stock Publishers. All rights reserved. Except for brief quotations in critical publications or reviews, no part of this book may be reproduced in any manner without prior written permission from the publisher. Write: Permissions, Wipf and Stock Publishers, 199 W. 8th Ave., Suite 3, Eugene, OR 97401.

Cascade Books
An Imprint of Wipf and Stock Publishers
199 W. 8th Ave., Suite 3
Eugene, OR 97401

www.wipfandstock.com

PAPERBACK ISBN: 978-1-7252-7438-9
HARDCOVER ISBN: 978-1-7252-7439-6
EBOOK ISBN: 978-1-7252-7440-2

Cataloguing-in-Publication data:

Names: Lee, Max J., editor. | Oropeza, B. J., editor.

Title: Practicing intertextuality : ancient Jewish and Greco-Roman exegetical techniques in the New Testament / edited by Max J. Lee and B. J. Oropeza.

Description: Eugene, OR: Cascade Books, 2021 | Includes bibliographical references and index.

Identifiers: ISBN 978-1-7252-7438-9 (paperback) | ISBN 978-1-7252-7439-6 (hardcover) | ISBN 978-1-7252-7440-2 (ebook)

Subjects: LCSH: Bible. New Testament—Relation to the Old Testament. | Intertextuality. | Bible—Criticism, interpretation, etc. | Greek literature, Hellenistic—History and criticism. | Rabbinical literature—History and criticism.

Classification: BS511.2 P73 2021 (print) | BS511.2 (ebook)

Contents

Contributors | vii
Abbreviations | ix
Preface | xv

Part I: Interactions, Intertextuality, and Readership in Greco-Roman Antiquity and Early Christian Discourse

1 A Taxonomy of Intertextual Interactions Practiced by NT Authors: An Introduction—*Max J. Lee* | 3
2 Quotations, Allusions, and Echoes: Their Meanings in Relation to Biblical Interpretation—*B. J. Oropeza* | 17
3 Intertextuality in Pompeian Plaster: Can Vesuvian Artifacts Inform Our Expectations about Intertextual Expertise among Early Jesus-Followers?—*Bruce W. Longenecker* | 27
4 Paul's Multi-Layered Use of Scripture: Taking Intertextuality One Step Further—*Konrad Otto* | 43
5 Intertextuality and Exegetical Techniques in Hebrews—*Susan Docherty* | 59

Part II: Practicing Intertextuality in the Gospels

6 The Church's One Foundation? Peter as the Messianic Temple Stone in Matt 16:18—*Bruce Henning* | 77
7 Scriptural Allusion and Bodily Age in Luke 1–2: Narrativizing Theological Continuity through Allusive Characterization and Plotting—*Julie Newberry* | 91

8 Vision and Re-Envision: Re-Tracing the Social Justice Relationship between Hannah's and Mary's Songs—*Alice Yafeh-Deigh and Federico A. Roth* | 109

Part III: Practicing Intertextuality in the Pauline Letters

9 "Consecrated by the Brother/Sister": The Norm of Religious Endogamy and Paul's Alternative in 1 Cor 7:14—*Judith M. Gundry* | 131
10 Negotiating Piety: Epicureans, Corinthian Knowers, and Paul on Idols and Idol Food in 1 Cor 8–10—*Max J. Lee* | 148
11 The Corporate Σῶμα in Epictetus and Paul —*Michael M. C. Reardon* | 167
12 Paul: Theologian, Historian, or Something Else?—*Rikk Watts* | 186

Part IV: Practicing Intertextuality in the General Letters

13 Precedents for Prosopological Exegesis and Features of Its Use in the Epistle to the Hebrews—*Madison N. Pierce* | 209
14 Humor in Hebrews: Rhetoric of the *Ridiculus* in the Example of Esau—*Jason A. Whitlark and Jon-Michael Carman* | 225
15 Intertextuality beyond Echoes: Cain and Abel in the Second Temple Jewish Cultural Context—*Ryder A. Wishart* | 246
16 Intertextual Echoes in Ephesus: "From the Beginning" in the City of Ephesus and the Letters of John—*Paul Trebilco* | 267

Bibliography | 289
Index of Subjects | 325
Index of Modern Authors | 328
Index of Ancient Sources | 336

Contributors

Jon-Michael Carman is a doctoral candidate in the Religion Department at Baylor University in Waco, Texas.

Susan Docherty is Professor of New Testament and Early Judaism at Newman University in Birmingham, United Kingdom.

Judith M. Gundry is Research Scholar and Associate Professor (Adjunct) of New Testament at Yale Divinity School in New Haven, Connecticut.

Bruce Henning is Professor of Bible and Theology at Emmaus Bible College in Dubuque, Iowa.

Max J. Lee is Professor of New Testament at North Park Theological Seminary in Chicago, Illinois.

Bruce W. Longenecker is Professor of Christian Origins and the W. W. Melton Chair of Religion at Baylor University in Waco, Texas.

Julie Newberry is Assistant Professor of New Testament at Wheaton College in Wheaton, Illinois.

B. J. Oropeza is Professor of Biblical and Religious Studies at Azusa Pacific University and Seminary in Azusa, California.

Konrad Otto is a Vikar of the Evangelical Church in Germany and until 2019 was a research fellow in the Collaborative Research Centre for Education and Religion at Georg-August-Universität Göttingen.

Madison N. Pierce is Assistant Professor of New Testament at Trinity Evangelical Divinity School in Deerfield, Illinois.

Michael M. C. Reardon is Academic Dean and Professor of Biblical Languages and Religious Thought at Canada Christian College in Whitby, Ontario, Canada.

Federico A. Roth is Professor of Biblical Studies at Azusa Pacific University in Azusa, California.

Paul Trebilco is Professor of New Testament at the University of Otago in Dunedin, New Zealand.

Rikk Watts is Research Professor of New Testament at Regent College, Vancouver, British Columbia, Canada.

Jason A. Whitlark is Professor of New Testament at Baylor University in Waco, Texas.

Ryder A. Wishart is a doctoral candidate in theology at McMaster Divinity College in Hamilton, Ontario, Canada.

Alice Yafeh-Deigh is Professor of Biblical and Religious Studies at Azusa Pacific University in Azusa, California.

Abbreviations

AB	Anchor Bible
ABR	*Australian Biblical Review*
ABRL	Anchor Bible Reference Library
AE	*Année épigraphique*
AGJU	Arbeiten zur Geschichte des antiken Judentums und des Urchristentums
AJA	*American Journal of Archaeology*
AOTC	Abingdon Old Testament Commentaries
AnBib	Analecta Biblica
ANRW	*Aufstieg und Niedergang der römischen Welt.* Ed by H. Temporini and W. Haase. New York: De Gruyter, 1972–
AnSt	*Anatolian Studies*
Apoc. John	*The Apochryphon of John*
ArBib	The Aramaic Bible
AS	*Aramaic Studies*
AUS	American University Studies
BBR	*Bulletin for Biblical Research*
BBRSup	*Bulletin for Biblical Research, Supplements*
BDAG	Bauer, Walter, F. W. Danker, W. F. Arndt, and F. W. Gingrich. *Greek-English Lexicon of the New Testament and Other Early Christian Literature.* 3rd ed. Chicago: University of Chicago Press, 2000.

BDF	Blass, Friedrich, Albert Debrunner, and Robert W. Funk. *A Greek Grammar of the New Testament and Other Early Christian Literature*. Chicago: University of Chicago Press, 1961
BECNT	Baker Exegetical Commentary on the New Testament
Bib	*Biblica*
BibInt	*Biblical Interpretation*
BibInt	Biblical Interpretation Series
BJS	Brown Judaic Studies
BT	*The Bible Translator*
BTB	*Biblical Theology Bulletin*
BThSt	Biblisch-theologische Studien
BHT	Beitrage zur historischen Theologie
BZNW	Beihefte zur Zeitschrift für die neutestamentliche Wissenschaft
CBQ	*Catholic Biblical Quarterly*
CErc	*Cronache Ercolanesi*
CIL	*Corpus Inscriptionum Latinarum*. Berlin, 1862–
CJT	*Canadian Journal of Theology*
CTM	*Concordia Theological Monthly*
CTR	*Criswell Theological Review*
CurBR	*Currents in Biblica Research*
CurBS	*Currents in Research: Biblical Studies*
CurTM	*Currents in Theology and Mission*
DRev	*Downside Review*
ECL	Early Christianity and Its Literature
EKK	Evangelisch-katholischer Kommentar zum Neuen Testament
FAT	Forschungen zum Alten Testament
FRLANT	Forschungen zur Religion und Literatur des Alten und Neuen Testaments
GBS	Guides to Biblical Scholarship
GELS	*A Greek-English Lexicon of the Septuagint*. Takamitsu Muraoka. Leuven: Peeters, 2009

Greg	*Gregorianum*
HNT	Handbuch zum Neuen Testament
HNTC	Harper's New Testament Commentaries
HTR	*Harvard Theological Review*
HUT	Hermeneutische Untersuchungen zur Theologie
Hyp. Arch	*The Hypostasis of the Archons*
IBC	Interpretation: A Bible Commentary for Teaching and Preaching
IBS	*Irish Biblical Studies*
ICC	International Critical Commentary
IEph	Wankel, Hermann, et al., eds. *Die Inschriften von Ephesos*. 8 vols. in 11. Inschriften griechischer Städte aus Kleinasien 11–17. Bonn: Habelt, 1979–84.
IJCT	*International Journal of the Classical Tradition*
Int	*Interpretation*
JAAR	*Journal of the American Academy of Religion*
JBL	*Journal of Biblical Literature*
JETS	*Journal of the Evangelical Theological Society*
JGRChJ	*Journal of Greco-Roman Christianity and Judaism*
JSJ	*Journal for the Study of Judaism in the Persian, Hellenistic, and Roman Periods*
JSNT	*Journal for the Study of the New Testament*
JSNTSup	Journal for the Study of the New Testament: Supplement Series
JSOT	*Journal for the Study of the Old Testament*
JTS	*Journal of Theological Studies*
KEK	Kritisch-exegetischer Kommentar über das Neue Testament (Meyer-Kommentar)
LCL	Loeb Classical Library
LHBOTS	The Library of Hebrew Bible/Old Testament Studies
LNTS	Library of New Testament Studies
LSJ	Liddell, H. G., R. Scott, and H. S. Jones. *A Greek-English Lexicon*. 9th ed. Oxford: Clarendon, 1996.

NAC	New American Commentary
NCBC	New Cambridge Bible Commentary
Neot	*Neotestamentica*
NIB	*The New Interpreter's Bible*
NICNT	New International Commentary on the New Testament
NICOT	New International Commentary on the Old Testament
NIDNTTE	*New International Dictionary of New Testament Theology and Exegesis.* 4 vols. Ed. by M. Silva. Grand Rapids: Zondervan, 2014.
NIGTC	New International Greek Testament Commentary
NovT	*Novum Testamentum*
NovTSup	Novum Testamentum Supplements
NTD	Das Neue Testament Deutsch
NTL	New Testament Library
NTS	*New Testament Studies*
PNTC	Pillar New Testament Commentaries
PRSt	*Perspectives in Religious Studies*
RB	*Revue biblique*
RBS	Resources for Biblical Study (SBL)
RIC	Mattingly, H., E. A. Sydenham, et al., *Roman Imperial Coinage* (1923–67); rev. ed. of vol. 1 only, C. H. V. Sutherland and R. A. G. Carson (1984)
SBL	Society of Biblical Literature
SBLDS	Society of Biblical Literature Septuagint Dissertation Series
SE	*Studia evangelica*
SEÅ	*Svensk exegetisk årsbok*
SHR	Studies in the History of Religions (supplement to Numen)
SJT	*Scottish Journal of Theology*
SNTSMS	Society for New Testament Studies Monograph Series
SNTW	Studies of the New Testament and Its World

SP	Sacra Pagina
SPhiloM	Studia Philonica Monograph Series
SR	*Studies in Religion*
SSEJC	Studies in Scripture in Early Judaism and Christianity
StBibLit	Studies in Biblical Literature (Lang)
STDJ	Studies on the Texts of the Desert of Judah
Str-B	Strack, H. L., and P. Billerbeck. *Kommentar zum Neuen Testament aus Talmud und Midrasch*. 6 vols. Munich: C. H. Beck, 1922–61.
SymS	Symposium Series
TANZ	Texte und Arbeiten zum neutestamentlichen Zeitalter
TBN	Themes in Biblical Narrative
TBT	*The Bible Today*
TDNT	*Theological Dictionary of the New Testament*. 10 vols. Ed. by G. Kittel and G. Friedrich. Trans. by G. W. Bromiley. Grand Rapids: Eerdmans, 1964–76.
TENTS	Texts and Editions for New Testament Study
Text	*Textus*
TJ	*Trinity Journal*
TLZ	*Theologische Literaturzeitung*
TNTC	Tyndale New Testament Commentaries
TSAJ	Texte und Studien zum antiken Judentum
TWNT	*Theologische Wörterbuch zum Neuen Testament*. 10 vols. Ed. by G. Kittel and G. Friedrich. Stuttgart: Kohlhammer, 1932–79.
TynBul	*Tyndale Bulletin*
WBC	Word Biblical Commentary
WGRW	Writings from the Greco-Roman World
WGRWSup	Writings from the Greco-Roman World Supplement Series
WTJ	*Westminster Theological Journal*

WUNT	Wissenschaftliche Untersuchungen zum Neuen Testament
ZNW	*Zeitschrift für die neutestamentliche Wissenschaft und die Kunde der älteren Kirche*
ZPE	*Zeitschrift für Papyrologie und Epigraphik*

Preface

THIS COLLECTION OF ESSAYS is the second of an ongoing series sponsored by the Intertextuality in the New Testament (INT) Section at the annual meeting of the Society of Biblical Literature. In this series, past papers in the session programming of INT have been further revised by their authors for publication in a single volume. The editors also commissioned some select new essays.

The first volume of essays was published in 2016 under the title *Exploring Intertextuality* and was edited by B. J. Oropeza and Steve Moyise. It focused on the diverse intertextual methods employed by biblical scholars to interpret NT texts. This second volume—entitled *Practicing Intertextuality*—publishes select papers since 2016 and a few newly invited essays. It describes how the NT authors employ ancient Jewish and Greco-Roman exegetical techniques in the process and production of early Christian discourse.

The NT writers cite, quote, and allude to the body of sacred texts traditionally known as the "Old Testament"—or alternatively called the "First Testament" or "Jewish Scriptures." They also interact with the interpretative traditions of their fellow Jewish contemporaries and the religious, political, social, and moral tenets of the wider Greco-Roman world. This volume seeks to map out how NT authors interpreted other bodies of discourse, and it suggests an initial taxonomy of intertextual practices. We editors hope that the essays will collectively help both the scholar and the student appreciate how the very process of intertextuality contributes to the meaning and composition of the New Testament.

The readers of this book can access its content in one of two ways. They can either selectively choose the essays that pique their individual interests, or they can get an overall sense of the essays' collective aims by reading along a recommended sequence of chapters. Readers are encouraged to examine first the wider discussion of ch. 1–5 in Part I, which investigates the literary relationship between ancient authors and their audiences. In these chapters, one can discover a suggested scheme for differentiating quotations, allusions, and echoes in NT texts (ch. 2), the literacy and intertextual capacities of the ancient audience (ch. 3), the different levels of an audience's proficiency to detect allusions in a given text (ch. 4), various Jewish and Greco-Roman exegetical techniques for the re-interpretation of Scripture available and employed by NT authors—using Hebrews as a test case (ch. 5), and a larger taxonomy of interactions on how ancient authors engage with other bodies of literature and traditions—Jewish or Hellenistic—within the wider Mediterranean world of the Roman Empire (ch. 1).

As part of one's inquiry into a taxonomy of seven interaction types, one may also find it helpful to read in conjunction with ch. 1 the extended discussion and illustration of the seventh interaction type in ch. 10. After engaging these chapters, it is then recommended that one move to the essays in Parts II–IV, which provide examples of ancient authors' practices and ancient audiences' literary capacities in the canonical order of the Gospels (chs. 6–8), Paul's letters (chs. 9–12), and the general letters (chs. 13–16).

A brief word is needed here about the conventions used in this book. Primary source abbreviations follow the SBL Handbook (2nd edition) and the *Oxford Classical Dictionary* (4th edition). For secondary sources, an abbreviations table is provided.

The editors and contributors would like to thank the following publishers for permission to reprint select sections of copyrighted material:

T. & T. Clark for the essay by Judith M. Gundry, "Children, Parents, and God/Gods in Interreligious Roman Households and the Interpretation of 1 Corinthians 7:14," in the *T. & T. Clark Handbook of Children in the Bible and the Biblical World* (edited by Sharon Betsworth and Julie Faith Parker; London: T. & T. Clark, 2019), 311–34.

Mediakor for the essay by Paul Trebilco, "'From the Beginning' in the Ancient City of Ephesus and in the Letters of John," in *Internationalising Higher Education from South Africa to England via New Zealand: Essays in Honour of Professor Gerald Pillay* (edited by Hoffie [J. W.] Hofmeyr and John Stenhouse; Highveld Park: Mediakor, 2018), 59–82.

Cambridge University Press for chapter 1 of the monograph by Madison N. Pierce, *Divine Discourse in the Epistle to the Hebrews* (SNTSMS 178; Cambridge: Cambridge University Press, 2020), 1–34.

E. J. Brill for chapter 4 of the monograph by Bruce Henning, *Matthew's Non-Messianic Mapping of Messianic Texts* (BibInt 188; Leiden: Brill, 2020), 139–79.

Special thanks are due to Megan Herrold Sinchi—associate pastor of Edgebrook Covenant Church, a freelance copy editor, and former teaching assistant of Max Lee—for her help in the editing process and compilation of the abbreviations table, indices, and bibliography. Thanks are also owed to the home institutions of the co-editors: North Park Theological Seminary, Azusa Pacific University, and the Henry Center of Trinity International University (where Max Lee conducted his sabbatical research as a 2020–2021 Henry fellow) for the space, time, and resources needed to complete the project.

Finally, our heartfelt thanks to the fantastic editorial team and staff at Cascade Books, but especially Chris Spinks, for their encouragement and support in publishing the work of the Intertextuality in the New Testament Section at SBL. We appreciate our continuing partnership.

Part I:

Interactions, Intertextuality, and Readership in Greco-Roman Antiquity and Early Christian Discourse

1

A Taxonomy of Intertextual Interactions Practiced by NT Authors

An Introduction

MAX J. LEE

THE ANCIENT WORLD OF the New Testament was as pluralistic and divided as ours is today, if not more so. When early Christianity emerged as a historical movement in the first century CE, it grew within a cosmopolitan Mediterranean environment of diverse religious and philosophical traditions which, with few exceptions, engaged one another in the marketplace of ideas in the public sphere. Religious groups did not develop their doctrines in an isolated vacuum. NT scholarship, however, has struggled to analyze this exchange of ideas, concepts, and traditions in ancient pluralism with nuanced precision. It is unfortunate that for the longest time (since the 1890s) the *Religionsgeschichtliche Schule* or the comparative religions approach focused on the questions of origins and the *derivation* of religious thought between two systems rather than other modes of engagement. Its legacy has either been an uncritical syncretism of concepts or the strict denial of shared traditions whatsoever between diverse philosophical schools or religious sects.[1]

---

1. Baird, *History of New Testament Research*, 2:222; 2:247–53; 2:361–95; 2:417–33; 2:469–70.

There is an enduring impulse on the part of some scholars even today to situate the message of the New Testament exclusively in the soil of Second Temple Judaism as if there were a strict divide between the thought world of Judaism and the Hellenism of its own immediate cultural and historical setting.[2] To move beyond this Judaism/Hellenism divide, scholars have developed (and many times debated over) various models of comparison between two bodies of discourse. It is exciting to see—even in the face of continuing debate—an emerging consensus that the analysis of parallels should not be restricted to questions of origins but provide more sophisticated types of interactions between rival sects and traditions.[3]

The hermeneutical stakes are high. NT authors demonstrate that their interactions with concepts and doctrines belonging to Judaism and Hellenism form an intrinsic part of the very process of interpretation and the production of their message.[4] They employ an arsenal of varied exegetical techniques to engage ideas in ways that go well beyond flat borrowing. It is in this vein of advancing more complex patterns of comparison between diverse religious, philosophical, and moral traditions that this volume of essays describes the intertextual practices of NT authors.

Types of Interactions between Religious and Philosophical Sects

In my book *Moral Transformation in Greco-Roman Philosophy of Mind*, I outline the six basic types of interactions between different ancient philosophies and religions during the early imperial period of Rome.[5]

---

2. See the discussion by Engberg-Pedersen, "Introduction: Paul Beyond the Judaism/Hellenism Divide," 1–16; and Meeks, "Judaism, Hellenism, and the Birth of Christianity," 17–27.

3. White and Fitzgerald, "*Quod est comparandum*," 13–39; Porter and Pitts, "Greco-Roman Culture in the History of New Testament Interpretation," 1–12; and the essays edited by Barclay and White, *New Testament in Comparison*, esp. the proposals by Engberg-Pedersen, "Past is a Foreign Country," 41–61, and Mitchell, "On Comparing," 95–124, with debate and rebuttal by Rowe, "Making Friends and Comparing Lives," 23–40, and Rowe, "Response to Friend-Critics," 125–41.

4. See the discussion by Engberg-Pedersen, "Introduction: A Historiographical Essay," 7–8, who speaks of interactions between different groups as "an intrinsic part of the kind of philosophizing the philosophers themselves did."

5. Lee, *Moral Transformation*, 493–518, but esp. 494 from which this summary of interaction types is drawn.

To these six, in my essay contribution to this volume (ch. 10), I also describe and add a seventh interaction type. Together, the taxonomy of interactions are as follows:

1) *Eclecticism* is the assimilation or appropriation of religious or philosophical material from another sect but the rationale or purpose for the appropriation remains unclear.

2) *Refutation* is the process where a quotation, paraphrase, or epitome of a rival school's doctrine is stated for the purpose of critically engaging the rival's major tenets, proving them false or inaccurate, and using them as a foil to introduce one's own beliefs.

3) *Competitive appropriation* is the adoption of another school's linguistic inventory—that is, a rival sect's technical terminology, syntactical phrasing, idioms, metaphors, or metonymies—in order to redefine and take over what these terms really mean with the result that one's own doctrines outdo the rival's. It is a hostile linguistic and semantic commandeering of the language deployed by a rival school in order to subordinate another's concepts to one's own.

4) *Irenic appropriation* is the non-hostile appropriation of another school's doctrinal teachings under the premise that such teachings do not conflict with those of one's own school. The newly appropriated material could critically *supplement* or *synchronize* with one's own doctrines without theoretical dissonance. An author may claim that the rival school even borrowed the idea originally from one's own founder.

5) *Concession* is a type of interaction between schools where an author admits that one's own founder or school might be wrong and inadequate on a particular issue and therefore the author accepts a rival school's teaching on the matter as a superior or a more satisfying answer to certain philosophical questions.

6) *Common ethical usage* is the appropriation of language and concepts that do not, or no longer, belong to any one school of thought but are part of a larger encyclopedia of knowledge shared between all philosophical schools and moral traditions in the Greco-Roman world.

7) *Doctrinal reformulation* is a mode of interaction between adherents within the *same* school of thought or tradition. It is a process where

a body of sacred texts or the founder's teachings are reinterpreted by subsequent followers who each think they adequately preserve their school's major doctrines but nevertheless, based on their individual exegetical work, can produce either congruent or competing interpretations within the same school.

Early Christianity, at its inception, was recognized as a sect (αἵρεσις) or school among other Jewish parties and rival philosophical groups by outsiders.[6] As a sect, the NT writers' literary output demonstrates several instances of the aforementioned interaction types. *Refutation* is exercised by Paul, for example, in his diatribe with an imaginary interlocutor in Rom 2. Regardless of whether one identifies the "so-called Jew" (Ἰουδαῖος ἐπονομάζῃ; Rom 2:17) as a Torah-observant Jewish pietist,[7] or as a gentile proselyte,[8] Paul sets out to dismiss the claims of his interlocutor one argument at a time by presenting "proofs" born from his own exegesis of Israel's Scriptures (Rom 2:17–29).

Anti-imperial language in the New Testament is an example of *competitive appropriation*.[9] Not all scholars are convinced that early Christianity appropriated key terms like κύριος from imperial discourse to make the alternative claim that Christ is Lord and Caesar is not.[10] Nevertheless, many have kept the debate alive by insisting that κύριος—along with such other terms as εὐαγγέλιον, υἱὸς τοῦ θεοῦ, σωτήρ, εἰρήνη καὶ ἀσφάλεια, παρουσία, κτλ.—has been "co-opted" by NT authors and

---

6. See, e.g., Acts 5:17 on the "sect of the Sadducees" (αἵρεσις τῶν Σαδδουκαίων), Acts 15:5 on the "sect of the Pharisees" (αἵρεσις τῶν Φαρισαίων), and Acts 24:5 on the disciples of Jesus of Nazareth as the "sect of the Nazarenes" (αἵρεσις τῶν Ναζωραίων); cf. Josephus, *J. W.* 2.162–64 on the Pharisees and Sadducees as a "sect" (αἵρεσις) or "group" (τάγμα); Josephus, *Life* 1.10–12 on several sects (αἱρέσεις), including the Pharisees, Sadducees, and Essenes, the first of whom he likens to the Stoics. Lucian of Samosata depicts Christians and Epicureans as schools comparable for their "atheism" toward traditional Greco-Roman religion (*Alex.* 38). See also the discussion by Alexander, "*IPSE DIXIT*," 103–27.

7. On the interlocutor as a representative of Paul's Jewish contemporaries, see, e.g., Cranfield, *Romans 1–8*, 136–40; Moo, *Letter to the Romans*, 135–85; Longenecker, *Epistle to the Romans*, 290–324.

8. On the interlocutor as a gentile proselyte, see, e.g., Thorsteinsson, *Paul's Interlocutor in Romans 2*, 196–234. Variations of Rom 2:17–29, expansions of the diatribe to Rom 3, and implications of Thorsteinsson's thesis for the whole of Romans are discussed in the essays edited by Rodriguez and Thiessen, *So-Called Jew*.

9. Lee, *Moral Transformation*, 498–500.

10. Barclay, "Why the Roman Empire Was Insignificant to Paul," 363–87; Kim, *Christ and Caesar*, 3–71; and most recently Robinson, "Hidden Transcripts?" 55–72.

redeployed as a critique against the Roman Empire and its imperial cult; yet, these said authors have also situated this critique into a larger discussion of how the cosmic powers use Rome as their pawn to dominate the human landscape.[11] If not Paul, then at the very least John of Revelation more explicitly articulates the gospel of Jesus Christ in antithesis to the claims of lordship and power held by Caesar.[12]

Another interaction type—*common ethical usage*—can be seen in Paul's use of the μιμεῖσθαι word group in his letters. *Imitatio Pauli* is part of a more broadly shared tradition called *psychagogy* that cuts across the sectarian divide.[13] Paul, as I argue elsewhere, offers his distinctly Christian understanding of spiritual mentorship and *exemplum*, but nevertheless his language of imitation constitutes a set of practices and traditions of moral instruction drawn, adapted, and modified from an encyclopedia of knowledge intrinsic to his larger Greco-Roman cultural environment.[14] Psychagogy—as one instantiation of a common ancient ethical tradition in the wider Mediterranean world—informed Paul's own understanding of discipleship and the moral formation of his congregation.

These are but a few interaction types exercised by early Christianity in relation to other religious and philosophical groups during the first century CE. I could provide further examples of other interaction types, but these should suffice as an introduction to the next section. For what follows, I will locate the various intertextual practices of the NT authors that are described by the essays in this volume within the above taxonomy of interactions.

---

11. Winn, "Striking Back at the Empire," 6–7; Lee, "Review of *Christ and Caesar*," 92–94; see also the collection of essays edited by McKnight and Modica, *Jesus Is Lord and Caesar Is Not*, and those edited by Winn, *Introduction to the Empire in the New Testament*.

12. Carey, "Book of Revelation as Counter-Imperial Script," 157–76. See also the entire issue of *Int* 63 no. 1 (2009), which is devoted to the theme of "Revelation as a Critique of Empire," esp. the articles by Koester, "Revelation's Visionary Challenge to Ordinary Empire," 5–18; Barr, "John's Ironic Empire," 20–30; Carter, "Accommodating 'Jezebel' and Withdrawing John," 32–47; and Callahan, "Babylon Boycott," 48–54.

13. Malherbe, *Paul and the Thessalonians*, 81–88; Malherbe, "Hellenistic Moralists and the New Testament," 301–4; Glad, *Paul and Philodemus*, 53–98; Thom, "Popular Philosophy in the Hellenistic-Roman World," 283–85; and Lee, *Moral Transformation*, 512–16.

14. Lee, "Ancient Mentors and Moral Progress," 55–70.

Mapping the Types of Interactions and the Cartography of Essays in This Volume

Theoretical Discussions on the Relationship between Author, Intertext, and Audience

Part I of this volume addresses more broadly theoretical issues of intertextuality between the NT author, ancient texts and their reception, and the ancient reader. In this *Chapter 1: A Taxonomy of Intertextual Interactions*, as noted above, I have mapped out the seven types of interactions between religious and philosophical groups in the ancient world. Intertextual techniques employed by the authors of the New Testament have an instrumental use in relation to these interaction types. A particular intertextual technique such as *metalepsis* (i.e., the phenomenon when a quotation, allusion, or echo evokes the larger literary context in which the quoted or echoed text is embedded),[15] for example, can be deployed by an author in more than one way to interact with one's own religious texts, traditions, and tenets, or with those of another sect. Many of the essays in this volume employ metalepsis, but the way by which they interact with text traditions varies, as we shall see in the chapter summaries ahead.

In *Chapter 2: Quotations, Allusions, and Echoes*, B. J. Oropeza calls for a refinement of the definitions and distinctions between different forms of intertextuality. Quotations usually have a citation formula but not always, and Oropeza marks out reasons why the formula may be omitted. Allusions employ direct or indirect literary patterns and rely on the reader's ability to access a cultural encyclopedia common with the author. Echoes require the greatest degree of audience competency for detection and may be missed by the reader. Oropeza then concludes by addressing briefly audience competency.

Bruce Longenecker, in *Chapter 3: Intertextuality in Pompeian Plaster*, examines the graffiti and artifacts of Pompeii to uncover a greater and surprising degree of literacy among the under-represented common masses "on the street." Most studies on audience literacy focus on the highly educated elite of Roman society. Longenecker's study, in contrast, focuses on the "material realia of ordinary people living in the Roman world," who not only quoted the likes of Ovid, Virgil, and Lucretius, but even satirized and subverted their literary works in creative ways.

---

15. See Brown, "Metalepsis," 29–41 for a history and description of its use among NT scholars and her own employment of the method.

In *Chapter 4: Multi-Layered Use of Scripture*, Konrad Otto adapts Christopher Stanley's taxonomy of readership to argue that in any given NT text, the ancient author's audience could be comprised of minimal, competent, and informed readers who each detect and interpret the various intertexts with different degrees of success. Using Paul's discussion of a "new covenant" in 2 Cor 2:14—4:6 as an example, Otto demonstrates that minimal audiences would likely follow Paul's rhetorical line of argumentation but miss most of the intertexts, while competent and informed readers would pick up many to all allusions to Exod 4:10–11; Jer 31:33; 38:33; Ezek 11:19; and other passages.

Some of the allusions and echoes analyzed by the studies that follow may, at first, draw skepticism as to whether they have enough "volume" to be detected. However, the findings by Longenecker and Otto together not only demonstrate a high literary competency among ancient readers, but also point to different levels of reading proficiency among the diverse members of early Christian congregations. Because detection is more likely than not by an ancient audience, defining more sharply the categories of quotations, allusions, and echoes—as Oropeza notes— becomes more important.

In *Chapter 5: Intertextuality and Exegetical Techniques in Hebrews*, Susan Docherty discusses various exegetical techniques employed by the author of Hebrews that were adapted from Jewish citation practices and more widely from Greco-Roman literary genres. Using the letter to the Hebrews as a test case, Docherty defines the phenomenon of textual pluriformity and how NT authors may choose variant scriptural traditions to assert a theological point. She also describes the Greco-Roman reading strategy of prosopological exegesis, the rabbinic technique of *gezerah shawa* or text-linking, rewritten Scripture, composite citations, and other intertextual practices.

Docherty's essay introduces well many of the studies in this volume that engage quotations, allusions, or echoes of the Old Testament— whether the LXX, the MT, or their textual variants. Her and others' essays focusing on the Old Testament in the New point to the practice of *doctrinal reformulations* by NT authors. I have described how this interaction works in Greco-Roman philosophical discourse (ch. 10). In the next section, I will apply this interaction type to describe the intertextuality between the testaments and explain how many of the essays in this book evince doctrinal reformulations.

In what follows, I deviate from introducing the volume chapters in numerical sequence. For the subsequent studies that focus on ancient practices of intertextuality in the Gospels, the Pauline letters, and the general letters (Parts II–IV), I arrange the chapter summaries by the kind of interactions each study catalogues. I describe here emerging patterns. I note each contributor's own assessment of their work and the kind of intertextual interactions they see employed by the authors of Second Temple Jewish literature, Greco-Roman literary and artifactual works, and the New Testament. I also selectively add my own editorial comments on what I think the essays of this volume indicate concerning the types of interactions practiced by NT authors.

Doctrinal Reformulations

In *Chapter 10: Negotiating Piety*, I set out to describe how the practices of the Corinthian γνῶσις group or "knowers" regarding idol food consumption fit within the context of philosophical discussions on cultic sacrifice. I begin by discussing how two Roman Epicureans—Philodemus and Lucretius—can take the unofficial collection of writings by their founder Epicurus as sacred texts and reinterpret his teachings for new social contexts. Despite the different applications of Epicurean piety in cultic settings by Philodemus and Lucretius, their variegated exegetical treatments or doctrinal reformulations remain well within the major tenets of Epicureanism. Then, I demonstrate that much like Philodemus (*contra* Lucretius), who justified Epicurean participation in temple feasts based on one's knowledge of the gods' true nature, the Corinthians analogously used their knowledge that "an idol is nothing" (1 Cor 8:4) to justify their consumption of εἰδωλόθυτα. Paul, in response, offers his own doctrinal reformulations concerning idol food, as compared to his Jewish contemporaries, that allow for the permissibility of consumption under certain non-cultic conditions. Cultic participation, however, was strictly forbidden by Paul.

The kind of doctrinal reformulations that take place in philosophical and religious discourses in Roman antiquity find analogues in the intertexts between the Old Testament and the New. NT authors have access to an unofficial canon of scriptural texts that they think of as authoritative for their communities within the wider context of Second Temple Judaism. In their individual exegeses of Scripture, the evangelists, Paul, and other NT writers produce new interpretations of the biblical texts that are either consonant or competitive with their fellow Jewish contemporaries.

In *Chapter 6: The Church's One Foundation?*, Henning intriguingly examines how OT texts that anticipate the arrival and mission of Israel's messiah find their fulfillment not solely in Christ but partially in the identity and work of Jesus' disciples, especially the apostle Peter. Henning's essay demonstrates a reformulation of messianic temple-foundation and temple-builder traditions such that Peter is the rock or foundation and Jesus is the builder of the church.

In *Chapter 7: Scriptural Allusion and Bodily Age in Luke 1–2*, Julie Newberry works with Richard Hays's figural reading of Scripture[16] to uncover the roles of old-age characters—i.e., Zechariah and Elizabeth, Simeon, and Anna—in the Lukan infancy narratives. Her study illuminates Luke-Acts's interpretation of age-pairing visions in the Old Testament (e.g., Joel 3) and the theological continuity of Abraham and Sarah with Lukan old-age figures to argue against a supercessionist-ageist reading of Scripture and for an anticipatory, proleptic reading of their roles in the arrival of God's kingdom. In *Chapter 8: Vision and Re-Envision*, Alice Yafeh-Deigh and Federico Roth co-author a study on the songs of Hannah and Mary. They argue that the restorative justice themes of Hannah's song in 1 Sam 2 are reformulated in Mary's *Magnificat* in Luke 1 to highlight Jesus' role as Israel's messiah to reshape existing social realities.

The work of Rikk Watts in *Chapter 12: Paul—Theologian, Historian, or Something Else?* paints a broader picture of Paul's use of intertexts. Watts provocatively argues that today's readers often fail to understand how a given scriptural allusion fits within Paul's overall line of argumentation because they do not place Paul within the lineage of Israel's prophetic tradition. While seeing Paul as a theologian and historian provides some limited hermeneutical insight, Watts nevertheless rejects these vantage points' ultimate value for interpreting Paul's letters. Watts instead guides us in a "thought exercise" of reading Rom 9 and its OT intertexts not through *theologia* or *historia* but through Israel's unique prophetic record that continues into Paul's own proclamation of the gospel.

---

16. For the most recent and developed description of Hays's figural interpretation method, see Hays, *Reading with the Grain of Scripture*.

Common Ancient Ethical and Religious Usage

In *Chapter 9: Consecrated by the Brother/Sister*, Judith Gundry situates Paul's instructions to believers in regard to their children and unbelieving spouses within the wider common traditions and practices of endogamy (i.e., marrying within one's own group) in the Greco-Roman world. Gundry—after rehearsing the debate on how to translate ἁγιάζεσθαι/ἅγια in 1 Cor 7:14—not only makes a convincing case that these terms should be understood in their transferred cultic sense as "to be consecrated" or "dedicated" to God, but also argues that Paul sets the premise in 1 Cor 7:12–16 to free believers from the restrictions of endogamy practiced in the Roman household.

Paul's approach to endogamy is a good example of a NT author drawing upon the common ancient ethical and religious traditions of one's day that cut across the sectarian divide and form part of a larger encyclopedia of knowledge shared between philosophical and religious groups in the Mediterranean world of the first century BCE to second century CE. Endogamy is but one *topos* (literally "common place") or topic among others that make up the moral universe and cultural encyclopedia shared between ancient authors and their readers.[17] My essay on negotiating piety (ch. 10) not only introduces the practice of doctrinal reformulations, but also describes another *topos*, that is, the anti-sacrificial discourse commonly held by various philosophical groups including the Socratics, Orphics, Pythagoreans, and Epicureans. Other common ethical and religious uses are investigated in the remaining essays.

Michael Reardon, in *Chapter 11: The Corporate Σῶμα*, analyzes Stoic tenets concerning how human beings, by virtue of their reason, all exist as members of one cosmic body. In comparison, Paul teaches that all believers—as members of Christ's ecclesial body—are united not by reason but by their reciprocal love for one another. Despite their different emphases, however, the σῶμα metaphor is commonly used by both Epictetus and Paul to describe non-hierarchal relationships and provides the ethical basis for mutual concern between its members.

What is more, Reardon concludes that both Epictetus's and Paul's conceptual uses of σῶμα individually participate in a larger encyclopedia

---

17. See the discussion by Thom, "Mind Is Its Own Place," 569–70, who suggests that the moral universe of the Greco-Roman world can be mapped out by showing the interconnectedness between various *topoi* across philosophical and religious traditions.

of knowledge. The Stoics and Paul are not the only ones who employ the corporate body metaphorically to emphasize the unity and diversity of a group. Other Greco-Roman authors use body language to describe solidarity among citizens and political assemblies.

In *Chapter 15: Intertextuality beyond Echoes*, Ryder Wishart analyzes the encyclopedia of knowledge concerning Second Temple Jewish interpretations of the Cain and Abel story. He argues for a broader understanding of intertextuality that moves beyond quotations, allusions, or echoes since these depend on key phrases or lexemes as the focal point for detecting intertexts. Wishart instead sees larger thematic formations in Jewish Greek and non-Greek (Hebrew/Aramaic) texts, organizes their conceptual domains, and examines how Hebrews, Jude, 1 John, and other NT texts access these larger domains of knowledge. This common religious usage takes on a different expression than described in the essays that engage Greco-Roman discourse. Wishart's work focuses on common *topoi* or knowledge domains *within* one of many cultures (but not across them) in the Mediterranean world. He focuses on common thematic formations within Second Temple Judaism and does not limit the scope of inquiry to any one Jewish sect. The usage still crosses the sectarian divide but stays within Judaism.

Lastly, in reference to the work of Longenecker (ch. 3), it may very well be that the epic stories and poems of Virgil's *Aeneid*, Lucretius's *On the Nature of Things*, and Homer's *Odyssey* and the *Iliad* were so popular and well-known that their narratives also contributed to this encyclopedia of knowledge shared among the general populace of the Roman Empire. As Longenecker's study and others indicate,[18] the average person on the street not only could recite famous lines from these works, even if crudely in their graffiti, but they also, at times, employed techniques such as metalepsis and hyptertextuality. Through the use of intertexts, these graffiti composers and artists propagated pro-Roman sentiments or in the opposite direction criticized Rome indirectly through political satire and humor. The use of humor in Greco-Roman literature brings us to the next interaction type.

---

18. See Longenecker's essay for audience literacy of Virgil and Lucretius; concerning Homer, see MacDonald, *Gospels and Homer*.

Refutation

Here I would like to suggest briefly that the intertextual uses of humor, parody, and satire can function as another interaction type, that is, *refutation*. Rather than engaging views against which one disagrees in an expository or diatribal manner, the ancient author can use intertexts and, through humor, indirectly refute those in power or defend oneself against external critique.

So Jason Whitlark and Jon-Michael Carman explore a different set of Greco-Roman intertexts in *Chapter 14: Humor in Hebrews*. They examine what Quintilian, Cicero, Aristotle, and other orators say about the purpose and mechanics of humor. Theirs is a detailed investigation into the various kinds of humor which utilizes comparison, analogy, ambiguity, brief remarks or "shafts of wit," tropes, caricatures, and other techniques to stir emotion, help the reader avoid folly, and deride opponents. Of particular interest is the notion of the absurd which the author of Hebrews applies to his reading of Esau (Heb 12:16) as a warning to the church against the folly of apostasy. Whitlark and Carman's study on humor also introduces another interaction type.

Irenic Appropriation

The analyses by Whitlark and Carmon (ch. 14) of a NT author's use of rhetorical techniques (in their case, techniques for generating humor) exhibit another interaction type besides refutation. The use of rhetoric is a kind of *irenic appropriation*, not of the kind where concepts or tenets are shared, but rather an appropriation of rhetorical devices and literary genres. Irenic appropriation as I have originally defined it earlier in this essay technically refers to the appropriation of another school of thought's teachings under the premise that the content of such teachings do not conflict with those of one's own school. The newly appropriated material could critically supplement one's own existing doctrines without theoretical dissonance. However, the kind of irenic appropriation or subtype that Whitark and Carmen catalogue in their study of humor is not the assimilation of a school's *content* but the *techniques*, devices, and genres of rhetorical education. Acquisition of intertextual techniques from other schools is an extended example of irenic appropriation.

Similarly, Madison Pierce has convincingly demonstrated in her essay how the writer of Hebrews appropriates prosopological exegesis for his own purposes to reassign quotations from Scripture as divine speech. In *Chapter 13: Precedents for Prosopological Exegesis*, Pierce describes the history of prosopological exegesis as a technique used by Greco-Roman rhetoricians and historians. She then traces how Hebrews and other NT authors employed προσωποποιΐα to interpret OT texts by reassigning the speeches of ambiguous or unspecified persons to new πρόσωπα or characters. When these new characters in Hebrews are the Father, Son, or Spirit, the OT speeches which they recite become reinterpreted christologically to illuminate the divine nature and actions of the triune God. The author of Hebrews's use of prosopological exegesis stands in continuity with its use in Greco-Roman rhetorical education and subsequent practices by such patristic fathers as Justin Martyr.

Competitive Appropriation

Lastly, in *Chapter 16: Intertextual Echoes in Ephesus*, Paul Trebilco examines the importance of antiquity or "foundations" for establishing the reliability of religious traditions within the cultural milieu of ancient Ephesus. What was "in the beginning" for Ephesus's past plays a crucial role for the present identity of the city's inhabitants. Trebilco examines the use of the phrase ἀπ' ἀρχῆς in the LXX, the Johannine letters, and other NT texts and convincingly argues that the particular Johannine use of ἀπ' ἀρχῆς in 1 John resonates most strongly with the foundation stories of Artemis and Androkolos. John's use of foundation stories establishes not the patron goddess Artemis but the eternal Son, Jesus Christ, as the one who was "from the beginning" and is the source of Christian identity for those living in Ephesus and Roman Asia.

Trebilco rightly identifies John's use of ἀπ' ἀρχῆς within the common ancient traditions on foundation myths in the wider Mediterranean world. Yet, he also suggests another interaction type beyond common ancient ethical and religious usage. Trebilco cautiously proposes that ἀπ' ἀρχῆς might be a form of *competitive* appropriation, that is, the adoption of another school of thought's linguistic inventory in order to commandeer what these religious terms or phrases really mean. In this case ἀπ' ἀρχῆς has been appropriated by John as an intended "polemical contrast" against the claims of one's immediate surroundings. Against the cultural milieu of ancient Ephesus, John assures the church within this milieu that their belief in Christ represents a foundation story that predates that of

Artemis or any other competing cult. Certainly this suggestion by Trebilco warrants further exploration.

Moving Forward

Arguably five of the seven types of interactions listed at the beginning of this essay have been demonstrated by the studies of this volume: that is, doctrinal reformulation, common ancient ethical and religious usage, refutation, irenic appropriation, and competitive appropriation. Not seen are examples of concession or eclecticism. These latter two categories, however, need not be represented. As stated elsewhere,[19] I make no claim that this taxonomy of interaction types is exhaustive, nor is it necessarily the case that the NT authors would exhibit all the types. It may very well be that we find no case of concession or eclecticism in the New Testament.

What is more, as the historian further investigates how ancient philosophical and religious groups interacted with one another in the pluralistic environment of the Greco-Roman world, one may discover additional interaction types. The data uncovered in this volume has certainly compelled me to modify or nuance existing types of interactions so that, for example, irenic appropriation is not limited to the content of a school's teachings but also expanded to the techniques, devices, and genres used by a school. What I can confidently conclude is that older models such as the *Religionsgeschichtliche Schule* which focus on questions of origins have proven inadequate to process and assess the complexity of early Christianity's interactions with its religious, moral, and cultural milieu. We need more sophisticated models to map the interactions and intertextuality demonstrated in the New Testament. The contributors and co-editors of *Practicing Intertextuality* present this volume of essays as an important start to this ongoing scholarly discussion in biblical studies.

19. Lee, *Moral Transformation*, 516–18.

2

Quotations, Allusions, and Echoes

Their Meanings in Relation to Biblical Interpretation

B. J. OROPEZA

BIBLICAL INTERPRETERS FREQUENTLY ASSUME that their readers know what they mean by the terms they use, but that is not always the case. With the rising tide of biblical studies related to intertextuality, it is important for interpreters to address what they mean by commonly used but ambiguous terms that are related to such studies. Intertextuality is in fact one such term.[1] It is not to be equated simply with the historical-critical inquiry of NT citations of the Old Testament.[2] Rather, intertextuality has

---

1. The theory and practice of intertextuality has evolved over the years. Its starting point in poststructuralism does not necessitate that biblical scholars today conform to that ideology if wanting to use the term, especially given that the person who coined it—Julia Kristeva—replaced it with "transposition" since she considered the latter to reflect her ideology in a more pristine way. In biblical scholarship, the use of intertextuality beyond poststructuralism has been attached prominently to Richard Hays and the figure of an echo. I discuss the meaning of intertextuality most thoroughly in Oropeza, "Ancient Midrash in the Age of Intertextuality," 9–17. See also Oropeza, "New Studies in Textual Interplay," 3–7; and for a succinct history of interpretation, see Oropeza, "Intertextuality," 453–63.

2. A useful study recognizing some differences is Moyise, "Intertextuality and Historical Approaches," 23–32.

to do with the presence of a text, or texts, in another text, the relationships of which prompt exploration into further text relationships, regardless of whether these relationships are diachronic, synchronic, literary, cultural, a combination of these, or something else.[3] Since intertextuality has been employed in diverse ways over the years, biblical interpreters who adopt it should explain what they mean by it and the way they intend to use it. The same holds true for other text-relational words. This study will elaborate on the terms "quotations," "allusions," and "echoes."

Quotations

By a "quotation," what is normally meant by biblical scholars is a recognizable set of words found in another text that is often signaled by a citation formula.[4] These markers may include phrases such as: "that the word might be fulfilled through the prophet Isaiah saying . . ." (Matt 8:17); "so that the Scripture might be fulfilled that says . . ." (John 19:24); "for David says with reference to him . . ." (Acts 2:25); "just as it is written . . ." (Rom 1:17); or "it is testified somewhere saying . . ." (Heb 2:16).[5] Quotations also may be signaled by an indirect marker such as "for" (γάρ), "that" (ὅτι), or, if in a string of quotes, with markers such as "again" and "and" (e.g., πάλιν and καί in Heb 1:5–13).

---

3. For intertextualists, "text" is not just Scripture but also the vast array of Second Temple and Greco-Roman literature, along with other sources and signifiers such as papyri documents, inscriptions, numismatics, oral communication, maxims, gestures, songs, and so on, whether communicated verbally, visually, or acoustically (see a succinct paradigm in Plett, "Intertextualities," 20). As Allen affirms: "In structuralist and poststructuralist theory the 'text' comes to stand for whatever meaning is generated by the intertextual relations between one text and another and the activation of those relations by a reader" (*Intertextuality*, 227). This is all to say that there is recognition that the social, cultural, and ideological world outside of the New Testament informed the writers and their recipients implicitly and explicitly. The biblical use of texts, then, is not limited to the study of quotations from earlier biblical sources.

4. How large or small a set? While there is no established number, Porter suggests at least three words are needed to "constitute meaningful minimal syntax" ("Pauline Techniques," 30).

5. All the same, the presence of a citation formula or mention of the Scriptures does not always mean that an actual quote will follow as in Luke 24:44–47; 1 Cor 15:3–4; and Gal 4:22. Even when a quote is apparently given, it is possible for the source to be unknown to us today (e.g., Jas 4:5). For further problems, see Porter, "Pauline Techniques," 29–30.

Occasionally there is no clear formula or marker provided, such as when Paul gives the command from Deuteronomy: "Drive out the wicked person from among you" (1 Cor 5:13 / Deut 22:21, 24; cf. 17:7; 19:19; 21:21; 24:27); or when he uses the expression from Isaiah: "Let us eat and drink for tomorrow we die" (1 Cor 15:32 / Isa 22:13). One reason introductory formulae may be obviated is that the author assumed the audience already was familiar with the words or maxim.[6] Interpreters today are able to determine such cases by noticing the combined set of words that have verbatim or near verbatim agreement with another text, whether from Scripture or another source.[7] Other criteria may include that the words are linguistically or syntactically set apart from the immediate context, or the author comments on the set of words, or that the source text is found elsewhere in the same context as the potential quote (such is the case with 1 Cor 5:13 and Deut 22:21–24 since the context of both refer to the same type of sexual impropriety; cf. 1 Cor 5:1 / LXX Deut 23:1).

Why do most NT authors use quotations in their works? Some reasons are as follows:[8]

1) Quotations of biblical Scripture establish the authority of the communicated words, since God or esteemed persons of the past are thought to be the originator of the words.

2) The author is able to deflect some responsibility for what is quoted since God or esteemed persons of the past are the ones speaking.

3) Quotations of biblical Scripture are used to support the fulfillment of prophesy.

4) Quotations validate the author as a credible and competent writer and teacher of the traditions cited.

---

6. Wagner, "Paul and Scripture," 164.

7. Nevertheless, theoretical distinctions between unmarked quotes and allusions are not always clear. The complexity of this issue is quite evident when consulting scholarly opinions. For discussions, see Koch, *Schrift als Zeuge des Evangeliums*, 11–24; Stanley, *Paul and the Language of Scripture*, 3–4; 31–61; Stanley, "What We Learned," 321–30, esp. 322–24; Kujanpää, *Rhetorical Functions of Scriptural Quotations*, 19–20; Moyise, "Quotations," 15–28; Porter, "Further Comments," 98–110; Porter, "Allusions and Echoes," 29–40; Beale, *Handbook on the New Testament*, 29–35.

8. Especially helpful to my thoughts in this list are Kujanpää, *Rhetorical Functions of Scriptural Quotations*, 332–34; and Wagner, "Paul and Scripture," 165–66.

5) Quotations provide a sense of continuity between the author and the tradition cited.

6) Quotations strengthen the solidarity of the author and the community addressed since they share the same traditions.

7) They support and fill in the author's words, whether arguments, teachings, narratives, exhortations, speeches, analogies, prophecies, or foreshadowing.

8) They add stylistic variation and decoration to the author's words.

9) They may help structure the composition of the writing.

Allusions and echoes may accomplish some of these things, too, but quotations are normally clearer and more explicit. We also notice from these points that, in terms of rhetoric, quotations help increase the author's persuasiveness by evoking *logos*, *ethos*, and *pathos*—that is, the communicator's arguments are validated and better received, the communicator's character is promoted, and the audience's emotions are stirred.

Among biblical scholars today there is general recognition that a number of NT authors use the LXX for their quotations. At the same time, NT quotations do not follow verbatim the extant sources, and sometimes the quotes resemble better the Hebrew text (e.g., Rom 11:35 / Job 41:32; 1 Cor 14:21 / Isa 28:11–12; 2 Tim 2:19 / Num 16:5 + Isa 26:13; Jude 12 / Prov 25:14; Jude 13 / Isa 57:20).[9] Other times they correspond with neither the LXX nor MT (e.g., 1 Cor 15:54–55 / Isa 25:8 + Hos 13:14; Eph 5:31 / Gen 2:24).[10] Apart from translation differences, several other factors may play into the comparative variations, such as the author's imperfect oral memory of the quotation, the author's reliance on earlier apostolic proclamation of the quote, the author's rhetorical inclusion or exclusion or paraphrase of the words when quoting, and the fact that

---

9. For Bauckham (2 *Peter, Jude*, 7–8), Jude's sources include the Hebrew text and literature from Palestinian Judaism.

10. This may be due to reliance on a Greek text that follows the Hebrew MT closer than the LXX (e.g., compare the later Theodotion, Aquila, or Symmachus versions). However, given that the original apostles are traditionally Palestinian Jews, and Paul claims a Pharisaic background, there is no reason to preclude that at least some of the NT quotations may originate from a Hebrew source. In Paul's case, helpful lists of quotations comparing the LXX and MT are presented in Ellis, *Paul's Use of the Old Testament*, 150–52; and Silva, "Old Testament in Paul," 631, though they are not always in agreement with every verse classification.

copyists have always made mistakes when copying Scripture from one scroll to another. This means that the author, if fortunate enough even to possess a scroll, had to depend on whichever copy of Isaiah, Exodus, Psalms, or other biblical text might be available to them with all its unique copyist errors intact.[11]

Scholars like me have learned from practice that it is through the quoted word that one often finds other words alluded to or echoed. The interpreter recognizes that the quote is only the tip of the iceberg. What is below the surface needs to be explored, and this often consists of examining not only the context of the quote but also the context of the pretext (the quote's source). Text connections combine and multiply this way.

Allusions

By the term "allusion," biblical scholars normally have in mind a portion of Scripture or some other text that is present in a given biblical writing but not quoted.[12] The pretext, the allusion's source, may be a direct or indirect reference having one or more agreements with the alluding text. Those agreements may include the same or similar word(s) or patterns, whether verbatim, conceptual, structural, thematic, or topical, and may refer to a person, place, action, or event.[13] Some examples of allusions are in the so-called "hall of faith" of Heb 11, Jesus' references to people and events in Matt 12:39–42 / Luke 11:29–32, and narratives from Israel's wilderness wanderings in 1 Cor 10:1–11.[14]

---

11. A fascinating study along these lines is Norton, *Contours in the Text*.

12. Similarly, see Porter, "Use of the Old Testament," 95. A number of potential allusions are provided in the margins and critical apparatus of NA[28], UBS[5], Hübner, *Vetus Testamentum in Novo*, and Schnelle et al., *Neuer Wettstein*. Dated but still of some use for Jewish parallels from the Tannaim and later eras is Str-B. Even the lists in these works, however, do not provide all potential allusions.

13. Porter ("Pauline Technique," 31–32) creates a distinct category independent of quotations and allusions called "paraphrase" that involves, for example, a change of wording (though words may remain in the same semantic range as the original) and change of word order from the pretext. Some verses that reflect elements of paraphrasing include 1 Cor 3:19 / Job 5:12–13, and Phil 2:10–11 / Isa 45:23. I prefer not to add another category in between quotation and allusion but would rather suggest that if such a "paraphrase" has a citation marker, it should be identified as a paraphrased quotation; and if it does not have such markers, it is an allusion.

14. Regarding the latter, apart from the quote in 1 Cor 10:7 (Exod 32:6), and arguably in 10:5 (Num 14:16), the rest of the references to the exodus-wilderness narratives are more readily identified as allusions.

Quite frequently, however, allusions are only indirectly referenced without clear indicators. Wagner affirms:

> This literary trope stimulates the hearer to scan the cultural 'encyclopedia' for the appropriate reference. By enlisting the listener's active cooperation in making the connections with a precursor text, allusion may evoke the competent hearer's pleasure at being 'in the know' and so foster a feeling of solidarity with the author.[15]

In the book of Revelation, for example, numerous allusions can be discerned, not only from Scripture, but also from Second Temple literature, mythology, coinage, and even geographical, socio-economic, historical sources related to the cities addressed in the discourse.[16]

Due to indirect referencing that characterizes many allusions, determination of which text or texts might inform which allusions should be argued by biblical scholars rather than assumed. Is Paul's cry of being a wretched, divided self in Rom 7:14–25 alluding to lamentations from the Psalms, a speech-in-character of Adam (or Eve), Medea in Euripides and Ovid, further Stoic discussions about Medea, something else, or not an allusion at all?[17] Even when allusions are directly referenced to an event, such as the wilderness travels in 1 Cor 10 above, it could still be unclear to audiences which event is featured when the Corinthians are charged not to grumble as some of wilderness generation did, "and were destroyed by the destroyer" (1 Cor 10:10). We search in vain in the Pentateuch for a grumbling event in the wilderness directly connected to punishment by "the destroyer," unless we extend our search to other sources both in and out of Scripture, and then make our case.[18] Such is the nature of allusions, and this is why scholarly studies are needed when exploring them.

---

15. Wagner, "Paul and Scripture," 166.

16. See, e.g., Jauhiainen, *Use of Zechariah in Revelation*; Beale and McDonough, "Revelation," 1081–161; Oropeza, *Churches under Siege*, 175–233, and other studies sensitive to Revelation's background.

17. For interpretative options, see, e.g., Wilder, *Perspectives on Our Struggle*; Schnabel, *Brief des Paulus an die Römer*, 121–23; Moo, *Romans*, 448–56.

18. Cases could be made for Ps 106:19–27 (LXX Ps 105); Wis 18:20–25; LAB 15.5–6; or Targum material. See Oropeza, *Paul and Apostasy*, 157–63.

Echoes

The more "subtle" allusions are sometimes understood by scholars (e.g., Richard Hays) as "echoes." An echo may be considered a faint resonance of a text, as small as a single word or phrase that evokes readers to "a reminiscence of an earlier text."[19] It could be derived from the thematic content or context of the pretext, or it could be used either consciously or unconsciously by the NT author.[20] There are some scholars (like me) who refuse to bend the knee to these meanings and simply prefer to identify echoes and allusions synonymously, as was typically done in biblical studies prior to the publication of Hays's *Echoes of Scripture in the Letters of Paul* in 1989. All the same, due to the slippery way the word "echo" is used in biblical scholarship today, it is advisable for all interpreters who use the term to state what they mean by it in their studies.

Some indirect references to texts do seem to be more "subtle" than others; we know this by the fact that scholars help us "hear" echoes we would have otherwise missed (or is it that the proposed echo does not really exist?). Some interpreters helpfully use criteria to assist in their discernment of these tracings. A popular set of norms for echoes, also applicable for allusions, originates from Richard Hays:[21]

1) *Availability*: was the purported pretext of the echo available to the NT author using it and the audience hearing it?

2) *Volume:* is the alluding text "loud" enough to hear in terms of its repetition of words and syntax from the pretext? How prominent was the pretext, and how much rhetorical stress does the NT author give it?

---

19. Hays, *Echoes of Scripture in the Gospels*, 10.

20. For further discussions on echoes and allusions, though not always in agreement with one another, see Hays, *Echoes of Scripture in the Gospels*, 10–13; Hays, "On the Rebound," 43; Shaw, "Converted Imaginations?" 234–45; Lucas, "Assessing Stanley E. Porter's Objections," 93–111; White, "Identifying Intertextual Exegesis," 169; Porter, "Further Comments," 107–9; Porter, "Allusions and Echoes," 29–40; Leonard, "Identifying Inner-Biblical Allusions," 241–65; Edenburg, "Intertextuality, Literary Competence," 144; Miller, "Intertextuality in Old Testament Research," 301; Gillmayr-Bucher, "Intertextuality," 18–20; Beale, *Handbook*, 31–40; Ben-Porat, "Poetics of Literary Allusion," 105–28.

21. Hays, *Echoes of Scripture in the Letters of Paul*, 29–32; Hays, *Conversion of the Imagination*, 34–45.

24   PRACTICING INTERTEXTUALITY

3) *Recurrence/clustering*: was the pretext quoted, alluded to, or echoed by the NT author or authors elsewhere?

4) *Thematic coherence*: does the echo fit well with the line of discourse or argument the NT author is developing?

5) *Historical plausibility*: could the NT author have meant the particular meaning derived from the pretext, and could the author's readers have understood that meaning?

6) *History of interpretation*: have other interpreters of the NT text, whether in ancient, medieval, or modern times detected the same echo?

7) *Satisfaction*: does the echo make sense of and make lucid the discourse, regardless of the confirmation of other criteria?

This set of criteria, however, is not without its detractors; their criticisms seem to center on a lack of clarity and the value of certain points in the list.[22] Other interpreters establish their own set of criteria,[23] or lay down rigid limitations,[24] whereas others deny that scientific precision can be made regarding echo/allusion types.[25] It is perhaps best to suggest that there should be room for scholarly artistry so that the force of the interpretation plays a role in the test of the echo's or allusion's presence.[26] It is up to the scholar, then, to argue a persuasive case for an allusive pretext's presence, and such are perhaps best determined on a case-by-case basis.

If we, the present readers and interpreters who are well-educated and informed about Scripture, often miss the echoes our fellow interpreters present to us, what can be said about ancient audiences of the

---

22. See, e.g., Porter, "Use of the Old Testament in the New Testament," 83–88; Shum, *Paul's Use of Isaiah*, 6–11; Heilig, *Hidden Criticism*, 35–36; 40–43.

23. See, e.g., Thompson, *Clothed with Christ*, 28–37; Allison, *Intertextual Jesus*, 5–13; Berkley, *From a Broken Covenant*, 60–64; White "Identifying Intertextual Exegesis," 174–87; White, *Erstlingsgabe in Neuen Testament*, 11–12.

24. See, e. g., Beetham, *Echoes of Scripture in the Letter of Paul to the Colossians*, 11–40. His definitions and limitations include, for example, that an unmarked quote must be verbatim (or near verbatim) with six words or more (17); allusions must point to a "single identifiable source" (18); the auditors of allusions are expected to remember "the original sense of the previous text" (19); and an echo is not dependent on the original sense of the prior text (21).

25. See, e.g., Jauhiainen, *Use of Zechariah in Revelation*, 13–35, esp. 33–34.

26. This perspective is in agreement with McAuley, *Paul's Covert Use of Scripture*, 31 (cf. 43–44), when he evaluates Hays's probability of allusion; and it is also compatible with Jauhiainen, *Use of Zechariah in Revelation*.

New Testament, a number of whom were illiterate, not well-educated, and often formerly pagan gentiles with little or no exposure to the Jewish Scriptures when growing up?[27] Christopher Stanley has contributed to scholarly awareness of reader competency by drawing our attention to three types of audiences: 1) the informed audience, such as Jews who know the Scriptures well; 2) the competent audience, who have a basic knowledge of the Scriptures, enough to understand the author's point of the quotation; and 3) the minimal audience, who have little or no knowledge of the Scriptures and were typically comprised of illiterate gentiles.[28] On one end of the spectrum, the informed hearers in an early Christian congregation may benefit from both the surface and deeper sub-textual contexts of the Scripture references; and on the other end, the minimal hearers would be able to comprehend only the surface meaning of the author's quotations in their new and rhetorical contexts. Stanley's study on Paul's undisputed letters suggests that most of his audience would fall under category three.

Certain other scholars suggest a better mixture of audience levels, with the informed members being able to assist and guide uninformed members to a better understanding of Jewish Scripture.[29] There is also a weak and strong way of reading allusions and echoes.[30] A weak orientation stays focused only on the NT authors' own use of texts and the contexts of those texts that might have informed them, whereas a strong orientation expects the audience also to know and appreciate those texts and their contexts. The scholar supporting a strong sense should not take for granted the audience's high level of Scripture competency without providing sufficient support.

---

27. See, however, Longenecker's essay in this volume which makes the case—through his study of Pompeian graffiti—for a greater literacy among Greco-Roman readers.

28. Stanley, *Arguing with Scripture*, esp. 62–71.

29. For a minimalist perspective, see Stanley, *Arguing with Scripture*; Stanley, "What We Learned," 325–27. For a non-minimalist perspective, see Abasciano, "Diamonds in the Rough," 153–83; Wagner, *Heralds of the Good News*; Wagner, "Paul and Scripture," 154–71; Oropeza, "1 Corinthians 10:1–22 in Light of the Corinthians' Knowledge." See also Otto's essay in this volume which argues for multiple levels of reading competency among Paul's letter recipients.

30. These categories are derived from Stanley, "Scripture in 1 Corinthians," 249–57.

Conclusion

New Testament writers were doubtless impacted by their hearing, reading, reflection, and recollections of the Scriptures in light of the Christ event, and they presumably used Scripture, as well as other texts, to formulate their own thinking, their gospel messages, and a number of their arguments, exhortations, and narratives in their writings. Markus Bockmuehl's perceptive words on the impact of Scripture are *apropos* here:

> It seems both a matter of fact and part of the biblical authors' intent that their engagement with the Old Testament is at least as much a function of the text's own agency in terms of its (divine) *claims and impact on them,* rather than merely of their 'use' of it. Could one say that [sic] that they speak as they do because they are thunderstruck by the pressure that Scripture *as a hermeneutical Other* exerts on their own view of things? In other words, perhaps what seems to the critic as a device or strategy of manipulation may have seemed to the authors mere faithfulness to the divine word's strong naming of the fresh reality God had worked in their midst.[31]

Such enthusiasm and Scripture-sharing with the biblical authors' congregations may suggest that they expected, through their trust in the divine Spirit's power and guidance, that the members would recognize, learn, obey, appreciate, and benefit from these Scriptures and traditions on multiple levels as they were able to hear them.

---

31. Private communication to Richard B. Hays recorded in Hays, *Reading Backwards,* x (italics in the original).

3

Intertextuality in Pompeian Plaster

Can Vesuvian Artifacts Inform Our Expectations about Intertextual Expertise among Early Jesus-Followers?

BRUCE W. LONGENECKER

FROM ITS MOST YOUTHFUL days, the emergent Jesus-movement frequently referenced the Scriptures of Israel in its theological discourse. Whether by direct quotation, allusion, echo, or any other technique we might want to define and discuss, Jesus-followers often made gestures to those scriptural precursors. In doing so, they accessed those texts across a spectrum of interpretative strategies, sometimes sticking closely to the sense of the precursor texts and sometimes seeming to stray far from any textual constraints.

Research in this field is now voluminous. Among that extensive literature, however, one avenue of consideration continues to be underrepresented—an avenue that I will explore here (and explain momentarily). It pertains to the question that Beverly Gaventa calls "one of the neuralgic points in contemporary Pauline study"—that is, "What did Paul's audiences know of Scripture, and how did he expect them to hear his quotations and allusions?"[1] It is one thing to imagine intertextual connections being sparked off in Paul's mind; it is another thing altogether to imagine

---

1. Gaventa, *When in Romans*, 59n17.

his audiences appreciating the extent of intertextual strategies that he (and other Jesus-devotees) employed. The issue is pressing precisely because Paul and other apostolic figures often referenced the Scriptures of Israel in ways that went "beyond" anything that might be deemed a "literal" reading of those texts. What would the first audiences have made of those instances of intertextuality?

Questions of this sort take us beyond closely related issues in this complex field of study—not least, the extent to which Jesus-groups in the Roman world would have been familiar with the Scriptures of Israel and the extent to which "catechetical instruction" regarding those Scriptures would have been carried out within those Jesus-groups.[2] Despite the importance of those issues, this essay will seek to discern the extent to which ordinary people in urban centers of the Roman world would have been familiar with the phenomenon of intertextual referencing and the discursive possibilities it afforded. Would the original audiences, comprised of ordinary urban residents in the Roman world, have been cognizant of the array of intertextual techniques utilized by authors of NT texts?

Judging from the literature of the time, the Greco-Roman elite seem to have employed intertextual resonances of various kinds within their own literary discourse. This is evident from any number of elite authors. Take, for instance, Seneca. As Chris Trinacty has demonstrated, Seneca's writings are often animated by significant intertextual allusions that help drive his discourse forward, with subtle allusions to Virgil (for instance) adding depth to the narrative's plot, characterization, and scenic vividness.[3]

The point could be made with regard to any number of Greco-Roman literary authors. But while it is not surprising that intertextuality was utilized by the educated elite of the Roman world, could the same be expected of those ordinary people who did not experience the benefits enjoyed by the educated elite? To what extent might people such as these (the very people whom leaders of the early Jesus-movement sought to influence) have appreciated intertextual functions and techniques?

---

2. When arguing that scholars "need a realistic set of assumptions concerning the literary capabilities of Paul's first-century audience," Christopher Stanley came to the conclusion that Paul overshot his readers' intertextual abilities when citing Jewish Scripture ("Pearls before Swine," esp. 144). Others are not so sure; see, e.g., Abasciano, "Diamonds in the Rough"; Williams, "From the Perspective of the Writer."

3. Trinacty, *Senecan Tragedy*, esp. 186–87; 234–35. See, more recently, Garani et al., *Intertextuality in Seneca's Philosophical Writings*, and esp. Lee, *Moral Transformation*, 493–518.

The great literature of the Greco-Roman elite does not give us much to go by when we ask questions of that sort. But beyond that literary corpus lies the Vesuvian towns of Pompeii and Herculaneum, destroyed in the eruption of Mount Vesuvius. The walls of those towns have over 8,000 graffiti scratched into or written onto them.[4] Do those data hold any clues regarding intertextual skills and strategies among the sub-elite? Can select graffiti from the Vesuvian towns help shed light on the extent to which we can imagine sub-elite recipients of Paul's letters (and other texts beyond them) being attuned to the phenomenon of intertextual resonance?

This essay explores this "road less traveled," sinking a few exploratory probes into the streets and residences of Pompeii to see what data might emerge in addressing questions of this kind—data from the material realia of ordinary people living in the Roman world. Consideration will be given to "intertextual graffiti"—that is, graffiti that appropriate precursor texts of the Greco-Roman "canon" in one manner or another. The database for such intertextual graffiti includes seventy-nine instances of exact or "loose" citations of Greco-Roman literature in Pompeian graffiti in the following proportion:[5]

- Homer, Seneca, and Tibullus are each referenced once
- Ennius is referenced four times
- Lucretius is referenced seven times
- Ovid is referenced eight times
- Propertius is referenced nine times
- Virgil is referenced forty-eight times

These intertextual graffiti usually involve making gestures toward short snippets of precursor texts from the literary canon of the first century CE. As we will see, a selection of these graffiti shed small shards of light on the issue of intertextual expertise among "the populace on the streets" of the Roman world.

---

4. Beyond them lie another 3,000 or so *dipinti*, i.e., notices painted on walls.
5. Cooley and Cooley, *Pompeii and Herculaneum*, 292–93 (Appendix 2).

Intertextuality and Virgil's *Aeneid*

Of the forty-eight citations of Virgil in Pompeian plaster, thirty-six of them cite the *Aeneid*. Twelve of those recall the famous first line of Book 1, fourteen recall the first line of Book 2, and ten others cite other texts from the *Aeneid*.

What are we to make of the relatively high concentration of Pompeian graffiti that reference Virgil's *Aeneid*? Are they snippets of text that have very little relationship to their precursor text? Might these simply be school-boy spelling exercises or memorization exercises, with walls being used to write on instead of wax tablets? Alternatively, since these are quotations from the most pro-Augustan narrative of the day, do these graffiti function as articulations of a pro-Roman sentiment, activating the *Aeneid*'s fervor for Roman rule?

Of course, in many instances such questions will need to go unanswered. We do not know the prosopography of any individual graffito author, nor the social context of any particular graffito (with a few rare exceptions), nor the author's motivation for etching something onto a wall. Nonetheless, more can perhaps be said. Kristina Milnor has recently adopted a minimalist position, proposing that these graffiti are instances of sub-elite "theft and redeployment of high literature."[6] She amplifies this claim in this way with regard to Virgil:

> [What Pompeians] knew of Virgil was not, in fact, the stories he told; instead, what was prized, and quoted, were individual pithy passages and lines, whose significance was not narrative or thematic but linguistic or gnomic. The Virgilian fragments are fragments, and were consumed as such, stripped of their original context and given new meaning as part of ancient urban street life.[7]

To the extent that Milnor is right about "textual theft," it would seem that the Virgilian precursor text was simply mined for solitary gems extracted from their original context and put to use without reference to that context.

While I wholly agree that we see a kind of "atomistic thievery" evidenced in some Pompeian graffiti, I nonetheless depart somewhat from viewing this as a blanket depiction of Virgilian graffiti in Pompeii, since

---

6. Milnor, *Graffiti*, 7; see also her "Literary Literacy in Roman Pompeii."
7. Milnor, *Graffiti*, 262.

I am not persuaded that Milnor's conclusions adequately deal with the full spread of the evidence.[8] The mere preponderance of graffiti drawing from the *Aeneid* tends to problematize a full commitment to atomistic theft of the precursor text. No doubt intertextual thievery might well represent what is going on in any given instance. But the fact that almost half of Pompeian intertextual graffiti cite the *Aeneid* in one fashion or another (in contrast to a single citation of Homer, for instance) suggests that this text was extremely popular among the residents of Pompeii.[9] Surely the text's pro-Roman program was not lost in this overwhelmingly pro-Roman town. Its material artifacts illustrate the point repeatedly, with architectural and artistic references to the *Aeneid* often illustrating a robust eagerness to support the Roman imperial order.[10] Why should we think differently with regard to the graffiti (in general) that reference the same popular work? If the *Aeneid* was "in the air," there must have been some underlying bedrock of interest in the work that went beyond simply using it for atomistic purposes. It should not surprise us, then, if some graffiti were meant to activate the pro-Roman sentiment of Virgil's text.

The most likely candidates for this would be the twelve graffiti that reference the opening line of the whole novel in line 1 of Book 1: *arma virumque cano*, that is, "I sing of arms and a man." This short sentence would seem to have little significance apart from its Virgilian context, and it resonates most in reference to that context. An analogy might serve to capture the point. During the US election cycle of 2016, if you entered a neighborhood in the United States with a preponderance of yard signs saying "Make America Great Again," you could be pretty sure that you

---

8. Nor does it seem to me valid to separate "the story of Aeneas" from Virgil's "epic poem which told his tale," as Milnor maintains (*Graffiti*, 262).

9. Hedrick doubts that we can say that the story of Aeneas created "a common base of knowledge and culture shared by every Roman, drawing together the disparate population of the empire and helping to create a sense of community" ("Literature and Communication," 168), but his reason for doing so is based on unconvincing grounds, including an unnecessary pessimism regarding literacy among the sub-elite. If we have learned anything from the Vesuvian remains, it is that we must now talk about levels of literacy among the sub-elite; see, e.g., Longenecker, *In Stone and Story*, 143–53. But even beyond the issue of literacy, Hedrick underestimates the extent to which architectural and artistic features commonly forced the Virgilian narrative of Aeneas into the public imagination. Nowhere is this more clear than in the Vesuvian remains.

10. See, e.g., the prominent Eumachia Building in the town's forum, with its pro-Roman inscription at its entryways resonating with its statues of Aeneas and Romulus at the front entrance; or the figures of Aeneas and Romulus at the entryway to the fullery at Pompeii 9.13.5 (further analyzed below).

were in Trump country. Even at the time of writing this essay, the bald slogan and its acronym, "MAGA," both conjure up Trump's much larger agenda on immigration, protectionism, and the like. This is not some decontextualized slogan; it resonates with a huge political program and posture. Of course, Bill Clinton used the same tagline in some of his 1992 speeches as a candidate for president, and then used it again in support of Hillary Clinton's 2008 campaign for the presidency. But these days, none of these associations are activated by the slogan and its acronym. They are indelibly associated with the Trump presidency.

Along similar lines, it is hard to imagine all of the dozen citations of "I sing of arms and a man" to be simple instances of textual thievery without intended reference to the precursor text. Unless other evidence suggests otherwise, these graffiti (or at least a significant portion of them) must have been meant to express and activate the sentiment of Virgil's pro-Roman and pro-Augustan text. That text had permeated the imagination of all levels of Roman society. Some must have imagined that writing "I sing of arms and a man" in a graffito would be an effective way to promote the pro-Roman sentiment of Virgil's larger storyline.[11] Perhaps these are instances of what others have called "metalepsis," in which a precursor text is cited or alluded to in order to evoke the larger context of that text.[12]

Another glimpse into intertextual relationality between Pompeian graffiti and Virgil's *Aeneid* is evident in a graffito written in rather small letters on the exterior wall of a fullery or laundry (at Pompeii 9.13.5).[13] It reads, "I sing of fullers and an owl, not arms and a man" (*fullones ululamque cano, non arma virumque*; *CIL* 4.9131). When it is recognized

---

11. Cf. the estimate of Graverini regarding "intertextual graffiti" in Pompeii: "These activities do not necessarily give evidence of a highly cultured society, but at least to some extent they are proof of the vitality and diffusion of sophisticated literary products that were by no means confined to the bookshelves of a narrow elite" ("Ovidian Graffiti," 28). More generally, note Pfister's estimate regarding the effective function of even short but selectively chosen intertextual gestures: "Mit dem pointiert ausgewählten Detail wird der Gesamtkontext abgerufen, dem es entstammt, mit dem knappen Zitat wird der ganze Prätext in die neue Sinnkonstitution einbezogen" ("Konzepte der Intertextualität," 29).

12. Brown, "Metalepsis."

13. The location of artifacts and graffiti at Pompeii are keyed by *regio* (region), *insula* (block), and *ianua* (entryway), so 9.13.5 is entryway 5 in block 13 of region 9. On the history of the numbering system devised by Giuseppe Fiorelli and later revised and expanded by Hans Eschebach, Jürgen Müller-Trollius, and Liselotte Eschebach, see Franklin, *Pompeis Difficile Est*, 3–4.

that the owl was the mascot of the fullers, the graffito on the wall makes sense as a parody of the opening line of Virgil's *Aeneid*.

These parodistic features are uncontested. Less obvious is the intended force of the graffito and its functionality. In my view, the graffito's force is probably not politically innocuous. The graffito replaces the great Roman hero Aeneas with laundry workers and replaces the military "arms" that prepared the way for Roman dominance with the mascot of the laundry business. The force of the graffito hangs on the negation, "not" (*non*)—"*not* arms and a man." And therein lies the poignancy of its political parody, involving political offense. If the person who wrote this graffito had intended simply to riff playfully off the *Aeneid* without a subversive nuance, he presumably could have written the first phrase and left it at that: "I sing of launders and an owl." Or he could have written "and" where instead he wrote "not." Or he could have composed a list containing the things of which he sings, such as, arms, a man, launderers, and an owl. Any of those possibilities would not have involved a negation of the pro-Roman story. But he did not choose any of those options. Instead, the macro-narrative of Roman power and authority is set aside in this graffito, with an eye-popping negation; instead, the micro-narrative of the laundry workers is presented as the only story to which the inscriber was committed.[14]

A further twist to the political agonism of the graffito is evidenced in the fact that this graffito was etched into an external wall just beneath a figure of Aeneas (at Pompeii 9.13.5).[15] In order to riff off of the opening

14. We might assume that an anti-imperial graffito would have been swiftly removed, but this graffito was quite small and may have remained under the radar of detection. Relatedly, offensive graffiti seem often to have been left in place. The curious case of Martha being ridiculed in her own "triclinium" (actually the toilet) is intriguing in this regard (*CIL* 4.5224). More telling is Salvius's graffito that insults Ampliatus (see *CIL* 4.3275, which reads: "Ampliatus, Icarus buggers you'—Salvius wrote this") in a residence that some think was occupied by Ampliatus himself (Pompeii 1.4.25); see, e.g., Hartnett, *Roman Street*, 126. Cf. also *CIL* 4.6893, which reads: "the mother of Augustus Caesar was a woman" (*Caesaris Augusti femina mater erat*). In one sense, this statement is perfectly true and politically innocuous, but in another sense, the very act of pointing out Augustus's non-divine origins might suggest that the inscriber felt the need to claw back extreme forms of devotion to the imperial family. Curiously, the graffito was found in the villa of Boscotrecase, which is often thought to have been originally built (at around the beginning of the first century CE by Agrippa Postumus, grandson of emperor Augustus.

15. In his reply to this essay at the Intertextuality in the New Testament Section at SBL 2018, Peter Oakes made the interesting suggestion that this graffito might simply have been a form of advertising the fuller's business. The suggestion needs to be

line of the *Aeneid*, this graffito activates the meaning of that line (which resonates with the display of Aeneas above it) in order to negate the political affirmation of the phrase. Contextual resonance is a necessary component of the graffito if its sentiment of political dissent is to be felt.[16]

Another Pompeian "intertextual graffito" may illustrate another way in which intertextuality was used creatively—not in the service of politics in this case but, instead, in the service of humor. A single word appears in a graffito on the wall of the town's main brothel (*CIL* 4.2213): *conticuere*. In their book on Pompeian inscriptions, Alison Cooley and M. G. L. Cooley list this as a citation of the first word of the second book of the *Aeneid*, which begins *conticuere omnes*, or "they were all silent."[17] The allusion to *conticuere* in the *Aeneid* is commonly recognized.[18]

---

considered, but is problematized by the fact that the graffito was written in small script and did not draw attention to itself (and, I think, by underestimating the force of the "not").

16. Others adopt much the same view of this graffiti. See, e.g., Milnor, *Graffiti*, 122–23; and Keegan, *Graffiti in Antiquity*, 153, who writes: "What the graffito... does with the best-known opening line of contemporary poetry in the Roman world is deliciously subversive.... [T]he reworked text foregrounds the priority of local personalities and issues... over and beyond national ideology—Romulus and Aeneas, the *Aeneid*, and underlying imperial claims." For another Pompeian example of the subversion of the story of Aeneas, see the artifact Museo Archeologico Nazionale di Napoli (MANN), no. 9089, as discussed in Longenecker, *In Stone and Story*, 138–39.

It is possible to speculate as to who the inscriber of the graffito might have been. That person was probably attached to this fullery in some fashion but was probably not the owner of the fullery. The "not" is provocative and it is unlikely that the owner would have wanted to articulate unpopular sentiments about Rome. Similarly, that person is unlikely to have been an offspring of the fuller. Consequently, it is most likely that the inscriber was a slave of the owner of the fullery. If this reasoning is correct, it would be another instance of a slave having a certain level of literacy. On slaves and workers undermining the interests of their owners and employers in the Roman world, see Joshel and Hackworth Petersen, *Material Life of Roman Slaves*, 121; 143. We know some of the names of dependents within the fullery: Calamus, Leno, Pegte, Ephebus, Ricinus, and Gerulus (see *CIL* 4.9116; 4.9125–32).

17. Cooley and Cooley, *Pompeii and Herculaneum*, 293.

18. We might want to question whether a single word is forceful enough to make an intertextual link. In this regard, however, we need to keep another Pompeian inscription in mind (whose provenance I am uncertain of). It reads *conticuere omnes* (*CIL* 4.6707), replicating the first two words of Book 2 of the *Aeneid* exactly. Notice, however, that the editors of *CIL* 4 (Supplement 2, 706) comment that *omnes* is written in a larger and sloppier hand than *conticuere*. This phenomenon usually suggests that the graffito resulted from the hands of more than one person. If that were the case in this instance, the first inscriber simply wrote *conticuere*, "they were silent," with the second adding *omnes*. Did the first inscriber intend to draw on the Virgilian classic

If this intertextual connection to the *Aeneid* has merit (as seems likely), it suggests something about the graffito's intended function. A graffito announcing "they were silent" was probably not etched into the plaster of the main brothel because the customer was bored and needed something to do. Since the brothel was probably not a place where people were silent, the statement "they were silent" must have served as a vehicle of humor.[19] This is not to say that the graffito loses sight of the Virgilian context; arguably, the humor of the graffito is rooted in the disjunction between the original literary referent and the word's new referent derived from its new context, with *conticuere* inviting new contours of significance. There would seem to be playfulness in this single-word graffito, with humor arising in the disparity between the word's function in the two quite different contexts, both of which are required to be in mind in order for the humor of the graffito to be effective.[20] Here we see a precursor text being both referenced and channeled into another stream of meaning simultaneously—an instance of what others have called "hypertextuality."[21]

Intertextuality and Lucretius's On the Nature of Things

In Pompeii's House of Fabius Rufus (at Pompeii 7.16.22), someone scratched the three Latin words that open Book 2 of Lucretius's *On the Nature of Things: suave mari magno.*[22] In Lucretius's rigorously Epicurean text, those three words introduce a short phrase within a much longer

---

with only one word, or did that Virgilian connection arise only when a second inscriber saw the possibility of creating a clever textual reference by adding *omnes*? We will never know the motives of the first inscriber, of course. The best guess is that that inscriber was referencing the first word of Book 2 of Virgil's *Aeneid*, with another inscriber taking the occasion to elaborate the reference.

19. Levin-Richardson has recently advocated this view as well; *Brothel of Pompeii*, 63.

20. This conforms to Quintilian's third category of humor, which arises by "taking words in a different sense from what was intended" (*Inst.* 6.3.24; Eng. trans. by Butler, LCL, 2:451).

21. Rosenberg, "Hypertextuality." With the *conticuere* graffiti in view, we might compare the way John's Gospel begins in a fashion that seems to activate the story of Genesis with two simple words (ἐν ἀρχῇ; John 1:1; LXX Gen 1:1), while transforming that story in relation to a new context of signification—the gospel of the Word, Jesus Christ.

22. Solin, "Die herkulanensischen Wandinschriften," 102n28.

complex sentence; in the graffito, by contrast, they stand as a short, self-standing, and simple sentence: "Pleasant it is over the great sea." The graffito applies Lucretius's three words to the situation of the grand residence—the four-story house with its splendid vistas overlooking the Mediterranean Sea. How pleasant that would have been.

In Lucretius's text, however, those three words served a different function. The full sentence in which they were embedded is as follows:

> *Suave mari magno turbantibus aequora ventis e terra magnum alterius spectare laborem; non quia vexari quemquamst iucunda voluptas, sed quibus ipse malis careas quia cernere suavest.*
>
> Pleasant it is, when over the great sea the winds trouble the waters, to gaze from shore upon another's great tribulation; not because any man's troubles are a delectable joy, but because to perceive you are free of them yourself is pleasant.[23]

Lucretius's point was that things are pleasant for the Epicurean in the same situations which other people find difficult. When the Epicurean sees other people in difficult situations, watching them struggle to survive the storms that come their way, although there is no pleasure in seeing their misfortune itself, the Epicurean nonetheless gains pleasure from the fact that one has not been engulfed in similar forms of emotional distress. The Epicurean stands above the fray of ordinary people who are disturbed by their troubles in life.

Was the graffito in the House of Fabius Rufus intended to import all this metaphorical meaning, espousing a kind of disengagement from the cares of those who struggle in life? We cannot rule this option out.[24] But even if that were the case, the graffito seems primarily to have force without necessarily relying on an Epicurean sentiment. It can simply stand

---

23. Lucretius, *DRN* 2.1; Eng. trans. by Smith, LCL, 95.

24. This would not be the first instance of a socio-economically privileged person adopting an Epicurean perspective. See, for instance, MacGillivray, "Popularity of Epicureanism." With reference to the graffito in Pompeii's House of Fabius Rufus, note the comment by Butterworth and Laurence: "Ungenerous as the attitude may have been, such *schadenfreude* [sic] was understandable. As men with mercantile interests, Fabius Rufus and his neighbours would have observed from their picture windows the fluctuation in their own fortunes as well as those of others connected to them" (*Pompeii, Living City*, 48 [43 in some editions]). The slight irony in this scenario is that this house was the place of death for at least four people who died in the dining room of the house, trying to avoid the "great tribulation" that was afflicting all the others within their town.

on its own, emphasizing how pleasant it was to reside in such an opulent setting. The original significance of the three Latin words in Lucretius's opening lines of Book 2 has been shifted by the new context of the graffito. This semantic shift (including a new syntactical function for *mari magno*) enables a new significance of the words and a new "concrete" application of the text taking precedence over the original metaphorical sense.

Arguably a similar case can be made with regard to several other graffiti (probably five in number) that cite the opening two words not of Book 2 but of Book 1—the very opening of Lucretius's long Epicurean text: *Aeneadum genetrix* (*DRN* 1.1; *CIL* 4.3072; 4.3118; 4.3139; 4.3913 [from Pompeii 1.2.21]; and 4.4373), "O mother of the Roman race." The "mother" referred to here is Venus (*DRN* 1.2), as Lucretius points out in the next clause, referring to her as "Venus most bountiful" and crediting her with filling creation with bounty ("since by your power creatures of every kind are brought to birth"; *DRN* 1.3–4).[25]

Lucretius's opening *encomium* to Venus is, of course, a complicated and highly nuanced piece of rhetoric. His strategy, both here and elsewhere in *On the Nature of Things*, is to articulate a literal understanding of the realm of the deities within Greco-Roman mythology only to demonstrate how seriously flawed that viewpoint is, at least as it was commonly understood. Lucretius wanted to educate his audience in knowing how to demythologize the myths of his day along Epicurean lines, educating people how to utter statements that fell in line with common perceptions while also meaning something completely alien to those common perceptions.[26] For Lucretius, the myths about the deities captured truths about the natural order of things, although the deities themselves were largely just placeholders for natural phenomena.

How then are we to interpret the handful of graffiti that reference the opening of Lucretius's text? Are they articulating (1) Lucretius's very nuanced and demythologized view of Venus and other deities, or (2) the view that Lucretius was trying to debunk, being held by (what he would consider to be) the uneducated masses? A dense pro-Roman sentiment had largely enshrouded the town, with no obvious foothold for

25. Eng. trans. by Knox and McKeown, *Oxford Anthology of Roman Literature*, 73.
26. Lucretius seems even to outline his rhetorical strategy in precisely these terms explicitly at key points; see, e.g., *DRN* 1.145, 933–950. In 4.11–25, he compares his task to that of a physician who, upon giving a cup of medicine to his patients, coats the rim of the cup with honey in order to sweeten its otherwise unpalatable contents.

a demythologized Venus detached from the Roman program.[27] For that reason, it seems likely that these graffiti were expressions of the popular sentiment that ran rampant in Pompeii, which held Venus literally to be the great protector of the town and promoter of the Roman order—that is, the "mother of the Roman race," in accordance with the standard understanding of popular Greco-Roman mythology.

Of course, we can never be sure of this, since we have no access to the social context in which these graffiti were written. It is always possible that this phrase was a uniquely Epicurean slogan that Pompeian Epicureans placed on walls to reinforce Lucretius's Epicureanism within the town. It seems more likely, however, that the widespread pro-Romanism within the town should tip us to expect these intertextual graffiti to be instances of putting textual data to use in ways unencumbered by the precursor text. The handful of people who inscribed these graffiti probably used Lucretius's words, "mother of the Roman race," to articulate a popular worldview that ran contrary to the function of those words within the larger context and rhetorical purposes of Lucretius's text. Some Pompeians may have been oblivious to this, of course, especially in view of Lucretius's complicated rhetorical strategy of articulating views in order to deconstruct popular (mis)conceptions. But that same strategy easily permitted this "naïve" form of intertextuality to emerge on Pompeian walls.

When assessing the graffiti that cited the opening words of Virgil's *Aeneid*, I argued that the pro-Roman sentiment that permeated large swaths of the Pompeian population should cause us to see those graffiti as referencing the pro-Romanism of the Virgilian novel, with the intertextual relationship being one in which Pompeian graffiti usually go with the grain of the precursor text (although not always with its sentiment, as in the case of the graffito outside the fullery). In the case of graffiti that cite the opening words of Lucretius's *On the Nature of Things*, however, I am arguing that that same pro-Roman sentiment should cause us to see those graffiti as instances in which the intertextual relationship is one of going against the grain of the precursor text (because of Lucretius's complicated rhetorical strategy).

---

27. Even the Roman emperor Nero and his wife, Poppaea, had sent gifts to honor the temple of "the most holy Venus" in Pompeii (*AE* [1985], 283–84). For further discussion of Venus in relation to Roman imperial ideology, see esp. Longenecker, *In Stone and Story*, 66–67.

Intertextuality and Cicero's *In Verrem*

As we have seen in the case of the fuller's graffito (discussed above), not all intertextual graffiti display pro-Roman sentiment, and the same is evidenced for one final example of Pompeian graffiti. This graffito is rarely discussed in Vesuvian literature, but when it is discussed, scholars usually suggest that it displays a radical form of intertextuality, drawing its significance from, but simultaneously reworking, a scene in Cicero's *In Verrem* (2.5.162).[28] In that scene, a Roman citizen is violently and unjustly tortured. Despite his sufferings, he keeps silent and does not cry out or moan in pain. Just before he dies, he repeats only one phrase in the hope of bringing his torment to an end: "I am a Roman citizen" (*civis Romanus sum*). His public pronouncement does nothing to change the course of his persecution, however; his life ends on a Roman cross in what Cicero depicts as a miscarriage of Roman justice.

If the graffito under consideration references that story, it does so by twisting its various components until they play new roles in a forcefully graphic sexual metaphor. Perhaps this is another instance of "hypertextuality" (as noted above), or what others have called "narrative transformation," in which a precursor text is referenced and simultaneously transformed in some fashion.[29] The components that carry over from Cicero's original story into this graffito would include three themes: citizenship, silence, and moans. The sexually graphic graffito is as follows: "Screwed, I say. With legs drawn back, the vagina of the citizens of Rome was screwed, and there was no sound except sweet and respectful moans" (*CIL* 4.1261).

In this new narrative, Rome takes its pleasures from the people, who oblige without protest, uttering moans that give Rome what it wants to hear. This graffito might be interpreted as a statement of support for Rome (assuming the citizens enjoy being "screwed"). But there is some scope for a more subversive interpretation, especially if the graffito is seen to riff off of Cicero's scene of the Roman citizen—a scene used by Cicero to condemn systemic injustice. If the creator of this graffito was drawing on that literary context, he (or, less likely, she) may be suggesting that the citizens were not, in fact, enjoying being "screwed" by Rome, just as Cicero's Roman citizen did not enjoy his unjust punishment and death.

---

28. As postulated by Cagusi, "Spunti di polemica politica in alcuni graffiti di Pompei."

29. Kirk, "Narrative Transformation."

Despite the "sweet and respectful moans," the sexual penetration mentioned in the graffito is the intertextual equivalent of the Roman citizen's death mentioned in Cicero's precursor text.

In this possible intertextual trope, the relationship of Rome to its citizens is more like a tragic and atrocious rape—a rape that is neither vocally protested nor physically resisted, but is unwanted and unjust nonetheless.[30] In situations where resistance is deemed to be futile and power is abusively overbearing, it is not unusual for people to feel that their survival strategies have been reduced to simply giving the oppressor what he wants, while saying what the oppressor wants to hear—and all this despite the absence of anything even closely approximating genuine consent.[31] Perhaps, then, this graffito "impart[s] a frisson of counter-culture and counter-hegemony" even while being "framed within the elite-oriented texts" and "related to and reflective of the elite's own agendas."[32]

If this graffito contains within it a subtle form of protest against the perceived atrocities of Roman rule, it is also marked out by strategic ingenuity.[33] This is because, as noted above, the graffito can also be heard as an

---

30. The sexual imagery of this graffito diverges notably from the script of sexual imagery normally reserved for descriptions of Roman imperial rule. For instance, during the reign of emperor Tiberius, the Roman historian Valerius Maximus depicted the female deity Chastity (*pudicitia*) as pervading the imperial household (*Memorable Doings and Sayings*, 6.1.1, which, e.g., states: "you [Chastity] never leave your post on the pinnacle of the Palatine"; Eng. trans. by Bailey, LCL, vol. 2, 3), just as a coin struck during the time of Hadrian put the emperor's image on one side and the deity Chastity on the other (*RIC* 2.135, 176–178, 343). Hylen notes, "[P]udicitia connoted political or civic virtue, and not only personal morality... Pudicitia was a goddess inhabiting and watching over sacred Roman space, and in particular, the imperial household. Human *pudicitia* pleased the divine and contributed to the security of the city" (*Women in the New Testament World*, 48). The imagery of the graffito may suggest that Rome, in fact, turns its citizens into (unwilling) whores.

The graffito may also draw on the sentiment that, on occasion, silence in adversity displays a form of bravery. Hylen so states: "silence was not simply viewed as mere passivity"; in some cases "it was an act of courage" (*Women in the New Testament World*, 39). The imagery of the graffito may suggest that the abused populaces are the ones of true courage.

31. On political subversion and the popular voice, see Zadorojnyi, "Transcripts of Dissent?" Of this graffito he notes that while "verbatim parallels [with Cicero] are minimal yet the flair and pathos look convincingly Ciceronian" (112).

32. Zadorojnyi, "Transcripts of Dissent?" 114.

33. For other evidence of subversion within Pompeian material remains, see Grant, *Cities of Vesuvius*, 130; Lessing and Varone, *Pompeii*, 83. For a similar phenomenon of indigenous resentment toward Rome among some residents in Philippi, see Nasrallah, *Archaeology and the Letters of Paul*, 119–22.

affirmation of Roman rule, even if it can also signal a protest. The graffito's potential to encapsulate double-but-independent meanings should not be surprising. People who consider themselves to be oppressed by empire sometimes choose not to articulate their disgruntlement explicitly; instead, they prefer to keep a low profile and articulate their sentiments through encoded discourse seemingly devoid of explicit articulation. Is this graffito an instance of that kind of thing? If pressed, the graffito composer could argue that all one (presumably) meant to say is that the citizens are enjoying the sweet penetration of Rome. If pressed, he/she could argue that the link to Cicero's famous scene is spuriously attributed to his/her otherwise innocent expression of political support for Rome. In other moments, a nod and a wink when alluding to Cicero's story takes the graffito's significance in the other direction altogether. Here, the fogginess of the link to Cicero can be seen as a tool of self-protection. That link can be appreciated in those moments when a subversive posture can be fostered, just as the same link can disappear from view in the very moment when a subversive posture would compromise one's strategies for survival and advancement.[34]

Summing Up

On the basis of Pompeian graffiti, I see little to suggest that the variety of intertextual strategies evidenced in the New Testament would have been foreign to the sub-elite of Pompeii. Expanding our survey to include Vesuvian wall paintings would help to triangulate this short study of Vesuvian graffiti, but would only reinforce our sense of variety with regard to the way precursor texts and narratives were activated among the Vesuvian sub-elite.[35] What we have seen is a spectrum of techniques for engaging

---

34. This graffito, then, conforms to the general pattern of "backstage discourse" or "hidden transcripts" outlined by Scott, *Domination and the Art of Resistance*; see, e.g., Joshel and Hackworth Petersen, *Material Life of Roman Slaves*, 7. Cf. the final words in the *Fables* by Phaedrus (15 BCE to 50 CE): "For a man of humble birth, it is not proper to protest in public" (3.34). Cf. also Euripides, *Phoen.* 392, where the condition of slavery is described as "not saying what one thinks" (μὴ λέγειν ἃ τις φρονεῖ).

35. Zanker captures the point this way: "For the Romans of that era, the use of myths to allude to the present seems to have been as natural as biblical references were in our own society not long ago. Ordinary people could use this relatively educated and 'international' language of allusion to express their claims to membership in dominant social and cultural circles, just as they did with wall paintings" (*Pompeii*, 22–23). Intertextuality within Pompeian frescoes is illustrated repeatedly in Tuck,

precursor texts of the Greco-Roman "canon" among Vesuvian sub-elite populations. Evidently, then, the techniques of intertextual referencing that we see in the texts of the early Jesus-movement were completely at home in the Roman world, at least if the "intertextual graffiti" of Pompeii are anything to go by. Those graffiti suggest that, with regard to method, the intertextual linkages and gestures that we see in NT texts would not have been seen as alien or illegitimate among sub-elite urban dwellers of the Roman world.

Pompeii. Further, see among many other contributions, Tuck, *History of Roman Art,* 175–76; Knox, "Ovidian Myths on Pompeian Walls"; Swetnam-Burland, "Encountering Ovid's Phaedra."

4

Paul's Multi-Layered Use of Scripture

Taking Intertextuality One Step Further

Konrad Otto

DETERMINING INTERTEXTUALITY IN PAUL is fraught with difficulty. Continuous critique notwithstanding,[1] intertextuality has garnered widespread acceptance as an umbrella term for research focusing on Paul's use of Scripture. Although interest in this field has been on a steady rise at least since Richard Hays's *Echoes of Scripture in the Letters of Paul*,[2] the research is far from following a unified approach or perspective. Thus, scholars have reached vastly different assessments of Paul's use of Scripture.[3]

Looking back at six years of SBL's Paul and Scripture Seminar, Christopher Stanley concluded in 2012 that all of the seminar's participants had realized the necessity of considering "the historical, social, and

---

1. See Porter, "Pauline Techniques of Interweaving Scripture into His Letters," 24–28.

*Work on the first drafts of this essay was funded by Deutsche Forschungsgemeinschaft's Collaborative Research Centre 1136—Education and Religion at the University of Göttingen.

2. Hays, *Echoes of Scripture in the Letters of Paul*.

3. For an overview on points of commonality and points of variety, see the essays edited by Wilk and Öhler, *Paulinische Schriftrezeption*.

rhetorical contexts in which [Paul] composed his letters" more deeply.[4] Moreover, they had realized the need not to confine their research to explicitly-marked quotations. Yet no consensus could be reached regarding what scriptural competency Paul presupposes for his audience and to what degree the context of the Scriptures Paul cites influences his reasoning.[5]

Today, some years later, one basic divide still runs between a maximalist and a minimalist view of the importance of scriptural references for Paul's meaning. On the one side of the debate, adherents to a maximalist view tend to identify even the slightest semantic or conceptual overlap as a biblical echo that determines the meaning behind Paul's words.[6] A common line of argument runs as follows: We can assume Paul to be well-versed in Scripture. Therefore, more often than not he takes his citation's context into account, adapts Scripture with a sense for minute exegetical detail, and expects an equally high proficiency in Scripture from his audience. Without such proficiency the reader simply cannot make sense of his writing and potentially can misconstrue it.[7]

On the other hand, those who pursue a minimalist approach tend to admit only clearly marked citations to contribute to Paul's line of thought. These scholars often consider Paul's addressees to be Greco-Roman converts who are unfamiliar with Israel's traditions. Obscure biblical allusions must be seriously called into question. While some exegetical intricacies might be intended by Paul, they are by no means crucial to his argument. For the sake of perspicuity, Paul clearly marks important citations and provides background knowledge for how he wants them to be understood.[8]

---

4. Stanley, "What We Learned—and What We Didn't," 322. See also the more recent assessment in Wagner, "Epilogue," 297.

5. Stanley, "What We Learned—and What We Didn't," 324–27.

6. The claim of new Exodus imagery in Paul provides a much debated example; see Keesmaat, *Paul and His Story*; Wright, "New Exodus, New Inheritance"; Morales, *Spirit and the Restoration of Israel*; Wright, *Paul and the Faithfulness of God*; cf. Das, *Paul and the Stories of Israel*; Moyise, "Wright's Understanding of Paul's Use of Scripture."

7. See Wright, *Paul and the Faithfulness of God*, 13, who argues that "Israel's scriptures were as familiar to Paul, and as readily available in his well-stocked mind, as Beethoven's sonatas to a concert pianist."

8. A main proponent of this minimalist approach is Christopher Stanley; see Stanley, *Paul and the Language*; Stanley, *Arguing with Scripture*; and Vegge, "Sacred Scripture in the Letters of Paul." See also the classical cautioning against "parallelomania" by Sandmel, "Parallelomania"; Porter, "Use of the Old Testament in the New Testament";

The aim of this essay is to demonstrate that choosing between a maximalist approach and a minimalist one might be choosing between false alternatives. Instead it proves instructive to bring the two perspectives together and combine an analysis of the texts' intentions (i.e., a mainly author-oriented perspective), with intertextual reconstruction of how different readers, coming from different cultural backgrounds and holding different levels of scriptural competency, might have understood the same text (i.e., a reader-oriented perspective). This essay argues for a tiered competency among Paul's readership.

The contested passage 2 Cor 2:14—4:6 shall serve as a case study to demonstrate that some Pauline texts allow readers with vastly different levels of scriptural competency to find meaning in Paul's scriptural allusions and thus to follow Paul's train of thought along different tracks toward the same argumentative goal. In order to make sense of this phenomenon, it is necessary to take the notion of intertextuality one step further so that it includes *both* the author's and the readers' interactions with relevant precursor texts or traditions.

2 Cor 2:14—4:6—An Overview

Perhaps more than any other Pauline text, 2 Cor 2:14—4:6 continues to baffle its interpreters. Not only are its intertextual dependencies widely debated, but the underlying theological concepts also elude scholarly consensus. Interpretations range from supersessionist to inclusivist, from casually intertextual to intricately linked with precursor texts and traditions.[9] The text is dominated by a clearly marked reference to the story of Moses returning from Mount Sinai in Exod 34:29–35. After encountering YHWH/the Lord on the mountain, Moses returns with a radiating, "glorified" face, which he later veils when talking to the Israelites. Paul takes this story as the starting point for an elaborate juxtaposition of his own preaching ministry with Moses' ministry.

---

or more recently "Schrifttüftelei" or "scriptural fiddling" by Zeller, *Der erste Brief an die Korinther*, 331.

9. For some major treatments see Hafemann, *Suffering and the Spirit*; Stockhausen, *Moses' Veil and the Glory of the New Covenant*; Belleville, *Reflections of Glory*; Hafemann, *Paul, Moses, and the History of Israel*; Duff, *Moses in Corinth*; and Cover, *Lifting the Veil*. For recent assessments of the role of Scripture in 2 Cor 3, see the essays edited by Wilk, *Paul and Moses*.

In fact, Linda Belleville and Michael Cover have each in their own way pointed out that Paul follows a common Hellenistic-Jewish commentary pattern when elaborating on the Exodus story.[10] Yet most of his exegetical finesse is hard to detect and easily missed if the reader is not an expert on the text. The significance of other even more subtle allusions to prophetic traditions that frame the Exodus reference is also debated. These difficulties make 2 Cor 2:14—4:6 an ideal test case for our purposes.

Here I will propose a reading of the passage from which we can then work our way back to the question of intertextuality. As 2 Cor 2:14—4:6 heads the section of 2 Cor 2:14—7:4, which is commonly known as Paul's "apology," the text is sensitive to bolster the speaker's character and trustworthiness through the rhetorical field of *ethos*. In this whole section, Paul argues for the validity of his apostolic ministry. He reacts to some (perceived) rejection of his person and preaching ministry. While all attempts to reconstruct the exact nature of the underlying debate have proven futile, the overall aim of his argumentation is clearly to present himself as a legitimate, competent, and crucial minister of the gospel (cf. 2:17; 3:3, 4–6; 4:1–6).[11]

Paul directly addresses the question of his competency in the opening verses of the passage. After portraying the life-and-death implications of his ministry, he rhetorically asks: "Who is sufficient for these things (καὶ πρὸς ταῦτα τίς ἱκανός; 2:16c)"? Some detect here the first allusion to the story of the Exodus.[12] In Exod 4:10, Moses objects to God's calling by stating: "I am not a man of words (לא איש דברים אנכי)." The LXX translates Exod 4:10 as "I am not sufficient (οὐχ ἱκανός εἰμι)."[13] In both accounts Moses, then, is enabled by God to fulfill his calling.

---

10. See Belleville, *Reflections of Glory*; Cover, *Lifting the Veil*.

11. See Wilk, "Zur Funktion von 2Kor 3,4–18 in seinem literarischen Zusammenhang."

12. See Hafemann, *Paul, Moses, and the History of Israel*, 49.

13. See Hafemann, *Paul, Moses, and the History of Israel*, 43. All English translations of scriptural texts from the Hebrew or Greek are my own unless otherwise noted.

Exod 4:10	2 Cor 2:16c
¹⁰ εἶπεν δὲ Μωυσῆς πρὸς κύριον δέομαι κύριε οὐχ <u>ἱκανός</u> εἰμι πρὸ τῆς ἐχθὲς οὐδὲ πρὸ τῆς τρίτης ἡμέρας οὐδὲ ἀφ' οὗ ἤρξω λαλεῖν τῷ θεράποντί σου	¹⁶ᶜ καὶ πρὸς ταῦτα τίς <u>ἱκανός</u>;

Paul does not directly answer the question regarding his competency. Instead he addresses two possible grounds on which he could argue for his sufficiency.

On the one hand, his sufficiency could theoretically depend on the qualities that lie in himself, like his moral conduct; but, on the other hand, his sufficiency could depend on his intimacy with God (2:17). Paul outright dismisses the first possibility and refuses any recommendation that is dependent on his own behavior or qualities (3:1).[14] Instead, he argues that his sufficiency is based on his relationship with God and the evidence for it is the spiritual fruit of his ministry, that is, the Corinthian community itself as the only valid "letter (of recommendation) written on our hearts" (3:2). By weaving together a series of interlocking metaphors, Paul makes his *apologia* that the proof of his apostleship lies not in his own moral character or rhetorical skills but in the Corinthian church whose lives in Christ function as a letter "written not with ink but with the Spirit of the living God, (and this) not on tablets of stone but on tablets of human hearts" (3:3).[15]

Confusing as the metaphors are, once the reader takes them under closer scrutiny, their basic message is clear. Since the Corinthians have encountered God's Spirit first and foremost through Paul's ministry, they are in no position to doubt the value of this very ministry.[16] The reference to the stone tablets of Mount Sinai aside, Paul apparently draws here—as some would argue—on texts from the books of Jeremiah and Ezekiel that promise covenantal renewal.[17]

14. For the reconstruction of Paul's overall argument, see Otto, "Zwischen den Welten."

15. See Thrall, *Critical and Exegetical Commentary on the Second Epistle to the Corinthians*, 1:226; Furnish, *II Corinthians*, 194.

16. See Duff, *Moses in Corinth*, 120; Land, *Integrity of 2 Corinthians and Paul's Aggravating Absence*, 121; Gerber, *Paulus und seine "Kinder,"* 180.

17. See Hafemann, *Suffering and the Spirit*, 204; Stockhausen, *Moses' Veil and the Glory of the New Covenant*, 54–59.

According to Ezek 11:19 and 36:36, God will give his people a new spirit (πνεῦμα καινόν) and a new living heart, while removing its old heart of stone (ἐκσπάσω τὴν καρδίαν τὴν λιθίνην ἐκ τῆς σαρκὸς αὐτῶν καὶ δώσω αὐτοῖς καρδίαν σαρκίνην). Similarly, LXX Jer 38:33 (MT 31:33) promises that God will write his law on the hearts of his people (καρδίας αὐτῶν γράψω) in the process of establishing a new covenant with them (διαθήσομαι τῷ οἴκῳ Ισραηλ καὶ τῷ οἴκῳ Ιουδα διαθήκην καινήν).

LXX Ezek 11:19 + 36:26	LXX Jer 38:31–34	2 Cor 3:6 + 3:2–3
11:19 καὶ δώσω αὐτοῖς καρδίαν ἑτέραν καὶ <u>πνεῦμα καινὸν</u> δώσω ἐν αὐτοῖς καὶ ἐκσπάσω τὴν <u>καρδίαν</u> τὴν <u>λιθίνην</u> ἐκ τῆς σαρκὸς αὐτῶν καὶ δώσω αὐτοῖς <u>καρδίαν σαρκίνην</u>	**38:31-32** ἰδοὺ ἡμέραι ἔρχονται φησὶν κύριος καὶ διαθήσομαι τῷ οἴκῳ Ισραηλ καὶ τῷ οἴκῳ Ιουδα <u>διαθήκην καινήν</u> **32** οὐ κατὰ τὴν διαθήκην ἣν διεθέμην τοῖς πατράσιν αὐτῶν ἐν ἡμέρᾳ ἐπιλαβομένου μου τῆς χειρὸς αὐτῶν ἐξαγαγεῖν αὐτοὺς ἐκ γῆς Αἰγύπτου ὅτι αὐτοὶ οὐκ ἐνέμειναν ἐν τῇ διαθήκῃ μου καὶ ἐγὼ ἠμέλησα αὐτῶν φησὶν κύριος	**3:6** ὃς καὶ ἱκάνωσεν ἡμᾶς διακόνους <u>καινῆς διαθήκης</u>...
36:26 καὶ δώσω ὑμῖν καρδίαν καινὴν καὶ <u>πνεῦμα καινὸν</u> δώσω ἐν ὑμῖν καὶ ἀφελῶ τὴν <u>καρδίαν</u> τὴν <u>λιθίνην</u> ἐκ τῆς σαρκὸς ὑμῶν καὶ δώσω ὑμῖν <u>καρδίαν σαρκίνην</u>	**38:33-34** ὅτι αὕτη ἡ διαθήκη ἣν διαθήσομαι τῷ οἴκῳ Ισραηλ μετὰ τὰς ἡμέρας ἐκείνας φησὶν κύριος διδοὺς δώσω νόμους μου εἰς τὴν διάνοιαν αὐτῶν καὶ ἐπὶ <u>καρδίας</u> αὐτῶν <u>γράψω</u> αὐτοὺς καὶ ἔσομαι αὐτοῖς εἰς θεόν καὶ αὐτοὶ ἔσονταί μοι εἰς λαόν **34** καὶ οὐ μὴ διδάξωσιν ἕκαστος τὸν πολίτην αὐτοῦ καὶ ἕκαστος τὸν ἀδελφὸν αὐτοῦ λέγων <u>γνῶθι</u> τὸν κύριον ὅτι πάντες εἰδήσουσίν με ἀπὸ μικροῦ αὐτῶν καὶ ἕως μεγάλου αὐτῶν ὅτι ἵλεως ἔσομαι ταῖς ἀδικίαις αὐτῶν καὶ τῶν ἁμαρτιῶν αὐτῶν οὐ μὴ μνησθῶ ἔτι	**3:2-3** ἡ ἐπιστολὴ ἡμῶν ὑμεῖς ἐστε, <u>ἐγγεγραμμένη</u> ἐν ταῖς <u>καρδίαις</u> ἡμῶν, γινωσκομένη καὶ ἀναγινωσκομένη ὑπὸ πάντων ἀνθρώπων, **3** φανερούμενοι ὅτι ἐστὲ ἐπιστολὴ Χριστοῦ διακονηθεῖσα ὑφ᾽ ἡμῶν, <u>ἐγγεγραμμένη</u> οὐ μέλανι ἀλλὰ <u>πνεύματι</u> θεοῦ ζῶντος, οὐκ ἐν πλαξὶν <u>λιθίναις</u> ἀλλ᾽ ἐν πλαξὶν <u>καρδίαις σαρκίναις</u>

After alluding to these traditions, Paul seems to finish his argument. He frankly states that his sufficiency is not coming from himself but from

God (3:4–5), who has made Paul and his coworkers "sufficient to be ministers of a new covenant" (3:6a), whereby Paul invokes LXX Jer 38:31 and its notion of covenantal renewal. At this point one could think Paul's argument to be complete. He has proven his sufficiency based on the Corinthians' own experience, and he has explained its divine origin.

Yet in the very same sentence, Paul picks up the motif of writing on stone tablets he mentioned earlier in passing and begins to amplify his argument from the Corinthians' spiritual experience.[18] First, he adds an argument from Scripture by paraphrasing and slightly embellishing Exod 34:29–30. His reasoning is from the lesser to the greater: If Moses' ministry—which Paul knows to have led to death—participated in God's glory (δόξα) as is evidenced in Moses' shining face, how much more will Paul's ministry participate in this glory since the latter is determined by God's life-giving Spirit (3:7–11; cf. 3:3).[19]

Paul then adds another supporting argument (3:12–18). As opposed to Moses, who had to veil his glorified face when speaking to the Israelites, Paul proclaims the gospel in bold freedom (πολλῇ παρρησίᾳ; 3:12).[20] Therefore, believers in Christ are free to encounter God's glory on the face of Christ as opposed to Israel, who could not stand to watch God's glory on Moses' face. Paul reasons that the Lord, who is the Spirit, enabled Moses to converse freely with him in the tent of meeting.[21] The same Spirit is active in Paul's ministry (3:16–17).

The passage culminates in an almost hymnic description of the believers who behold God's glory "as in a mirror" and thereby are transformed by it (τὴν δόξαν κυρίου κατοπτριζόμενοι τὴν αὐτὴν εἰκόνα μεταμορφούμεθα; 3:18). Finally, Paul sums up his argument in 2 Cor 4:1–6. Again, the idea of seeing God and being transformed by his glory hearkens back to Moses being transformed by an encounter with God's glory in Exod 34. Along those lines, the language of seeing God in a mirror, too, might point to Moses who, according to ancient Jewish exegetical

18. See Duff, *Moses in Corinth*, 133; Hellholm, "Moses as διάκονος of the παλαιά διαθήκη—Paul as διάκονος of the καινή διαθήκη."

19. See Thrall, *Critical and Exegetical Commentary on the Second Epistle to the Corinthians*, 1.240; Stockhausen, *Moses' Veil and the Glory of the New Covenant*, 28; Duff, *Moses in Corinth*, 139–43.

20. On παρρησία see Becker, *Lukas und Dion von Prusa: das lukanische Doppelwerk im Kontext paganer Bildungsdiskurse*, 112–20.

21. On the translation of ἀπὸ κυρίου πνεύματος in 3:18, see Furnish, *II Corinthians*, 216; Thrall, *Critical and Exegetical Commentary on the Second Epistle to the Corinthians*, 1.287.

traditions on Num 12:6–8, did exactly that (Lev. Rabb. 1.14; Philo, *Leg.* 3.99–101).[22]

Adapting Christopher Stanley's Taxonomy of Readers

Reading 2 Cor 2:14—4:6 as a coherent, highly intertextual argument like this makes perfect sense, yet none of these scriptural references are explicitly marked other than the two paraphrases of Exod 34 that start off Paul's juxtaposition with Moses. How, then, can the more subtle allusions be said to be crucial to Paul's meaning? How do they serve his line of thought? And how would readers with different levels of scriptural competency have understood Paul's argument? At this point, multiple layers of intertextuality come into view.

In his book *Arguing with Scripture*, which decidedly argues for a reader-oriented approach, Christopher Stanley posits three classes of hypothetical readers:

(1) a *minimal audience* "with little specific knowledge about the content of the Jewish Scriptures"[23]

(2) a *competent audience* "who knows just enough of the Jewish Scriptures to grasp the point of Paul's quotations"[24]

(3) an *informed audience* "who knows the original context of every one of Paul's quotations"[25]

Admittedly, this taxonomy is far too schematic to reconstruct comprehensively historic reality, but it is a useful tool to map a broad range of historically plausible interpretations. Thus we can adapt Stanley's taxonomy to fit our text's specific needs.

In the Corinthian community, we would have likely found a majority of converts coming from the city's immediate Greco-Roman surroundings, possibly some former God-fearers, and a minority from a Jewish-Hellenistic background (cf. 1 Cor 6:11; 7:18–19; 8:7; 12:2).[26] Therefore it

---

22. See the analyses by Litwa, "Transformation through a Mirror"; and Back, *Verwandlung durch Offenbarung*.

23. Stanley, *Arguing with Scripture*, 69.

24. Stanley, *Arguing with Scripture*, 68–69.

25. Stanley, *Arguing with Scripture*, 68.

26. See Engels, *Roman Corinth*, 107–10; O'Connor, *St. Paul's Corinth*, 78–80. For a reappraisal of the category "God-fearers," see Gupta, "Thessalonian Believers."

seems likely that Paul's letter recipients comprised of (a) a group with ample knowledge of Hellenistic culture but only an elementary knowledge of Israel's Scriptures; (b) a group with a Greco-Roman or Jewish-Hellenistic education with a knowledge of biblical themes and stories; and (c) a group with a Jewish-Hellenistic scribal background who was familiar with the very texts Paul alludes to.

I will borrow Stanley's terminology and refer to these three groups of readers respectively as the (a) "minimal," (b) "competent," and (c) "informed" audiences. Yet my classification differs from Stanley's as his three classes are defined by their overall comprehension of Paul's train of thought as is evident from Stanley's description of the "competent" and "informed" audiences. In contrast, the hypothetical groups of readers I posit here are defined by their scriptural competency irrespective of the Pauline text.

The reading I proposed earlier mostly corresponds to the middle group's understanding, which Stanley calls the "competent audience." Speaking about the second half of our text, Stanley concludes that the minimal audience would have had a hard time following Paul's reasoning, while the informed audience might likely rebel against his idiosyncratic interpretation of Scripture.[27] Strikingly, an intertextual analysis of 2 Cor 2:14—4:6 will show that the passage allows for varied intertextual readings which, in turn, lead towards the same argumentative goal. All three groups of potential readers would have been able to follow the main thrust of Paul's argument, their different levels of scriptural competency notwithstanding.

A Multi-Layered Intertextual Reading

Going through the text verse by verse, some detect the first allusion to the story of the Exodus in Paul's rhetorical question: "Who is sufficient for these things?" (2:16c). Admittedly, it is doubtful that the competent middle group would have easily identified this as an allusion to Moses before knowing where Paul's argument was headed. Still they would have likely been familiar with the concept of prophetic sufficiency in Second Temple Jewish literature.[28] Overall, sufficiency

---

27. See Stanley, *Arguing with Scripture*, 110–13.
28. See the discussion by Aernie, *Is Paul Also Among the Prophets?* 116–20.

is a common theme in prophetic calling narratives.²⁹ In his treatment of 2 Cor 3, Scott Hafemann has convincingly argued that a pattern of theophany–calling–objection–empowerment, modelled after the example of Moses, is also applicable to the train of thought in 2 Cor 3 and was well-known to Paul's readers in his day.³⁰

Thus, both for competent and informed readers who were familiar with the general prophetic call tradition, the rhetorical question would have foreshadowed Paul's claim to be made sufficient by God alone (3:5). Moreover, a scribal, informed reader might have been able to trace this tradition back to its origins in Exod 4:10. Close familiarity with the entire narrative of Exod 4 might also have brought to light other parallels between the Exodus account and 2 Cor 3. In the very next verse, Exod 4:11, for example, insists on God's direct agency to empower speech and sight or to cause blindness and deafness (καὶ τίς ἐποίησεν δύσκωφον καὶ κωφόν βλέποντα καὶ τυφλόν οὐκ ἐγὼ ὁ θεός),³¹ a claim that corresponds with the motif of hardened and blinded minds (ἐπωρώθη τὰ νοήματα αὐτῶν; 3:14 // ὁ θεὸς τοῦ αἰῶνος τούτου ἐτύφλωσεν τὰ νοήματα; 4:4) and veiled hearts (κάλυμμα ἐπὶ τὴν καρδίαν αὐτῶν; 3:15) in 2 Cor 3:12—4:6.³²

Neither of these echoes alluding to Exod 4:10 or 4:11 would have been noticed by a minimal audience, although even these readers would know enough to track the direction of Paul's argument. Stripped of its biblical background, the rhetorical question—"Who is sufficient for these things?" (2:16c)—still preempts an objection that might be brought up

---

29. According to Hafemann (*Paul, Moses, and the History of Israel*, 59–62), the *topos* of sufficiency does not even depend on the use of the actual term ἱκανός. See also Theobald, *Die überströmende Gnade*, 171.

30. Hafemann (*Paul, Moses, and the History of Israel*, 47–62) points to Gideon, Isaiah, Jeremiah, and Ezekiel as other biblical examples. Aernie (*Is Paul Also Among the Prophets?* 118–20) continues this line of inquiry and states: "Moses is seen as a 'fountainhead' for the entire prophetic tradition" (119).

31. See Danker, "Hardness of Heart," 89, who interprets Exod 4:11 as key to the motif of Israel's hardness of heart in the entire book of Exodus.

32. The more familiar one is with both texts and relevant exegetical traditions, the more parallels are there to discover or rather to construct. The LXX, for example, commonly translates דברי יהוה as ῥήματα (τοῦ) κυρίου. Strikingly, at the end of this very chapter, the translators deviate from this habit. According to LXX Exod 4:28, Moses passes πάντας τοὺς λόγους (!) κυρίου on to Aaron. To suspect an influence of this verse on the wording of 2 Cor 2:17; 4:2 might stretch credibility, but that alone is not an argument in itself. Moreover, in another example, Hafemann (*Paul, Moses, and the History of Israel*, 81–89; 100–106) points to rabbinical traditions that understand the calling of Moses as an act of new creation (cf. 2 Cor 5:17–21).

against the validity of Paul's ministry and thereby starts a line of reasoning that leads even the minimal reader to the claims of 2 Cor 3:5 that ultimately "we are not sufficient by our own agency... but our sufficiency comes from God (οὐχ ὅτι ἀφ' ἑαυτῶν ἱκανοί ἐσμεν... ἀλλ' ἡ ἱκανότης ἡμῶν ἐκ τοῦ θεοῦ)."[33] It is worth noting that the Corinthians would have been familiar with ἱκανός terminology in connection with Paul's ministry from 1 Cor 15:9. There he insists on not being worthy of his own accord to be called an apostle (ὃς οὐκ εἰμὶ ἱκανὸς καλεῖσθαι ἀπόστολος). Overall, Paul's argument gains coherence the more biblically competent or informed an audience is, but it has rhetorical coherence for a "minimal" audience as well.

The case of Paul's metaphorical tapestry about the Corinthians as a living letter of recommendation is more intricate. The competent middle group would have likely recognized the metaphor of being written on Paul's heart and that of the Spirit's writing on tablets of living hearts as an allusion to the prophetic traditions about the restoration of God's covenant with Israel. The concept of God renewing his covenant by somehow changing the heart of his people is a biblical commonplace, whether the Lord is imagined to write on the heart (LXX Jer 31:33; 38:33), substitute the heart (Ezek 11:19; 36:26), or circumcise it (Deut 30:6).[34]

A scribal, informed audience might have further been aware of the very texts Paul alludes to and those passages' wider contexts, that is, topics such as God's initiating his people's repentance (LXX Jer 38:18) and the correlation of spirit, life, and knowledge (LXX Ezek 37:6). These themes all contribute to the growing development of Paul's argument in 2 Cor 3.[35] Again, close familiarity with the texts to which Paul alludes allows the informed reader to construct various points of contact between the prophetic texts and the developing argument of 2 Cor 3. For example, LXX Jer 38:32 contrasts the new covenant with the covenant of the Exodus.[36] As opposed to "the covenant which I made with their fathers in

---

33. A typical feature of this use of rhetorical questions in antiquity is the lack of a direct answer. See Watson, "1 Corinthians 10:23—11:1 in the Light of Greco-Roman Rhetoric," 315–17. On the significance of the term ἱκανός in 3:5, see Hafemann, *Paul, Moses, and the History of Israel*, 97–109.

34. For the prevalence and the interdependency of these three concepts, see Coxhead, "Cardionomographic Work of the Spirit," and Robson, *Word and Spirit in Ezekiel*, 262.

35. See Kuschnerus, *Die Gemeinde als Brief Christi*, 154.

36. See Ezek 20:9–18 and 36–44 for unambiguous Exodus allusions in Ezekiel.

the day I took them by the hand to bring them out of the land of Egypt," the promised new covenant will be eternal (διαθήκην αἰωνίαν; LXX Jer 39:40; see also Ezek 37:26). Likewise Paul can speak of his ministry as that which "remains (τὸ μένον; 2 Cor 3:11)." What is more, the new covenant will bring knowledge of God (LXX Jer 38:34), just as Paul claims it for his own ministry (2 Cor 4:6).

All of these promises for a new covenant are based on the sins of Israel being forgotten according to Jeremiah (LXX Jer 38:34), but according to Paul they are based on the Spirit's work through Christ (2 Cor 3:6, 14–17; 4:5–6.). In fact Ezekiel's distinct interest in God's Spirit culminates in the very passage Paul alludes to, that is, Ezek 36:26—37:14 where 11 out of 36 instances of πνεῦμα in LXX Ezekiel can be found.[37] Notably the structure of Ezek 37 makes clear "that word and Spirit need to be united to achieve the aim of bringing people to God."[38] This aim corresponds to the necessity of the Spirit according to 2 Cor 3:6, which states: "The (mere) letter kills, but the Spirit gives life (τὸ γὰρ γράμμα ἀποκτέννει, τὸ δὲ πνεῦμα ζῳοποιεῖ)." Thus, again, given a high scriptural competency, the reader is guided by these allusions to follow Paul's extended line of argumentation.

But even a reader with minimal scriptural competency would not have been at a loss when following Paul's thought, although one would have contextualized the metaphors differently. To speak of one's heart, and even writing on the heart, is a common *topos* of the antique discourse on friendship which might here be understood as a rhetorical technique of pacifying an adversary with endearing speech or promises.[39] In fact, this is exactly what you would expect in a letter of recommendation: an emphasis on the friendly terms between the participating parties.[40] It is

---

37. Block ("Prophet of the Spirit", 30–31) notes that more than half of all the instances describing the Spirit as an "agency of animation" are found in Ezek 36:26—37:14.

38. Schafroth, "Exegetical Exploration of 'Spirit' References," 70. See also Robson, *Word and Spirit in Ezekiel*, 230.

39. See Becker, *Schreiben und Verstehen*, 209. For examples, see Thucydides, *P.W.* 2.43.2; and Schrenk, "γράφω, γραφή, κτλ.," in *TWNT* 1:770. For the "'heart'-motif" as "part of the larger theme of Paul's 'fatherhood,'" see Hafemann, *Suffering and the Spirit*, 193. For the general "idea of precepts being written in the soul," see Oropeza, *Exploring Second Corinthians*, 211.

40. See Klauck, *Die antike Briefliteratur und das Neue Testament*, 76. For *philophronesis* as a *topos* in letter-writing, see Koskenniemi, *Studien zur Idee und Phraseologie des griechischen Briefes*, 115–27; and Thraede, *Grundzüge griechisch-römische Brieftopik*, 124–46.

not uncommon for Paul to describe his good relations to the addressees by referring to his heart (2 Cor 7:3; 1 Thess 2:17; Phil 4:1) and even within the Corinthian correspondence Paul speaks of the heart as the place where God's Spirit is at work (1 Cor 1:22). What is more, for minimal readers, the reference to God's life-giving Spirit as the agent of writing would probably remind them of their own conversion experience. Mark Goodwin has shown how both the notion of the living God and of God's Spirit played a crucial role in early Christian missionary preaching.[41]

Thus, all three reading groups would have understood Paul as addressing the spiritual life of the Corinthian community, which was brought about through his preaching, as an argument for the legitimacy of his ministry. The higher one's scriptural competency, the more a reader is likely to hear the overtones that characterize this spiritual life as an instantiation of God's eschatological saving work. But even though a minimal reader might at first miss out on this dimension, it would have been retroactively added to one's understanding of Paul by the explicit mention of a "new covenant" (καινῆς διαθήκης; 3:6). Even if the minimal audience did not know about the provenance of the phrase, it would have been familiar to them through the dominical words of Jesus at the Lord's Supper—"This cup is *the new covenant* in my blood (τοῦτο τὸ ποτήριον ἡ καινὴ διαθήκη ἐστὶν ἐν τῷ ἐμῷ αἵματι)"—attested in 1 Cor 11:25. The phrase "new covenant" would urge even a minimal audience to link all they had heard from Paul in his past preaching and teaching with what Paul writes now in 2 Cor 3 concerning the new order of salvation that Christ had instituted. So the minimal reader would arrive at similar conclusions as a more competent reader of Paul's letter.

An audience's ability to detect the allusions to Jeremiah's new covenant would not only enhance their own comprehension of Paul's arguments but also confirm for them Paul's own scriptural competency and establish Paul's trustworthy character or *ethos*.[42] The sudden antithesis between living hearts and stone tablets in 3:3 might have made an odd impression on a competent audience and just a slightly less odd impression on an informed one until the allusions to the Exodus texts further clarified what Paul was saying.

---

41. Goodwin, *Paul, Apostle of the Living God*, 15–64; 169–70.

42. See Quintilian's remarks on persuasion by foreshadowing in *Inst.* 9.2.65, 68, 77; 9.1.14; see also the discussion by Lampe, "Quintilian's Psychological Insights in His *Institutio Oratoria*," 189.

The minimal reader would likely miss the additional Exodus echoes. But even if the minimal readers did not grasp any allusion to the Exodus story, the contrast between dead stone and living flesh would have been familiar to them as it is attested widely in Greco-Roman and Hellenistic literature.[43] Probably the minimal audience would have perceived some jarring notes during a first reading of Paul's text, but odd points would not have hindered their general understanding of Paul's line of reasoning. To the contrary, points of unclarity might have encouraged an audience to engage in the process of intra-communal inquiry, discussion, and teaching, where more informed readers at Corinth could help elucidate Paul's fuller arguments and allusions.

These examples give an impression that intertextual references can work on different levels towards the same argumentative goal. In the remainder of the passage, other features of Paul's scriptural citations can be found that are in accordance with our observations. In 3:7 and 3:12, Paul openly refers to parts of the Exodus story. He does so according to Hellenistic-Jewish commentary patterns.[44] Yet it is by no means necessary to be familiar with these patterns to follow Paul's reasoning. Starting with 3:7, Paul essentially amplifies the argument he has already made in 2:16—3:6, and then he paraphrases the Exodus story providing details only relevant to his argument (3:7, 13–17). Rather than being irritated by his selective focus and seemingly random interpretive approach to the story, a competent and informed audience would likely have recognized Paul's adherence to commentary conventions and appreciated his use of them.

Paul's covert scriptural allusions in 2 Cor 3 are not crucial to his main argument. Even the notion of transformation through viewing God's glory in a mirror in 3:18 can be construed from a less scripturally informed vantage point. It can easily be understood along the lines of Greco-Roman concepts of mirror optics, which assumed that "a mirror transforms rather than reflects reality." Thus, as Weissenrieder aptly puts it, "looking can transform a person."[45]

---

43. See Dio Chrysostom, *Or.* 76; Philo, *Spec.* 4.149–50, where it is in fact applied even to the issue of laws. Similarly, the superiority of internalized *ethos* over exterior written laws is arguably a matter of common sense; see the discussion by Thrall, *Critical and Exegetical Commentary on the Second Epistle to the Corinthians*, 1:227; and Furnish, *II Corinthians*, 195.

44. See Cover, *Lifting the Veil*; and Belleville, *Reflections of Glory*.

45. Weissenrieder, "Blick in den Spiegel," 313.

This multivalent reading of 2 Cor 3–4 demonstrates that Paul's argument grows more compelling the more his audience is rooted in Israel's Scriptures. The more informed Paul's audience is, the more they will perceive the coherence of his biblical allusions and understand how these allusions influence and anticipate Paul's train of thought. But his *main* argument is comprehensible for all three readings groups.

Conclusion

For the classic minimalist or maximalist approach to Paul's use of Scripture, intertextuality takes place between Paul and his source texts. This is obviously the case with an author-oriented approach, but the same is true for a reader-oriented approach. Even though the latter focuses on Paul's audiences, it does so mostly to establish some limitations to Paul's intertextual use of Scripture based upon the extent of knowledge that he could have presupposed from his audience. This essay has tried to sketch a way to widen the notion of intertextuality by examining the reading competencies of the various members of Paul's original audience. Intertextuality is not confined to the relationship between Paul and his source texts, but it also "happens" between Paul's letter and the audience's cultural encyclopedia.

Not only does this approach clarify the coherence of Paul's thought in 2 Cor 2:14—4:6, it also reveals an astonishing interplay between the intertextual competency of the author and his readers. These findings shed new light on Paul's use of Scripture and the question of its intentionality. They portray Paul as a thinker and preacher who is himself deeply embedded in Scripture, yet sensitive to his readers' cultural background. Paul deliberately crafted at least this text, if not the whole of 2 Corinthians, in a way that his letter appeals to readers with different levels of scriptural competency. The christological focus aside, Paul's treatment of the precursor texts dealt with in this essay is largely in continuity with the exegetical traditions of his day.

Indeed Paul develops a distinct interpretation of Exod 34:29–35 in 2 Cor 3:7–18, but the exceptional feature of 2 Cor 2:14—4:6 lies not in the exegetical methods applied, nor in the ingenious interpretations offered, but in its multi-layered intertextual strategy. This strategy allows Paul to engage his audience at different levels of reading competency. The higher their scriptural competency, the more they will appreciate

Paul's fleeting allusions as an indicator of his own exegetical expertise. From this vantage point, the intertextual strategy undergirds Paul's *ethos*. The lower their scriptural competency, the more likely they are to perceive Paul's train of thought as somewhat disjointed. Still it would make enough sense for all readers to remain engaged with the argument. In this way, Paul enables the members of his minimal audience to formulate questions that draw their interest towards a deeper understanding of his intertextual allusions.[46] These findings also coincide with some recent studies on Paul's use of Scripture in the Corinthian correspondence. Florian Wilk, for example, has repeatedly argued that Paul uses intertextual ambiguity as a means of guiding the Corinthian community towards an active engagement with Scripture.[47]

Looking at Paul's use of Scripture, we can discern not only Paul's progressive use of scriptural allusions as his rhetorical argument unfolds but also layers of possible understanding by the audience as they follow his line of reasoning. Both Paul's layered use of allusions and the layers of understanding by different reading groups interact with each other to expose their respective scriptural competencies. Yet this multi-layered use of Scripture can only be discovered by taking the notion of intertextuality one step further to include both author and readers alike.

---

46. I argue for this extensively on the basis of 1 Cor 10 and 2 Cor 3 in my forthcoming doctoral dissertation "Zwischen den Welten."

47. See most notably Wilk, "Durch Schriftkenntnis zur Vollkommenheit," and Wilk, "Schriftauslegung als Bildungsvorgang."

5

Intertextuality and Exegetical Techniques in Hebrews

SUSAN DOCHERTY

HEBREWS PROVIDES ONE OF the fullest and richest examples of intertextuality within the entire New Testament as it is intrinsically shaped by extensive engagement with the Jewish Scriptures. The letter is structured around a series of key—and often lengthy—formal citations,[1] and its argument throughout is supported by appeal to scriptural texts, themes, and symbols. Indeed, it seems that, for its author, scriptural language is even more essential to the expression of the significance of Christ's life and death than the words of the historical Jesus himself (e.g., Heb 2:11–13; 10:5–7). George Guthrie has aptly concluded, "Simply stated, the uses to which Hebrews has put the Old Testament are the book's bone and marrow."[2]

Hebrews offers uniquely valuable insights, therefore, into the way(s) in which Israel's Scriptures were understood and re-used by the first followers of Jesus, illustrating in particular the continuing application to these authoritative texts of Jewish exegetical techniques. However, given

---

1. For further detail on the main proposals regarding the letter's structure, see e.g., Caird, "Exegetical Method"; and France, "Writer of Hebrews."

2. Guthrie, "Hebrews' Use of the Old Testament," 272.

that it was composed in a Diaspora setting,[3] and since Second Temple Judaism as a whole did not operate in isolation from wider Hellenistic culture, connections between the hermeneutical methods of this author and Greco-Roman literary practices are also in evidence.

The interpretation of the Scriptures within Hebrews is a vast and well-ploughed field of study, so this chapter does not aim to offer a comprehensive survey of it.[4] Rather, the focus will be on selected aspects of this subject which are significant in themselves, and which have also been impacted by recent developments within NT scholarship more broadly. The fundamental question of the nature and range of the text form(s) available to the author, and the implications of this for his citation practice, will be explored first.[5] Two key components of his exegetical method will then be examined, and compared to other forms of interpretation, both early Jewish and Greco-Roman: his treatment of quotations containing direct speech, and the frequent juxtaposition of texts from different parts of the Scriptures. The final section of the chapter will highlight some features of the implicit use of Scripture in Hebrews, an area that has received relatively limited attention to date, and which thus offers scope for fruitful further investigation.

Text Form and Citation Practice

Textual Pluriformity

Many of the scriptural citations in Hebrews exhibit divergences, both minor and more substantial, from the form of the text found in the major early witnesses to the Septuagint. In seeking to explain these differences, commentators divide into two camps, broadly speaking. One school of thought, reflected particularly in the studies produced by a former generation of scholars such as Kenneth Thomas and Graham Hughes,

---

3. This is widely assumed by commentators, on the basis of evidence such as the high-quality Greek in which the letter is written, and the reference in the text to the sending of greetings from those in Italy (Heb 13:24); see, e.g., the discussion of authorship and audience in Cockerill, *Epistle to the Hebrews*, 2-23.

4. I have offered somewhat fuller treatments elsewhere; see Docherty, "How Hebrews Reads Scripture"; and Docherty, *Use of the Old Testament in Hebrews*.

5. The author will be referred to throughout with masculine pronouns, as the case made by some commentators for female authorship of the letter (e.g., Hoppin, *Priscilla's Letter*) has not won widespread support; for further discussion of this question, see also e.g., Attridge, *Hebrews*, 1-6.

emphasizes the author's readiness to adapt his quotations for theological or rhetorical purposes.[6]

More recently, however, there has been a growing acceptance of the possibility that, on the whole, the author is faithfully reproducing his *Vorlagen*, which may have included some variants that are now lost to us. This shift in thinking towards the second position is represented especially in the work of Cecil McCullough and Martin Karrer,[7] and it has been largely prompted by the unassailable evidence from Qumran of the multiple forms in which the Jewish Scriptures circulated in the late Second Temple period. It is against this backdrop that Gert Steyn is pioneering an exemplarily thorough approach to investigating the citations in Hebrews, which engages seriously with the pluriformity of texts that would realistically have been available to the first Christians.[8] He highlights, for example, readings parallel to those in the letter found in the writings of the contemporary Jewish author Philo (e.g., Exod 25:40 / Heb 8:5; cf. *Opif.* 136; Deut 31:6 / Heb 13:5; cf. *Conf.* 166) and in minor Septuagint manuscripts such as Papyrus Bodmer XXIV (e.g., Ps 104:4 [103:4 LXX] / Heb 1:7). He also helpfully considers the potential influence on the author of liturgical versions of the Psalms and other texts widely cited in the letter (e.g., the Song of Moses, Deut 32:1–43).[9]

I have argued elsewhere, on the basis of a full evaluation of the extant textual witnesses, that the author of Hebrews generally quotes his scriptural sources faithfully.[10] A comparison of the formal quotations with other kinds of appeal within the letter to the same passage further confirms this view. The Psalm text used to establish Christ's priesthood (Ps 110:4 [109:4 LXX]), for instance, is reproduced exactly in two explicit citations: "You are a priest forever according to the order of Melchizedek" (Heb 5:6; 7:17).[11] Almost all of the numerous definite allusions to this

---

6. See, e.g., Thomas, "Old Testament Citations in Hebrews"; and Hughes, *Hebrews and Hermeneutics*; cf. Bateman, *Early Jewish Hermeneutics and Hebrews 1:5–13*.

7. See, e.g., Karrer, "LXX Psalm 39:7–10 in Hebrews 10:5–7"; Karrer, "Die Schriften Israels im Hebräerbrief"; McCullough, "Old Testament Quotations in Hebrews"; and McCullough, "Some Recent Developments."

8. Steyn, *Quest for the Assumed LXX Vorlage*.

9. For an earlier study placing the citations in Hebrews in the context of early Jewish and Christian liturgical tradition, see Kistemaker, *Psalm Citations in Hebrews*.

10. See especially Docherty, "Text Form of the Old Testament Citations in Hebrews Chapter 1."

11. All biblical citations are taken from the NRSV unless otherwise noted.

verse in Hebrews (Heb 2:17; 3:1; 4:14–15; 5:1, 5, 10; 6:20; 7:26–28; 8:1; 9:11; 10:21) depart, however, from the Septuagint in introducing Jesus as a *high* priest to support more effectively the overall argument of the epistle. Nevertheless, the accuracy of the author's citation practice remains a contested issue. Scholarly advances in two areas in particular have contributed new information to this debate and so will be explored further below: (1) the development of more nuanced approaches to analyzing possible authorial alterations to the wording of citations; and (2) a greater appreciation of the conscious employment of a variety of scriptural forms in early Jewish exegesis.

Authorial Adaptation of Citations

Even small linguistic differences between the citations in Hebrews and known Septuagintal forms are regarded by some commentators as intentional and theologically significant. The quotation from Jer 31:31–34 [38:31–34 LXX] at Heb 8:8–12 contains a number of such variants, including, for example, the verbs λέγει ("he says") and ἐπιγράψω ("I will write"), where the Septuagint has the virtual synonyms φησὶν and γράψω (Heb 8:8, 10; cf. 10:16). Thomas, however, suggests that the author of Hebrews changes an original γράψω to ἐπιγράψω because this more clearly signals the permanency of the laws which will ultimately be written by God on the hearts of the people. He argues also that the verb used in the Septuagint to describe the establishment of the covenant, διαθήσομαι/ διεθέμην, is deliberately replaced in Hebrews by either συντελέσω or ἐποίησα, in order to draw a contrast between the future covenant which will be kept (συντελέσω, Heb 8:8) and the first covenant with Israel, which was broken (ἐποίησα, Heb 8:9).[12]

Too much weight is placed by Thomas on these minor variations in vocabulary, however, and it seems unlikely that the subtle distinctions in meaning between words that he proposes can be maintained. The author of Hebrews certainly does not do so consistently, as the verb διαθήσομαι (and not συντελέσω) is actually applied to the making of the *new* covenant later in the citation, in agreement with the majority of Septuagint manuscripts (Heb 8:10; cf. Jer 31:33 [Jer 38:33 LXX]). This increases the probability that he is accurately reproducing his *Vorlage*, given that these

---

12. Thomas, "Old Testament Citations in Hebrews," 310–13; for a different view, see, e.g., McCullough, "Old Testament Quotations in Hebrews," 364–67.

terms are all reasonable Greek translations of the underlying Hebrew, especially when there is concrete evidence from Qumran and elsewhere that the book of Jeremiah circulated in multiple textual forms during this period.

Even if the case for the presence of significant theologically motivated changes to the text of the major scriptural quotations in Hebrews is not fully persuasive, though, there is still the possibility that minor linguistic alterations have been introduced for stylistic reasons. It is difficult to achieve clarity and objectivity in defining what constitutes a "stylistic improvement," especially in an ancient text, but Karen Jobes has attempted to do so by drawing on the recorded principles of Greco-Roman rhetoric. She emphasizes that, since Hellenistic texts were largely written to be read aloud, features such as rhythm and *paronomasia* were highly valued in this cultural context. A NT writer may have sought, therefore, to enhance the representation of his scriptural sources specifically in respect of these elements.[13]

In her investigation into the form of one of the major citations in Hebrews (Ps 40:6-8 [39:7-9 LXX] / Heb 10:5-7), Jobes focuses on the passage as a whole rather than on the individual variants from the major Septuagint witnesses. This enables her to point to ways in which these differences combine to produce greater phonetic assonance (or a more pleasing sound), while at the same time serving to foreground phrases in it that are particularly significant for the author's argument. She suggests, for example, that the plural form of the word for "burnt offerings," ὁλοκαυτώματα, is a careful substitution for the more usual singular ὁλοκαύτωμα, made in order to produce a rhyming couplet with the crucial phrase σῶμα δὲ (Heb 10:5-6). Similarly, the verb εὐδόκησας may have been chosen for the end of the third line of the quotation because its three syllables provide a more effective pair for ἠθέλησας in the first line than do the two syllables of the Septuagint term ᾔτησας (Heb 10:5-6; cf. Ps 40:6 [39:7 LXX]).[14]

Jobes's holistic approach to analyzing the form of the scriptural citations in the letter demonstrates the potential rhetorical significance of even apparently minor linguistic alterations to a quotation. However, her conclusions can only be speculative given the lack of concrete data about authorial intention. It is also important to recognize that even if a stylistic

---

13. Jobes, "Function of Paronomasia in Hebrews 10:5-7."
14. Jobes, "Rhetorical Achievement," 390-91.

adaptation of this kind can be identified, it may have originated earlier than Hebrews. In this case, for example, the plural noun ὁλοκαυτώματα is attested in a number of Septuagint manuscripts, including Papyrus Bodmer XXIV, an important early witness to the Psalms. It is also closer to the reading in the MT, and so it is probably a genuine variant reflecting a Greek translation revised towards the Hebrew.[15] Although the possibility that the author amended his quotations slightly to enhance their rhetorical power cannot be entirely discounted, the situation of widespread textual pluriformity in the first century CE still appears to be the decisive factor for explaining his citation practice. The burden of proof, then, falls firmly on those who would argue for any deliberate theologically or stylistically motivated changes to a scriptural source on the part of the author.

Exegetical Exploitation of Textual Pluriformity

A second development relevant to understanding the citation practice of the author of Hebrews is a growing appreciation of the way in which the exploitation of textual pluriformity functioned as an early Jewish exegetical technique. An awareness of alternative scriptural versions is clearly visible within the Qumran literature, for instance. The best-known example of this occurs in the *Habakkuk Pesher* (1QpHab XI, 9–13), where Hab 2:16 is quoted in a Hebrew form parallel to that attested in the Septuagint translation (הרעל; LXX διασαλεύθητι καὶ σείσθητι, i.e., "stagger" or "shake and quake"), while the ensuing commentary includes reference to the MT reading הערל, or "be uncircumcised."[16]

A similar appeal to Scripture in more than one form may underlie a puzzling section of Hebrews, the treatment of Ps 95:7–11 [94:7–11 LXX] in chapter 3. The period of "forty years" is, unusually, linked in the formal citation of this passage with God's miracles in the wilderness through the introduction of the connective conjunction διό (Heb 3:10). The following explanation, however, assumes the traditional understanding of this timeframe as relating to the duration of God's anger (Heb 3:17). Commentators like Peter Enns regard the form of the quotation as integral to its interpretation in the letter, enabling its application to both the Israelites of the early post-exodus age, who *angered* God with their

---

15. As argued, e.g., by Steyn, *Quest for the Assumed LXX Vorlage*, 285–89.
16. This and other examples are highlighted in Lim, *Pesharim*, 54–63.

disobedience, and to the new wilderness generation, the community of Christ-followers to whom the letter is addressed and who are presently experiencing not divine anger and punishment but God's blessing and *miraculous* signs of the coming eschatological age (cf. Heb 1:2; 2:4, 14–15; 4:3, 9–10; 6:4–5; 12:18–29).[17] Enns does not, however, consider the possibility that the author may have known this Psalm in two versions, and so derived his exegesis from this variant text.

Early Jewish interpreters sometimes had access to scriptural texts in more than one form, then, and so had the opportunity to exercise a choice about which one of the available versions to quote, depending on their theological or rhetorical aims.[18] This possibility arises especially in cases of the citation of those passages where the extant evidence attests to a level of textual variety. The first verse of the quotation in Hebrews discussed by Jobes and others (see above) falls into this category: that is, Ps 40:6 [39:7 LXX] at Heb 10:5.[19] The difficult Hebrew phrase in this sentence "ears you have dug" is variously translated into Greek, with some manuscripts retaining the word "ears" (ὠτία), while others render it as "a body (σῶμα) you have prepared."[20] The letter's theology clearly depends on the reading "body," so that Jesus' death can be presented as a replacement for the sacrifices required by the Mosaic Law (Heb 10:5–10). While the author may simply have reproduced the psalm in the only form known to him, it is also quite feasible that he made an intentional selection of the version most effective for his argument. This possibility opens up intriguing new lines of inquiry into his hermeneutical techniques and axioms.

---

17. Enns, "Creation and Re-Creation," 272–75.

18. For further discussion of this exegetical technique and possible example of its use within the New Testament, see Docherty, "New Testament Scriptural Interpretation," 3–7.

19. For a fuller treatment of this text, see Gheorghita, *Role of the Septuagint in Hebrews*, 147–224. See also, e.g., Hab 2:4, quoted at Heb 10:38 and in a slightly different form in Rom 1:17 and Gal 3:11.

20. For further detail, see Karrer, "LXX Psalm 39:7–10 in Hebrews 10:5–7."

Exegetical Techniques

Citing Scriptural Speech

This section will focus on two particularly characteristic features of the exegetical method of Hebrews. First, almost all of the passages selected for citation are presented in their original context as first-person direct speech. This emphasis on Scripture as a spoken word (cf. Heb 1:1) is intensified in the letter through the re-contextualization of these texts as either a personal and immediate address to the audience (e.g., Heb 3:7–11; 12:5–6; 13:5), or a conversation between God and Jesus (e.g., Heb 1:5–13; 5:5–6; 10:5–7). The author's willingness to attribute scriptural words to Christ and other speakers in this way has long attracted scholarly interest, and this technique can fruitfully be compared with both contemporary Jewish and Greco-Roman literary and interpretative practice.

Greco-Roman Interpretative Context

It has been argued that Hebrews contains examples of the ancient Greco-Roman reading strategy of prosopological exegesis. This form of interpretation involves assigning characters, or "faces" (πρόσωπα), to speakers, addressees, or other events in classical texts, in order to resolve any apparent difficulties within them and clarify their meaning. It is certainly applied by patristic authors, including Justin Martyr and Augustine, to the Jewish Scriptures in their efforts to relate them to Jesus, but its use by Christians at an earlier period remains contested. Matthew Bates is most closely associated with the view that it is widely practiced within the New Testament.[21]

Most recently, Madison Pierce has sought to demonstrate how prosopological exegesis operates specifically in Hebrews to provide the framework for the interpretation of scriptural passages as forming part of a dialogue between three divine characters: the Father, the Son, and the Holy Spirit.[22] This reading of the letter has obvious implications for the author's Christology, as it assumes that he understood Christ as present and active in the events recorded in Scripture, a claim previously

---

21. See Bates, *Hermeneutics of the Apostolic Proclamation*.

22. See further Pierce's contribution to this volume (ch. 13) and her *Divine Discourse in the Epistle to the Hebrews*.

made by, for instance, Anthony Hanson and Markus Barth.[23] There is no scholarly consensus, however, about when a firm belief in Jesus' divinity and preexistence actually crystallized among his followers, and how far it is reflected in Hebrews.[24] Whether or not the author employed this form of exegesis explicitly, it is significant that he makes the same initial interpretative move as other Greco-Roman exegetes of ascribing a new and definite speaker to a potentially ambiguous earlier authoritative text.

Early Jewish Interpretative Context

This technique of specifying a new speaker, addressee, or context for a scriptural speech, especially one with an originally general or imprecise referent, is an important component of early Jewish, as well as Greco-Roman, exegesis.[25] It is widely attested in the Targumim and Midrashim, as highlighted especially in the studies of Alexander Samely,[26] and is operative also in the *Biblical Antiquities* of Pseudo-Philo (e.g., LAB 23:2 [cf. Num 22:19]; 35:6 [cf. Gen 18:30–32]; 48:1 [cf. 1 Kgs 17:4]; 50:3 [cf. Ps 43:3]; 56:6 [cf. Jer 1:6]). It is evidenced in the NT Gospels, too, as exemplified in the debate between Jesus and the scribes (Mark 12:35–37; Matt 22:41–45; Luke 20:41–44) about the identity of the two "lords" who converse in Ps 110:1 [109:1 LXX]. So, in Hebrews, such "gapped" texts are applied to Christ, who can thereby be introduced as the unspecified "priest like Melchizedek" (Ps 110:4 [109:4 LXX]; cf. Heb 5:6; 7:17, 21), for instance, or as the unnamed "one who comes to do God's will" (Ps 40:7 [39:6 LXX]; cf. Heb 10:7, 9).

A further striking element of the treatment of scriptural direct speech in the letter also corresponds to wider patterns within early Jewish exegesis—the author tends to formally quote direct speech even when he is paraphrasing the larger episode within which it occurs. Short speech citations are included, for example, in his summaries of Abraham's life (Heb 11:17–18; cf. Gen 21:12), the Sinai theophany (Heb 12:20 [Exod 19:12–13], 21 [Deut 9:19], 26 [Hag 2:6]), and the establishment of the

---

23. Barth, "Old Testament in Hebrews"; Hanson, "Christ in the Old Testament."

24. For an overview of this issue and different approaches to it see, e.g., Dunn, *Did the First Christians Worship Jesus?*

25. See further, Docherty, "Exegetical Techniques in the New Testament and 'Rewritten Bible.'"

26. Samely, *Interpretation of Speech in the Pentateuch Targums*; and Samely, *Rabbinic Interpretation of Scripture*.

Mosaic covenant (Heb 9:20; cf. Exod 24:8). A similar pattern occurs in Stephen's outline of Israel's history in Acts (Acts 7:3, 7, 26–28, 32–34, 35, 37, 40), and this technique is commonly employed also in the works of rewritten Scripture. Pseudo-Philo's condensed account of the flood, for instance, includes no fewer than seven direct speech citations (LAB 3:1–12; cf. Gen 6:1—9:29), and the spoken words found within the underlying narrative are largely retained in his retelling of other incidents, including the building of the Tower of Babel (LAB 7:1–5; cf. Gen 11:1–9), the meeting between Balaam and Balak (LAB 18:1–14; cf. Num 23:1–30), and the call of Samuel (LAB 53:1–13; cf. 1 Sam 3:1–18).[27]

This practice may point, then, to a previously overlooked early Jewish hermeneutical principle shared by the author of Hebrews, imbuing scriptural speech with an especially solemn status. These words have a meaning and relevance that extends beyond the single situation in which they were first uttered, so that later interpreters take care to repeat and continuously re-apply them to new characters and circumstances. In this way they are enabled quite literally to "speak" to God's people for all time, as Scripture is regarded as a divine and still-living word, not only a record of Israel's past.

Juxtaposition of Scriptural Texts

A second significant exegetical operation widely employed in Hebrews is the bringing together of texts from different parts of Scripture so that they become mutually interpretative. Examples of this technique include the linking of citations on the basis of a common word, such as "son" (υἱός/ υἱόν; Heb 1:5; cf. Ps 2:7; 2 Sam 7:14) or "rest" (κατάπαυσίν/κατέπαυσεν; Heb 4:4–5; cf. Ps 95:11 [94:11 LXX]; Gen 2:2). This practice also places the author firmly within his early Jewish context, as it demonstrates his commitment to the fundamental underpinning axiom of the coherence of Scripture. His approach has frequently been compared, therefore, to both the characteristically rabbinic technique of *gezerah shawa*,[28] and to the collecting of purposeful anthologies of scriptural excerpts at Qumran (e.g., 4Q174, 4Q175, 4Q176, 4Q177).[29] Scriptural passages are juxtaposed

27. For further discussion of these examples plus others drawn from *Jubilees* and the *Genesis Apocryphon*, see Docherty, "Why So Much Talk?"

28. See, e.g., Boyarin, "Midrash in Hebrews / Hebrews as Midrash."

29. See, e.g., Albl, "*And Scripture Cannot Be Broken.*"

in the letter in a great variety of ways, however, and three further and less obvious forms of text-linking merit particular highlighting.

First, citations are consistently presented in pairs, as has been comprehensively established by Steyn.[30] They may be coupled on the basis of shared theme rather than catch-word (e.g., Ps 22:22 [21:23 LXX] and Isa 8:17-18 at Heb 2:12-13; Deut 31:6 and Ps 118:6 [117:6 LXX] at Heb 13:5-6), or so that the dual authority of both the Torah and the Psalms or Prophets can be claimed in support of the argument being made (e.g., Exod 25:40 and Jer 31:31-34 at Heb 8:5, 8-12; Deut 9:19 and Hag 2:6 at Heb 12:21, 26).

Second, scriptural *narratives* can be conflated through the citation of a text taken from one episode within the summary of another. These apparently misplaced quotations are often noticed by commentators, but neither the purpose of this technique nor its relationship to the author's overall exegetical method has been investigated in detail. In a lengthy allusion to the Sinai theophany (Heb 12:18-24), for instance, Moses is presented as saying, "I tremble with fear" (ἔκφοβός εἰμι καὶ ἔντρομος; Heb 12:21). In none of the Pentateuchal accounts of this event (Exod 19:9-24; 20:18-21; Deut 4:11-12), however, does Moses declare that he is afraid. It is, rather, at the time of the casting of the golden calf that he makes this statement, when he fears that this act of idolatry will provoke God's anger towards the Israelites (Deut 9:19). The author may intentionally be connecting these two incidents, then, in order to imply that dread is always attached to the encounter with God under the former dispensation. This heightens the contrast he seeks to draw with the joy and immediacy of the divine access that he claims is now on offer in Jesus (Heb 12:21-24).

Similarly, when recounting the faith of Jacob in Heb 11, the author pictures the patriarch "bowing in worship over the head of his staff" when bestowing his death-bed benediction on his grandsons (Heb 11:21; cf. Gen 47:31). Yet, according to the Genesis narrative, it was, in fact, before this that Jacob bowed over his staff, in response to Joseph swearing that he would bring his father's body back from Egypt to Israel for burial (Gen 47:29-31). Both of these episodes involve Jacob and Joseph, include the same verb προσκυνέω ("to worship"; Gen 47:31 and 48:12), and relate to the end of Jacob's life. Conflating them in this way enables the author to add a sense of divine solemnity to the utterance of the very blessings

---

30. Steyn, *Quest for the Assumed LXX Vorlage*, esp. 25-28.

in which he promises that his audience will share if they only remain faithful (Heb 11:39-40).³¹

Furthermore, he is here purposefully connecting episodes which are adjacent to one another in the Scriptures, an exegetical technique employed in several forms of early Jewish interpretation, especially the rewritten Scriptures. A causal link, for instance, is made between the pronouncement of the law about tasseled garments and Korah's rebellion against Moses (LAB 16.1; cf. Num 15:37—16:3). Abraham is also inserted into the account of the building of the Tower of Babel in the *Biblical Antiquities*, so that his refusal to take part in the enterprise is presented as an early demonstration of his faith in the one true God (LAB 6:3-18; cf. Gen 11:1-9; 11:31—12:5).³²

Third, throughout Hebrews there is appeal to texts that evoke a number of scriptural contexts or examples. The final chapter, for instance, includes an exhortation to show hospitality to strangers, grounded in a reference to those in the past who have done so and thereby found themselves entertaining angels (Heb 13:2). This may be an allusion to the actions of either Abraham (Gen 18:1-15), Lot (Gen 19:1-22), Gideon (Judg 6:11-24), or Manoah (Judg 13:2-23), but it is possibly intended to call to mind all of these figures, given the plural reference (τινες). The review of Israel's faithful ancestors ends with a similarly indefinite allusion to various unnamed people who endured persecution (Heb 11:35-39), and who should, therefore, act as inspiration for the letter's recipients. Furthermore, the precise scriptural source of a surprising number of citations in Hebrews is disputed (e.g., Heb 1:6 [Deut 32:43 and Ps 96:7 LXX]; 12:29 [Deut 4:24; 9:3]; cf. 2:13a [Isa 8:17 and 2 Sam 22:3]; 10:30 [Deut 32:36 and Ps 134:14]; 13:5 [cf. Gen 28:15; Deut 31:6, 8; Josh 1:5; 1 Chr 28:20]). This raises the possibility, then, that the author's selection of texts with multiple potential referents is part of a deliberate exegetical strategy, designed perhaps to emphasize the widespread scriptural support for his position.

The relative absence in Hebrews of one widely attested ancient form of textual juxtaposition, however, sets this author apart from both his early Jewish context and the broader Hellenistic literary culture. Composite citations are widely employed throughout Greco-Roman and patristic

---

31. For a fuller discussion of this aspect of the author's exegetical method, see Docherty, "Composite Citations in Hebrews," 200-202.

32. For rabbinic use of this method, see e.g., Num. Rab. 16:3; b. Sanh. 110a; cf. Tg. Yer. I on Num 16:2.

literature, as well as in Jewish sources written in Hebrew and Greek,[33] but there is only one definite example in the letter of this phenomenon, at Heb 10:37–38, where Hab 2:3–4 is combined with three words drawn from Isa 26:20 (μικρὸν ὅσον ὅσον).[34] This is a striking contrast to the figures for other NT writings. According to the most recent study, approximately 20 percent of the scriptural quotations in Paul's letters and the Synoptic Gospels are composite or conflated, and the total for the Fourth Gospel is over half.[35] The author's general avoidance of this technique is relevant for an understanding of his use of sources, making it appear less likely that he depended on an extract collection or "Testimony Book," for instance, in which key texts were already combined. It also provides additional support for the view that he prefers to reproduce his scriptural *Vorlagen* accurately in direct citations.

Areas of Future Possibility

The issues discussed thus far, namely the text form of the citations and the main techniques employed in their interpretation, are central to any investigation of the re-use of Scripture in Hebrews. Other aspects of this subject have received less scholarly attention to date, however, and so they offer scope for further fruitful exploration, especially in the light of recent currents in NT studies more broadly.

Scriptural Allusions

First, there is considerable potential for deeper analysis of the scriptural allusions within the letter. Following the publication of the work of Richard Hays on "echoes," and the burgeoning application of the tools of literary theory to the New Testament, this has become a very significant strand in the study of the Gospels and the Pauline Epistles over the past

---

33. Specific examples of this phenomenon in texts ranging from the Qumran *Temple Scroll* and the *Book of Jubilees* to the *Letter of Aristeas* and *4 Maccabees* are discussed in detail in the various contributions collected in Adams and Ehorn, *Composite Citations in Antiquity*, vol. 1.

34. See the fuller discussion of this passage and of other possible but far less probable examples of composite citation within the letter (Heb 8:5; 13:5) in Docherty "Composite Citations in Hebrews," 193–200.

35. Adams and Ehorn, "Composite Citations in Antiquity: A Conclusion," 210.

three decades.[36] This research has not made an impact on Hebrews commentary to the same extent, however, mainly because the direct citations are so prominent and integral to its argument and structure that they have naturally dominated the discourse. Nevertheless, closer investigation of the more implicit uses of Scripture may result in a fuller understanding of the author's exegetical method. For example, the allusions indicate the wide range of scriptural influences beyond the Psalms on his thought, including Isaiah in particular (e.g., Isa 53:12 / Heb 9:28; Isa 26:11 / Heb 10:27; Isa 35:3 / Heb 12:12; Isa 66:22 / Heb 12:27; Isa 63:11 / Heb 13:20; cf. possibly Isa 45:17 / Heb 5:9). This distribution of allusions situates him more firmly within his early Jewish context, as it is comparable to that found elsewhere in the New Testament, and in other contemporary corpora, such as the Qumran scrolls.[37]

Second, the author's implicit re-use of the Scriptures parallels his treatment of direct citations in some respects, especially in the frequent juxtaposition of texts from different locations. There is a possible example of a composite allusion in Heb 13:15 (ἀναφέρωμεν θυσίαν αἰνέσεως, or "a sacrifice of praise"; see Pss 50:14; 107:22; 116:17; and καρπὸν χειλέων, or "the fruit of lips"; Hos 14:3 LXX), and verses from Haggai (Hag 2:6; cf. 2:21) and Isaiah (Isa 66:22) are also brought together, if not formally conflated, at Heb 12:27.

More often, however, a number of scriptural allusions are combined and reworked in a kind of pastiche, a style employed in the book of Revelation and in other early Jewish apocalyptic writings and prayers (e.g., Ezek 38–39; Dan 9:4–19; the throne vision in 1 En. 14:8–25; the Qumran *Thanksgiving Hymns* and *Songs of the Sabbath Sacrifice*; cf. for a legal text employing this form, the *Temple Scroll*).[38] The opening paragraph thus recalls the language and motifs of several Psalms as well as of the Book of Wisdom (Heb 1:1–4; cf. 2 Sam 7:23; Pss 2:7, 8; 110:1 [109:1 LXX]; Wisd 7:26), for instance,[39] and the closing chapter draws widely on the Pentateuch and the Prophets (Heb 13:10–20; cf., e.g., Exod 33:7–11; Lev 16:27; 17:3; Ezek 34).

---

36. Hays, *Echoes of Scripture*.

37. See, e.g., the discussion of this overlap and the data presented in Evans, "Why Did the New Testament Writers Appeal to the Old Testament?" 36–38.

38. For further discussion of this form of scriptural re-use, see Tooman, *Gog of Magog*, 200–224.

39. For a more detailed analysis of the scriptural texts evoked in Heb 1:1–4, see Ellingworth, *Epistle to the Hebrews*, 92–106; 708–29; and Guthrie, "Hebrews," 923–25.

This concentration of allusions in certain parts of the letter in particular warrants further exploration. In addition to its occurrence in these transitional paragraphs, this kind of dense appeal to scriptural allusions also appears frequently within ethical exhortation (e.g., Heb 6:4–14 with Gen 1:11–12; 3:7–18; 22:16–17; Deut 11:11; Ezek 18:24; and Heb 12:12–17 with Gen 25:33; Deut 29:17; Job 4:3; Prov 4:26; Isa 35:3; Sir 25:23). It is also characteristic of the introductions to the extended exposition of key citations (e.g., Heb 3:1–6; cf. Num 12:7; 1 Sam 2:35; 1 Chr 17:14), in which allusions serve an essential function in enabling the author to lead his audience to the desired understanding of these texts. Moses is presented as "servant" rather than "son" (Heb 3:2–6) in advance of the quotation of Ps 95 (Ps 94 LXX), for example, so that the ensuing interpretative emphasis on his failure to lead the wilderness generation to their promised "rest" comes as no surprise (Heb 3:16—4:3; cf. Ps 95:7–11 [94:7–11 LXX]).

Appeal to Scriptural Characters and Narratives

A second thriving area of contemporary scholarship is the investigation of the re-use of scriptural characters, themes, and narrative frameworks within the writings of the New Testament. This development also has potential implications for understanding Hebrews, as demonstrated by, for instance, recent holistic studies of the author's interaction with specific scriptural books, especially Deuteronomy and Genesis,[40] and important treatments of his appeal to figures like Abraham, Moses, and Joshua.[41] Nevertheless, these characters are frequently considered only in terms of their function within the letter as either a foil to establish the superiority of Jesus (e.g., Heb 3:1–6; 7:1–25), or as models of ethical behavior, both positive and negative (e.g., Heb 11:1—12:1; 12:15–17; 13:2). A fuller picture of this aspect of the author's re-use of Scripture might be achieved by applying to Hebrews the insights of current research on characterization in Greco-Roman literature and in the New Testament.[42]

---

40. See, e.g., Allen, *Deuteronomy and Exhortation in Hebrews*; and Docherty, "Genesis in Hebrews."

41. See, e.g., D'Angelo, *Moses in the Letter to the Hebrews*; Eisenbaum, *Jewish Heroes*; and Ounsworth, *Joshua Typology*.

42. See, e.g., Bennema, *Theory of Character*.

Conclusion

This study has explored key elements of the intertextual relationships between the letter to the Hebrews and Israel's Scriptures, connections that are fundamental to the epistle's structure, argument, and language. It has, firstly, demonstrated the extent to which this author's exegetical methods reflect the literary context in which he operated. His most characteristic techniques—the identification of new speakers for indefinite or ambiguous texts and the interpretative juxtaposition of passages from different locations—are widely employed in early Jewish and/or wider Greco-Roman interpretative literature. Second, however, it has uncovered one particular feature of his treatment of Scripture that marks him out from his cultural environment, namely, the relative absence in his writing of the phenomenon of composite citation. Finally, some ways in which contemporary approaches in biblical studies might cast fresh light on central and long-running debates about his re-use of Scripture have also been highlighted, including new contributions to the effort to determine the level of accuracy with which he reproduces his direct citations. Further investigation of the multiple implicit forms of appeal to the Scriptures in Hebrews, including allusions to particular texts, wider narratives, and significant characters, also offers considerable scope for developing this well-worked but by no means exhausted field of inquiry.

Part II:

Practicing Intertextuality in the Gospels

6

The Church's One Foundation?

Peter as the Messianic Temple Stone in Matt 16:18

Bruce Henning

WHO DO PEOPLE SAY that Peter, the son of Jonah, is? Some say an apostate, some say an apostle, or some say one of the popes. But who do you say that he is? Jesus answers and says to him: σὺ εἶ Πέτρος, καὶ ἐπὶ ταύτῃ τῇ πέτρᾳ οἰκοδομήσω μου τὴν ἐκκλησίαν (Matt 16:18). This study will tread on the tumultuous waters of this famously disputed text and argue that as Peter's declaration of Jesus' true identity far exceeded popular opinion in some circles, so too Jesus' statement of the role and position of Peter exceeds what many attribute to him. In particular, I aim to demonstrate that, although only of Jesus will Matthew allow us to say: Σὺ εἶ ὁ Χριστός, Jesus' response to Peter: Σὺ εἶ Πέτρος shockingly portrays Peter with imagery traditionally used for the messiah. While this text affirms that Peter is not the Christ, Jesus' portrayal of him nonetheless places him in a position of one who shares in the messianic vocation predicted in the First Testament. Jesus alone does not inhabit the space of the predicted agent to usher in the eschaton; he invites others to inhabit that space as well, sharing in some (though certainly not all) aspects of this role. Matthew's Gospel presents a robust and rich theology of discipleship and apostleship as those who are great in the kingdom, and no text bears this out more than this one.

To demonstrate that the role ascribed to Peter evokes traditionally messianic imagery, first, I will build my temple imagery case for Matt 16:18. Then, we will see how the image of the temple foundation was traditionally seen as messianic. Lastly, I will demonstrate that the referent of πέτρᾳ is Peter. Since the building in Matt 16:18 is the temple, and the temple foundation stone is a messianic image, Jesus' description of Peter as this stone places him in surprising proximity to the messiah himself.

The Underlying Imagery of the Temple in Matt 16:18

Scholarship has not reached a consensus that temple imagery stands behind Jesus' declaration to Peter, but five factors strongly suggest this is the case when taken together.[1] First, other texts show Matthew has a keen interest in new temple imagery. Matt 12:6 has prepared the reader that τοῦ ἱεροῦ μεῖζόν ἐστιν ὧδε, that is, "some*thing* [not necessarily some*one*] greater than the temple is here."[2] Temple language and related ideas occur significantly during the Passion Week. Space does not allow a full exploration here, but Jesus' dramatic entry to the temple (21:1–11), his "cleansing" (or pronouncement of destruction; 21:12–13), his healing in the temple (21:14–16), his allusion to Isa 5 with its temple background (21:31–41), his citation of the rejected cornerstone text (21:42), his eschatological discourse regarding the temple's destruction (24:1–31; cf.

---

1. Examples of those who see a temple allusion in Matt 16:18 include Davies and Allison, *Matthew*, 2:624–30; Hillyer, "'Rock-Stone' Imagery," 58–81; Barber, "Jesus as the Davidic Temple Builder," 935–53; Beale, *Temple*, 187; McKelvey, *New Temple*, 193–94; Meyer, *Aims of Jesus*, 185–202; Wright, "Jerusalem in the New Testament," 57; Shäfer, "Tempel und Schopfung," 126; Schweizer, *Evangelium nach Matthaus*, 222; Fletcher-Louis, "Revelation of the Sacral Son of Man," 272–74. Examples of those who are less convinced or argue against it include Nolland, *Gospel of Matthew*, 672; Gundry, *Peter—False Disciple*, 20–22; and Witherington, *Matthew*, 317 (though he advocates for it in *Jesus, Paul*, 89). Schreiner, "Peter, the Rock," 99–117 argues that Dan 2 stands behind Matt 21 and 16. The textual difficulty of 21:44 is not discussed, but if the allusion exists in the wicked tenant parable, then Schreiner's argument that both texts have Dan 2 in view may be valid. This approach would only confirm a similar finding to the one proposed here, though temple imagery creates a louder echo than an allusion to Dan 2.

*Some of the material in this study comes from my monograph *Matthew's Non-Messianic Mapping of Messianic Texts*, used here with permission from E. J. Brill.

2. France, *Gospel of Matthew*, 623.

23:38—"your house is left to you desolate"), and the accusations against Jesus that he would destroy and rebuild a temple (25:61; 27:40) all point to a significant temple interest. This theme is so prominent that Piotrowski states: "Once Jesus reaches Jerusalem . . . all of his actions and words in the rest of the gospel bear directly on the temple."[3] Though surely an overstatement, his remarks nonetheless rightly stress the strong presence of this interest in the temple. Certainly these references do not all contain "construction" imagery, but they do demonstrate the temple is a significant Matthean motif. While they do not refer to every building in Matthew as the temple, they show that the possibility of a temple reference in 16:18 warrants serious consideration.

Second, the seemingly disparate images of building on a rock (v. 18a) and conflict with πύλαι ᾅδου ("gates of hell"; v. 18b) point to the need for an underlying scheme to unite them. The Targums and later rabbinic writings portray the temple as resting on a cosmic stone which covered the underworld. For example, Tg. Ps.-J. Exod 28:30 (in the cultic context describing Aaron's garments) describes "the foundation stone (אבן שתייה) with which the Lord of the world sealed up the mouth of the great deep/abyss (תהומא רבא) at the beginning."[4] This matches nicely with the following description in Matt 16:18: πύλαι ᾅδου οὐ κατισχύσουσιν αὐτῆς. Moreover, the cosmic stone was not only seen as something that covers the abyss, but also as the foundation of the temple. The Mishnah describes it as the stone upon which the ark rested, three finger lengths above ground: "a stone was there from the days of the earlier prophets; it was called 'Foundation' (שתיה; m. Yoma 5:2)."[5]

Data concerning the cosmic stone comes later, but the idea here fits quite well with the presence of a rock that is the foundation of a significant structure, as well as being in contact and conflict with the underworld, and this would entail the significant structure being the temple. This narrative coheres well with the common tradition of cultic sites being connected to a special stone.[6] In other words, the concepts of building on a rock and conflict with πύλαι ᾅδου at first seem to be unrelated. But

---

3. Piotrowski, "'Whatever You Ask,'" 99. His argument focuses on Mark, but easily applies to Matthew.

4. Translation mine; see Hillyer, "Rock-Stone Imagery," 79; Meyer, *Aims of Jesus*, 185.

5. Translation mine. Rabbi Yose in the *Tosefta* takes this to mean, "from it the world was carved," playing on שתיה; see Eliav, "Temple Mount," 62–63.

6. E.g., Gen 28:10–22; Zech 4:7–9; *m. Yoma* 5:2; *b. Yoma* 53b, 54b; *T. Sol* 23:6–8.

if the underlying image is that of a temple, then these formerly disparate ideas are properly linked if the rabbinic tradition extends back to the time of our text.

Third, several scholars have proposed that Matt 16:18 alludes to Isa 28:16, which depicts YHWH laying a foundation stone.[7] Isa 28:16 likely has the temple in view since the laying of the stone is located in Zion, and 1 Pet 2:6–8 confirms this understanding by citing the same passage in an explicitly temple context. The 1 Peter text, as well as Rom 9:33, also joins Isa 28:16 to another Isaianic stone (Isa 8:14), the latter of which is also in a temple context. Several similarities between Isa 8 and 28 exist, and the two seem to describe the same situation.[8] The proposed allusion of Matt 16:18 to Isa 28:16 fares quite well with Hays's criteria.[9] An allusion to Isa 27:13 in Matt 24:31 and a citation of Isa 29:13 in Matt 15:8–9, not to mention frequent other references to Isa 28:16 in the New Testament (i.e., Rom 9:33; 10:11; 1 Pet 2:6), demonstrate that the proposed allusion satisfies the criteria of availability and recurrence, and even has popular familiarity. In fact, 1QS 8:4–8 also references Isa 28:16 and then describes a figurative temple. There is also sufficient volume with significant similarities. The annulment of the covenant with death (מות/θάνατος) and sheol (שאול/ᾅδης)[10] would correspond to the church's conflict and victory over the πύλαι ᾅδου.[11] There is certainly thematic coherence, too, as Matthew applies many of Isaiah's deliverance motifs.[12] Thus, there is

---

7. Keener, *Gospel of Matthew*, 428; Davies and Allison, *Matthew*, 2:630. Derret ("Thou art the Stone," 276–85) believes Matt 16:18 alludes to Isa 28:16 and especially Isa 54 to argue that πέτρα refers to a precious stone. He notes the messianic understanding of 28:16 but does not discuss if or how a messianic text can be applied to Peter. Hillyer ("Rock-Stone Imagery," 80), too, sees in 28:16 a parallel between Peter and the one who believes. As with most allusions, the direction of this reasoning could be reversed: temple construction behind Matt 16:18 would contribute to the likelihood that an allusion is being made to the temple image of Isa 28:16.

8. Snodgrass, "Christological Stone Testimonia," 27–28.

9. E.g., Hays, *Echoes of Scripture in the Letters of Paul*, 29–31.

10. Based on other usage, one would expect the LXX to have θάνατος before ᾅδης (Isa 28:15). It is not clear why the order is seemingly reversed.

11. Evans (*Matthew*, 314) suggests that the Aramaic saying originally referred to a storm (שער) instead of a gate (שער). This would increase the volume of the allusion since Isa 28 refers to a storm: שוט שותף / καταιγίς (vv 15, 17, 18). However, the gates of Hades seem to be implicitly contrasted with the gates of the kingdom, to which Peter is given the keys (Marcus, "Gates of Hades," 443–55).

12. The last three of Hays's criteria, more minor, are difficult to establish here, but less significant. One difficulty that arises is later uses of Isa 28:16 to make Christ the

sufficient indication that this proposed allusion is valid and therefore suggests the building of Matt 16:18 is a temple.

A fourth reason for seeing temple imagery behind Matt 16:18 can be found in the significance of Jesus being portrayed as both the messiah and as the one who would build this new edifice. Certainly the central idea of this pericope (16:13–28) is the revelation of Jesus as the messiah, and this suggests that the following image of Jesus' building activity utilizes a view in the first century of the messiah as a temple builder, which has recently received attention from a number of scholars.[13] Although it is too soon to say this image of the messiah as a temple builder is generally accepted as scholarly consensus, it has much in its favor. Space does not allow a full exploration, but a brief summary of the argument will suffice. The idea can be traced back to one of the most significant messianic texts in the Hebrew Bible, that is, 2 Sam 7. Playing on the ambiguity of בית, YHWH promises that although David will not build a בית for him (vv. 5–7), YHWH himself will build a בית for David (v. 11). However, YHWH promises that one of David's descendants will build the בית for YHWH: יבנה־בית לשמי (v. 13), which is then connected to (1) the promise that his throne would be established forever (עד־עולם). Especially given the predicted consequences of iniquity (vv. 14–15) and wider literary context (e.g., 1 Kgs 5–6), this seems to have Solomon (at least primarily) in view.

However, later interpreters make a messianic connection more explicit. The account in 1 Chr 17 omits any reference to discipline for sinning and thus shows signs that a more messianic interpretation was underway.[14] Zech 6:12–13, which was understood as messianic, likely builds on the Davidic covenant, and describes a "branch/sprout" (צמח) who will build YHWH's temple.[15] Similarly, Isa 44:28—45:1 refers to

---

foundation stone (following the New Testament, as in Barnabas, *Ep.* 6:2 and Ambrose, *De Offic.* 1.29.142). But this complication touches the nerve of this project, that there are times when the Matthean Jesus takes passages which are easily and naturally used of the messiah but does not make the expected application.

13. E.g., Juel, *Messiah and Temple*, 198–99; Wright, *Jesus and the Victory of God*, 411; Ådna, *Jesu Stellung zum Tempel*, 50–53; Chester, *Messiah and Exultation*, 471–96; Fitzmyer, *One Who is To Come*, 172; Perrin, *Jesus and the Temple*, 80–113; Macaskill, *Union with Christ*, 100–27; 147–71.

14. Surely by the first century the one who was to sit on David's throne was seen as the messiah (e.g., Heb 1:5). But citations or allusions connecting Jesus with 2 Sam 7 do not necessarily require the temple building function to map to the messiah.

15. This is connected to the Davidic covenant and the referent is not Joshua or Zerubbabel but the messiah (Petterson, *Haggai, Zechariah and Malachi*, 186; Boda,

Cyrus as רעי and משיחו who will lay the foundation of the temple. The Targums confirm a messianic interpretation of temple builder texts (Zech 4:7–9; 6:12–13)[16] and render Isa 53:5 as follows:

> And he will build a holy temple (והוא יבני בית מקדשא), which will be cleansed of its guilt.[17]

In its midrash of 2 Sam 7:11–14, *The Eschatological Midrashim*—also called *4QFlorilegium* (4Q174)—connects the messiah ("the Branch/Sprout") with the work of rebuilding the temple. After citing portions of that Scripture, the text explains:

> This is the Sprout of David [הואה צמח דויד], who will arise with the interpreter of Torah, who will [arise] in Zi[on in the lat]ter days, as it is written, "And I shall raise up the hut of David [סוכת דויד] that is fallen." This is the fallen hut of David [סוכת דויד], [w]hom He shall raise up to save Israel (3.11–13).[18]

This "hut" has the temple in view since the earlier discussion centers around the building of a new temple (esp. 3:3, 6). Matthew's scriptural roots and his contemporary fellow interpreters demonstrate that scholarship's understanding of the messiah as temple builder has much in its favor. Since the passage at hand focuses on Jesus as the messiah, it is reasonable to connect Matthew's imagery with this concept of the messiah as temple builder.

Fifth, the location in Caesarea Philippi may also confirm this interpretation. Witherington argues against a reference to the Jerusalem

---

Book of Zechariah, 397–403). Interestingly, Zech 6:15 describes those who will come from afar and will build (in?) the temple of YHWH (ובנו בהיכל יהוה; καὶ οἰκοδομήσουσιν ἐν τῷ οἴκῳ κυρίου). ב is not normally used with בנה to identify the object (as with את for example), and so it seems these returned exiles are building something inside the temple. Either way, this still describes an eschatological temple building by someone besides the messiah. However, the text does not seem to have had much significance during the first century.

16. However, it is possible that the "messiah" in Tg. Ps.-J. only refers to a postexilic character. Besides the identification of the צמח (Zech 6:12) and האבן הראשה (4:7) as משיחיה, there are no substantial differences to require an eschatological orientation if one was not there already. See Shepherd, "When He Comes, Will He Build It?" 89–107.

17. Tg. Isa. 53:5; Shepherd, "When He Comes, Will He Build It?" 98; Eng. trans. my own.

18. Eng. trans. my own; contra Wise et al., *Dead Sea Scrolls*, which translates the text as "this describes the fallen Branch of David," and does not convey the temple reference in 4 סוכת דויד. Q174's citation of portions from 2 Sam 7:11–14 is connected with Amos 9:11.

temple by pointing to the temple of Pan and other shrines at Caesarea Philippi. He writes:

> Neglected in the discussions by Schweizer and many others is the fact that at Caesarea Philippi an underground stream surfaced and can still be seen today. There were traditions that this was one of the gates to the underworld and the river Styx. Both the saying of Peter and the saying of Jesus take on special relevance and poignancy if they were given in the locale of all these shrines to other sons of the gods and next to the river thought to go into the underworld, and it seems to me that the other parallels are frankly more remote.[19]

On the one hand, it is uncertain if Matthew's readers (probably in Antioch) would have known the connections to Pan and the nearby temple to Caesar.[20] Thus, this consideration is not as strong as the four features just considered. On the other hand, the reference Witherington notes and the allusions to the temple are not necessarily exclusive since allusions often converge multiple images or backgrounds at once. Instead, Witherington's explanation fits nicely with the approach advocated here—Jesus' temple outdoes the pagan ones.

Thus, the presence of the temple motif elsewhere in Matthew, the cohesion which comes from connecting the stone to the cosmic stone of rabbinic Judaism, the allusion to Isa 28:16, and the messiah-as-temple-builder motif, as well as the presence of the grotto of Pan—when taken together—strongly suggest the edifice that Jesus builds in Matt 16:18 is a figurative temple.

The Traditionally Messianic Understanding of the Temple Foundation

What, then, is the significance of the foundation stone? Though the temple *builder* was seen to be the messiah, the imagery becomes complicated in that first-century Judaism, particularly the kind represented by Matthew and his audience, would have seen the temple *foundation* as a messianic image as well. Many references to a rock in the First Testament

---

19. Witherington, *Matthew*, 318. He also states: "The problem with this conclusion is that the term 'temple' does not come up here." But this reasoning contradicts the vast majority of intertextual theorists. Though an allusion could be more overt, this does not discredit its existence. To say so is to rule out the majority of allusions.

20. Wilson, *Caesarea Philippi*, 206n61; Phillips, "Peter's Declaration," 286–96.

are metaphors for YHWH himself. This is so frequent that the LXX often translates צוּר ("rock") with θεός ("God," e.g., Deut 32:4; Ps 18:31; 62:2). This may explain why the messiah could so easily be linked with stone and rock imagery.[21] For example, Justin's *Dialogue with Trypho* (36) has Trypho the Jew simply conceding that "Christ is called a Stone." But the messianic connotations increase when the picture goes from just a stone to the temple foundation. Seen in other NT references (e.g., 1 Cor 3:10; Eph 2:20), the most significant for our purposes are the ones which cite Isa 28:16, since we have seen this text likely stands behind Matt 16:18 and another significant Matthean messianic temple-stone text—Matt 21:42.

The messianic use of Isa 28:16 may be seen as early as the LXX. Whereas the MT has המאמין לא יחיש ("the one who believes will not hasten"), the LXX has ὁ πιστεύων ἐπ' αὐτῷ οὐ μὴ καταισχυνθῇ ("the one who believes in him/it will not be put to shame"). The addition of ἐπ' αὐτῷ makes the object of faith the previous temple stone. Not only does this reinforce the link between Matt 16:18 and Isa 28:16 (cf. Rom 9:33 and 1 Pet 2:6–7, which significantly also understand Isa 28:16 as messianic), it also shows the messianic understanding of the foundation stone from the LXX itself. A messianic interpretation of Isa 28:16 is also used in later Christian texts.[22] The Targum similarly gives a messianic interpretation of Isa 28:16:

> Therefore, thus says the Lord God, "Behold, I appoint in Zion a king, a strong, mighty king (מלך מלך תקיף גיבר), and the one who believes will conquer."[23]

Thus, the foundation stone of Isa 28:16 was widely conceived as messianic, and there is no reason to doubt this perception would not have been shared by Matthew and his readers. If the allusion to Isa 28:16 in Matt 16:18 is certain, then this evokes messianic stone imagery. But the case is made stronger against the backdrop of temple imagery since not only was the temple stone of Isa 28:16 understood messianically, but the motif in general was as well.

---

21. Jeremias, "Λίθος, Λίθινος," 4:273. This connection only expanded in later Christian literature. Snodgrass ("Christological Stone," 5) explains: "The post-apostolic Church found the Old Testament to be an abundant quarry from which nearly every rock or stone, from the one Jacob used as a pillow (Gen 28:11f.) to that which killed Goliath (1 Sam 17:49), could be understood of Jesus."

22. E.g., Barn. 6:2–3; Ambrose of Milan, *Off.* 1.29.142; Irenaeus, *Haer.* 3.21.7.

23. Tg. Isa. 28:16; Eng. trans. my own.

The messianic use of a temple foundation can also be seen in the saying "the stone the builders rejected has become the cornerstone (οὗτος ἐγενήθη εἰς κεφαλὴν γωνίας)" in Matt 21:42, citing Ps 118:22-23. Time does not allow an in-depth consideration of this passage, but a few observations suffice to show that there, too, the image of a temple stone is messianic. Ps 118 easily lends itself to a messianic interpretation with its portrayal of a victorious warrior fighting on behalf of Israel and then coming to the temple to celebrate in worship. The Targum of the passage and the apocryphal *Songs of David* (A.18) from Cairo Geniza seem to have David in view, though this could have messianic overtones, or at least pave the way for later messianic interpretation.[24]

However, Acts 4:11 and 1 Pet 2:6-7 clearly show a messianic interpretation. Most significantly, Matt 21:42 certainly connects the stone with Jesus. In addition to the "stone"/"son" (אֶבֶן/בֵּן) connection, the feature of being rejected links the images. The fact that the stone is rejected then vindicated in the reference to Ps 118:22-23 probably clarifies the lack in the wicked tenant parable, in which the son is only rejected but with no mention of vindication or future significance. Moreover, though there is debate about the exact nature of the κεφαλὴ γωνίας, it is possible that this is a "foundation stone" and not a "capstone" since 1 Pet 2:6-7 connects it with Isa 28:16, where the image is certainly that of a foundation.[25] If so, this would only strengthen the text's relevance as a demonstration of why the stone of Matt 16:18 would be seen as messianic since there the stone is clearly built upon.

Πέτρος as the Πέτρα

If the πέτρα of Matt 16:18 is to be connected to the messianic temple foundation, who (or what) is this rock? Jesus' saying clearly plays on the name Πέτρος. The simplest understanding of this word play is that Peter is the rock on which Jesus will build. There are variations of this

---

24. Blomberg, "Reflections on Jesus' View," 677; de Moor, "Targumic Background of Mark 12:1-12," 77.

25. Blomberg (*Matthew*, 73) rightly observes that רֹאשׁ/κεφαλὴν does not require the stone to be on top, but could indicate primacy. Cahill ("Not a Cornerstone!" 345-57) argues strongly that a cornerstone is not in view in Ps 118, but allows that a different sense may occur in the New Testament due to the influence of Isa 28:16. For a good argument on the meaning of "cornerstone" in Matt 21:42, see Silva, "γωνία," in *NIDNTTE* 1.627; McKelvey, "Christ the Cornerstone," 352-59.

approach, such as Peter being the rock in his confession,[26] Peter being a representative of the band of apostles (a view which would find support in the portrayal of the twelve apostles as the foundation of the new temple in Rev 21:14),[27] and Peter being a representative of all believers,[28] but these subdivisions are outside of the purview of this essay. Peter is under consideration immediately before and after the *logion* in question, and it would be unlikely for the referent to be changed without any indication.

Moreover, the connective καί most naturally continues or expands on the identification given before rather than contrasting it (i.e., "*You are Peter, but* [καί?] *on this Rock* I will build"). Sometimes commentators observe that Peter being the rock is confirmed since any differences in Greek are unlikely to have occurred in Aramaic (כיפא). However, this last point is speculative and is only of limited, if any, value since our attention is on what Matthew was communicating to his readers, and his composition is in Greek.

However, many Protestant commentators have argued that Jesus is not referring to Peter as the rock but either to himself[29] or to Peter's confession.[30] Support for these views fall into three categories. First, objections are presented focusing on the differences between the words. Πέτρος is masculine and refers to an individual stone; πέτρα is feminine and refers to bedrock. However, these distinctions require too much precision for metaphorical speech.[31] Moreover, the distinction between the masculine and feminine can be easily explained since πέτρα is the expected word for "bedrock," but obviously Peter's name must be given in the masculine. Furthermore, studies have shown that there was not a strict differentiation in usage during the first century CE. Caragounis's monograph, which is devoted to arguing for πέτρα being Peter's confession, acknowledges and states:

> Although in earlier literature πέτρα was used mostly with the sense of 'rock', 'boulder' and πέτρος with the sense of (free-standing) 'stone', the two terms were occasionally used

26. Nolland, *Gospel of Matthew*, 669.

27. Turner, "*Primus inter pares?*" 179–201; Viviano, "Matthew," 660.

28. E.g., Calvin, *Commentary on a Harmony*, 291.

29. Lenski, *St. Matthew's Gospel*, 625–27; Walvoord and Dyer, *Matthew*, 222; Wilcox, "Peter and the Rock," 73–88.

30. Caragounis, *Peter and the Rock*; McNeile, *St. Matthew*, 241; Toussaint, *Behold the King*, 201–2 (who says it is both the confession and Christ himself).

31. Turner, *Matthew*, 406.

interchangeably. In later literature this interchangeability becomes more frequent, until finally πέτρος falls into disuse, πέτρα comes to signify 'stone', and its older sense of 'rock' is taken by βράχος. This interchangeability during the transition period is evidenced also in LXX and NT usage.[32]

Caragounis then argues that Jesus must have been purposefully juxtaposing the words since they could have been used similarly. This seems speculative and overly confident in the reconstruction of the etymology. The argument requires the two being synonymous, but at most we can say that some used the words interchangeably. We cannot say that all would have used the words this way. The fact that Jesus does use them separately in Matt 16:18 suggests that Matthew at least would have understood πέτρα as "bedrock" and πέτρος as "stone."

A second objection focuses on smaller details in the way Jesus expresses the saying. The demonstrative pronoun is said to point away from Peter back to Jesus or the confession of faith since it does not match the second person address to Peter.[33] Similarly, objections are given that had Jesus meant himself, he would have clarified as much. Lenski writes: "If by 'this rock' Jesus had Peter himself in mind, he could easily have said ἐπὶ σου, 'on thee' will I build my church; or, 'on thee, Peter,' adding his name."[34] However, by saying ἐπὶ ταύτῃ Jesus is developing his building imagery. One can always wish that Jesus would have clarified the exact nature of the imagery, but this sword cuts both ways. One could easily argue that had Jesus meant himself, he would have said "ἐπὶ μου—'on me' will I build my church." Similarly, Quarles argues: "If attention were being shifted from Simon as the rock to another rock, one would have expected the remote demonstrative pronoun (ἐκείνη)."[35] Thus, one's reasoning that "had Jesus meant the other position, he would have said . . . " can be used by either side of the argument. Instead, interpreters must base their case on what stands written.

---

32. Caragounis, *Peter and the Rock*, 116. See also Quarles, *Matthew*, 188.

33. E.g., McNeile notes: "If he is the 'rock,' ταύτῃ is strange after the direct σὺ εἶ. It would be more natural if the Lord were speaking of him in the third person to the other disciples" (*St. Matthew*, 241).

34. Lenski, *St. Matthew's Gospel*, 625.

35. Quarles, *Matthew*, 188.

A third objection concentrates on problematic theology that would arise from identifying Peter as the rock.[36] We have already seen how the image of a rock, especially a foundation stone, is often mapped to Jesus Christ. In fact, the incongruence of Jesus being the expected rock and the link here with Peter has cast doubt by some on its historicity.[37] Alternatively, some have argued that since the rock imagery can only legitimately be applied to Jesus due to its messianic connotation, then this demonstrates that the πέτρα simply cannot be Πέτρος.[38]

However, this last argument requires Matthew to have a narrow mapping scheme in which messianic texts or images from the First Testament can only map directly to Jesus. One must leave open the possibility that others, especially Jesus' band of disciples, share in some aspects of the messianic vocation.[39] In fact, the very next verse (16:19) provides another example of this phenomenon in which Peter is the one who has the keys of the kingdom, an allusion to Isa 22:22, which also was seen as messianic (cf. Rev 3:7). Investigation of these texts must be reserved for

36. Gundry (*Peter—False Disciple*, 20–21) presents a unique argument against Peter being the rock, but it has not gained much acceptance. He argues that 16:18 alludes to 7:24–27, where the foundation is Jesus' words. He claims that this excludes temple imagery, but some (e.g., Wright, *Jesus and the Victory*, 292) have seen it in 7:24–27, too, so that it might only increase the volume of the allusion. But even if the allusion to 7:24–27 is granted, this does not require the referent to be the same. We have already seen similarities between 16:18 and 21:42, which create a louder echo than the one between 16:18 and 7:24–27. But in 21:42, the referent is Jesus. Gundry does not account for the flexibility of the imagery. After all, Peter's and Jesus' words are not entirely exclusive—one only has to imagine Peter communicating Jesus' words.

37. See, e.g., Seitz, "Upon This Rock," 340, who states: "In view of the long persisting primitive tradition in which Christ himself is claimed as the church's one foundation, the Matthean interpolation in its present form proves to be nothing more than an exceedingly insecure, late fabrication, to build upon which would be to build on sand. In contrast to this stands the unshakable consensus of testimony to the more ancient tradition concerning the rock on which the church and its faith was founded, and that rock was Christ." Cf. Harnack, "Der Spruch über Petrus," 646. Similarly, Wilcox ("Peter and the Rock," 73–88) argues that for these reasons the original saying must have had Jesus as the rock, but Matthew's redaction is a play on words to be connected with σκάνδαλον εἶ ἐμοῦ (16:23).

38. See, e.g., Lenski, *St. Matthew's Gospel*, 626; Walvoord and Dyer, *Matthew*, 222.

39. The research presented here is part of a larger project that examines several case studies in which this is the case, namely the Matthean Jesus' application of the messianic shepherd to the disciples (Matt 10:6), his use of the messianic caretaker of the eschatological vine (Matt 21:41, 43), his use of the messianic temple-builder imagery (Matt 21:42), and the eschatological herald of Isa 61:1–3 (Matt 5:3–4; 11:6). See Henning, *Matthew's Non-Messianic Mapping*.

another study, but the fact that the phenomenon may occur elsewhere means that a strict messianic hermeneutic cannot be presumed in Matt 16:18. Furthermore, passages like Eph 2:20 and Rev 21:14 answer any reluctance to seeing the apostles as the eschatological temple foundation on theological grounds since the identification there is undeniable. In light of the ease of the reading, as well as the weakness of arguments against the identification, the case for identifying Πέτρος as the πέτρα seems "rock solid."

Conclusion

Thus, Matt 16:18 does describe Peter in terms traditionally reserved for the messiah. We have seen that the saying evokes temple imagery—as supported by the prevalence of Matthew's temple motif elsewhere—the cohesion that comes from seeing the saying against the background of rabbinic Judaism's cosmic stone, the allusion to Isa 28:16, the first-century view of the messiah as a temple builder, and the presence of the nearby grotto of Pan and temple to Caesar. We have seen that the resulting picture of a temple foundation was widely understood as messianic, especially by first-century Christ followers and most significantly by Matthew. We have also seen that the πέτρα is Πέτρος since the pieces immediately before and after concern Peter, and the conjunction καί joins Matt 16:18a to 18b.

Peter's response to Jesus' question acknowledges that the then current popular opinion of their teacher fell woefully short. Jesus had been proclaiming the nearness of the kingdom (e.g., Matt 4:17). Peter and the apostles had done so as well (10:7). In ch. 16, Peter confesses the unique and unrivaled role Jesus is to play in this kingdom as its Christ. In response, Jesus affirms this answer, but asserts that Peter, too, is great in the kingdom, so great that he even shares a part in Jesus' messianic vocation. How Peter shares in this task depends on the meaning of the following text regarding the keys of the kingdom and binding and loosing. We cannot discuss this much-disputed text here. Instead, our investigation has demonstrated that Peter's role and activity are being portrayed with messianic connotations.

The Matthean Jesus plays with concepts surrounding eschatological temple construction so that both he and Peter are mapped to distinct messianic images. Intertextual scholars often investigate the technique that maps a concept originating from the Old Testament (as opposed to an allusion to a specific text) to Jesus. But what we have been considering here differs by using what we could call "referential opacity."[40] Instead of having a one-to-one scheme, in which a messianic image exclusively maps to Jesus, here Peter is bundled together with Jesus, in such close proximity that the messianic mapping also lands on him. Certainly the overall theology of Matthew precludes taking Peter as the messiah, and Matthew does not use direct messianic vocabulary for anyone but Jesus. But allusions allow for an element of ambiguity so that Matthew can maintain a necessary gap in order to distinguish Peter and Jesus, while simultaneously bringing the two together in extremely close proximity by sharing imagery which was traditionally used of the messiah. Though this may seem surprising, what ultimately matters is not popular flesh and blood opinion, but the significance of Jesus' declaration: σὺ εἶ Πέτρος, καὶ ἐπὶ ταύτῃ τῇ πέτρᾳ οἰκοδομήσω μου τὴν ἐκκλησίαν.

---

40. This terminology comes from Cognitive Metaphor Theory. For a further exploration of this concept and how it can be used in intertextual studies, see ch. 1 of Henning, *Matthew's Non-Messianic Mapping*.

7

Scriptural Allusion
and Bodily Age in Luke 1–2

Narrativizing Theological Continuity
through Allusive Characterization and Plotting

JULIE NEWBERRY

DESPITE GROWING INTEREST IN the New Testament's treatment of a range of body-related themes, age and especially old age remain underexplored areas of bodily description in NT studies.[1] As Richard B. Hays and Judith C. Hays observe, this may be partly because advanced age is not a

---

1. On the age of one or more characters in Luke 1–2, see Helyer, "What about Anna?"; Autero, "Social Status in Luke's Infancy Narrative," 43–44; de Jonge "Sonship, Wisdom, Infancy," 317–24; 353–54; Krückemeier, "Der zwölfjärige Jesus im Tempel"; and Billings, "At the Age of 12." For (old) age in the New Testament more generally, see Hays and Hays, "Christian Practice of Growing Old"; Barclay, "There is Neither Old Nor Young?"; LaFosse, "Age Matters"; and Reinmuth, "Das Alter würdigen." The journal *Interpretation* devoted its April 2014 issue to the topic of aging. Young age, especially childhood, has received more attention. See, e.g., Aagaard, "Paul as a Child"; Miller-McLemore, "Jesus Loves the Little Children"; Bunge et al., *Child in the Bible*; Murphy, *Kids and the Kingdom*; Betsworth, *Children in Early Christian Narratives*; Allen, *For Theirs Is the Kingdom*; Parker and Betsworth, *T. & T. Clark Handbook of Children in the Bible*; MacDonald, "Reading the New Testament Household Codes"; and Punt, "Not Child's Play."

pressing concern in much of the New Testament, perhaps for historical-demographic reasons.[2] Simply put, "fewer people lived to old age" then than do today, and "those who did were honored and esteemed" so that aging—unlike death—"was not seen by the early Christians as a 'problem' to which some sort of religious solution was required."[3] Nevertheless, (old) age descriptions are not entirely absent from or merely incidental in NT texts. As Hays and Hays also note, advanced age figures prominently in the Lukan infancy narrative (Luke 1:5—2:40).[4] The same chapters also highlight young age, as shown below. Moreover, because Luke 1–2's handling of age both evokes Israel's Scriptures and anticipates a key scriptural quotation in Acts, this motif cannot be properly analyzed without attending to Luke's intertextual practice.[5]

After sketching the problem of how to characterize Luke's intertextual approach as it relates to age, I will survey relevant data, highlighting the prominence of old age in Luke 1–2, summarizing the Old Testament's portrayal of old age and the ways in which older adults in Luke 1–2 evoke the Scriptures through their elderliness, and drawing attention to the prominence of young-age categories here and elsewhere in Luke-Acts. Taken together, this evidence might seem to support a supercessionist-ageist interpretation of Luke's intertextual practice in relation to elderliness. However, further intertextual analysis problematizes this conclusion. The quotation of LXX Joel 3:1 in Acts 2:17—the only other Lukan passage that immediately juxtaposes "old" and "young" people—suggests that old age is in fact a Janus-faced motif in the infancy narrative, pointing back to Israel's Scriptures but also looking ahead to Acts 2.[6] Rather than marking a supercessionist-ageist sense of disjuncture in salvation history, Luke's intertextual practice as it relates to age serves to emphasize (age-inclusive) theological continuity, precisely at moments of radical surprise in the unfolding of God's saving work.

2. Hays and Hays, "Christian Practice of Growing Old," 3; 14.
3. Hays and Hays, "Christian Practice of Growing Old," 3–4.
4. Hays and Hays, "Christian Practice of Growing Old," 6.
5. This essay is thus also a case study of whether scholarship at the intersection of scriptural allusion and human embodiment might shed fresh light on intertextuality in the New Testament. See also, e.g., Spencer, "Ethiopian Eunuch and His Bible"; García Serrano, "Anna's Characterization in Luke 2:36–38," 479.
6. See, e.g., Green's narratological analysis of how repetition links Luke 1–2, Israel's Scriptures, and Acts, highlighting theological continuity ("Problem of a Beginning," 79–82).

Age and Intertextuality in Luke 1–2: Supercessionist-Ageist Appropriation?

Luke's infancy narrative includes four older adults: Zechariah (1:7, 18), Elizabeth (1:7, 18, 36), Anna (2:36–37), and Simeon (2:25–26, 29). As discussed below, foregrounding the elderliness of these characters helps to link Luke's Gospel to Israel and its Scriptures.[7] However, these older adults more or less vanish after Luke 2,[8] while the youngest characters in Luke's opening chapters—the infants John and Jesus—play important roles in the ensuing narrative. The dearth of aged characters elsewhere in Luke-Acts, together with the privileging of children and babies in several other Lukan passages (e.g., Luke 9:48; see below), raises important questions about old age in Luke 1–2. Might it be the case, as F. Scott Spencer wryly suggests in an article on young men in Acts, that "in Luke's narrative scheme, older seers have had their day" well before Peter's Pentecost sermon[9]—namely, in the infancy narrative? Moving beyond the aim of Spencer's tongue-in-cheek remark, we might further ask: Are the older adults of the infancy narrative, and perhaps also the faith of Israel with which they are so closely associated, simply *superseded* by the youthful John and Jesus and a correspondingly new period of salvation history?[10]

Such a conclusion would be broadly consistent with the view that Luke-Acts assumes sharply divided eras of salvation history, as in Hans Conzelmann's well-known schematization of Lukan *Heilsgeschichte* into three periods, focused successively on Israel, Jesus, and the church. Conzelmann (in)famously excludes the infancy narrative from his analysis,[11] and some have thought that these chapters undermine his proposal. As Paul S. Minear puts it, "It is only by . . . ignoring the birth narratives that

---

7. Green, "Problem of a Beginning," 79–83; Green, *Gospel of Luke*, 61–63; Hays and Hays, "Christian Practice of Growing Old," 7.

8. Zechariah is named in 3:2 but not narratively present.

9. Spencer, "Wise Up, Young Man," 35, commenting (apparently in jest) on the reordering of Joel's age categories in Acts 2:17; Spencer does register the inclusive import of the citation ("Wise Up, Young Man," 34). On "young men" in Acts, see also Spicq, "La place ou le rôle des jeunes."

10. Scholarly diction sometimes unreflectively points in this direction: Brown describes the OT-evoking older adults of Luke 1–2 as "the *final* representatives of the piety of Israel" (*Birth of the Messiah*, 242, emphasis mine).

11. Conzelmann, *Theology of St. Luke*, 172.

Conzelmann can appear to establish his thesis that Luke visualized the story of salvation as emerging in three quite distinct stages."[12]

At first glance, however, Luke's handling of age categories might seem to mitigate this objection—or rather, to create space for a modified form of Conzelmann's position, one that still marks a strong divide between the periods of Israel and of Jesus, albeit with John the Baptist shifting somewhat in the schema.[13] If Luke dispenses with the OT-evoking older adults following his opening chapters and instead privileges younger characters in the rest of Luke-Acts, perhaps the older adults of the infancy narrative call Israel's story to mind simply as a means of relegating it to a period of salvation history that is sharply divided from the dawning era that John announces (Luke 1:16–17, 41–44, 76–77; 3:3–6, 15–18; see also 16:16).

If Luke did engage with Israel's Scriptures in this fashion, we might describe his age-related intertextual practice as *supercessionist (and ageist) appropriation*: evoking Israel's Scriptures only to sideline them as outmoded in light of his central (Christian) story. In what follows, I hope to clarify why such a view might arise and then to propose an alternative interpretation. Far from expressing supercessionism figured by ageism, Luke's age-related intertextual practice *narrativizes theological continuity through allusive (and ultimately age-inclusive) characterization and plotting*.

Old Age in Luke 1:5—2:40 and in Israel's Scriptures

Early in Luke 1, the narrator concludes an extended description of Zechariah and Elizabeth with the first of several references to old age. John's parents-to-be are childless, "because Elizabeth was barren and they were both advanced in their days (προβεβηκότες ἐν ταῖς ἡμέραις αὐτῶν

---

12. Minear, "Luke's Use of the Birth Stories," 121. See also Brown, *Birth of the Messiah*, 242–43; Rasco, "Hans Conzelmann y la 'historia salutis,'" 289n8; Talbert, "Shifting Sands," 383; Tyson, *Luke, Judaism, and the Scholars*, 83–84. As Minear notes ("Luke's Use of the Birth Stories," 120), some who accept much of Conzelmann's proposal object to his dismissal of Luke 1–2 (e.g., Oliver, "Lucan Birth Stories"; Tatum, "Epoch of Israel").

13. Conzelmann locates John on the Israel "side" of the Israel/Jesus divide (*Theology of St. Luke*, 22–23; see Wilson's critique, "Lukan Eschatology," 330–36); the argument sketched above emphasizes John's connection with Jesus.

ἦσαν; 1:7).''[14] Zechariah reinforces the age motif in his query to Gabriel (1:18), using the same expression to describe Elizabeth's advanced age (προβεβηκυῖα ἐν ταῖς ἡμέραις αὐτῆς) and calling himself an "old man" (πρεσβύτης). As Joel B. Green notes, Zechariah is merely telling the angel what the narrator earlier told readers/hearers.[15] However, Zechariah departs from the narrator's account in one important respect: he does not mention Elizabeth's barrenness, only their shared old age. Given that the scene treats their basic problem as childlessness, this is a striking omission, suggesting that elderliness is a more important part of the couple's characterization than one might expect. Lest the reader miss the point, Gabriel refers yet again to Elizabeth's old age (γῆρας) when addressing Mary (1:36).[16]

Nor are these the only aged figures in Luke 1–2: Simeon is not explicitly called elderly, but allusions to his impending death may imply that he is older (2:26, 29).[17] Moreover, Luke introduces Simeon in tandem with Anna, who is "very advanced in days" (προβεβηκυῖα ἐν ἡμέραις πολλαῖς; 2:36). Scholars differ over how to calculate her exact age, but Anna is at least 84 years old (2:36–37).[18] Given Luke's oft-noted tendency to pair similarly situated male and female characters, her elderliness indirectly corroborates the impression that Simeon, too, is an older adult.[19]

Why make so much of these characters' agedness? Though this question could be approached from several angles, the infancy narrative's extensive engagement with Israel's Scriptures suggests that we would do well to consider how the Old Testament uses Luke 1–2's old-age-related terms.[20] Space does not allow a comprehensive survey here, but examination of old age in Israel's Scriptures confirms what the experience and

14. Unless otherwise noted, English translations are my own.

15. Green, *Gospel of Luke*, 78.

16. Hays and Hays, "Christian Practice of Growing Old," 6. On the Abraham/Sarah parallels, see further Newberry, "You Will Have Joy," 111–20.

17. Many see Simeon as elderly (e.g., Hays and Hays, "Christian Practice of Growing Old," 6–7), interpreting his comment about "releas[ing] your servant" (2:29) as referring to (imminent) death (e.g., Figuera, "Syméon et Anne," 89). However, cf. Green, *Gospel of Luke*, 147. With Chen, I see the phrase as "a double-entendre" (*Luke*, 39).

18. Elliott, "Anna's Age (Luke 2:36–37)"; Thurston, "Who Was Anna?" 49; Varela, "Luke 2.36–37"; and García Serrano, "Anna's Characterization in Luke 2:36–38," 469–71.

19. Seim, "Gospel of Luke," 729–32; Thurston, "Who Was Anna?" 48.

20. I.e., προβαίνω ἐν [ταῖς] ἡμέραις [πολλαῖς] (1:7, 18; 2:36); πρεσβύτης (1:18); and γῆρας (1:36). Πρεσβύτερος is not used for old age in Luke 1–2.

observation of aging even today might lead one to expect: Old age in the Old Testament does not have a single, stable meaning or value. It is an ambiguous life stage that, like others, is better or worse depending both on individuals' choices and on the circumstances in which they find themselves. Thus, old age and older adults are conventionally honored (LXX Prov 30:17); some older adults are depicted as exceptionally wise (LXX Num 10:31); and merely reaching old age is sometimes assumed to be a blessing (Gen 15:15), perhaps specifically the reward of righteous living (LXX Prov 16:31). However, this period of life also brings challenges, such as bodily weakness—including decreased sexual and procreative capacities (e.g., Gen 18:11; 21:7; see also 1 Kgs 1:1–4; 2 Kgs 4:14)—as well as diminished physical and emotional resilience (Gen 42:38; 44:29, 31; 1 Sam 4:18; Tob 3:10); limited social-political influence (Josh 13:1; LXX 1 Sam 2:22–25; 3:21; but cf. Phlm 1:9), and even moral and cognitive deterioration (1 Kgs 1:1–37).[21]

Returning to Luke 1–2, one finds similar nuance in the depiction of old age. Luke's further characterization of the four older adults in the infancy narrative confirms that, in their cases, advanced age does underscore long-term faithfulness.[22] Indeed, as others have suggested, through the intersection of their old age and devotion (e.g., 1:5–9; 2:25–26, 37), these characters embody faithful Israel's protracted waiting for the divine deliverance now begun in the infants John and Jesus (1:41–45, 67–79; 2:25–38).[23] However, the advanced age of the older adults also involves age-related trials, seen particularly in Zechariah's reference to elderliness as a barrier to having a child (1:18).

Zechariah's concern relates to one of several more direct intertextual connections perceptible in the infancy narrative. Luke's emphasis on the age of these older characters evokes specific scriptural passages, not least in the case of John's parents. Though God heals infertility numerous times in Israel's Scriptures (e.g., Judg 13; 1 Sam 1–2), the combination of elderliness and infertility in Zechariah and Elizabeth's case particularly

---

21. On ancient stereotypes concerning elderly men's sexual impotence, see Cokayne, *Experiencing Old Age in Ancient Rome*, 115–33, also discussed in relation to Luke 1 in Wilson, *Unmanly Men*, 81. On Roman views of moral and intellectual decline in old age, see Cokayne, *Experiencing Old Age in Ancient Rome*, 57–112.

22. On the honor attached to their advanced age, see Green, "Social Status of Mary," 463.

23. Green, "Problem of a Beginning," 79–83; Green, *Gospel of Luke*, 61–63; Hays and Hays, "Christian Practice of Growing Old," 7.

recalls Abraham and Sarah.[24] Importantly, as Green argues, this intertextual link serves less to imply a one-to-one typological correspondence between the couples than to situate Luke's narrative "in tradition," thereby tacitly "invit[ing] [Luke's] auditors to hear in *this* story [Luke 1-2] the reverberations and continuation of *that* story [Gen 11-21] as [Luke] attempts to give significance to the *present* one."[25] Luke forges this intertextual link through a variety of literary techniques, including brief verbal and thematic echoes,[26] as well as the repetition of key phrases from the Abraham-Sarah narrative.[27] Most important for the present study, however, is both couples' elderliness, an aspect of their characterization which proves central to the plot of Genesis and of Luke as each couple moves toward unexpected late-life procreation.[28]

When Abraham learns that he will have a son by Sarah within the year (LXX Gen 18:10), both are "old people" (πρεσβύτεροι), "advanced in days" (προβεβηκότες ἡμέρων; 18:11). The latter phrase is close to the narrator's description of Zechariah and Elizabeth in Luke 1:7 and to Zechariah's portrayal of his wife in 1:18. In the same passage in Genesis, Sarah refers to Abraham as "older" (πρεσβύτερος) while making a comment that may gesture toward impotence (LXX Gen 18:12). Her reflection finds a near echo in Zechariah's self-designation as an "old man" (πρεσβύτης), which in Luke 1 likewise implies concerns about advanced age inhibiting procreation (1:18). The elderliness of Elizabeth and Sarah is also a perceived hindrance to childbearing in both passages (cf. LXX Gen 18:14; 21:7; Luke 1:36). Indeed, the Genesis parallel may account for the curious fact, noted above, that Zechariah makes no reference to Elizabeth's barrenness when questioning Gabriel's promise (Luke 1:18; cf. 1:7). So also in Genesis: despite the narrator's previous description of Sarah as barren (11:30), in Gen 17:17 Abraham reflects on his own and

---

24. See, e.g., Chen, *Luke*, 16.

25. Green, "Problem of a Beginning," 77; see also, e.g., González, *Luke*, 19, 24-27; Brown, *Birth of the Messiah*, 451.

26. Cf. Luke 1:6 / Gen 15:5-6; Luke 1:6 / Gen 17:1; Luke 1:7, 36 / Gen 11:30; 16:1; and Luke 1:58 / LXX Gen 21:6; see also Green's tables ("Problem of a Beginning," 68-71; *Gospel of Luke*, 53-55) and Wilson, *Unmanly Men*, 86-87.

27. Cf. Luke 1:18 / LXX Gen 15:8 and Luke 1:37 / Gen 18:14; Green, *Gospel of Luke*, 55; 78; 91.

28. Green, "Problem of a Beginning," 70-71.

his wife's advanced age, but not the latter's barrenness, as an obstacle to having a child (cf. 18:11–12).[29]

More could be said about the scriptural reminiscences in Luke 1–2's characterization of and plotting related to aged figures, through which these characters come to represent Israel.[30] Jesus' reception by the elderly Simeon may echo young Samuel's reception by Eli, for instance (1 Sam 1:24–28; 2:22).[31] Anna, as a pious older widow, resembles Judith (Jdt 16:22–23).[32] Given the greater prominence of Abraham and Sarah in first-century Christian literature, however, Luke's intertextual practice in relation to this couple provides the easiest point of comparison to the intertextual practices of others in his time and tradition. Early Christians such as Paul (Rom 4:18–21) and the author of Hebrews (11:11) mention Abraham's (and Sarah's) old age and late-life procreation explicitly, in connection with the theme of trusting God's promise even in the face of seeming impossibility. Though Luke can also refer overtly to Abraham and God's promise to him (1:55, 73; see also Acts 7:4–8),[33] the infancy narrative's allusion to Abraham and Sarah's old age is less direct and serves a distinct theological purpose. Luke evokes the Genesis couple's elderliness through characterization and plotting, as part of a broader narrative strategy to convey continuity between Israel's Scriptures and Luke's own narrative.[34]

Young Age in Luke 1:5 — 2:40 and Beyond

The need to establish continuity with the Old Testament cannot exhaustively account for Luke's marked interest in age in the infancy narrative,

---

29. On how Zechariah's fixation with Elizabeth's age reinforces the Abraham/Sarah connection, see also Brown, *Birth of the Messiah*, 280.

30. On the representative character of one or more of the older adults, see Minear, "Luke's Use of the Birth Stories," 127; Wolter, *Luke 1–9:50*, 59; De Long, *Surprised by God*, 222.

31. Green, *Gospel of Luke*, 149.

32. Elliott, "Anna's Age (Luke 2:36–37)," 100–102; Thurston, "Who Was Anna?" 49. Less plausibly, Figueras proposes Simeon and Anna symbolize the Law and the Prophets, respectively ("Syméon et Anne").

33. On children in Acts 7, see Green, "Tell Me a Story," 215–16; on Abraham in Luke-Acts, see Dahl, "Story of Abraham in Luke-Acts."

34. See also Green, "Problem of a Beginning," 77. Craddock also registers the emphasis on continuity in Luke 1, commenting on Zechariah and Elizabeth: "The old (in this case, an old couple) will usher in the new" (*Luke*, 26).

however, because this line of reasoning does not explain the third evangelist's complementary emphasis on *youth* in these chapters. Luke repeatedly draws attention to the young age of the two infants welcomed by the older adults discussed above.[35] John the Baptist (1:41, 44) and Jesus (2:12, 16) are each repeatedly described as a βρέφος, a relatively uncommon term in the New Testament[36] that denotes unborn (John) or recently born (Jesus) babies.[37] Slightly later in their young lives, each is also referred to as a παιδίον, a (young) child.[38] Luke applies this diminutive form of παῖς to the two boys seven times in two chapters,[39] with παιδίον often standing in for the child's name so that age becomes a primary identifying trait (1:59, 66, 76, 80; 2:17, 27, 40). John's father even addresses him by the term παιδίον in 1:76—after having just given him a proper name through a fraught process recounted in the preceding verses (1:59–66).[40]

While it is thematically appropriate to focus on babies and small children in annunciations and birth narratives,[41] Luke's many references to old *and* young age in the infancy narrative are striking. Why not have Zechariah address his recently named son *by name* in 1:76? Why describe Anna's age at length while only summarizing her witness to Jesus

---

35. As a παρθένος, Mary is presumably rather young herself (unlike Elizabeth)—even if Luke 1:34 indicates that Luke's primary interest is in Mary's sexual status, not her age (Seim, "Virgin Mother," 97–98). On the age contrast between Mary and Elizabeth, see Just, *Luke*, 10; Guite, "Visitation." Later Christian tradition emphasized Joseph's advanced age, as seen in the *Prot. Jas.* 9 (Goodacre, "Protoevangelium of James," 64).

36. See also Luke 18:15; Acts 7:19; 2 Tim 3:15; 1 Pet 2:2; Betsworth, *Children in Early Christian Narratives*, 104; 107.

37. BDAG, s.v. βρέφος, ους, τό, 183 (def. 1 and 2); Allen, *For Theirs Is the Kingdom*, 9–10.

38. BDAG, s.v. παιδίον, ου, τό, 749 (def. 1).

39. Of Luke's 13 uses of παιδίον, seven occur in the infancy narrative. The term παῖς, from which the diminutive παιδίον is formed, appears in Luke 1:54 and 1:69, but not until 2:43 does it unambiguously imply young age (rather than servanthood). Elsewhere in Luke-Acts, παῖς often occurs in contexts where it clearly indicates a character's relatively young age (e.g., Luke 8:51, 54; 9:42; Acts 20:12). See BDAG, s.v. παῖς, παιδός, ὁ or ἡ, 750 (def. 1–3). For discussion of whether παιδίον and παῖς designate different age brackets, see Allen, *For Theirs Is the Kingdom*, 10–12; Betsworth, *Children in Early Christian Narratives*, 105.

40. Thanks to Laura Robinson for pointing this out (personal communication).

41. Interestingly, παιδίον, which is first applied to John at his circumcision (1:59), makes its inaugural canonical appearance when God gives Abraham the covenant of circumcision (Gen 17:12; see also Green, "Problem," 70). Luke's use of παιδίον in growth summaries (1:80; 2:40) may also reflect OT intertexts (esp. Gen 21:8; Brown, "Annunciation to Zechariah," 487).

(2:36–38)?⁴² Cumulatively, Luke's multiple mentions of age in the infancy narrative suggest that this motif serves a more profound purpose than might be anticipated.

At this point, it is worth returning to the observation that Luke sometimes seems to elevate youths over their elders.⁴³ Later in Luke 2, we hear of Jesus' precocious piety as an older child who impresses adults in the temple (2:41–52).⁴⁴ Luke's account of Jesus' earthly ministry⁴⁵ also includes two instances in which Jesus raises from the dead a person whose youth is explicitly noted: a "young man" (7:11–17) and a twelve-year-old girl (8:40–56).⁴⁶ Children and babies *as such* are also honored as representatives of Jesus, recipients of his blessing, and models for his followers (e.g., 9:46–48; 18:15–17).⁴⁷

Admittedly, assuming Markan priority, much of the children-privileging material in the body of Luke's Gospel is not original to Luke. The fact that he retains this material is significant, however, as is his addition

---

42. Figueras, "Syméon et Anne," 93–94; García Serrano, "Anna's Characterization in Luke 2:36–38," 464; 473. There may be gendered dynamics at work in the omission of Anna's words. Thurston notes that the same pattern of relating the male character's words and only summarizing the female character's occurs in relation to Zechariah/Elizabeth and Simeon/Anna ("Who Was Anna?" 48).

43. E.g., Betsworth, *Children in Early Christian Narratives*, 99–126; Carroll, "What Then Will This Child Become?"

44. On this portrayal of Jesus as a child in relation to ancient biographical conventions, see Krückemeier, "Der zwölfjärige Jesus im Tempel"; Billings, "At the Age of 12"; Betsworth, *Children in Early Christian Narratives*, 108–12; Ibita and Bieringer, "Beloved Child."

45. Luke describes Jesus as roughly thirty when beginning his public ministry (3:23). According to Spencer's analysis of the age-boundaries of νεανίσκος ("Wise Up, Young Man," 35–36), this places Jesus toward the older end of being a "young man." On the category's fluidity, see Allen, *For Theirs Is the Kingdom*, 3; 12–14. Jesus is never an *older* adult in Luke-Acts; see Hays and Hays, "Christian Practice of Growing Old," 11–14.

46. Luke uses νεανίσκος in 7:14; ἐτῶν δώδεκα in 8:42; παῖς in 8:51, 54. Note that παῖς is a term of address in 8:54, as is νεανίσκε in 7:14 and παιδίον in 1:76.

47. Green, *Gospel of Luke*, 76; Allen, "*Theirs* is the Kingdom." A few Lukan passages portray youth more ambiguously. Jesus draws an unflattering analogy between implacable children and those who reject him and John (Luke 7:31–35; see Betsworth, "Children Playing in the Marketplaces"; Carroll, "What Then Will This Child Become?" 191–93). He also makes a notoriously puzzling comment about old (παλαιός) and new ("young," νέος) wine (5:39). See Allen, *For Theirs Is the Kingdom*, 15–16; Eriksson, "Old Is Good," 53n4; Dupont, "Vin vieux, vin nouveau (Lc 5:39)"; and Kee, "Old Coat and the New Wine." Space does not allow detailed discussion of these passages, but they do not fundamentally undermine my point.

of further references to young age—including within triple tradition. Particularly striking is Luke's substitution of "the younger" (νεώτερος, 22:26) for Mark's "the last" (ἔσχατος, Mark 9:35) as the one who is "greatest" among Jesus' followers. By comparison, outside of the infancy narrative, overt references to elderly adults are scarce in Luke's Gospel.

Nor is this foregrounding of the young limited to Luke's Gospel. As Spencer has shown, Acts features "young men" repeatedly, even if not always in an unambiguously positive light.[48] In contrast, aside from a single reference to Moses' age and subsequent allusions to the passing of time during his life (Acts 7:23, 30, 36), the only explicit description of an old(er) individual in Acts is the vague characterization of a healed man as "over forty" (Acts 4:22). Even here, though, mention of this man's age—like the earlier comment about him being "lame from his mother's womb" (3:2)—serves primarily to underscore the wonder of his instantaneous healing, not to categorize him by his age. Acts does mention "elders" (πρεσβύτεροι) in the Jewish or early church communities (e.g., Acts 4:5; 15:2; 21:18), but the emphasis in Luke's usage of this term falls on elders' community standing, not their biological age.[49] Luke-Acts's only use of πρεσβύτερος specifically to denote advanced age occurs in the quotation of LXX Joel 3:1 in Acts 2:17, to which I will return below.[50]

The greater prominence and the sometimes more positive portrayal of younger characters across Luke-Acts raises the question of whether the evangelist favors youth over old age, perhaps for theologically weighty reasons. Two passages appear to provide important corroboration of this view. First, within the infancy narrative, the angel Gabriel arguably privileges the younger generation by describing the Baptist's mission in terms of "turn[ing] back the hearts of the parents (fathers, πατέρων) to the children (τέκνα)" (Luke 1:17). Scholars debate the meaning of this scripturally evocative phrase,[51] but the most straightforward interpreta-

---

48. Spencer, "Wise Up, Young Man"; Spicq "La place ou le rôle des jeunes." However, there are fewer explicitly identified children in Acts than in Luke (Green, "Tell Me a Story").

49. On age, social status, and communal authority as qualifications for a πρεσβύτερος in ancient Jewish and Christian communities, see Campbell, Elder; Campbell, "Elders in Jerusalem"; van Campenhausen, Ecclesiastical Authority and Spiritual Power; Elliot, "Elders as Leaders," 549–50; Harvey, "Elders," 318–22; and Merkle, Elder and the Overseer.

50. Πρεσβύτερος refers to relatively older age (*not* elderliness) in Luke 15:25.

51. See LXX Mal 3:23 and discussion in Marshall, Gospel of Luke, 59–60; Culpepper, "Luke," 47; Chen, Luke, 17; and Brown, Birth of the Messiah, 278–79. Carroll

tion—particularly in light of the parallelism between parents/children and disobedient/righteous (1:17)—is that the older generation needs to turn to the younger, presumably because the former are erring.[52]

A second passage, occurring at a similarly pivotal point in the narrative of Luke-Acts, might also seem to evince a preference for the young. When adducing LXX Joel 3:1–5 as an explanation for the strange events of Pentecost (Acts 2:17–21), the Lukan Peter makes several changes to this intertext,[53] including by inverting Joel's age categories. Whereas Joel mentions old men before young men, Peter lists "young men" (νεανίσκοι) and then "old men" (πρεσβύτεροι)[54] as groups upon whom God's Spirit was to be—and now has been—poured out (Acts 2:17; cf. Joel 3:1). Luke's transposition of these age categories has been variously interpreted. Among those who view the reordering as significant,[55] Spencer sees a "sligh[t]" privileging of youth, though he recognizes the generally inclusive import of the citation.[56] Conversely, Hays and Hays suggest that Luke's postponing of older adults places more emphasis on them.[57] While these scholars perhaps too readily assume that the change in word order highlights the age category under investigation in their respective studies, Christopher M. Blumhofer has drawn attention to another possibility—one with the advantage, as we will see, of building on clearer evidence elsewhere in Luke-Acts. Following cues provided by John Chrysostom's interpretation of the passage,[58] Blumhofer ponders whether the transposition of age

---

proposes that the direction of turning may involve "surprising reversal" within the household (*Luke*, 32–33; see also discussion below of Blumhofer, "Luke's Alteration of Joel 3.1–5").

52. Carroll, "What Then Will This Child Become?" 181. Allen sees this passage as privileging children "[i]n an adult-dominated world" (*For Theirs Is the Kingdom*, xiii), though (as she recognizes) "children" can include adult children (xiv).

53. Blumhofer, "Luke's Alteration of Joel 3.1–5"; Runge, "Joel 2.28–32a in Acts 2.17–21."

54. The juxtaposition of age terms and pattern of contrasting pairs confirm that πρεσβύτεροι here functions as an age category; see Hays and Hays, "Christian Practice of Growing Old," 5.

55. Blumhofer comments: "Few interpreters offer a theological rationale for Luke's inversion of these lines" ("Luke's Alteration of Joel 3.1–5," 509).

56. Spencer emphasizes: "This is not a geriatric slap: both young and old experience the Spirit's blessing, and visions and dreams amount to about the same thing" ("Wise Up, Young Man," 35).

57. Hays and Hays, "Christian Practice of Growing Old," 10n3.

58. Blumhofer, "Luke's Alteration of Joel 3.1–5," 510n31, citing John Chrysostom, "Homily v on Acts ii.14."

categories in Acts 2:17 might point to "eschatological reversal."[59] Perhaps, he suggests, "Luke's placement of young men over old is a sign that the reversals of the new age, once spoken of by the angel who announced John's birth, are now realized in the church."[60]

Building off of Blumhofer's proposal—and taking it, I should underscore, in a very different direction than he does—one might argue that this third interpretation of Acts 2:17 corroborates the proposal, sketched above, that Luke's intertextual practice with respect to age can be categorized as *supercessionist-ageist appropriation*. To review: In part through their biological age itself, the older adults of the infancy narrative recall Israel's Scriptures. However, these elders essentially disappear after Luke 2, whereas the younger generation (John and Jesus) remains central to Luke's narrative. Further, Luke valorizes babies and youths elsewhere, especially in his Gospel, and he arguably privileges the younger generation over the older in scripturally resonant terms at key turning points in both the Gospel (Luke 1:17) and Acts (2:17). It might seem, then, that Luke's allusive handling of age implies a sharp disjuncture between the story of Israel—related in earlier Scriptures and evoked by the older adults of the infancy narrative—and the remainder of Luke-Acts and the salvation-historical developments that it recounts.

Age in Acts 2:17 and the Proleptic Fulfillment of LXX Joel 3:1 in Luke 1:5—2:40

In the space remaining, I will propose an alternative interpretation of Luke's references to age in the infancy narrative and in Acts 2. The atmosphere of surprised joy in Luke 1–2 does indeed suggest that God is doing something new in the births of John and Jesus.[61] However, Luke does not simply abandon the "old folks" of the infancy narrative as representatives of an "old age" rendered obsolete by the ministries of John, Jesus, and the early church. To the contrary, through their close pre-Pentecost relationship to the Holy Spirit, the scripturally evocative older adults of Luke 1–2 prove to be proleptic participants in narratively future movements

---

59. Blumhofer, "Luke's Alteration of Joel 3.1–5," 510.

60. Blumhofer, "Luke's Alteration of Joel 3.1–5," 510.

61. See, e.g., 1:14, 44, 58; 2:10. On joy in Luke 1–2 with attention to intertextuality, see Wenkel, *Joy in Luke-Acts*, 28–70; Newberry, "You Will Have Joy and Gladness," 55–253; De Long, *Surprised by God*, 135–80; and Inselmann, *Die Freude im Lukasevangelium*, 11; 146–91.

in God's redemptive work.[62] Their allusive old age thus anticipates and creates continuity with scripturally resonant events not recounted until the beginning of Acts.[63]

It is helpful here to revisit the age binary in Acts 2:17 and the question of whether Luke's inversion of Joel's age categories[64] suggests eschatological reversal. Luke-Acts does foreground eschatological reversal.[65] Given children's vulnerability in the ancient world,[66] the reversal motif may indeed be in play in the privileging of the young in several Gospel passages (e.g., Luke 22:26).[67] Nevertheless, there is good reason to conclude that eschatological reversal is not the point of transposing Joel's age categories in Acts 2:17.

For one thing, Luke does not invert Joel's other pairs. Peter still mentions sons before daughters (LXX Joel 3:1 / Acts 2:17) and male before female slaves (Joel 3:2 / Acts 2:18). If the aim of reversing Joel's age groups were to underscore eschatological reversal, one might have expected Luke to carry that project through by reversing the gendered pairings.[68] As the citation stands, the eschatological overtones of the other pairs are bound up with inclusivity, not reversal.[69] Additional details in

62. On the anticipatory character of the Spirit's work in Luke 1–2, see Figueras, "Syméon et Anne," 94; Doohan, "Zechariah, Elizabeth, and John," 384–85; and López Mauleón, "Τὸ Πνεῦμα (τὸ) ἅγιον en san Lucas," 281.

63. Contra Conzelmann's judgment that "nowhere in [Luke's] writings is a figure from the past brought into direct connection with the future eschatological events" (*Theology of St. Luke*, 22). Brown helpfully describes Luke 1–2 and Acts 1–2 as "bridge passages" in which "characters from the material that precedes encounter characters from the material . . . to follow" ("Annunciation to Zechariah," 483). I would add that the elderly characters of Luke 1–2 also *participate* in future redemptive-historical events proleptically, through pre-Pentecost experiences of the Spirit.

64. Old/young in LXX Joel 3:1; young/old in Acts 2:17.

65. See, e.g., York, *Last Shall Be First*.

66. We should balance recognition of children's marginal status with the recognition that they were valued in various ways (Allan, *For Theirs Is the Kingdom*, 16–17; 26–29).

67. Carroll, "What Then Will This Child Become?" 178–79.

68. Admittedly, the Magnificat varies the order in which it lists eschatologically reversed pairs, without negating the emphasis on reversal (e.g., Luke 1:52–53); however, its pairings form a chiasm (Green, *Gospel of Luke*, 99), and Mary mentions reversal—unlike Peter (Acts 2:17).

69. On the inclusive implications of the Joel citation, see Spicq, "La place ou le rôle des jeunes," 514; Spencer, "Wise Up, Young Man," 34. On whether the expectations thus created are met within Acts, see Spencer, "Wise Up, Young Man," esp. 34–36; Williams, "'Upon All Flesh': Acts 2, African Americans, and Intersectional Realities."

the quotation—notably, the reference to "all flesh" (Joel 3:1 / Acts 2:17)[70] and the mention of (even)[71] slaves as recipients of the Spirit (Acts 2:18; cf. Joel 3:2)—further highlight inclusivity. Likewise, we should understand the reference to young and old men as underscoring inclusion, rather than inversion.

Specifically, the age terms are two poles of a "merism," a rhetorical device in which the mention of two extremes implies the inclusion of both poles and everything in between.[72] When age merisms occur in Israel's Scriptures, the order in which old and young are mentioned does not affect the (all-encompassing) import of this literary device (e.g., Gen 19:4; Exod 10:9; Ps 148:12; Lam 2:21; Ezek 9:6; 1 Macc 14:9). Accordingly, rather than attempting to account for the reordering of Joel's age terms in Acts 2:17, we should ask how the juxtaposition of these categories—understood as a merism—might retrospectively inform our interpretation of the dual emphasis on very elderly and very young characters in Luke 1:5—2:40.

In short, through the Spirit's work in both old and young characters, Luke's opening chapters narrate a proleptic fulfillment of Joel 3:1–5, foreshadowing the age-inclusivity of Pentecost.[73] As Hays and Hays observe, Luke 1–2 and Acts 2:17 share an emphasis on the Holy Spirit's work in the aged.[74] The elderly Elizabeth is "filled with the Holy Spirit" (Luke 1:41), and while her words are not labeled as prophecy, the mysteriously knowing blessing she pronounces over Mary qualifies for that designation (1:42–45).[75] Zechariah, too, is "filled with the Holy Spirit" and then prophesies (1:67). As for Simeon, the Holy Spirit is "upon him" (2:25).[76] He has received a special revelation from the Spirit (2:26), obeys

---

70. "All flesh" is presumably age-inclusive (Green, "Tell Me a Story," 224).

71. On Luke's addition of γέ, see Blumhofer, "Luke's Alteration of Joel 3.1–5," 508; Runge, "Joel 2.28–32a in Acts 2.17–21," 107–9.

72. Without using this term, Keener interprets the pairing similarly (*Acts*, 885).

73. As Minear suggests, "Surely the whole sequence of events from the conception of John to the arrival of Paul in Rome belongs within the orbit of Luke's testimony to the ways in which God is pouring out his Spirit 'on all flesh'" ("Luke's Use of the Birth Stories," 120).

74. Hays and Hays, "Christian Practice of Growing Old," 10. Brown also notes the Spirit's role in both passages, though he focuses more on gender than on age ("Annunciation to Zechariah," 483). See also Oliver, "Lucan Birth Stories," 224–25.

75. Hays and Hays describe both Zechariah and Elizabeth as prophets ("Christian Practice of Growing Old," 6); see also Seim, "Virgin Mother," 97–98.

76. Green, *Gospel of Luke*, 145.

the Spirit's promptings (2:27), and speaks prophetic words over Jesus and Mary (2:29–32, 34–35). Finally, although Luke does not mention the Holy Spirit in relation to Anna, she is called a prophet (προφῆτις, 2:36), again implying Spirit-filling.[77]

The youngest characters in these chapters, John and Jesus, also have marked experiences of the Spirit. John the Baptist, who will be a pivotal prophet (Luke 1:76; 7:24–28; 16:16), is already filled with the Holy Spirit "from his mother's womb" (1:15), as evidenced by his in-utero response to Mary's greeting (1:40–44).[78] Jesus—who will also be characterized (albeit not exhaustively) as a prophet (e.g., 4:24)[79]—is conceived through the activity of the Holy Spirit (1:35), and Luke's wider narrative underscores his unique relationship with the Spirit (3:22; 4:1, 14, 18; 10:21; 24:49; Acts 1:1–8; 2:33).

Also significant is the fact that πίμπλημι—the verb used to describe John (Luke 1:15), Elizabeth (1:41), and Zechariah (1:67) as being "filled with the Holy Spirit"—is the very same verb used in Acts 2:4, when Jesus' followers are filled with the Holy Spirit on Pentecost.[80] Admittedly, the Spirit-empowered activities that Luke 1–2 attributes to young and old characters do not correspond exactly to the description and distribution of spiritual experiences in Joel 3:1 / Acts 2:17. For instance, Joel 3:1 / Acts 2:17 might lead one to expect dreams for older adults and "visions" (ὅρασις) for younger characters, yet the elderly Zechariah is the only one who has a "vision" (ὀπτασία) that is identified as such in the infancy narrative (Luke 1:22).[81] Meanwhile, unlike Matthew (1:20; 2:12, 13, 19, 22), Luke describes no one in the infancy narrative—young or old—as receiving a revelatory dream. However, if, as argued above, the juxtaposition of old and young men in Joel 3:1 / Acts 2:17 does not suggest opposition so

---

77. Helyer, "What about Anna?" 5–6; Green, *Gospel of Luke*, 150; and Chen, *Luke*, 39.

78. Green, *Gospel of Luke*, 95. Regarding the emotional overtones of John's leaping, see Inselmann, "Emotions and Passions in the New Testament."

79. Minear, "Luke's Use of the Birth Stories," 118.

80. Marshall, *Gospel of Luke*, 58; Culpepper, "Luke," 46. Ἐπέρχομαι in Luke 1:35 "anticipates Acts 1:8" (Green, *Gospel of Luke*, 90). Tatum recognizes that the Spirit's work in Acts 2 recalls the infancy narrative, but he sees a substantive difference between these cases ("Epoch of Israel," 191). Unlike Tatum, I attribute this difference not to a strongly periodized Lukan *Heilsgeschichte* but to the (merely) proleptic quality of the Spirit's work in Luke 1–2.

81. On ὀπτασία elsewhere in the Bible, see Green, *Gospel of Luke*, 80; Brown, "Annunciation to Zechariah," 485.

much as inclusion, then presumably the point of the age-group pairing is not that one set will see visions while the other will dream dreams but rather that people of all ages will be filled with the Holy Spirit, resulting in new revelatory experiences[82]—as indeed does occur already in the infancy narrative.[83]

Conclusion

Interpreted in light of Luke's allusive references to age in Acts 2, then, the infancy narrative's emphasis on contrasting age categories does not drive a wedge between generations—much less between periods of salvation history or halves of what would become the Christian canon. Instead, like the age merism in Joel 3:1 / Acts 2:17, the age categories of Luke 1–2 reflect an age-inclusive vision of the in-breaking of God's kingdom. The infancy narrative's older adults may not personally live to see the fullness of the salvation-historical events in which they proleptically participate.[84] Nevertheless, at a narrative-theological level, the inclusion of these scripturally evocative Jews in the Spirit's anticipatory work in Luke 1–2 indicates that faithful Israel is taken up into the salvation-historical developments that Zechariah, Elizabeth, Simeon, and Anna glimpse in later life.

This theologically and pastorally important conclusion arises from careful attention to Luke's distinctive intertextual practice in relation to biological age. Whereas some early Christians explicitly refer to specific scriptural figures' elderliness (e.g., Rom 4:18–21; Heb 11:11), the Lukan infancy narrative evokes the Old Testament's treatment of old age more implicitly, through characterization and plotting that recall such figures as Abraham and Sarah. Though Luke's handling of age might at first glance appear to be a supercessionist-ageist appropriation of this OT motif, further intertextual analysis has confirmed that Luke's portrayal of old and young age in fact contributes to his narrativization of theological

---

82. Talbert, *Reading Acts*, 44; Spencer, "Wise Up, Young Man," 35.

83. Luke 1–2's older adults also anticipate narratively later developments in other ways. E.g., Anna's consistent presence in the temple foreshadows believers' practice in Luke 24:53 and Acts 2:46, while her extended widowhood previews the church's elevation of this state of life (Thurston, "Who Was Anna?" 51–52; see also Acts 6:1–6).

84. As Joel Marcus pointed out to me (personal communication). John and Jesus will have died before the sending of the Spirit, too—though the latter will also have been resurrected.

continuity that reaches from the infancy narrative back to Israel's Scriptures and forward into Acts.[85]

---

[85]. Thanks to Brittany E. Wilson for commenting on an earlier version of this study and to Mary Lynn Myers for copy editing.

8

Vision and Re-Envision

Re-Tracing the Social Justice Relationship between Hannah's and Mary's Songs

ALICE YAFEH-DEIGH AND FEDERICO A. ROTH

THIS ESSAY EXAMINES THE relationship between the Song of Hannah (1 Sam 2:1–10) and Mary's *Magnificat* (Luke 1:46–55). The former is related to the latter on the basis of "reversal" themes, that is, both songs highlight the overturning of expected social norms. Intertextually, Hannah's song is regularly related to Mary's *Magnificat* on the grounds of several basic similarities. Both songs are delivered by lowly, unlikely women awaiting (as in the case of Mary) or reflecting (as in the case of Hannah) on the significance of miraculous childbearing events. Both songs highlight the foolishness of overwrought pride (1 Sam 2:3; Luke 1:51). Both songs signal imminent transformation for parents in particular and for Israel more widely. Both songs feature the power of God to reimagine expected socio-economic norms. Both songs praise God for male children. Both children—Samuel and Jesus—act as transformative agents in their own right, inspiring a deeper faith for God's people. Finally, for Hannah, the birth of Samuel signals that God is capable of overcoming barrenness in life and can author more life-giving moments through the coming monarch. For Mary, Jesus as a child growing up signals God's intent to reshape existing social realities.

We contend that, while these narrative and thematic similarities are clearly evident in both texts, they nevertheless fail to account for the precise correlative elements that serve to unify these poems. Here we make the case that:

1. Both poems understand God's work to be of a social and justice-making nature. To this end, we aim to show that at the core of each poem are parallel rhetorical structures and verbal-tense shifts that set the social justice theme in relief.

2. Both poems reconceptualize social justice—not as a program that re-inscribes destructive binaries by way of crude reversals—but in a way that re-envisages justice as being redemptive and restorative for *both* the rich and the poor. The *Magnificat* looks to Hannah's song, not simply because of plot resemblances between the female characters, but also because in the life and ministry of Jesus the Lukan Evangelist sees the theme of social justice as a humanizing and dignifying force for the wealthy and privileged *along with* the despoiled and disenfranchised.

3. Both poems work to create anticipation for the justice-making king—a future anticipation in the Song of Hannah and a proleptically realized anticipation in the *Magnificat*.

4. The promise of Hannah's song is reinforced, reconfigured, and rearticulated in the *Magnificat* in order to give the Gospel of Luke an orientation and vision for Jesus' ministry. It is Jesus' work for the poor and the oppressed that will serve as the final, climactic, divine act of social justice. In so doing, Jesus reiterates, reaffirms, expands, and legitimizes the prophetic restorative justice framework shared by both Hannah and Mary.

The Social-Justice Dimensions in the Song of Hannah

The Song of Hannah may be structurally conceived of as consisting in four discreet units. Sections 1–4 begin with introductory lines that stress (A) the physical features of the body as metonymies for human and divine characteristics and follow the pattern of (B) acknowledging God's sovereign actions over human history and the cosmos; (C) a description of the social realities experienced (or to be experienced) by God's people; and (D) a reiteration of God's sovereignty over the affairs of individuals, nations, and all creation.[1] This literary pattern is summarized in the following chart which further details the structural coherence of Hannah's song:

The Literary, Rhetorical Pattern of Hannah's Song (1 Sam 2:1–10)				
Literary Themes	Section 1: Exultation (vv. 1–3)	Section 2: Reversals (vv. 4–8)	Section 3: Restoration (vv. 9–10b)	Section 4: Promise (v. 10c–e)
A) Images of Physicality	heart, horn, mouth (1)	gird/strength (4), hungry/fat, births (5)	guard, feet (9)	strength (10d)
B) Cosmic Sovereignty	YHWH's incomparability (2a–b) and rock-like grandeur (2c)	YHWH's sovereignty over life and death, Sheol (6)	darkness (9b)	judge of all the earth (10c)
C) Social Contexts and Realities	exhortation for proper social behavior and humble speech (3a–b)	*YHWH as ruling over socio-economic realities; poverty and wealth (7–8d)*	didactic affirmation that might does not yield success (9c)	give strength to his king (10d); exalt the power/ horn of the anointed (10e)
D) Cosmic Sovereignty Reiterated	appeal to YHWH's omniscience and justice (3c–d)	YHWH's possession and establishment of cosmic pillars (8e–f)	YHWH's power and incomparability reaffirmed, thunder in heaven (10a–b)	[lacuna]

1. We see a chiastic pattern in the themes B–C–D which repeat throughout all four sections. This repeating chiastic structure functions as the intertexture of the Song of Hannah and gives the text its literary coherence. Commentary on this structure, however, though adding to the persuasive argument of this essay, will be kept to the notes. See also Overland's four-part criteria for avoiding over-detection in "Chiasm," 55, as well as Tsumura's description of a "rondo form (ABABAC)" in *First Book of Samuel*, 141.

Section 2C (vv. 7–8d) is the single largest unit of the poem and it explicitly addresses social justice as its central theme. In 7a the poet makes a claim to the sovereignty of God. Only YHWH makes poor and makes rich. In 7b spatial terms are revisited (cf. v. 6). God "brings low" and "exalts" (from רום). In 8a God "raises up" (from קום) and in 8b God "lifts" (again from רום). The subunit 8c–d finishes as 7b began, with another verb connoting a downward movement, that is, the poor and needy "sit" (ישב).

Therefore, what we see in this central unit is the roots for רום framing the word קום. In the hiphil (active causative) form, when combined with דל ("poor"), the sense of the pairing is that of raising in order to help up (cf. Ps 113:4 for the nearly identical line). The Hebrew Bible uses קום in this way to instruct community members to help lift injured animals (Deut 22:4), a fallen companion (Qoh 4:10), one who stumbles (Jer 50:32; Job 4:4), one suffering illness (Hos 6:2), or one who is grieving and fasting (2 Sam 12:17). In these contexts, the hiphil of קום implies ideas of deliverance, rescue, and restoration. Here we find the core of Hannah's song. It expresses that God "raises" the poor from the "dust" (עפר), a term that echoes the creation dust of Genesis (Gen 2:7; 3:19) and also substitutes for human frailty (as in Job 42:6). Hannah's God is imminent and intimate, identifying vulnerability and exercising divine will to create an inversion that establishes the poor with honor and dignity. God is the one who raises up.

As a unit, verses 7–8d bring an end to the poem's contrasting language. Indeed, all of the poem's reversals take place in Section 2 (vv. 4–8), in the shape of antithetic parallelism:

> 4 The bows of the mighty are broken,
> *but* (ו) the feeble gird on strength.
> 5 Those who were full have hired (נשכרו) themselves out for bread,
> *but* (ו) those who were hungry are fat (חדלו) with spoil.
> The barren has borne (ילדה) seven,
> *but* (ו) she who has many children is forlorn (אמללה).

Verse 5, in particular, features a collection of perfect verbs which together signal supreme assurance in actions that have been completed and verified.[2] As Ralph Klein points out, it is also important to note that these verses are conveyed in the passive voice and with no direct identification

---

2. Tsumura, *Samuel*, 145.

of God.³ God will be identified in the immediate verses that follow as a way to intensify the theme of cosmic sovereignty.

In vv. 6–7 reversal language is intensified as the poet makes a statement about God's role as sovereign over the beginning and end of a person's life. This is hardly the type of heavy-handed and generalized reversals of fortune we have seen to this point.

> ⁶ The LORD kills (ממית) and brings to life (ומחיה);
> he brings down (מוריד) to Sheol and raises up (ויעל).

What is more, the series of perfect verbs (v. 5) now give way to a string of three consecutive participles (the last verb is a waw consecutive). The God who *was* now *is*. Verse 7 again employs a similar parallelism:

> ⁷ The LORD makes poor (מוריש) and makes rich (ומעשיר);
> he brings low (משפיל), he also exalts (מרומם).

As with verse 6 (and unlike vv. 4–5), the prime mover is explicitly identified as God. It is God—seen here again as sovereign over wealth—who is emphasized as the agent of reversal and restoration. As with three of the four verbs in verse 6, verse 7—following the divine name—is made of participles. Taken together, both couplets (vv. 6–7) help effect the transition, not only by playing with time (past to present, i.e., from the perfect to the participle), but also by moving from simplistic forms of parallelism (i.e., antithetical in vv. 4–5 and synonymous in vv. 6–7) to the more sophisticated form of synthetic or advancing parallelism in verse 8.⁴

So the poet exclaims:

> ⁸ He raises up the poor from the dust; he lifts (ירים) the needy from the ash heap,
> to make them sit with princes and inherit (ינחלם) a seat of honor.

Here in verse 8 the reader encounters the most complexity. Utilizing imperfect verbs, the poem shifts beyond the present to the future. The poet expounds on the very understanding of what is meant by reversal. What one might expect given the pattern of preceding antithetical couplets is for princes to feel the sting of poverty and find *themselves* sitting amidst the dust and ash heap of the city dump. But the humiliation of the

---

3. Klein, *1 Samuel*, 14.

4. This type of parallelism may be defined as thought rhyme in which the sentiment or sense of a subsequent line enhances, develops, specifies, or heightens the sense of a previous line.

wealthy is never realized. Unexpectedly, the poor are *brought up* to sit in the company of the royal court without the rich being correspondingly cast down.

The difference, so it seems, is the presence of the sovereign God. Where God is absent, overturning is possible, but it is indelicate, raw, and coarse. The appearance of God marks an indelible humanizing shift in the discourse of the poem. Thus, in the final climactic lines of its central unit the poem resists the urge to re-victimize by returning violence to the privileged. Rather, the poem affirms the role of God in social spheres as one whose decree expands the kingly guest list to create equity and inclusiveness for all. The momentum of imperfect verbs is continued into verses 9–10b of Section 3 where the poet promises that God will guard (ישמר) the faithful and will destroy (ידמו) the wicked.

Section 4 (vv. 10c–e) forms a worthy conclusion to Hannah's song by recalling the central message of the poem as a whole:

> 10c The LORD will judge the ends of the earth;
> 10d he will give strength to his king,
> 10e and exalt the power (horn) of his anointed.

Section 4 (vv. 10c–e) closes the song by incorporating a pair of already familiar and striking terms. First, the lexical *inclusio* that is made by repeating קרן (horn)—translated by the NRSV as "power" in 10e—finishes what has been started in 1b where the term is glossed in English Bibles as "strength." The difference, however, is that Hannah's horn, exalted as a sign of triumph over enemies in verse 1, is now the horn of the coming king. It is his horn that *will be* lifted up, as was Hannah's. What God has done for Hannah attests to what God *will do* for the future king. Here again, divine agency benefits the once disempowered Hannah and the powerful monarch. Second, the verb used in the final phrase "and *exalt* the power (horn) of his anointed" is built from the now familiar Hebrew word רום of verses 7b and 8b. We recall that this was the verb that envelops the word קום at the very heart of the poem. The God who "exalts" the rich (v. 7b) and "lifts the needy" (v. 8b) now *also* raises up the king. What is more, this very word *also* governs the reference to Hannah's lifted horn in verse 1. So, the reuse of the theme verb רום in verse 10 has the effect of echoing these previous claims. The poet affirms that God does not wish to replace one violence with another. The status of the vulnerable *and* that of the powerful king are preserved. God exalts those on either end of the socio-economic spectrum.

Perhaps more strikingly, 10c–e offers the finale to the poem by pulling from all the main categories outlined in our grid (physicality, cosmic sovereignty, and social realities). The reference to "strength" in 10d and the *inclusio* formed by the repetition of "horn" (v. 10e) bespeaks the theme of *physicality* of the prior sections (cf. vv. 1, 4–5, 9). The phrase in 10c—"The LORD will judge the ends of the earth"—reiterates already familiar themes of cosmic sovereignty, omniscience, and justice-making capabilities (cf. vv. 2, 6, 9b; 3c–d, 8e–f, 10a–b). Here, in the final moments, the poet affirms that YHWH's historical program will include the human institution of monarchy with the reference to the king in vv. 10d–e (cf. 3ab, 7-8d, 9c).

The final lines contain an important omission. The reader—now familiar with the movement from literary pattern of physicality, cosmic sovereignty, social realities, and cosmic sovereignty reiterated—anticipates a final line beyond 10e to reference God's action in history according to his sovereign end. But it never comes. Leaving aside the unknowable possibility that the final line might have been corrupted or lost, the reader finds that the canon leaves a jarring, abrupt ending. The text focuses on a terrestrial figure, "his anointed." No mention of omniscient knowledge (3c–d), prowess over primordial pillars (8e–f), darkness (9b), or astral terminology like "thunder/heaven" (10b) is in view. The rhetorical effect of omitting the cosmic sovereignty element in the final line puts into relief the remaining *social* focus of the poem as a whole.

The poem's conclusion serves to reinforce the urgent and emphatic theme of social justice as a terrestrial necessity. It points to a future king as YHWH's anointed, left as we are with him and him alone, and means to instill hope that the most destitute will, aided by the coming king, experience YHWH-ordained social justice. For as 10c–d make clear, YHWH's power to judge will be bestowed as "strength" to the king.[5] According to Walter Brueggemann, "The coming king will be an agent for the poor, needy, hungry, barren. This poem anticipates the hope placed in kingship for time to come" and "articulates the criteria by which subsequent kings are to be evaluated."[6] This, then, forms the "vision" (to borrow from our title) of Hannah's song. It is one of hopeful waiting for a figure that will enact and reenact socio-economic praxis. The song reimagines the status

---

5. Brueggemann, *First and Second Samuel*, 20.
6. Brueggemann, *First and Second Samuel*, 20.

quo in ways that reaffirm the value of all human beings—the disenfranchised and the powerful alike.

Therefore, the song means to persuade, encourage, perhaps even entice its reader to hope for a way out of the degradation of the Judges period, which forms its immediate literary and historical context. Perhaps as YHWH has done for Hannah (in birthing Samuel), so YHWH will do for Israel. Israel can also experience a new type of coming to life. Hannah's poem makes it clear that YHWH's commitment to Israel will develop in social spheres that feature the recasting of expected social norms, the elevation of those on history's undersides, and the humanization of the affluent. Work towards these ends will come to define the character profile of the coming king.

Sadly, however, the reader's exuberance is arrested by the storyline that follows. The ensuing narratives in 1 Samuel (2:12—3:21) show Eli, Hophni, and Phinehas as each a scoundrel in his own right. The arrival of King Saul offers no solution. By the end of his reign, he has attempted and vowed murder on several occasions (1 Sam 18:10–11; 19:8–10; 20:31; 23; 24; 26), accomplished it for the whole city of Nob (1 Sam 22), and infamously disobeyed even his own pro-Yahwist decree (1 Sam 28). Saul, it turns out, is not Hannah's justice-making king. Neither, for that matter, is David. Indeed, his depravity is well-documented. He nearly slaughters the males of Nabal's family over an interpersonal offense (1 Sam 25), orders numerous executions (2 Sam 1; 4; 11; 1 Kgs 2), and rapes Bathsheba (2 Sam 11:4), to name but a few of his crimes. Like Saul, David is a spectacular disappointment. It is clear, in the light of these failures that the wider rhetorical function of Hannah's song is to create and maintain yearning. Who will function as YHWH's conduit for justice? What is the identity of this righteous ruler?

Mary's Song (Luke 1:46–55)

At the end of the book of Samuel, the unrealized hope begs an essential question: "Who is this ideal King?" Mary's song proleptically claims that Jesus is the righteous ruler, God's final, climactic, justice-making King. Mary's song extrapolates from Mary's personal experience of God's restorative grace in her life to assert confidently that God's ultimate restorative justice process has begun. God is already intervening on behalf of the subalterns—all the underprivileged and disenfranchised oppressed by power holders. They are the paradigmatic victims of systemic injustices.[7] Mary's song links God's climactic actions to God's restorative justice commitment to Israel. The prophetic restorative justice framework of Mary's song will show that Jesus' actions fit neatly into the character profile of the coming King.

The second part of this essay argues that the central theme of restorative justice presents Hannah's song as the prominent intertextual candidate for Mary's song. Through an intertextual analysis between the two songs, we will claim that the Lukan Mary's social justice vision is couched predominantly in terms of restorative justice like Hannah's rather than a retributive or punitive justice.

Inner-Texture Analyses of Mary's Song[8]

A literary-rhetorical examination of the inner texture for Mary's song leads us to uphold the commonly suggested two-part division: Section 1 (vv. 46–50) and Section 2 (vv. 51–55).[9] Linguistic, thematic, and conceptual markers further reveal three subsections (A–C) within each of the two main sections—that is, Section 1 (A: vv. 46–47, B: vv. 48–49a, and C: vv. 49b–50) and Section 2 (A: v. 51, B: vv. 52–53, and C: vv. 54–55).[10] The various subsections share a mosaic of structural features and give the Song a cohesive, unified fabric. Two of the most prominent structural features driving the Song are repetition and parallelism. They are the most conspicuous formal devices.

The following chart details the significant linguistic, thematic, and structural coherence of Mary's song:

---

7. For a detailed understanding of the term "subaltern," see Spivak, "Can the Subaltern Speak?" 271–313; Spivak, "Gayatri Spivak on the Politics of the Subaltern," 85–97.

8. This section of the essay follows the socio-rhetorical criticism of Vernon Robbins; see notably, Robbins, *Tapestry of Early Christian Discourse*, 108–18; Robbins, *Exploring the Texture of Texts*, 58–63.

9. Cf. Talbert, *Reading Luke*, 27.

10. For Mary's song's sophisticated poetic structure, see Tannehill, "Magnificat as Poem," 263–75; and Bailey, "Song of Mary," 29–35.

Literary Structure of Mary's Song	Themes and Emphases
Section 1: God's graciousness and restorative justice for Mary (vv. 46–50)	**Emphasis on God's action for Mary as an individual**
A. A fervent, heartfelt outburst of joyous gratitude 46 Καὶ εἶπεν Μαριάμ· Μεγαλύνει ἡ ψυχή μου τὸν κύριον, 47 καὶ ἠγαλλίασεν τὸ πνεῦμά μου ἐπὶ τῷ θεῷ τῷ σωτῆρί μου	1) Five first-person singular pronouns emphasize focus on Mary as individual: ἡ ψυχή μου (v. 46), τὸ πνεῦμά μου (v. 47a), τῷ σωτῆρί μου (v. 47b), μακαριοῦσίν με (v. 48), ἐποίησέν μοι (v. 49a)
B. Rationale through three parallel constructions (with two ὅτι clauses) 48 ὅτι ἐπέβλεψεν ἐπὶ τὴν ταπείνωσιν τῆς δούλης αὐτοῦ. ἰδοὺ γὰρ ἀπὸ τοῦ νῦν μακαριοῦσίν με πᾶσαι αἱ γενεαί, 49a ὅτι ἐποίησέν μοι μεγάλα ὁ δυνατός.	2) Synonymous parallel: ἡ ψυχή μου, τὸ πνεῦμά μου (v. 46b) Μεγαλύνει, ἠγαλλίασεν (v. 47) 3) Titles used for God: τὸν κύριον (v. 46b), σωτῆρί μου (v. 47), ὁ δυνατός (v. 49a)
C. Two attributes of God: holy and merciful 49b καὶ ἅγιον τὸ ὄνομα αὐτοῦ, 50 καὶ τὸ ἔλεος αὐτοῦ εἰς γενεὰς καὶ γενεὰς τοῖς φοβουμένοις αὐτόν.	4) Emphasis on God's attributes: ὁ δυνατός (v. 48), ἅγιον (v. 49a), τὸ ἔλεος (v. 50), τοῖς φοβουμένοις αὐτόν (v. 50)
Section 2: God's restorative actions for all marginalized as promise-fulfillment (vv. 51–55)	**Emphasis on the universal scope of God's mercy as God's covenant faithfulness**
A. God's mighty arm against the proud 51 Ἐποίησεν κράτος ἐν βραχίονι αὐτοῦ, διεσκόρπισεν ὑπερηφάνους διανοίᾳ καρδίας αὐτῶν·	1) Antithetical parallelism chiastically arranged (vv. 52–53) 2) Synonymous parallel at the center of the chiasm καὶ ὕψωσεν ταπεινούς (v. 52b) πεινῶντας ἐνέπλησεν ἀγαθῶν (v. 53a)
B. God's restorative justice on behalf of the poor and powerless 52 καθεῖλεν δυνάστας ἀπὸ θρόνων καὶ ὕψωσεν ταπεινούς, 53 πεινῶντας ἐνέπλησεν ἀγαθῶν καὶ πλουτοῦντας ἐξαπέστειλεν κενούς.	3) Pervasive use of kinship language in the closing section: Ἰσραὴλ παιδὸς αὐτοῦ (v. 54a), τοὺς πατέρας ἡμῶν (v. 55a), τῷ Ἀβραὰμ (v. 55b), τῷ σπέρματι αὐτοῦ (v. 55b)
C. God's merciful actions as faithfulness to his covenantal promise 54 ἀντελάβετο Ἰσραὴλ παιδὸς αὐτοῦ, μνησθῆναι ἐλέους, 55 καθὼς ἐλάλησεν πρὸς τοὺς πατέρας ἡμῶν, τῷ Ἀβραὰμ καὶ τῷ σπέρματι αὐτοῦ εἰς τὸν αἰῶνα	

The song's two main literary sections are equally bonded together by repeating keywords and phrases. A significant structural term that establishes thematic connections between the two units is the repetition of words, especially the term ἔλεος or "mercy" (vv. 50, 54; cf. 58, 72).[11] Mercy is an overarching theme that integrates the two sections. The term ἔλεος serves as a thematic marker that unifies the Song's literary units. It alerts the reader to the theological importance of God's mercy construed as God's covenant faithfulness, revealed by both God's actions and God's attributes. This enduring covenant faithfulness characterizes and emphasizes God's act of restorative justice in favor of Mary and anyone who fears God (vv. 46–50), as well as Israel, God's covenant people (vv. 51–55).

Section 1: God's Graciousness and Restorative Justice on Behalf of Mary (vv. 46–50)

The tense shift in the first section reveals an intriguing progression. Following the present tense μεγαλύνει ("magnifies"; v. 46), the tense switches to the two aorist verbs ἠγαλλίασεν ("rejoiced"; v. 47) and ἐπέβλεψεν ("looked"; v. 48a), then to the future tense verb μακαριοῦσίν ("will bless"; v. 48b), and then back to the aorist tense with ἐποίησέν ("did"; v. 49a). The use of three verb tenses—present, aorist, and future—discloses advancements in time and plot sequence. Yet the progression exhibits an awkward chronological sequence as the narrative moves from the present, then to the past, and finally towards the future. Shifts in verb tense are deliberate and purposeful. Notably, the use of the present μεγαλύνει (v. 46) makes the Song immediate. However, Mary's outburst of joyful praise is rooted and firmly established in God's subversive, countercultural, and transformative actions that began earlier in the chapter. As such, the aorist ἠγαλλίασεν ("rejoiced"), in verse 47 functions as a gnomic aorist.[12] The peculiarity of the gnomic aorist's use here is that it summons a retrospective memory or recollection of past events (vv. 26–45). Mary's joy-filled celebration culminated in her hermeneutical reflections on the activities

---

11. Unless otherwise indicated, all English translations are taken from the NRSV.

12. For useful discussions of the change in tenses, see Carroll, *Luke*, 48; Fitzmyer, *Gospel according to Luke I-IX*, 366; Bovon, *Luke 1*, 60; Méndez, "Semitic Poetic Techniques in the Magnificat," 557–74.

that began with the annunciation (vv. 26–38),[13] her visit with Elizabeth (vv. 39–45), Elizabeth's Spirit-empowered prophetic affirmation that Mary has been chosen to become the mother of Elizabeth's Lord/Messiah (vv. 42–43), and Elizabeth's declaration that Mary is blessed because she is a model of faithful obedience (v. 45).

The liberating action of ὁ δυνατός ("the Mighty one"; v. 49a) on behalf of Mary are actions that are grounded in τὸ ἔλεος αὐτοῦ ("his [God's] mercy"; vv. 50, 54). Mary interprets this liberative initiative of God in light of her current reality (ἐπέβλεψεν ἐπὶ τὴν ταπείνωσιν τῆς δούλης αὐτοῦ ["he has looked with favor on the lowliness of his servant"]; v. 48). God's recent restorative intervention on Mary's behalf becomes paradigmatic for God's future actions. Mary's celebratory exclamation that God has looked upon her underprivileged status (v. 48a) implies that Mary embraces the phrase τὴν ταπείνωσιν τῆς δούλης αὐτοῦ as an identity marker that underscores her low socio-economic position.[14] Mary sees herself as quintessentially defined by her role as God's servant, a position secured through single-minded devotion and obligation to God. As Seim puts it, this singular commitment and dedication to God make Mary "the very prototype of the Lord's servant."[15]

Mary's personal experiences propelled her to make a prophetic announcement, an affirmation that future generations will remember God's redemptive and saving actions in her life ("Surely, from now on all generations will call me blessed"; v. 48b). Mary is convinced that when future generations witness God's actions on her behalf, they will recognize, legitimate, and celebrate her ascribed honor.[16] With the child in her womb and God's action in her life, the restorative justice process has already begun. The future is now being realized. Mary's ascribed honor is due to the unilateral initiative of God.

The universal emphasis of God's mercy-driven faithfulness foreshadowed here will become a prominent theme in the Gospel of Luke (see, e.g., 1:79; 2:10, 14; 2:29–32; 3:6; 3:38; 4:16–30; 7:2–9; 10:30–37; 17:11–16; 24:47). Mary pioneers new hope for the subalterns; yet, the

---

13. Cf. De Long, *Surprised by God*, 146.

14. Bock points out that τὴν ταπείνωσιν is better construed here as a technical term denoting social status; see Bock, *Luke 1:1–9:50*, 150; and Farris, *Hymns of Luke's Infancy Narratives*, 122.

15. Seim, *Double Message*, 175.

16. For details on honor and shame dynamics in antiquity, see Neyrey, *Honor and Shame*; Malina, "Social-Scientific Methods in Historical Jesus Research," 3–26.

God who is subverting conventional expectations is not just interested in Mary (τῆς δούλης αὐτοῦ; v. 48a) or Israel (παιδὸς αὐτοῦ; v. 54), but in all people, particularly "those who fear God" (τοῖς φοβουμένοις αὐτόν; v. 50). Analogously, examples of God's mighty acts in the next section will show that God's holiness is revealed in God's relentless pursuit of social justice for the subalterns.

Section 2: God's Restorative Actions for all Marginalized as Promise-Fulfillment (vv. 51–55)

As noted previously,[17] the content and the focus of the song shift in this second section. One of the most salient features of this next section is the parallel construction of aorist action verbs in vv. 51–54 that characterize God's social justice actions, including: ἐποίησεν ("has shown"), διεσκόρπισεν ("scattered"), καθεῖλεν ("brought down"), ὕψωσεν ("lifted up"), ἐνέπλησεν ("filled"), ἐξαπέστειλεν ("sent away"), and ἀντελάβετο ("helped"). Different suggestions have been proposed for the specific meaning of the aorist in this section.[18] I contend that the aorist verbs are used proleptically or prophetically, in anticipation of future events described as sure realities. The song recognizes that the proleptic actions have already been inaugurated in the events that elicited the song. As Levine insists, "in Mary's imagination, God has already performed these social reversals. For Mary, the victory is already won."[19] The song further acknowledges that God's recent actions on Mary's behalf—actions celebrated in Mary's song—are on the continuum with God's restorative activities in Israel's narrative.[20] Israel still occupies a pride of place as evidenced in the use of the kinship language such as Ἰσραὴλ παιδὸς αὐτοῦ, τοὺς πατέρας ἡμῶν, and τῷ Ἀβραὰμ καὶ τῷ σπέρματι αὐτοῦ (vv. 54–55). Mary's song appeals to the unity and continuity between God's present social justice actions and God's enduring covenant faithfulness with Israel for legitimation and credibility. God's covenant faithfulness serves as an anchor for envisioning proleptically the "not yet" of God's restorative justice actions.

17. Please see the chart above for details.
18. Many exegetes take the aorists in verses 51–53 as gnomic; see, e.g., Méndez, "Semitic Poetic Techniques in the Magnificat," 559.
19. Levine and Witherington, *Gospel of Luke*, 42.
20. Cf. Levine and Witherington, *Gospel of Luke*, 41.

There is a striking use of strong action verbs at the beginning of the sentence with God as the subject/agent (verb-object; v. 52). Changing expected word order allows the poem to foreground the actions of "the Mighty One," the implied subject/agent of all the verbs. Thus, by placing verbs at the beginning of the antithetical structure (vv. 52–53), key divine actions are emphasized. The first subunit is a judgment directed against the arrogant in general (v. 51). As signaled earlier, God's mighty arm against the proud establishes an antithetical relationship with God's mercy to "those who fear God" (v. 50a). God's redistributive justice will radically change the present reality of the proud and rich.

Levine makes a crucial point when she states:

> The refrains of what God has done—shown strength, brought down and lifted up, filled and sent away, helped—are not only metaphors. The hungry who are filled are not just spiritual seekers; they are people who do not have enough to eat. The oppressed are those who face oppression. Mary is thus issuing a political manifesto: when the promises of God come to fruition, people will have enough to eat; the rich will no longer exploit the poor.[21]

Lukan scholars have continued to understand God's social justice actions in terms of an inverted pyramid.[22] Interestingly, the song does not precisely say that the disenfranchised groups are lifted to the throne. It merely says that they are lifted up (ὕψωσεν ταπεινούς, v. 52). Restorative justice necessitates status readjustment or realignment. The mighty are on the throne at the expense of the subaltern being made marginal, displaced, or relegated to the bottom of the status ladder. Justice for the subaltern requires that they be restored to their rightful place in society. Even the mighty are not brought down to the bottom of the ladder. They are displaced to where they rightfully belong. The focus is on dismantling social and religious norms that sustain discriminatory practices.

To be sure, everyone will feel the redistributive effects of God's social justice activities. The subalterns will thrive, flourish, and have full and meaningful participation in society. The powerful/mighty who are usurping thrones will be deposed/displaced and forced to go back to their rightful positions in society. If the song were declaring a reversal of status, there would be nothing revolutionary or radically new about

---

21. Levine and Witherington, *Gospel of Luke*, 42.
22. Cf. Stein, *Luke*, 96.

God's kingdom in-breaking actions. Once the lowly are lifted up to the throne, they become the new oppressors, and the "power-over" paradigm continues, but inverted with the "same system, [just] different suffering players."[23] In stark contrast, Mary's song makes an unprecedented claim that God's in-breaking kingdom activities interrupt, challenge, and dismantle oppressive systems and promote restorative justice. This restorative justice on behalf of the subalterns has already begun based on her personal experiences. God's present activity on behalf of Mary is the lens through which the not-yet-realized prophetic vision for the future is to be understood.

The repetition of the song's thematic word ἐλέους (v. 54b) connects the two main literary sections of the song and reasserts God's characteristic attribute "mercy." The final subunit (Section 2C; vv. 54–55) indicates that God's action of social justice is inextricably tied to God's loyalty to his servant Israel (v. 54, Ἰσραὴλ παιδὸς αὐτοῦ). In addition to divine attributes of power, holiness, and mercy that have been strategically woven into the song's fabric, God's covenant faithfulness is another characteristic attribute of God. A central hypothesis here is that God's faithfulness to his covenant with Abraham ties Mary's song to that of Hannah. The unrealized promise that creates social justice expectations in Hannah's song is being fulfilled in Mary's. Therefore, the closing subunit fundamentally functions as an appeal to God's attribute of mercy and God's prevailing promise as powerful tools of legitimation for the proleptic declarations made in Mary's song. The prepositional phrase εἰς τὸν αἰῶνα ("in perpetuity"; v. 55) appropriately concludes the song on a solemn note. It accentuates the permanent nature of God's covenant faithfulness.

Building Bridges between Two Prophetic Voices: Central Social-Justice Thematic Parallels in Hannah's and Mary's Songs

The preceding discussion has focused primarily on the fabric of inner texture. Through an inner-textual analysis on the *Magnificat*'s rhetorical structure, we have established that, structurally, social justice categories couched in terms of restorative justice are at the core of Mary's song. A close reading of intertextual elements shows that, although Mary's song is a tapestry woven from different scriptural threads (vv. 52–53), the *Magnificat,* for the most part, is intricately connected to Hannah's song,

---

23. Levine and Witherington, *Gospel of Luke,* 41.

especially to 1 Sam 2:7–8. Both songs are masterpieces sung by female characters, where the dominant theme of social justice stands as the focal point and unifying theme. Especially important are the parallels between the two songs that emphasize not a retributive justice against the powerful and wealthy, but a restorative justice for the poor and lowly. The chart below tracks the literary and thematic parallels between 1 Sam 2:7–8 and Luke 1:51–53 as follows:

The Song of Hannah (1 Sam 2:7–8)	The Song of Mary (Luke 1:51–53)
	51 He has shown strength with his arm; he has scattered the proud in the thoughts of their hearts.
7 The LORD makes poor and makes rich; he brings low, he also exalts.	52 He has brought down the powerful from their thrones, and lifted up the lowly;
8 He raises up the poor from the dust; he lifts the needy from the ash heap, to make them sit with princes.	53 he has filled the hungry with good things, and sent the rich away empty.

An intertextual analysis of the songs' literary structures reveals that social justice is at the core of the two songs. There are striking conceptual and thematic parallels between the two songs. Critical social justice concepts exhibited in the songs are signaled by terms in both songs concerning the "mighty," "arrogant," "humiliation," "feeble," "full," "hungry," "poor," "rich," "needy," "princes," "faithful," and "wicked." Both songs create tensions through an antithetical relationship, that is, a series of values that are opposite. The following, for instance, stand in an antithetical relationship: "mighty and feeble," "full and hungry," "exalts and puts down," "high and low," "poor and rich," "needy and princes," "powerful and lowly," "filled and empty-handed," and "servant and children."

The antithetical parallels notwithstanding, the overarching theme at the core of the literary units is God's merciful restorative justice in favor of the subalterns. God's justice is reparative—the needs of the poor and vulnerable come first but do not necessitate a kind of reversal that does violence to the powerful and rich. To be sure, God's redistributive policies are confrontational; hence, they are broadly framed in terms of contrasts. However, they focus more on restoring full dignity and respect to the victims of unjust social, religious, political, and economic institutions of society rather than the destruction of those in power. Accordingly, the two songs' vision of social justice emphasizes God's restorative actions in favor of subalterns so there is equity between all parties, including those who once monopolized power and have since been dislodged from a position of privilege.

A key literary feature shared by both songs is their dramatic movement from the particular to the general. The songs turn quickly to establishing a bridge between the particular and the national or universal. Both Mary's and Hannah's hermeneutical reflections about God's redemptive and restorative actions on their behalf led them to conclude that God's victorious interventions in their lives provide the quintessential example of what God's saving actions will look like for Israel (in the case of Hannah) and all humanity (for Mary). In both songs, the women are given a prophetic role.

Mary's song transforms the meaning of Hannah's song by broadening the scope of God's restorative activities to include all humanity. From a historical perspective, the intertextual reader is aware of the differences between the divergent social locations of the texts. They address different socio-political and cultural realities and experiences. Nevertheless, they both envision a broadening scope of God's justice from the individual to Israel and to every nation.

Mary's song provides a definitive response to the open-ended, lingering question of the book of Samuel: "Who is the righteous ruler, the ideal justice-making King?" Brueggemann pointedly notes that the ideal King's legitimacy will be measured by his commitment to confronting social injustices perpetrated against the subalterns.[24] Mary proleptically claims that the child she is bearing is the justice-making, triumphant King envisioned by Hannah's song. For Mary, Hannah's song has been prophetically realized through God's apocalyptic in-breaking into the cosmos in the events of the child she is bearing. Thus, Mary's song is designed to continue and compliment Hannah's prophetic voice.

Mary's song uses prophetic aorists to underline a series of God's actions in her life as an instantiation of restorative justice for all. By recontextualizing Hannah's song's social vision, Mary's prophetic proclamation of God's restorative justice asserts that the unrealized promise that creates a situation of hopelessness in Hannah's song is transformed into hopeful

---

24. Cf. Brueggemann, *First and Second Samuel*, 20.

anticipation.²⁵ Mary's song therefore has an anticipatory orientation toward the future events that are yet to unfold. It creates a sense of curiosity in the reader and builds anticipation for the foreshadowed events. The onus is now on Jesus' ministry to serve as evidence of Mary's claim and give legitimacy to her prophecy.

Lastly, the strategic position of Mary's song in the entire narrative of Luke's Gospel gives primacy to Mary's song over the inaugural speech in Nazareth as the programmatic text that sets up the central vision and orientation of Jesus' ministry. The programmatic importance of the inaugural sermon, which functions as an explicit overture to Jesus' ministry, is that Jesus explicitly reiterates, reaffirms, expands, and legitimizes Mary's prophetic restorative justice framework. This perspective, to be sure, stands in contradistinction to most conventional readings of Luke's Gospel.²⁶

Conclusion

This essay's premise was that the intertextual relations between Hannah's and Mary's songs are essential to the understanding of Mary's distinctive vision in Luke 1:46–55. We have claimed that both songs evoke similar underlying social justice themes that invite readers to remember Hannah's song as they read Mary's, even though they are both inscribed in different cultural and historical settings. Hannah's song functions as a

---

25. On the contextual function of recontextualization, see Linell, "Discourse across Boundaries," 143–57.

26. The majority of Lukan scholars identify Jesus' inaugural address in Luke 4:16–30 as the programmatic passage of Luke's Gospel. See, e.g., Lieu, *Gospel of Luke*, 31; Brawley, *Luke-Acts and the Jews*, 12; Garland, *Luke*, 189; Bock, *Theology of Luke and Acts*, 136; Talbert, *Reading Luke*, 57; Marshall, *Gospel of Luke*, 177–78; Bruno, "'Jesus is our Jubilee' . . . But How?" 84; Sloan, *Favorable Year of the Lord*, 174; Tannehill, *Narrative Unity of Luke-Acts*, 1:62; Green, *Theology of the Gospel of Luke*, 76; Barker, "Time is Fulfilled," 22–32; Abogunrin, "Jesus' Sevenfold Programmatic Declaration at Nazareth," 227. While a comprehensive analysis of the close relationship between the two pericopae (Luke 1:46–51 and 4:16–30) is beyond the scope of this essay, our basic contention is that Luke has placed Mary's song at the opening chapter of the Gospel because of its crucial programmatic role. The inaugural sermon in Luke 4:16–30 enhanced the programmatic effectiveness of Mary's song by reinforcing the essential theme of restorative justice on behalf of the powerless and disenfranchised as the goal of Jesus' *basileia* ministry, thereby legitimizing Mary's prophetic song. Jesus' appropriation of the restorative vision of Isa 61:1–2 occurs in the context of an explicit echo of Mary's song, albeit not necessarily using the same wording.

crucial intertext and provides a unique template for understanding the themes in Mary's song concerning God's restorative justice. Our claim is that Mary's song draws from Hannah's, but reconfigures and recontextualizes it along the theme of social justice to address Mary's own historical and socio-economic location. Mary's song also broadens the scope of God's actions beyond Hannah's song so that restoration and justice are experienced not just for Israel, but for all humanity. The intertextuality between the songs demonstrates a kind of metalepsis that reconfigures past texts to new contexts, but also a broadening of the text's scope and relevance for the reader.

We also maintain that God's "already" and "not yet" restorative activities provide new foundations for continuing the essential social justice themes of Hannah's song in our day. The thematic echoes are not just decontextualized from the literary context of Hannah's song. On the contrary, Mary's song exhibits a strong sense of thematic continuity with Hannah's song, and the thematic continuity adds new layers of interpretive possibilities for the present reader. We concluded that Mary's song explicitly employs the social dimensions of Hannah's song as a springboard for framing Jesus' ministry of restorative justice for subalterns. This ministry was continued in the work of the early Christian church in Acts and throughout the centuries until our present times.

Part III:

Practicing Intertextuality
in the Pauline Letters

9

"Consecrated by the Brother/Sister"

The Norm of Religious Endogamy and Paul's Alternative in 1 Cor 7:14

JUDITH M. GUNDRY

IN 1 COR 7 Paul prohibits divorce in Christian marriages based on Jesus' prohibition of divorce (7:10–11), but adopts a more nuanced stance in cases of marriages between Christ-believers and unbelievers, or inter-religious marriages (7:12–16).[1] Paul writes that if the unbeliever wants

---

1. Jesus' teaching on divorce (Mark 10:2–12; Matt 19:3–12; Luke 16:18) presupposes religious endogamy and was thus not applicable to the Corinthians' interreligious marriages. The Corinthians may have wanted to divorce their unbelieving spouses based on the widespread norm of religious endogamy in Greco-Roman antiquity. As Collins (*First Corinthians*, 265–66) notes, in the ancient Mediterranean world in general "people are expected to marry within their own group whether 'the group' be defined racially, ethnically, socially, or religiously (cf. Deut 7:3; Neh 13:25)." It is also plausible that the Corinthians thought Paul's prior instructions not to associate with "the immoral," including the idolater (εἰδωλολάτρης, 5:9), implied they should divorce an unbelieving, polytheistic spouse. Paul's clarification in 5:10–12 rules out such an implication—he meant not to associate with "the so-called brother/sister" who is "a sexually immoral person," "an idolater," etc.

*Parts of this essay are drawn from my previous work on "Children, Parents, and God/Gods in Interreligious Roman Households and the Interpretation of 1 Corinthians 7:14" in the *T. & T. Clark Handbook of Children in the Bible and the Biblical World*, used here with permission from Bloomsbury Press.

to "live together" with the Christ-believer, the Christ-believer should not initiate divorce (7:12–14), but if the unbeliever wants to divorce, the Christ-believer should "let him/her separate" (7:15–16).

Against divorcing an unbelieving spouse willing to remain, Paul argues that "the unbelieving husband ἡγίασται by the wife, and the unbelieving wife ἡγίασται by the brother" (7:14a). This assertion is apparently not self-evident, so Paul gives a proof: "For otherwise, your children[2] would be impure, but as it is, they are ἅγια (7:14b)."[3] Both the proof and the assertion it supports are difficult to interpret, leading to a wide variety of translations and interpretations.

A consensus has yet to emerge.[4] After critiquing several interpretations, I shall support one based on the parallel in Rom 11:16, where the same terminology is used in a cultic (or transferred cultic) sense and being "consecrated" to God implies hope of future salvation for unbelievers. Then I shall offer a new explanation for Paul's interest in the consecration

---

2. Τέκνον can denote a child of any age (see BDAG, s.v. τέκνον, ου, τό, 994 [def. 1]). Paul may be referring to very young children or infants here, since he describes them neither as believing nor unbelieving and omits injunctions to obey parents (contrast Col 3:19–21; Eph 6:1–4; 1 Tim 3:4, 12; 5:4, 8; 2 Tim 1:5; Tit 1:6; 2:4). Nevertheless, there was a relative lack of rigidity in age demarcation in first-century CE Roman society; see Rawson, *Children and Childhood*. Paul mostly refers to *metaphorical* children (and parents) in his letters (e.g., Rom 16:5, 10; 1 Cor 3:1–2; 4:14–21; 2 Cor 6:11–12; 12:14b–15a; Gal 4:19; Phil 2:22; 1 Thess 2:7, 11); on Paul's metaphorical references to children, see Aasgaard, *Beloved Brothers and Sisters*; Aasgaard, "Like a Child," 249–77; Gerber, *Paulus und seine 'Kinder'*; Gaventa, *Our Mother St. Paul*.

3. With Lindemann (*Korintherbrief*, 166), there is no difference in meaning between ἡγίασται and ἅγια ἐστιν in 1 Cor 7:14. See also Beasley-Murray (*Baptism*, 193), who argues against an allusion to infant baptism in 1 Cor 7:14: "Above all it is to be recognized that the holiness of the child is commensurate with that of the unbelieving parent; a valid explanation of the former must account also for the latter . . . it is impermissible to draw a distinction between two conceptions of holiness here, on the ground that the parent is said to be only ἡγίασται whereas the child is ἅγιος." Contrast Jeremias (*Infant Baptism*, 37–40; 44–48), whose earlier work appealed to Jewish proselyte baptism as a parallel to early Christian infant baptism in 1 Cor 7:14, which he then recanted. Cf. Hofius, "Glaube und Taufe," 253–75.

4. See Thiselton, *First Epistle to the Corinthians*, 528, for alternative translations of 7:14. Scholarly discussions of 1 Cor 7:14 abound; see, e.g., Delling, "Nun aber sind sie Heilig," 84–93; Ford, "Hast Thou Tithed," 71–79; Murphy-O'Connor, "Works Without Faith," 349–61; O'Neil, "1 Corinthians 7.14 and Infant Baptism," 358–59; Best, "1 Corinthians 7:14," 158–66; Tomson, *Paul and the Jewish Law*, 103–24; Collins, *Divorce*, 40–64; Müller, *In der Mitte*, 356–64; Adewuya, *Holiness and Community*, 139–46; Gillihan, "Jewish Laws on Illicit Marriage," 711–44; MacDonald and Vaage, "Unclean but Holy Children," 526–46; Horrell, "Ethnicisation," 439–60.

of unbelievers to God: the expectation of a uniform religious identity and practice in Roman households, of which the Corinthians' interreligious marriages fell short. Here, Paul supplies an alternative form of religious unity in support of his paraenesis on divorce.

The Status Quaestionis on 1 Cor 7:14

Scholars disagree whether Paul in 7:14 describes the Corinthian Christ-believer's unbelieving spouse and children as "saints"—those who share a Christian identity and are members of the Christian community—or rather, simply as morally "holy," ritually "pure," or "consecrated" to God in a transferred cultic sense.

Paul's frequent use of the term ἅγιος for Christ-believers as "saints"[5] is cited in favor of the children's being "saints" (ἅγια), despite (implicitly) being unbelieving or unbaptized. Likewise, Paul's use of the term ἁγιάζεσθαι to refer to Christ-believers' "being sanctified"[6] is cited in favor of the unbelieving spouse's being "sanctified" (ἡγίασται) despite being "unbelieving."

David Horrell explains Paul's statement about the children as ἅγια in terms of "the principle of heredity": "Paul is in effect establishing a principle of heredity: children already belong within the Christian community."[7] Horrell continues: "Christian identity . . . can be passed on by either parent . . . through the family, and specifically through the rearing of children."[8] Conversion was not the only way to become a Christian. Paul's words in 1 Cor 7:14 attest that the early Christians, like other ancients, envisioned the possibility of acquiring a religious group identity through the family—"ethnicisation"—which idea is further developed in the Pauline tradition (Colossians, Ephesians, and the Pastoral Epistles) and 1 Pet 3.[9]

Horrell eschews, however, appealing to Paul's use of the cognate verb ἡγίασται in the case of the unbelieving husband or wife as evidence for a Christian identity obtained through the family. Rather, Horrell claims:

---

5. E.g., Rom 1:7; 1 Cor 1:2; 2 Cor 1:1; Phil 1:1. Cf. Trebilco, *Self-Designations*, 122–63.
6. E.g., 1 Cor 1:2; 6:11; 1 Thess 5:23.
7. Horrell, "Ethnicisation," 439–60.
8. Horrell, "Ethnicisation," 451–52.
9. Horrell, "Ethnicisation," 452–60.

> Notable here is the difference in Paul's description of the unbelieving spouse and the children: the former is 'sanctified' (ἡγίασται) by the believer, despite remaining ἄπιστος . . . Only the children are emphatically and unambiguously described as ἅγιος.[10]

The unbelieving spouse is not a "saint."[11] But the distinction which Horrell imposes on the usage of the cognate terms is unpersuasive, for as already noted, Paul's argument depends on the semantic equivalence of ἅγια ἐστιν and ἡγίασται: the status of the children is a proof for the *same* status of the unbelieving spouse, which was open to dispute, apparently. In 1 Cor 1:2 Paul uses the same cognate terms with no semantic difference but as stylistic variants: ἡγιασμένοις ἐν Χριστῷ Ἰησοῦ, κλητοῖς ἁγίοις ("to those consecrated in Christ Jesus, called as consecrated ones").

In support of a principle of heredity in 7:14, Horrell rightly does *not* appeal to Rom 11:16:

> Now if the firstfruits [is] consecrated (ἁγία) [to God], so also the lump of dough [is consecrated to God]. And if the root [is] consecrated (ἁγία) [to God], so also the branches [are consecrated to God].

As James Dunn has argued, neither here nor in 1 Cor 7:14 does Paul teach "a doctrine of transmission of holiness in strict genetic terms," for in Rom 11:5-6 it is clear that "the promise . . . comes to expression *through grace*" (emphasis mine).[12] Dunn's argument, however, also invalidates Horrell's notion of inheriting Christian identity "through the family, and specifically through the rearing of children."

Margaret MacDonald and Leife Vaage explain Paul's use of the ἅγιος lexicon for unbelievers as "saints" in the light of their "complex social reality" (referring to interreligious marriages or possibly the sexual use of Christian slaves by unbelieving masters), resulting in an "ambiguous social identity and paradoxical (including irregular) presence."[13] They have contradictory statuses: both "saints" (ἅγια) and "sanctified"

---

10. Horrell, "Ethnicisation," 450-51.

11. Horrell, "Ethnicisation," 450-51.

12. Dunn, *Romans 9-16*, 660. Käsemann (*Romans*, 308) rejects the view that Paul is referring to "the inheriting of religious qualities (*contra* Dodd), nor does he speak of natural holiness (*contra* Jülicher)."

13. MacDonald and Vaage, "Unclean but Holy Children," 533; 537; 546. Cf. MacDonald, *Power of Children*, 24-25.

(ἡγίασται), or members of the *ekklēsia* / "us" and "saved,"[14] and "impure" (ἀκάθαρτα), or nonmembers of the *ekklēsia* / "not us" and "not saved."[15] MacDonald and Vaage argue that 7:14b should be translated: "Since then (ἐπεὶ ἄρα), your children are impure, but now (νῦν δέ) they are holy,"[16] instead of the more common translation, "since otherwise (ἐπεὶ ἄρα), your children would be impure, but as it is, they are holy." Paul's allegedly "contradictory" instructions on divorce in 7:12–13 and in 7:15–16, where some Christ-believers are prohibited from divorcing an unbeliever, while others are told not to resist an unbeliever's initiation of divorce are cited as evidence for Paul's "logical jumble" in 7:14.

But against this interpretation, the only other Pauline occurrence of ἐπεὶ ἄρα … νῦν δέ, is found at 5:10–11 and has the sense, "since otherwise … but now," and is thus to be preferred in 7:14b.[17] Furthermore, Paul only refers to the *potential future* salvation of the unbeliever: "For how do you know, woman, whether you *will save* [σώσεις] your husband? Or how do you know, man, whether you *will save* [σώσεις] your wife?" (7:16). And Paul's instructions on divorce are hardly contradictory; rather, as Peter Tomson has argued, they can be compared with Jewish *halakha*, which is tailored to individual circumstances.[18]

MacDonald and Vaage do not explain how their interpretation can be reconciled with 1 Cor 14, where Paul distinguishes carefully between members and nonmembers who attend the Corinthians' assemblies. When "the church" (ἐκκλησία) "gathers together in one place," "the uninitiated or the unbelievers (ἰδιῶται ἢ ἄπιστοι) may enter (εἰσέλθωσιν)," or "the one who fills the place of the uninitiated" (ὁ ἀναπληρῶν τὸν τόπον τοῦ ἰδιώτου; 14:23). The Corinthians should prophesy intelligibly so that these unbelievers will understand, be convicted, and confess the one true God: "If all prophesy, and some unbeliever or uninitiated person should come in, is convicted by all, examined by all, [and] the secrets of

---

14. MacDonald and Vaage, "Unclean but Holy Children," 536–37. Similarly, Mitchell (*Rhetoric of Reconciliation*, 123n352) takes Paul to mean that "if an unbeliever becomes 'sanctified' (ἁγιάζεσθαι), this means that they join the community … Their contact with 'the body of Christ' through their spouse may bring sanctification."

15. MacDonald and Vaage, "Unclean but Holy Children," 531.

16. MacDonald and Vaage, "Unclean but Holy Children," 535–36; see also Vaage, "Translation of 1 Cor 7:14c," 557–71; MacDonald, *Power of Children*, 24.

17. With Horrell, "Ethnicisation," 449n47; see also BDF §456 [3]; BDAG, s.v. ἐπεί, 360 (def. 2).

18. Tomson, *Paul and the Jewish Law*, 116–22.

[the person's] heart are revealed, in this way, [the person] will fall down on their face and worship God, proclaiming, 'God is truly in your midst' (14:24–25)."[19] There is no third category of persons who are unbelieving "saints," though this would be the perfect opportunity to refer to one, since a "complex social reality" is in view. Despite its appeal, MacDonald and Vaage's interpretation of 7:14 as a "strikingly generous expression of early Christian inclusiveness"[20] lacks conviction.

Yonder Moynihan Gillihan proposes that Paul's "saints" and "sanctified" unbelievers in 7:14 are "licit" children and marriage partners. By repurposing a Pharisaic-rabbinic tradition on betrothal in which "to sanctify" refers to a licit betrothal resulting in licit offspring, Paul predicates to the Corinthians' unbelieving spouses and children a "holy status," being "counted among the ἅγιοι," being "eligible to participate in the religious life of the community," "hav[ing] full access to the temple constituted by the sanctified community," and being able to "come and go and interact freely with the holy community."[21]

Gillihan goes to great lengths to compare Jewish *halakha* concerning marriage, where "the verb 'to sanctify' [קדש] is used consistently to describe an act of licit betrothal," which guarantees that the children will be licit.[22] Prohibited marriages—those that did not meet certain genealogical criteria for permitted marriage—resulted in the production of illicit children (ממזרים), who were a source of moral defilement for the Temple, the community, and the land and who had to be eliminated, according to some sources.[23] He concludes that Paul's "ἡγίασται ἐν appears to be a faithful appropriation of מתקדשת/מקדש ב."[24] The unbelieving spouse "is sanctified/betrothed by" the Christ-believer "in the sense of 'is eligible' for licit marriage to a believer."[25] On this basis, Paul can claim that the children of this couple are licit. So 1 Cor 7:14 constitutes a "linguistic proof that the sanctification of the spouse and the licitness of the union were guaranteed," despite falling short of the criterion of marriage "only

19. All Eng. trans. of primary texts are my own unless otherwise noted.
20. Tomson, *Paul and the Jewish Law*, 539–40.
21. Gillihan, "Jewish Laws," 715–35.
22. See m. Qidd. 2.1: "A man betroths [a woman] by himself or through his agent. A woman is betrothed by herself or through her representative. A man betroths his daughter [to another] ... either by himself or through his representative."
23. See further Hayes, *Gentile Impurities*, 68–91.
24. Gillihan, "Jewish Laws," 717.
25. Gillihan, "Jewish Laws," 716.

in the Lord" (μόνον ἐν κυρίῳ; 7:39). Paul is motivated by Jesus tradition against divorce in making an exception for preexisting marriages to unbelievers: "[The Pharisaic-rabbinic tradition on licit betrothal] has come under the influence of the commandment of the Lord against divorce, so that licitness of marriage is now judged on the basis of the indissolubility of the marital bond (by the believer) rather than on the basis of the premarital status of each spouse."[26]

There are numerous discrepancies, however, between the Pharisaic-rabbinic tradition on licit and illicit betrothals, on the one hand, and Paul's discussion on preexisting religiously mixed marriages, on the other hand. These discrepancies are noted by Gillihan himself and others.[27] Further weaknesses of this interpretation can also be mentioned. Both Paul and the Corinthian Christ-believers assume that their children are ἅγια; this status requires no justification and thus undermines the suggestion that Paul wanted to clarify that the Corinthian Christians' marriages to unbelievers, as well as their children, were licit despite these unions' falling short of the criterion of marriage "only in the Lord." If these marriages are here declared licit, Paul's insistence that the unbeliever be allowed to divorce seems to go in the wrong direction. Why not urge the Corinthians with unbelieving spouses to actively seek to keep these marriages together? Also, while Paul gives extensive instructions "on the virgins" (7:25–38), nowhere does he address the issue of licit or illicit betrothals.[28] Whether the Corinthian Christ-believers, who were predominantly former gentiles, would have been familiar or concerned with a Pharisaic-rabbinic tradition on betrothal is hard to say, but it seems unlikely.[29]

The three interpretations discussed above assume that ἅγια in 7:14 is used substantively for "saints." But its anarthrous character speaks against this assumption. Most Pauline occurrences of ἅγιος for "saint"

---

26. Gillihan, "Jewish Laws," 719; 728–29.

27. Gillihan, "Jewish Laws," 719; 728–29.

28. On the possibility that female virgins were included in "your children" in 1 Cor 7:14, see MacDonald and Vaage, "Unclean but Holy Children," 540.

29. Gillihan ("Jewish Laws," 721n31) refers to a "lack of concern for the illegitimate status of children born of forbidden marriages" in a Roman milieu. Nevertheless, he argues that former gentile polytheists in Corinth were under the influence of Jewish legal rulings on permitted and prohibited marriages and the implications of these prohibited marriages for the moral defilement of the community; see Gillihan, 712–13 with n6.

are arthrous.³⁰ It is thus preferable to take ἅγια in 7:14 as an adjective, as in the interpretations discussed below.

William Loader argues that in 7:14, Paul describes the Corinthians' children as ritually "pure" (ἅγια), as opposed to ritually "impure" (ἀκάθαρτα), and that this statement functions as the proof that the unbelieving spouse "is [ritually] pure" (ἡγίασται) through (ἐν) the Christ-believing spouse.³¹ Loader suggests that while the Corinthian Christ-believers feared ritual contamination by their unbelieving spouses, Paul indicates that the latter are "counter-contaminated" by the former, just as the (unbelieving) children are "counter-contaminated" by the Christ-believing parent. Loader notes, however, that Paul posits counter-contamination only for preexisting marriages, not new marriages, since he stipulates that marriage is to be "only in the Lord" (7:39).

Loader, however, does not explain why Paul makes a distinction between preexisting and new marriages in this regard, or why the Corinthian Christ-believers were apparently unafraid of being religiously contaminated by their unbelieving children, for Paul asserts without argument that these children are ἅγια (in Loader's view, ritually "pure"). It is problematic to assume that the predominantly former gentile Corinthians were concerned about ritual purity (as Jews might have been) and that Paul had any interest in ritual purity in their regard.³² Furthermore,

30. See Rom 12:13; 15:25, 31; 16:2, 15; 1 Cor 6:2; 14:33; 16:1, 15; 2 Cor 1:1; 8:4; 9:1, 12; Phil 1:1; 4:21; 1 Thess 3:13; 2 Thess 1:10; no article is needed for the substantival use in the following constructions: πάντα ἅγιον (Phil 4:21); κλητοῖς ἁγίοις (1 Cor 1:2; Rom 1:7); ὑπὲρ ἁγίων (Rom 8:27).

31. Loader, *New Testament on Sexuality*, 202; cf. Ciampa and Rosner's translation "concerns about purity" (*First Letter to the Corinthians*, 297); BDAG, s.v. ἁγιάζω, 10 (def. 2), citing 1 Cor 7:14b: "by contact w. what is holy." Some recent German commentators preserve the older interpretation that "external" purity or impurity is implied; so, e.g., Schrage, *Korinther*, 2.105: "An objective, though not exactly material [*dinglich*]-magical, concept of holiness is present here . . . the unbeliever is drawn into [the force field in which the Christ-believer lives] with a magnetic power" (my translation); see also Conzelmann, *1 Corinthians*, 122.

32. Murphy-O'Connor ("Works Without Faith," 44–45) opines: "Not only is there no hint that the primitive church was influenced by this Jewish attitude, but it is explicitly contradicted by the practice of the most conservative Christian community" (citing Acts 9:43; 10:25–26, 28; Rom 14:14); similarly, Lindemann, *Korintherbrief*, 165. Contrast Thiselton (*First Epistle to the Corinthians*, 297), who suggests the influence of Jewish assumptions about ritual purity on the Corinthians, including biblical texts such as Leviticus and Hag 2:11–14. Some scholars suggest that Paul's own teaching in 2 Cor 6:14—7:1 is the source of the Corinthians' concern about purity and impurity. But the Pauline authorship of this text is disputed. For further discussion, see the sources cited in Gillihan, "Jewish Laws," 712n3.

though Loader's interpretation explains why Corinthian Christ-believers may have wanted to divorce their unbelieving spouses, it *fails* to explain why unbelieving spouses may have wanted to divorce their Christ-believing spouses.

Jerome Murphy-O'Connor argues that in 1 Cor 7:14 Paul is referring to the *moral* "holiness" or "sanctification" of unbelievers. In support, Murphy-O'Connor appeals to the unbeliever's willingness to remain in the marriage: "[This] brings his/her behavior into line both with the intention of the Creator concerning marriage . . . and with the dominical directive prohibiting divorce," such that "the behavior of the pagan is identical with the conduct that Paul expects of Christians, and so the predication of 'holiness' is justified."³³ Furthermore, Murphy-O'Connor appeals to the "simple fact of experience that children assimilate the behavior pattern of their parents."³⁴

But there is no evidence that Paul refers to the good deeds of unbelievers with the language of sanctification that he uses for Christ-believers' moral holiness. And in any case, Paul regards moral holiness as the work of the Holy Spirit,³⁵ not the result of the moral influence of Christ-believers on unbelievers. Murphy-O'Connor's interpretation thus does not explain Paul's formulation, ἡγίασται ἐν τῇ γυναικὶ . . . ἐν τῷ ἀδελφῷ, where a Christian wife or "brother" (i.e., husband) is an agent of the "holiness" of the unbelieving family member.³⁶ Finally, since there is no indication of the age of the Corinthians' children, it is impossible to assume morally holy conduct by them.³⁷

Beverly Gaventa suggests the children's "holiness" probably refers to their "location in the body of Christ through God's calling of their

---

33. Murphy-O'Connor, "Works Without Faith," 356-57. Contrast Hayes (*Gentile Impurities*, 92-98), who argues that Paul considered unbelievers immoral *by definition* and thus ruled out sexual or social intimacy with unbelievers as "a kind of *porneia*" (cf. 1 Cor 6:12-20). In her view (94-95), Paul's statement that the unbelieving spouse ἡγίασται "is promulgating a legal fiction" necessary in order to enforce the Lord's command not to divorce. The Corinthians, however, were unlikely to have heeded Paul's command on this clearly refutable ground; this unlikelihood renders Hayes's suggestion problematic.

34. Murphy-O'Connor, "Works Without Faith," 361.

35. For sanctification as the work of the Holy Spirit, cf. Rom 5:5; 14:17; 15:13; 1 Cor 6:19; 12:3; 2 Cor 6:6; 1 Thess 1:5; 4:8.

36. With Schrage, *Korinther*, 2:105.

37. See my discussion of τέκνον above at n2.

household," not their faith or achievement.³⁸ But household conversions are not in view, as Paul's reference to unbelieving husbands and wives in 7:12–16 indicates.

The editors of BDAG cite 1 Cor 7:14 for ἅγιος in the cultic sense, "dedicated to God, holy, sacred, i.e. reserved for God and God's service," and for ἁγιάζω in the sense, "consecrate, dedicate, sanctify" or "include a pers. in the inner circle of what is holy."³⁹ Gordon Fee adopts this usage in his commentary on 7:14. In support, he appeals to the close parallel in Rom 11:16: "[The analogy] seems to be the same analogy put forth here [in 1 Cor 7:14]."⁴⁰ Fee is referring to the analogy in Rom 11:16 between the consecration of the firstfruits and (by extension) the lump of dough, on the one hand, and the consecration of the root and (by extension) the branches, on the other hand:

> Now if the firstfruits [is] consecrated [ἁγία] [to God], so also the lump of dough [is consecrated to God]. And if the root [is] consecrated [ἁγία] [to God], so also the branches [are consecrated to God].

---

38. Gaventa, "Finding a Place for Children," 236; see also 233–48. Gaventa disputes my earlier suggestion that Paul is referring to these children as being "consecrated to God through their familial or genealogical relationship to believers" (Gundry-Volf, "Least and the Greatest," 51). Gaventa argues that "it seems unlikely that God's action is altogether absent here, especially in light of the discussion of divine calling in 1 Corinthians 7:17–24" (236). But my earlier discussion implies that *God's action* toward the children began with their "consecration to God" through the human agency of family members and would hopefully continue with the children's calling to faith through the further human agency of the preachers of the gospel. See 1 Thess 5:23 for the wish that God might "consecrate you completely" (αὐτὸς δὲ ὁ θεὸς τῆς εἰρήνης ἁγιάσαι ὑμᾶς ὁλοτελεῖς). Cf. Gundry-Volf, "Least and the Greatest," 29–60.

39. See BDAG, s.v. ἅγιος, ία, ον, 10–11 (def. 1.a.β); s.v. ἁγιάζω, 10 (def. 2). The editors comment that moral associations are necessarily implied in this usage. But that assertion can be disputed. For example, moral associations are not necessarily implied in 1 Cor 1:2 (see below, n65); 6:11. In 1 Cor 7:34, Paul refers to the unmarried, chaste woman as "consecrated (ἁγία) both in body and in spirit," i.e., not dedicated to childbearing. No moral associations are implied here either. Cf. Rom 15:16, where cultic associations are prevalent throughout: "With the result that I am a cultic minister (λειτουργὸν) of Christ Jesus to the Gentiles, who renders priestly service (ἱερουργοῦντα) to the gospel of God, so that the offering (ἡ προσφορά) of the Gentiles might be acceptable (εὐπρόσδεκτος), consecrated to God by the Holy Spirit (ἡγιασμένη ἐν πνεύματι ἁγίῳ)." For further discussion, see Downs, *Offering of the Gentiles*, 146–57.

40. Fee, *First Epistle to the Corinthians*, 333.

As Dunn notes in his commentary, here Paul claims that the consecration of a cultic object is extended to a non-cultic object (e.g., Neh 11:1, 18; Isa 11:9, where the temple's consecration to God extended to Jerusalem and its hills).[41] Furthermore, the Pharisees aimed "to extend the holiness of the temple throughout the land . . . [by observing] in daily life the level of purity/holiness required in the law only in relation to the temple."[42] This tradition enables Paul to draw an analogy between the firstfruits and the lump of dough, on the one hand, and the Jews who disbelieve the gospel ("the branches" who "were cut off in unbelief" [Rom 11:20] and are not "sharers in the fat root of the olive tree" [Rom 11:17]) and the Israelite patriarchs/matriarchs (the "holy root"), on the other hand. Those who are unbelieving are yet consecrated to God by extension, and hence, by God's power they may be "grafted back onto the olive tree in faith" (Rom 11:23–24).[43]

On the basis of the parallel in Rom 11:16, Fee concludes: "If the husband or wife is 'holy,' then the unbelieving spouse is also 'holy,' that is, set apart in a special way that hopefully will lead to their salvation (v. 16)."[44] But Fee argues that this result is dependent on an "intact" relationship: "[The unbelieving husband or wife] is sanctified in [ἡγίασται ἐν] their relationship with the believer . . . as long as the marriage is maintained, the potential for the spouse's realizing salvation remains. To that degree

---

41. In Num 15:20–21, the firstfruits are consecrated to God in sacrifice, but the lump of dough is set free for common use and is *not* consecrated to God.

42. Dunn, *Romans 9–16*, 658–59. Similarly, Dunn (659) notes that Paul's teaching on "the whole people . . . as 'saints' [ἅγιοι; Rom 1:7] and 'consecrated' [ἡγιασμένοι; Rom 15:16]" relies on the notion of "consecration to God" by extension.

43. With Käsemann (*Romans*, 307–8), Rom 11:16a is best taken literally, and 11:16b is best taken metaphorically: "[The first ἅγιος] supplies the aspect from which the second [ἅγιος] is seen: Holy means consecrated to God."

44. Fee, *First Epistle to the Corinthians*, 332; similarly, Beasley-Murray, *Baptism*, 196–97; 199; Collins, *Divorce*, 53. Collins (*First Corinthians*, 266) notes: "In v. 14a–b Paul expresses something akin to the biblical tradition of holiness by association (cf. Exod 29:37; Lev 6:18; Rom 11:16)." Contrast Gillihan ("Jewish Law," 735), who argues *against* consecration by extension based on Rom 11:16. He appeals to "Paul's Greek" as indicating that "the children's holiness proceeds out of the unbeliever's sanctified status" (rather than the Christ-believer's) and that "the statuses of the unbelieving spouse and of the children are clearly of different origins." I find these arguments unpersuasive. For a more general discussion of 1 Cor 7:14 in relation to Jewish Scripture, see Rosner, *Paul, Scripture and Ethics*, 168–71.

the unbeliever is 'sanctified' in the believing spouse."[45] Fee maintains that this construction refers to "a relationship with the believer rather than a relationship to God 'through' the believer."[46]

But Rom 11:17–24 disfavors this view, since the branches who were "cut off in disbelief" explicitly "do not share in the holy root" and have no "intact" relationship to it, yet "are consecrated" to God and potentially saved. With Ernst Käsemann, "The issue [in Rom 11:16b] is the relation between beginning and result, as earlier [in Rom 11:16a] that between the part and the whole. The two cannot be separated as though they had nothing to do with each other."[47] Furthermore, Paul's use of the perfect tense verb ἡγίασται probably emphasizes the lasting results of the consecration of the unbeliever to God,[48] and this emphasis disfavors Fee's interpretation.

In conclusion, with Fee, in 1 Cor 7:14 as in Rom 11:16 Paul uses the adjective ἅγιος in the transferred cultic sense, "consecrated to God, dedicated to God," and the cognate verb ἁγιάζεσθαι in a transferred cultic sense, "to be consecrated to God, dedicated to God," to refer to the consecration of unbelievers to God with a view to their potential, future salvation as believers in God. This notion reflects a biblical and Jewish tradition on the extension of the consecration of a cultic object to a non-cultic object.

Support for this interpretation may also be found in 1 Cor 1:2: ἡγιασμένοις ἐν Χριστῷ Ἰησοῦ, κλητοῖς ἁγίοις. Here, "the ones who are consecrated in Christ Jesus" are "called [to faith] as ones [having been] consecrated" or are "called [to faith] to be holy." The implication is that prior to calling to faith through the preaching of the gospel God

---

45. Fee, *First Epistle to the Corinthians*, 332 with n145; 333. For a critique of the older view that Paul is referring to the consecration of the wife or husband "through natural corporal union of one human being with another," see Thiselton, *First Epistle to the Corinthians*, 528–29.

46. Fee *First Epistle to the Corinthians*, 332n145; similarly, Yarbrough, "Parents and Children," 129.

47. Käsemann (*Romans*, 308) continues: "Paul is stressing the continuity of God's *hidden* faithfulness in Israel's history" (emphasis mine), just as Paul earlier described "the selection which breaks earthly continuity again and again" and "prevents interpretation along the lines of an immanent process of development" (Rom 9:6–33).

48. Collins, *First Corinthians*, 266. Paul's requirement of complying with an unbelieving spouse's wish to divorce (1 Cor 7:16) makes it unlikely that Paul thought the consecration of unbelievers was effected by an intact marriage with a Christ-believer. It is likely that he views the unbeliever's unwillingness to remain in the marriage as a sign of *lack* of consecration to God.

consecrates those who then place their trust in God when called. If Paul taught that Christ-believers were "consecrated to God" prior to being called to faith in God and believing the gospel, then it is plausible that he thought the Corinthians' unbelieving children and (some) spouses were consecrated to God prior to being called to faith and believing the gospel. Indeed, the Corinthians themselves thought that their children were "consecrated to God" prior to believing the gospel.

In the next section I shall explore how 1 Cor 7:14 advances Paul's argument for not divorcing an unbelieving spouse who is willing to remain married and is, like the children, "consecrated to God" by extension.[49]

1 Cor 7:14 and the Role of Religion in the Roman Household

The larger context for interpreting 1 Cor 7:12–16, as Raymond Collins and Caroline Johnson Hodge have suggested, is the norm of endogamy in the ancient Mediterranean world. Collins notes: "People are expected to marry within their own group whether 'the group' be defined racially, ethnically, socially, or religiously (cf. Deut 7:3; Neh 13:25)."[50] In 1 Cor 7:12–16 the problem is religious exogamy. Johnson Hodge highlights the role of religion in Roman households. She notes various religious rituals that were a matter of household life. Some of them are associated with meals and involved sacrifice, others with simple entering and exiting and similarly mundane tasks.[51] Still other religious rituals are associated with special occasions. In *On Marriage*, the early second-century CE Stoic Hierocles refers to "the gods who preside over weddings, births and hearths (θεοῖς γαμηλίοις γενεθλίοις ἐφεστίοις)."[52]

---

49. Perhaps Paul was inspired by Jesus' argument against divorce in Matt 19:6: "What God has joined together [συνέζευξεν], let no human separate."

50. Collins, *First Corinthians*, 265.

51. For the suggestion that 1 Cor 7:12–16 should be interpreted in the light of the expectation that wives adopt the gods of their respective husbands, see Johnson Hodge, "Married to an Unbeliever," 7. For a general discussion of the relationship between food/drink and sacrifice in the Greco-Roman world, see McGowan, *Ascetic Eucharists*, 60–67.

52. Ramelli, *Hierocles*, 76–77; Eng. trans. by Malherbe, *Moral Exhortation*, 102; cf. Ramelli's translation of "the gods of marriage, generation, and the hearth" (77); see comments by Johnson Hodge, "Married to an Unbeliever," 11n41.

Roman household members, with the exception of slaves, were expected to observe a common religious practice as defined by the *dominus*. Slaves may have had their own religious rituals devoted to gods other than those of the *dominus* and were thus not allowed to perform the rituals that were the domain of the *domina*.[53] Wives, on the other hand, were expected to adopt their husbands' gods and give up their own gods. For example, in *Advice to Bride and Groom*, Plutarch writes: "A married woman should therefore worship and recognize the gods whom her husband holds dear, and these alone. The door must be closed to strange cults and foreign superstitions. No god takes pleasure in a cult performed furtively and in secret by a woman."[54] Plutarch implies that the gods will retaliate or withhold favor from the household if wives worship gods other than those of their respective husbands.

Correspondingly, Roman husbands were to teach their wives how to perform religious duties in the household to ensure a common religious practice. In *Oec*. VII.8, Xenophon writes that Socrates asked Ischomachus, after the latter instructed his young wife in her household duties, "Did your wife sacrifice along with you and offer the same prayers (καὶ ἡ γυνή σοι συνέθυε καὶ συνηύχετο ταυτὰ ταῦτα)?" He answered, "Oh, yes, very much so (καὶ μάλα γ')."[55] Xenophon's discussion on the household in *Oeconomicus* influenced Roman philosophers such as Cicero, Philodemus, and Columulla.[56]

Johnson Hodge does not discuss the roles of children in the common religious practice of the Roman household. But she cites the following pertinent text by the first-century CE Roman elegist Tibullus in which a child is instructed by her mother how to pray to "Juno of the birthday" and make sacrifices to the goddess:

> Juno of the birthday, receive the holy piles of incense which the accomplished maid's soft hand now offers thee. Today she has bathed for thee; most joyfully she has decked herself for thee, to stand before your altar a sight for all to see. 'Tis in thee, goddess, she bids us find the reason for this apparelling... They are making an offering to thee, holy goddess, thrice with cake and thrice

---

53. Johnson Hodge, "Married to an Unbeliever," 6; 12.

54. Plutarch, *Conj. Praec.* 140D; Johnson Hodge, "Married to an Unbeliever," 1; 9–13. For a similar discussion of the expectation of religious conformity in the Roman household, see Harrison, "Paul and the Gymnasiarchs," 172–77.

55. Pomeroy, *Xenophon*, 139.

56. Pomeroy, *Xenophon*, 69–73.

with wine, and the mother eagerly enjoins upon her child what she must pray for.[57]

The point of Johnson Hodge's article is that Paul is tolerant of religious difference in marriage in a way that challenges the hierarchical Roman expectation that wives give up their own gods and worship only their respective husbands' gods, viz., early Christian women married to polytheists were free to do otherwise.[58] But Johnson Hodge does not explain how, in Paul's view, the Corinthians' interreligious marriages were tenable. Nor does she attribute significance to 7:14 in this regard.[59] Does Paul express not only tolerance of religious difference in the household but also a reason to remain in an interreligious marriage?

I suggest that in 7:14 Paul asserts that the Corinthian Christ-believers' unbelieving spouses and children are "consecrated" to God, like Christ-believers are "consecrated" to God, in order to show that there is an imperceptible yet divinely wrought religious *uniformity* in their religiously *mixed* households which ought to relieve the pressure on the Corinthian Christians to divorce their unbelieving spouses on the grounds of the norm of religious endogamy. In support of this suggestion, consider a similar comment by the Stoic philosopher Hierocles about the common consecration of husbands and wives to the gods: "The beauty of a home," he writes, is not "expensive buildings and marble walls," but rather, "the union of a husband and wife who *share each other's destinies and are consecrated to the gods* (συγκαθειμαρμένων ἀλλήλοις καὶ καθιερωμένων θεοῖς) of marriage, generation, and the hearth, in concord with each other and setting everything in common up to their very bodies, or rather up to their very own souls."[60] A similar implication may be

---

57. Tibullus, *Poem* III.12.1–5; 14–15; Eng. trans. by Postgate and Goold, LCL, 331; cited by Johnson Hodge, "Married to an Unbeliever," 6.

58. Johnson Hodge's main aim is to reconstruct the experience of the Corinthian women, not to interpret Paul's text.

59. Johnson Hodge ("Married to an Unbeliever," 14–18) adopts the interpretation criticized above that Paul is addressing the issue of "purity," and overturning the view that impurity is contagious to the Christ-believer.

60. Ramelli, *Hierocles the Stoic*, 76–77 (italics mine). See Harrison, "Paul and the Gymnasiarchs," 174–77, for a similar discussion of Eph 5:18–33 in the light of household harmony as "the divine ideal for marriage in antiquity." Harrison argues that Ephesians modifies the Colossian household code "by demoting the Graeco-Roman gods from their privileged position as guardians of the household and its social relations" (177).

present in the comment of the Stoic Musonius Rufus that marriage is under the superintendence of "the great gods," Hera, Eros, and Aphrodite.[61]

If a Corinthian wife's polytheistic husband was willing to "live together" with her, then we can postulate that he may not have subscribed so fervently as the Greek husband Ischomachus to the ideal of "cultivating the good will of the gods," as in Xenophon's *Oec.* XI.8–9:

> I start by cultivating the good will of the gods. And I try to behave so that it may be right for me when I pray, to acquire good health, physical strength, distinction in the city, good will among my friends, survival with honour in war, and wealth that has been increased by honest means . . . It's a pleasure to honour the gods magnificently.[62]

Whether in Roman Corinth the unbelieving husbands or wives amenable to living with their Christ-believing spouses were simply backsliders who did not faithfully worship the gods, or perhaps sympathetic to the early Christian monotheists, we do not know.[63] What we do know is that such spouses were not strict when it came to the norm of religious endogamy, and on that basis Paul apparently concludes they are "consecrated" to God and hoped for their future salvation.

Concluding Remarks

Paul's stance on unbelieving spouses as "consecrated" to God, however, does not negate the inevitable difficulties that must have plagued the Corinthians' interreligious marriages. If idolatrous rituals were practiced in their households, how could the Christ-believing spouses "flee idolatry" so as to avoid the punishment of the wilderness generation, as Paul advised (1 Cor 10:1–14)? If their everyday meals were accompanied by sacrifices to the household gods, should they then refuse to "partake of the cup of demons" and "the table of demons" so as not to "provoke the Lord to jealousy" (1 Cor 10:21–22)?[64] And would they then be blamed

---

61. Musonius Rufus, *Or.* 14.20–32 (Lutz, "Musonius Rufus," 94–95).

62. Pomeroy, *Xenophon*, 165.

63. Cf. 1 Cor 10:14–33 for Paul's advice on maintaining one's religious distinctiveness at private dinner parties with Gentile polytheists.

64. On the demonic reality to which Paul points here, see Hofius, "Einer ist Gott," 173. Paul refers to divine judgment among the Corinthians in 1 Cor 11:17–34 ("many among you are weak and sick, and a number sleep," v. 30), which could be related to engagement in polytheistic rituals on the occasion of meals.

for the gods' withdrawal of favor from the household? If they did not abstain from food on their own tables that was "idol food," would they be complicit in encouraging unbelievers to worship idols, and injuring their "conscience" (1 Cor 10:28–29)? Not to mention, how should they deal with the religious education of their children? No naïve ideal of a frictionless domestic life with the religious "other" is being assumed here.[65] Nevertheless, in Paul's view there were reasons to abandon the norm of religious endogamy in some cases. On the bright side, wives who endured in interreligious marriages with amenable husbands would not be deprived of their children, for according to Roman custom, children remained with their fathers after divorce.

Household relationships between husbands and wives and parents and children are important avenues of God's redemptive work, in Paul's view, as the interpretation of 1 Cor 7:14 here demonstrates. These relationships are not primarily means of establishing and preserving a family line, or more generally, of preserving the human race, city, or nation. Rather, whatever the composition of Christ-believers' households, they derive their unity from God's consecrating activity at work through the "brother/sister."

---

65. Contrast Johnson Hodge ("Married to an Unbeliever," 23n82): "Perhaps it [this mixing of gods] would not have bothered Paul." She cites 1 Cor 8:4–13; 10:23–33 for the view that "Paul is remarkably tolerant of other religious traditions." But in both of these texts, Paul is concerned precisely about the problem of Christ-believers' misuse of "freedom" to "build up" (sarcastic!) Gentile polytheists in their idolatrous ways of thinking. So Paul would not have tolerated a Christ-believer's participation in the polytheist spouse's religious practices. For a later discussion on the Christian wife married to the tolerant pagan husband, see Tertullian, *Ux.* 2.5–7.

10

Negotiating Piety

Epicureans, Corinthian Knowers, and Paul on Idols and Idol Food in 1 Cor 8–10

Max J. Lee

LUCIAN OF SAMOSATA, IN his well-known satire *Alexander the False Prophet*, narrates an episode in which Alexander of Abonoteichus, as a self-declared prophet of a new serpent god Glycon,[1] leads an angry mob to oust the atheists among them. What is surprising about his invective against the atheists is his lumping together of two very different sects or schools. Alexander so exclaims:

> If any atheist or Christian or Epicurean has come as a spy of our secret rites, let this person flee (Εἴ τις ἄθεος ἢ Χριστιανὸς ἢ Ἐπικούρειος ἥκει κατάσκοπος τῶν ὀργίων, φευγέτω); but let those who believe in god perform them by Good Providence (οἱ δὲ πιστεύοντες τῷ θεῷ τελείσθωσαν τύχῃ τῇ ἀγαθῇ).[2]

---

1. Lucian, *Alex.* 18.

*This essay was made possible through the support of the Henry Center for Theological Understanding, funded by a grant from the John Templeton Foundation, as part of a larger 2020–2021 project on a theory of pleasure. The opinions expressed in this publication are those of the author and do not necessarily reflect the views of the John Templeton Foundation.

2. Lucian, *Alex.* 38; Eng. trans. modified from Harmon, LCL, 4:225.

The episode ends with Alexander shouting: "Out with the Christians (Ἔξω Χριστιανούς)!", and with the crowds chanting back: "Out with the Epicureans (Ἔξω Ἐπικουρείους)!

By the second century CE, Christians and Epicureans were seen together as enemies of traditional Greek and Roman religion(s). Both groups refused to practice divination and denied the prophetic power of pagan oracles. Both would argue that idols have no real existence apart from the wood or stone from which they were crafted. In the words of 1 Cor 8:4, to them, an idol is nothing (οἴδαμεν ὅτι οὐδὲν εἴδωλον).[3]

Yet while Christians segregated themselves from pagan cultic ritual (1 Cor 10:1–22), the Epicureans, by contrast, actually participated in cultic sacrifice, ate at the idol's table, and participated in the festivals even though they themselves believed that the gods do not meddle in human affairs.[4] Why then did Epicurus and his disciples participate in cultic feasting when he himself believed that the gods could not be propitiated?

Philodemus records Epicurus declaring:

> "Let us sacrifice to the gods," says he [Epicurus], "piously and nobly on the appropriate days (ἡμ[εῖς θεοῖς| θύμεν φησιν [ὁσί|ως καὶ καλῶς οὗ [καθ|ηκει κα[ὶ κ]αλῶ<ς>), and let us nobly practice all these things in accordance with the laws (πάν|τα πράττωμεν [κα|τὰ τοὺς νόμους)."[5]

Elsewhere Philodemus notes:

> In his *Symposium* concerning temple rites (ἐν δὲ τῷ Σ[υμπο|σίῳ περὶ τῶν [ἱερῶν], [Epicurus says]: "Let us gather for the festivals and make noble sacrifices to god . . . (τὰς ἑορτὰς [συνάγω|μεν καὶ θεῷ[ι καλλι|θυτειν ειλ[. . .)[6]

---

3. Ghisalberti, *Soteriology and the End of Animal Sacrifice*, 96–137; Koch Piettre, "Paul and the Athens Epicureans," 48–51; Erler, *Epicurus*, 139–41; and Simpson, "Epicureans, Christians, Atheists," 372–76.

4. Obbink, "Atheism of Epicurus," 194–215; Obbink, *Philodemus on Piety*, 411–12; 435–43; Erler, *Epicurus*, 84–99; Clay, "Diogenes and His Gods," 89–92; Festugière, *Epicurus and His Gods*, 51–65; Mikalson, *Greek Popular Religion in Greek Philosophy*, 43–45; 58–59; 85; 94.

5. Philodemus, *Piet.*, PHerc 1098, col. 31.879–84; Eng. trans. modified from Obbink, *Philodemus on Piety*, 167. All citations from Philodemus' *De pietate* are based on Obbink's critical Greek text and cited by treatise, PHerc no., column no., and line no., with corresponding pages from the Eng. trans. Diacritical marks follow the apparatus by Obbink, *Philodemus on Piety*, 103. Throughout the essay, the lunar sigma has been replaced with the regular sigma, and the iota subscripted where applicable.

6. Philodemus, *Piet.*, PHerc 452, col. 62B.1784–91; Eng. trans. modified from Obbink, *Philodemus on Piety*, 229.

How does the Epicurean sage insist on a theology that places the gods *outside* of human history while at the same time participate in a system whose very religious underpinnings were based on the gods' constant interaction *within* history? Does the Epicurean stance on cultic participation in any way illuminate the practices of the Corinthian γνῶσις group (1 Cor 8:1–4) who likewise denied the existence of idols (or rather, the gods represented by the idols) yet also participated in the feasts? How did the apostle Paul respond to the slogans and practices of the Corinthian "knowers" who ate εἰδωλοθύτα (i.e., "meat/food sacrificed to an idol") without problems of conscience? In what ways is Paul's rejoinder both consistent with his Diaspora Jewish heritage yet also distinct within it? These are the questions this essay seeks to explore and answer.

Common Criticisms of Traditional Religion among Greco-Roman Epicureans

The essence of Epicurean theology is stated succinctly in the first of the forty Principle Doctrines of Epicurus (Κύριαι Δόξαι):

> The blessed and eternal being neither has troubles itself, nor does it produce them for any other (Τὸ μακάριον καὶ ἄφθαρτον οὔτε αὐτὸ πράγματα ἔχει οὔτε ἄλλῳ παρέχει), so that it is neither moved by bouts of anger nor by expressions of grace, for every such thing is done in weakness (ὥστε οὔτε ὀργαῖς οὔτε χάρισι συνέχεται ἐν ἀσθενεῖ γὰρ πᾶν τὸ τοιοῦτον).[7]

And in his *Letter to Menoeceus*, Epicurus further explains:

> For indeed, the gods do exist, and the knowledge of them is visibly clear. And they are not of the sort as many customarily acknowledge them (θεοὶ μὲν γάρ εἰσιν. ἐναργὴς δέ ἐστιν αὐτῶν ἡ γνῶσις· οἵους δ' αὐτοὺς <οἱ> πολλοὶ νομίζουσιν, οὐκ εἰσίν) . . . Truly impious is not the one who takes up the gods of the many but fastens oneself to the *opinions* of the many about the gods (ἀσεβὴς δὲ οὐχ ὁ τοὺς τῶν πολλῶν θεοὺς ἀναιρῶν, ἀλλ' ὁ τὰς τῶν πολλῶν δόξας θεοῖς). For they are not correct preconceptions but false notions (οὐ γὰρ προλήψεις εἰσίν, ἀλλ' ὑπολήψεις ψευδεῖς αἱ τῶν πολλῶν ὑπὲρ θεῶν ἀποφάσεις).[8]

---

7. Diogenes Laertius, *Lives* 10.139 (= Epicurus, *KD* 1); Eng. trans. modified from Hicks, LCL, 2:663.

8. Epicurus, *Ep. Men.* 123–24 (= Diogenes Laertius, *Lives* 10.123–24); Eng. trans. modified from Hicks, LCL, 2:649–51 (italics added).

In these two excerpts, Epicurus argues that "the gods do exist" (θεοὶ μὲν γάρ εἰσιν) but they are not the kinds of gods commonly and mistakenly construed by the opinions of the masses (τὰς τῶν πολλῶν δόξας θεοῖς). Common folk attribute to the gods false notions (ὑπολήψεις ψευδεῖς) and opinions (δόξας θεοῖς) that generate fear and misunderstanding concerning their true divine nature. The Garden made a hard distinction between traditional (Homeric or Hesiodic) Greek and Roman religion (θρησκεία/religio) as a superstition (δεισιδαιμονία/superstitio) versus genuine Epicurean expressions of piety (εὐσέβεια/pietas).[9]

The first-century BCE Roman Epicurean Lucretius, in his epic poem *De rerum natura* ("On the Nature of Things"), lists some of the popular ideas concerning the gods entertained by many during the late Republic. In *DRN* 5.1198–1240, Lucretius describes the heart of Roman religion as worshipers who veil their heads and men who prostrate themselves before altars from fear of the gods (*formidine divum*; 1223) as they participate in cultic rites. Most believe that the gods can cause war, exact revenge, destroy cities with earthquakes, inflict disease, and crash ships with storms. They try to appease the gods for their grace or favor by sprinkling the blood of four-footed beasts on altars (*aras sanguine multo spargere quad quadrupedum*; 1201–2), making vows with the gods (*divom pacem votis*; 1229), and offering prayers in a system of divine-human reciprocity. Human beings worship, sacrifice, and pray to the gods; the gods, in turn, avert disaster and bless their loyal subjects.[10] Yet all of these religious practices do not constitute true piety (*nec pietas*; 1198) according to Lucretius.[11] In fact, in *DRN* 2.646–50, Lucretius insists that the very nature of divinity (*per se divom natura*; 646)—because it does not concern itself with human affairs and needs nothing from human

---

9. Spinelli and Verde, "Theology," 101–10; Erler, *Epicurus*, 79–81; Summers, "Lucretius and the Epicurean Tradition of Piety," 33; Festugière, *Epicurus and His Gods*, 51–57; Wynne, *Cicero on the Philosophy of Religion*, 102–3. Cf. Cicero, *Nat. d.* 1.117, who defines *superstitio* as fearing the gods versus *religio* as worshiping the gods.

10. Rüpke, *Religion of the Romans*, 12–15; 162–67; Price, *Religion of the Ancient Greeks*, 25–39; Mikalson, *Greek Popular Religion in Greek Philosophy*, 43; Osborne, "Sacrificial Theologies," 247–48; Ghisalberti, *Soteriology and the End of Animal Sacrifice*, 22–23.

11. Summers, "Lucretius and the Epicurean Tradition of Piety," 35–38; Erler, *Epicurus*, 79–81; Ghisalberti, *Soteriology and the End of Animal Sacrifice*, 120–26.

beings—can neither be propitiated with good deeds nor swept up by anger (*nec bene promeritis capitur neque tangitur ira;* 651).[12]

His contemporary Philodemus of Gadara likewise quotes Epicurus's injunction against the many who think that the gods can be propitiated for favors or to avert their wrath. In a satiric tirade, Epicurus exclaims: "if only the gods were propitious (θεῶν εἴλε[ων ὄν|των; lines 931–32; cf. 936–37)," then a person might call upon their help in times of war (κἂν πόλ[ε]μ[ος ᾖ; line 929), or his friend Polyaenus could live—and continue to live—a pure life with his slave Matron (καθαρὰν τ[ην ζωὴν| διηχέναι κ[αι διά|ξειν σὺν αὐτ[ῷ|Μάτρωνι; lines 933–37), or Epicurus's older brother Neocles might learn to disperse aid from his money "piously for the gods" (εἶναι τη[ν] ἀπ' ἀρ[γυ|ρείου β[ο]ήθειαν [θεοῖς |ὁσίως δέον [ν]έμ[ειν; lines 950–52).[13] In other words, if the gods could be propitiated, perhaps they could help people in times of calamity or motivate good behavior among mortals. However, such is neither the state of the world nor the gods' engagement with it; this system of propitiation and divine favor is, in the end, an inaccurate and superstitious depiction of how the gods interact with human beings and the cosmos.

In contrast to such popular notions, Epicurus insisted that a god is blessed and eternal (μακάριον καὶ ἄφθαρτον), and not moved by bouts of anger nor expressions of grace (οὔτε ὀργαῖς οὔτε χάρισι συνέχεται). A god is angry neither at one's unethical living nor lack of veneration; a god shows no grace towards us, neither for one's acts of worship nor for practice of virtue.[14] Instead, a god demonstrates real power precisely by the fact that it is not troubled or disturbed by anything (οὔτε αὐτὸ πράγματα

---

12. Cf. Lucretius, *DRN* 1.45, which reads: "For the very nature of divinity (*per se divom natura*) necessitates enjoyment from the immortal life with utmost peace (*inmortali aevo summa cum pace*), remote and separated from our everyday affairs (*semota ab nostris rebus seiunctaque longe*); for without any pain, without danger, itself flourishing by its own resources, not needing us, it [divinity] is neither propitiated with good deeds nor swept up by anger (*nec bene promeritis capitur neque tangitur ira*)"; Eng. trans. modified from Rouse/Smith, LCL, 7.

13. Philodemus, *Piet.*, PHerc 1098, col. 33.928–57; Eng. trans. modified from Obbink, *Philodemus on Piety*, 171.

14. See also P. Oxy. 215, col. 2.8–11 (Obbink, "Sulla religiosità e il culto popolare," 172–74), which reads: "But henceforth, do not create fear in—nor the notion of being graced with favor by—the gods (δέος |δὲ μὴ πρόσα[γε] ἐνταῦθα |μηδ' ὑπόληψιν χαριτωνί[ας θεοῖς), since you practice these things" (Eng. trans. my own); cf. Seneca, *Ben.* 4.4.1; Us. 388 (= Codex Parisinus 1168, fr. 115). That P. Oxy. 215 is excerpted from Epicurus, see Obbink, "Sulla religiosità e il culto popolare," 188–91; Mikalson, *Greek Popular Religion in Greek Philosophy*, 44–45.

ἔχει οὔτε ἄλλῳ παρέχει).¹⁵ The gods in their true divine nature—unlike the capricious personalities narrated by Hesiod or Homer—do not participate in the affairs of this world, for if they did, they would be agitated by the vanity, errors, vice, and evil perpetuated by human beings. Instead, the tranquility (ἀταραξία) of the gods—i.e., their freedom from all forms of disturbance—is what makes their lives blessed.¹⁶ As the only truly free beings—free because nothing in the world can cause them pain or suffering—the gods understandably become not only the subjects of veneration for the Epicurean sage but also the objects of imitation.¹⁷

Can I Have My Idol Food and Eat It Too? Competing "Doctrinal Reformulations" between Lucretius and Philodemus on Cultic Observance

While both Lucretius and Philodemus ultimately reject the beliefs behind the propitiatory system of cultic sacrifice as something superstitious and impious, they nevertheless differ on the socio-ethical implications of their rejection and whether an Epicurean could participate in the cult or not. Lucretius appears to take the radical position that Epicurus's teachings on the true nature of the gods demand from his followers a withdrawal from all participation in temple worship. The key text of *DRN* 5.1198–1203, which has already been summarized above but is also quoted in full below, is the most derisive passage by Lucretius against cultic observance from which scholars such as Ghisalberti and Summers conclude that the Epicurean poet must have taught complete non-participation in all cultic rites.¹⁸

---

15. Diogenes Laertius, *Lives* 10.139 (= Epicurus, *KD* 1); cited in full above. See also the quotation of *KD* 1 in Latin by Velleius the Epicurean in Cicero, *Nat. d.* 1.45, which reads: "The famous maxim of Epicurus truthfully expounds that (*vere exposita ilia sententia est ab Epicuro quod*) 'the blessed and eternal can neither have troubles itself nor produce troubles for others, and therefore can feel neither anger nor favor, since all such things are only for the weak-minded (*beatum aeternumque sit id nec habere ipsum negotii quicquam nec exhibere alteri, itaque neque ira neque gratia teneri quod quae talia essent imbecilla essent omnia*)'"; Eng. trans. modified from Rackham, LCL, 47.

16. Epicurus, *Ep. Herod.* 76–78 (= Diogenes Laertius, *Lives* 10.76–78).

17. Erler, "Epicurus as Deus Mortalis," 167–80; Festugière, *Epicurus and His Gods*, 57–61; Spinelli and Verde, "Theology," 111–13; Shakhnovich, "Theological Paradox in Epicurus," 162–63.

18. Ghisalberti, *Soteriology and the End of Animal Sacrifice*, 120–26; Summers, "Lucretius and the Epicurean Tradition of Piety," 45–48.

Lucretius so states:

> It is neither piety to show oneself often with covered head (*nec pietas ullast velatum saepe videri*), turning towards a stone and proceeding towards every altar (*vertier ad lapidem atque omnis accedere ad aras*), nor to fall prostrate upon the ground and to spread open the palms before the shrines of the gods (*nec procumbere humi prostratum et pandere palmasante deum delubra*), nor to sprinkle altars with much blood from four-footed animals (*nec aras sanguine multo spargere quadrupedum*), nor to bind vow to vow (*nec votis nectere vota*). To the contrary, it [piety] is to be able to survey all things with a tranquil mind (*sed mage placata posse omnia mente tueri*).[19]

Lucretius further warns the Roman worshiper:

> To the contrary, since you yourself will determine them [the gods], who are tranquil with a quieting peace, as rolling out great waves of anger (*sed quia tute tibi placida cum pace quietos constitues magnos irarum volvere fluctus*), you will not be able to approach the shrines of the gods with a tranquil heart (*nec delubra deum placido cum pectore adibis*).[20]

In the above two passages, Lucretius so "sharply criticizes procedures of religious observance"—i.e., the head coverings, the march toward the altar, the open-palms posture of prayer, the splattering of blood from the sacrificial animal upon the altar, and the exchange of vows between deity and the cultic participant—he "presents a deviation from his master's original intent on the matter" so that "the religious ideas of Epicurus, especially as expressed by Philodemus, cannot be harmonized with the more revolutionary ones of Lucretius."[21] Lucretius expresses his doubts to the reader that an Epicurean or any Roman worshiper can approach, let alone sacrifice at, the shrines of the gods with a tranquil heart (*nec delubra deum placido cum pectore adibis*). Since everything about the setting of the temple bombards the participant with false notions of wrathful gods who seethe with waves of anger (*magnos irarum volvere fluctus*), ready to punish someone with disaster, the participant cannot remain

---

19. Lucretius, *DRN* 5.1198–203; Eng. trans. modified from Rouse/Smith, LCL, 471–73.

20. Lucretius, *DRN* 6.73–75; Eng. trans. modified from Rouse/Smith, LCL, 499.

21. Summers, "Lucretius and the Epicurean Tradition of Piety," 32–33.

undisturbed.[22] So Ghisalberti rightly concludes: "In several examples of animal sacrifices in his poem, Lucretius has been insistent: sacrifice can in no way be considered an act of authentic piety."[23] Therefore, according to Lucretius, no devout Epicurean would participate in the cult and so risk perpetuating the false belief system behind it.

While Ghisalberti is correct in his description of Lucretius's own prohibitive stance toward the cult, he overstates the influence of Lucretius's teaching on cultic non-participation when he insists that Lucretius's position constitutes an exclusively orthodox Epicurean viewpoint. Ghisalberti makes Lucretius's prohibitions normative for Epicurean piety as an overall inherited tradition and even argues that it is the original stance of Epicurus himself, despite a consensus view among scholars and ancient *testimonia* to the contrary.[24] Ghisalberti argues instead for an alternative theory that Epicurus did *not* participate in the cult and Lucretius represents well Epicurus's teaching on religious matters. Ghisalberti's argument is based upon a problematic rejection of Philodemus's testimony in favor of Lucretius's.[25]

Summers, however, as stated above, believes that Lucretius marks "a deviation" from Epicurus's approach to sacrifice.[26] While Lucretius preserves Epicurus's redefinition of the gods as remote from, and uninvolved in, human affairs, Lucretius nevertheless infers from the founder's theology different implications for Epicurean religious practice. Summers has adequately explained that Philodemus's statements should not be rejected nor harmonized with the more radical and anomalous position of Lucretius.[27] Lucretius's rejection of cultic participation should nevertheless be understood as one of multiple diverse interpretations and applications of the founder's teachings *within* Epicureanism in the Greco-Roman era.

In other words, Lucretius has reinterpreted and recontextualized the Hellenistic teachings or doctrines of Epicurus to address Roman

22. Summers, "Lucretius and the Epicurean Tradition of Piety," 32–34; 44–45; 47–48.

23. Ghisalberti, *Soteriology and the End of Animal Sacrifice*, 125.

24. See my discussion above and note 4 on scholarship favoring Epicurus's participation in cultic rituals.

25. Ghisalberti, *Soteriology and the End of Animal Sacrifice*, 126–36.

26. Summers, "Lucretius and the Epicurean Tradition of Piety," 33 (italics added).

27. Summers, "Lucretius and the Epicurean Tradition of Piety," 54–57; *contra* Erler, *Epicurus*, 90–93, who harmonizes Lucretius with Philodemus by arguing the opposite extreme that they both allowed for the permissibility of cultic practice.

readers in a different way than Philodemus does. Yet, both Philodemus and Lucretius believe that theirs is a faithful reformulation of the scholarch's theological tenets. Even though Epicureanism enjoyed the reputation of having an unbroken chain of successive scholarchs in Athens from the time of its founding (307/306 BCE) until the third century CE,[28] the continuity of the Garden's leadership and tradition did not mean subsequent Epicureans were unoriginal thinkers who just parroted the dogmas of their founder. Current scholarship has started to recognize some creative innovations in the teachings of the Garden especially among Greek Epicureans like Philodemus who wrote to a Roman audience.[29] What we have here are two Epicurean exegetes who had access to the unofficial canon of Epicurus's treatises, personal letters, epitomes, and maxims and reinterpreted them for their own contemporary setting in ways which best preserved the school's doctrines.[30] *Lucretius and Philodemus provide examples of what I would label as* "doctrinal reformulations" *of a founding philosopher's teachings by subsequent followers who each think they adequately preserve their school's tradition and major tenets but nevertheless, based on their individual exegetical work, can produce competing interpretations* within *the same school.*[31]

Returning to the previously cited excerpt by Philodemus concerning Epicurus's teaching on religion, we read it in its expanded form as follows:

> "Let us sacrifice to the gods," says he [Epicurus], "piously and nobly on the appropriate days (ἡμ[εῖς θεοῖς |θύμεν φησιν [ὁσί|ως καὶ καλῶς οὗ [καθ|ηκει κα[ὶ κ]αλῶ<ς>), and let us nobly practice all these things in accordance with the laws (πάν|τα πράττωμεν [κα|τὰ τοὺς νόμους), while simultaneously not disturbing ourselves with [false] opinions in matters concerning the most excellent and august of beings (μ[η|θὲ[ν] ταῖς δόξαις α[ὑ|τοὺς ἐν τοῖς περὶ|τῶν ἀρίστων κ[αὶ |σεμνοτάτων δια|

---

28. Diogenes Laertius, *Lives* 10.9–10; see also Dorandi, "School and Texts of Epicurus," 30–37, on the history of "successors" (διάδοχοι) for the Garden at Athens.

29. Fish and Sanders, "Introduction," 1; Wurster, "Changing Perceptions," 21.

30. Snyder, *Teachers and Texts in the Ancient World*, 45–65.

31. The category of "doctrinal reformulation" is taken from the translation of the Greek term διδασκαλία into the Latin *doctrina* and refers to the reinterpretation of a school's "teaching" or tenets by its adherents to address new situations not anticipated by its founder(s). Doctrinal reformulation demarcates a seventh interaction type I would add to the six that I name in *Moral Transformation*, 494–516; see the introduction to this volume.

ταράττοντε[ς). Yet let us sacrifice *rightly*, based on the opinion which I was stating [i.e., the correct view of the gods' true nature]. For in this way it is possible for mortal nature, by Zeus, to live in likeness to Zeus . . . (ἔτι |δὲ καὶ δίκαιο[ι θύω|μεν ἀφ' ἧς ἔλε[γον δό|ξης· οὕτω γὰρ [ἐν|δέχεται φύσ[ιν θνη|τὴν ὁμοίω[ς τῷ Διῒ |νὴ{ι} Δία <διά>γειν)."[32]

Philodemus also insists Epicurus practiced what he taught:

By his very own actions, he [Epicurus] is found participating in all the ancestral festivals and sacrifices (καὶ δι[ὰ τῶν |ἔργων αὐτῶν ϛ[ὑρίσ|κεται πάσαις ταῖς |πατρίοις ἑορταῖς |καὶ θυσίαις κε[χ]ρη|μένος).[33]

The key principle for the Epicurean participation in sacrifices according to Philodemus is knowing how to "sacrifice rightly" (καὶ δίκαιο[ι θύω|μεν; lines 879–80). The sage must rid oneself of all false opinions (ταῖς δόξαις; line 885) about the gods and especially that they meddle in human affairs. Instead, the gods should be admired on account of their true nature as "the most excellent and august of beings" (περὶ |τῶν ἀρίστων κ[αὶ |σεμνοτάτων; lines 887–88).[34] If the sage rejects popular beliefs that the gods should be feared or propitiated, beliefs that are false and "empty opinions" (ταῖς κεναῖς δόξαις) in the end,[35] and enters into the sacred rite admiring the gods for who they really are—blessed, eternal, and free from disturbance—it is possible for the Epicurean to live

---

32. Philodemus, *Piet.*, *PHerc* 1098, col. 31.879–95; Eng. trans. modified from Obbink, *Philodemus on Piety*, 167.

33. Philodemus, *Piet.*, *PHerc* 1098, col. 28.792–97, Eng. trans. modified from Obbink, *Philodemus on Piety*, 161.

34. See also Philodemus, *Piet.*, *PHerc* 1077/1093, col. 45.1282–92; Eng. trans. modified from Obbink, *Philodemus on Piety*, 195, which reads: "Divine beings are the most excellent, most august, and most worthy of emulation (τ]ῶν ὄντων ἄριστον |κ]αὶ σεμνό[[ν]]τατον |καὶ ἀξιοζηλωτότατον), and having dominion over all good things, unburdened by [human] affairs (καὶ |πάντων [τ]ῶν ἀγα|θῶν κυριεύοντα κὰ|πραγμάτευτον), and exalted, high-minded, and high-souled (καὶ ὑψηλὸν καὶ μεγαλό|φρονα καὶ μεγαλό|ψυχον) . . . the ineffable pre-eminence of divine strength and perfection (τὴν ἄφραστον ὑπεροχὴν τῆς ἰσχύος τοῦ θε[ί]ου καὶ τελειό||[τητος])."

35. Spinelli and Verde, "Theology," 113; Asmis, "Psychology," 211; O'Keefe, *Epicureanism*, 124–27. False opinions have the technical designation of "empty opinions" (δόξαι κεναί) in Epicurean discourse; see, e.g., Epicurus, *KD* 29–30. Though in this text, Philodemus simply refers to "opinions" or the "opinions of the many," elsewhere he does use "empty opinions" to describe traditional religion; see, e.g., Philodemus, *Piet.*, *PHerc* 1098, col. 43.1231 (δοξῶν] κενῶν); and *PHerc* 1077, col. 50.1430–31 (κε|ναῖς δόξ[αις).

"in likeness to Zeus" (ὁμοίω[ς τῷ Διΐ; line 894), or in other words, to become like the gods in their blessedness, tranquility, and freedom. If the goal (τέλος) of the blessed life (τοῦ μακαρίως ζῆν) is the tranquil soul (καὶ τῆς ψυχῆς ἀταραξίαν),[36] then imitating the gods for their tranquility (ἀταραξία), self-sufficiency (αὐταρκεία), and freedom (ἐλευθερία) enabled the Epicurean to come one step toward reaching this goal.[37] To do this, the sage actively reconceptualized the gods with the right knowledge (γνῶσις) concerning their divine nature so that when one participated in any segment of the cult, the worshiper did so—not thinking of the false Olympian gods of Greek and Roman religion—but the true divinities who epitomized the undisturbed life.[38]

Hence Philodemus concludes:

> They [the masses] will suppose that the gods are terrifying tyrants (δεινοὺς ὑπολή|ψονται τυράννους), and most of all they—because of their own consciences—will expect great misfortune from them [the gods] (δι' ἃ συνοίδασιν |αὐτοῖς μεγάλας ἐ|ξ αὐτῶν συμφο|ρὰς προσδοκήσου|σιν) . . . but those who believe our "oracles" about the gods will first wish to imitate their 'blessed-blessedness' in so far as mortals can (οἱ δὲ πει<σ>θ[έν|τες οἷς ἐχρησμῳ|δήσαμεν περὶ θε|ῶν πρῶτον μὲν |ὡς θνητοὶ μειμε[ῖσ|θαι τὴν ἐκείνων εὐδαι{δαι}μονίαν θελήσουσιν)."[39]

Philodemus, as well as some doxographers,[40] provide *testimonia* that Epicurus taught—and his followers practiced—that the Garden's adherents could indeed participate in temple sacrifices, festivals, vows, prayer, and other aspects of traditional Greek and Roman religion *if they re-theologized their conception of the gods to justify their observance*

---

36. Epicurus, *Ep. Men.* 128.

37. Epicurus, *VS* 77 (Arrighetti).

38. Diogenes Laertius, *Lives* 10.123.

39. Philodemus, *Piet.*, PHerc 229, col. 71.2031–50; Eng. trans. modified from Obbink, *Philodemus on Piety*, 247.

40. See, e.g., Plutarch, *Suav. viv.* 1102B (= Us. 30); *Adv. Col.* 1112C; Diogenes Laertius, *Lives* 10.120; Us. 390 (= Origen, *Cels.* 7.66); Cicero, *Nat. d.* 1.56. See also Diogenes of Oinoanda, fr. 19.II.12–III.5, which reads: "O you! What is it, then? We [Epicureans] are pious to the gods both in the religious festivals and in secular matters, both in public and private (τοὺς μὲν θεοὺς εὐσε|βῶμεν, v καὶ ἐν ἑορταῖς |καὶ ἐν βε[βήλοις καὶ |κοινῇ κ[αὶ ἰδίᾳ καλῶς), and we observe closely our ancestral customs"; Eng. trans. modified from Smith, *Epicurean Inscription*, 376.

of religious ritual.[41] As Epicureans had true knowledge of the gods and could maintain a correct mental disposition towards divinity, they could transform religious rites into acts of genuine piety even as they engaged in cultic worship. Some second-century CE Epicureans such as Tiberius Claudius Lepidus of Amastrias and Aurelius Belius Philippus of Apamea even served as cultic priests.[42]

Epicureans and the Corinthian "Knowers" in Analogical Comparison

When we compare Epicurean theological teachings and the Corinthian slogans embedded in Paul's instructions concerning idol food (1 Cor 8:1–13; 10:1–22; and 10:23–30), we can notice areas of coherence between the two bodies of discourse. Like the Epicureans, those who eat idol food at Corinth do so on the basis that:

> "All have knowledge" (πάντες γνῶσιν ἔχομεν; 8:1)
> "There is no idol in the world" (οὐδὲν εἴδωλον ἐν κόσμῳ; 8:4a)
> "Food will not bring us closer to God" (βρῶμα δὲ ἡμᾶς οὐ παραστήσει τῷ θεῷ; 8:8)

The authors of the above slogans have been identified by NT scholarship under several designations—including the Corinthian "knowers," "the strong," or "the wise."[43] To avoid confusion, the Corinthian elitist group who argued for the permissibility of eating idol food will primarily be identified as the "knowers" since the γνῶσις/γινώσκειν word group is the most prominent in 1 Cor 8–10.[44]

---

41. Erler, *Epicurus*, 88–94; Spinelli and Verde, "Theology," 111–13.

42. Spinelli and Verde, "Theology," 110–11.

43. Hurd, *Origin of 1 Corinthians*, 61–94; Kwon, "Critical Review," 386–427; Brookins, *Corinthian Wisdom, Stoic Philosophy, and Ancient Economy*, 82–103; Watson and Culy, *Quoting Corinthians*, 84–97.

44. The knowers, the wise, and the strong appear in separate but overlapping texts. The language of γνῶσις/γινώσκειν occurs in 1 Cor 8 (Paul's teaching on idol food; 8:1–3; 8:7; 8:10–11) but also in 1 Cor 1–4 (Paul's critique of worldly wisdom; 1:5; 1:21; 2:8; 2:11; 2:14; 2:16; 3:20; 4:19). The terms σοφία/σοφός primarily occur in 1 Cor 1–3 (1:17; 1:19–22; 1:24–27; 1:30; 2:1; 2:4–7; 2:13; 3:10; 3:18–20) but the alternative term φρόνιμος is used in 4:10 and 10:15. The term ἰσχυρός can be found in 1 Cor 1–4 (1:25; 1:27; 4:10) and 1 Cor 10:22, with its counterpart ἀσθενής/ἀσθένεια/ἀσθενεῖν in 1 Cor 1–4 (1:25; 1:27; 2:3; 4:10) and 1 Cor 8–10 (8:7; 8:9; 8:10–12; 9:22).

The previous section described how Epicureans use their knowledge (γνῶσις) and freedom (ἐλευθερία) to participate in traditional festivals and sacrifices (πάσαις ταῖς |πατρίοις ἑορταῖς |καὶ θυσίαιας κε[χ]ρη|μένος),[45] eat at the sacred table of the temple (τὴν κα[θ' ἱερᾶς τρα|πέζης),[46] and celebrate a meal (δεῖπνον; presumably including idol meat) with other revelers at the temple precincts.[47] Because they have the knowledge of the gods' true imperturbable nature (ἀταραξία) and imitate (μιμεῖσθαι) the blessed tranquility of the gods, the sage can share in all aspects of the cultic rituals without disturbing one's soul.[48]

Likewise the Corinthian γνῶσις group makes the claim that knowing "no idol exists in the world" (οὐδὲν εἴδωλον ἐν κόσμῳ; 8:4a) and "there is no God except one" (οὐδεὶς θεὸς εἰ μὴ εἷς; 8:4b) enables them to eat idol food while they are participating in the various aspects of the cult. With the right understanding of the nature of God, the Corinthians—like the Epicureans—participated in the festivals and feasted without feeling perturbed or having problems of conscience (συνείδησις; 8:7). Contrary to the popular religious idea that the consumption of idol food symbolized communion with the divine—that is, there is a sharing of the sacrifice at the religious feasts between the gods who receive the offerings and the human worshipers who ate the remaining parts of the animal[49]—the Corinthians insisted that "food will not bring us closer to God" (βρῶμα δὲ ἡμᾶς οὐ παραστήσει τῷ θεῷ; 8:8). There is no real presence of the gods at cultic meals and rites for the Corinthian knowers. What is more—like the Epicureans who defined "the weak" (ἀσθενής) or "weak-minded" (*imbecillus*)[50] as those who do not have knowledge (of the gods' true nature) and therefore are perturbed by their own guilty consciences (σύνοιδα) and irrational fear of divine retribution[51]—the

---

45. Epicurus, VS 77 (Arrighetti); Philodemus, *Piet.*, PHerc 1098, col. 28.792–97.

46. Philodemus, *Piet.*, PHerc 1077, col. 30.843–84.

47. Philodemus, *Piet.*, PHerc 1077, col. 29.1078.

48. Philodemus, *Piet.*, PHerc 229, col. 71.2031–50.

49. See Veyne ("Inviter les dieux," 3–42) on understanding the gods as hosts of the ritual meals (cf. Xenophon, *Anab.* 5.3.9–13). Rüpke (*Religion of the Romans*, 142–45) and Klauck (*Religious Context of Early Christianity*, 38–39) understand the gods as guests (cf. Plutarch, *Suav. viv.* 1102A–C). Smith (*From Symposium to Eucharist*, 77–78) allows for both variations of the temple meal traditions.

50. See Diogenes Laertius, *Lives* 10.139 (= Epicurus, *KD* 1); Philodemus, *Piet.*, PHerc 1077, col. 36.1036. Cicero translates ἀσθενής into Latin as *imbecillus* or "weak-minded" in *Nat. d.* 1.45 (= Epicurus, *KD* 1).

51. Philodemus, *Piet.*, PHerc 229, col. 71.2022–43.

Corinthian knowers are faulted by Paul as showing contempt towards a group of "weak" Christians who eat idol food as if an idol were real and consequently suffer from a wounded conscience themselves (ἡ συνείδησις αὐτῶν ἀσθενὴς οὖσα; 8:7; cf. 10:25–29).

The Epicureans and the Corinthian knowers share a commitment to a cognitive program of restructuring their belief system about the true nature of divinity versus the idols of traditional religion so that they could participate in the cult, eat εἰδωλόθυτα, and celebrate the festivals without harm to themselves. This program not only stands in sharp contrast to Roman religion but also is distinct among other anti-superstitious philosophical and religious groups who rejected sacrifice and chose to withdraw from the temple cult. The Pythagoreans, for example, refused all types of blood sacrifice, excluded oxen and sheep, and withdrew from the cultic celebrations.[52] The Orphics likewise refrained from eating (idol) meat, eggs, and beans and drank no wine.[53] While these philosophical and religious groups, and others like them, critiqued popular religion by *withdrawing* from the ceremonies of the pagan temples, most Epicureans (with the exception of Lucretius) provided a cognitive basis for a reengagement with the cult by infusing within the old structures of sacred rites their own understanding of the gods' true nature.

An elitist group of Corinthians did the same with the new knowledge that "there is but one God" when they converted to Christianity. In an analogous way, their self-identification as those with knowledge (γνῶσις; 8:1–4), as the wise (φρόνιμοι; 10:15), and as the strong (ἰσχυρός; 10:22), coupled with their dismissive attitude toward the weak (ἀσθενής; 8:7–13), make a comparison with Epicurean philosophical tenets an illuminating exercise. In my comparison between the Epicureans and the Corinthian knowers, it is important to note, however, that I am not arguing here for the origin of the Corinthian slogans to be found in Epicurean doctrines.[54] Other scholars have argued for different philosophical traditions, especially Stoicism, as the source of knowledge and wisdom of the Corinthian elitist group.[55] Instead, a comparison between two

52. Ghisalberti, *Soteriology and the End of Animal Sacrifice*, 12–15.

53. Ghisalberti, *Soteriology and the End of Animal Sacrifice*, 15–16.

54. Past attempts for situating the slogans in Epicurean doctrines in essay-length treatments have proven only suggestive; see, e.g., Tomlin, "Christians and Epicureans in 1 Corinthians," 51–72.

55. The most thorough and updated case for a Stoic origin of the slogans is by Brookins, *Corinthian Wisdom, Stoic Philosophy, and Ancient Economy*, 153–200.

bodies of discourse—Epicurean and Pauline—allows for the language of one ancient literary corpus to provide new categories and new modes of description for the other.[56] As Barclay points out, the aim of the comparison between two bodies of ancient traditions is "defamiliarizing our own assumptions" and "unsettling the very concepts by which we compare" so that we as current readers can reinterpret familiar texts like 1 Cor 8–10 with fresh language and concepts.[57]

Paul's Rejoinder to the Corinthian Knowers and his "Doctrinal Reformulations" within Diaspora Judaism

Paul responds to the slogans of the Corinthian knowers by addressing three specific social and religious settings where a believer might encounter idol meat and gives a different set of admonitions for each occasion. In 1 Cor 8:1–13 (and 10:23–30), he agrees with the elitist members of the congregation that "an idol is nothing" (8:4). First, Paul makes an allowance for εἰδωλόθυτα sold in the marketplace to be eaten in the private banquet settings of their own homes (10:23–26) or on the occasion when hosts invite them as guests to a meal (10:27–30).[58] It was the habit of pagan priests in the ancient world to sell surplus meat sacrificed to idols in the public square. This meat was often bought by clientele, brought home,

---

56. See, e.g., the following works which compare Epicurean discourse with Paul's: Glad, *Paul and Philodemus*, 185–336; Allison, *Saving One Another*, 124–201; and Fitzgerald et al., *Philodemus and the New Testament World*, 272–321.

57. Barclay, "O wad som Pow'r the giftie gie us," 9–10.

58. This "traditional reading" of 1 Cor 8–10 is well represented by Willis, *Idol Meat in Corinth*, 37–64; Fisk, "Eating Meat Offered to Idols," 49–70; Barrett, "Things Sacrificed to Idols," 45–56. Some scholars argue that Paul thought idol food was inherently idolatrous and therefore prohibited on all occasions; see Cheung, *Idol Food in Corinth*, 82–164; Gooch, *Dangerous Food*, 73–97. Others insist Paul's stance in 1 Cor 8–10 is prohibitive not because of the food itself but because every setting for εἰδωλόθυτα is tied to cultic feasting; see Fee, "Εἰδωλόθυτα Once Again," 181–95; Witherington, "Not So Idle Thoughts," 238–51. There are diverse mediating positions. Fotopolous recognizes the agreement between Paul and the knowers theologically but concludes that Paul, nevertheless, doubts their knowledge can make them "strong" enough to resist the dangers of idolatry (*Food Offered to Idols*, 208–63). Others understand Paul's *theological* recognition of Corinthian freedom to eat idol food but see Paul asking the knowers *ethically* to relinquish their freedom for the weak; see Horrell, "Theological Principle or Christological Praxis," 105–9; Still, "Paul's Aims Regarding ΕΙΔΩΛΟΘΥΤΑ, 334–41; Allison, *Saving One Another*, 124–43.

and served during a private meal.⁵⁹ Here Paul advises the Corinthians to eat without problems of conscience because anything that the earth produces is from the Lord and a part of God's good creation (10:26; cf. Ps 24:1; 50:12; 89:11).

Second, Paul also has no theological objections to the eating of idol food on the temple grounds during non-cultic occasions (8:1–13) since the lavish facilities of temple dining rooms could be rented for private family gatherings, trade association or civic meals, birthdays, funerals, weddings, or other celebrated events.⁶⁰ This concession by Paul to the Corinthian knowers appears anomalous compared to the more strictly prohibitive stance of some Diaspora Jewish writers such as Philo and the author of 4 Maccabees—or other authors of early Christian works such as Revelation (2:14; 2:20) and the *Didache* (6:3)—all of whom see any instance of idol food consumption as a moral compromise and a boundary-breaking action which pushes the violator outside the community.⁶¹

Paul's understanding of the *Shema* (ἄκουε Ισραηλ κύριος ὁ θεὸς ἡμῶν κύριος εἷς ἐστιν; LXX Deut 6:4) in 1 Cor 8:4-6 (οὐδεὶς θεὸς εἰ μὴ εἷς . . . καὶ εἷς κύριος Ἰησοῦς Χριστός) and his allusion to the double commandment of loving God (καὶ ἀγαπήσεις κύριον τὸν θεόν σου; LXX Deut 6:4) and one's neighbor (καὶ ἀγαπήσεις τὸν πλησίον σου; Lev 19:18) in 1 Cor 8:1-3 (τις ἀγαπᾷ τὸν θεόν / ἡ γνῶσις φυσιοῖ, ἡ δὲ ἀγάπη οἰκοδομεῖ)—and possibly also Jesus' own teachings that all foods had been declared clean (καθαρίζων πάντα τὰ βρώματα; Mark 7:15-19)⁶² in 1 Cor 8:8 (βρῶμα δὲ ἡμᾶς οὐ παραστήσει τῷ θεῷ)⁶³—provide the cogni-

59. Tite, "Roman Diet and Meat," 186-87; Cadbury, "*Marcellum* of Corinth," 134-41; Murphy O'Connor, *St. Paul's Corinth*, 186-91.

60. On non-religious uses of temple dining halls, see Willis, *Idol Meat in Corinth*, 37-64; Oster, "Use, Misuse, and Neglect of Archaeological Evidence," 64-67; Still, "Paul's Aims Regarding ΕΙΔΩΛΟΘΥΤΑ," 335-36.

61. See 4 Macc 5:1-12; 5:22-24; Philo, *Leg*. 3.155-57; *Flacc*. 85-96; and the discussion by Waaler, Shema *and the First Commandment*, 292-94; deSilva, *4 Maccabees*, 127-28; Cheung, *Idol Food in Corinth*, 197-220.

62. On the echo of Mark 7:15-19 in 1 Cor 8-10 and Rom 14-15, see Kim, "*Imitatio Christi* (1 Corinthians 11:1)," 202-7. While Kim's article establishes the likelihood of the echo, the interpretation of Mark 7 needs to be revisited in light of recent works; see, e.g., van Maaren, "Does Mark's Jesus Abrogate Torah?" 21-41; Thiessen, *Jesus and the Forces of Death*, 187-95.

63. While 1 Cor 8:8 originates as a Corinthian slogan, Paul affirms his agreement with the knowers that "food does not bring us closer to God." As Oropeza notes (*1 Corinthians*, 112), Paul's stance here is consistent with his view on food elsewhere in his letters (e.g., Rom 14:14; cf. 1 Cor 9:4; 10:30-31).

tive basis for Paul to restructure the believers' eating practices (including meat sold in the marketplace whose origin may not be known; 10:25–27) in alignment with one's convictions on the nature of God.[64] This reading of the Pentateuch (especially Deuteronomy) and the Jesus tradition by Paul provides the theological basis for believers to consume idol meat in non-liturgical settings without a violation of conscience (συνείδησις; 10:25, 27–29).[65]

Yet, at the same time, the allusion to the second commandment to love one's neighbor so that one's knowledge "does not puff up" but out of love "builds up" fellow believers shifts the discussion from a theological confession of "one God" and "one Lord" to ethical imperatives.[66] Though Paul and the Corinthian knowers are free to eat εἰδωλόθυτα in non-liturgical settings, Paul does not exercise his freedom to eat, but instead reapplies his freedom to love rather than insist on his own rights; he expects the knowers to do the same.[67] The apostle calls the knowers out of their love for God and each other to avoid stumbling (σκανδαλίσαι; 8:13) the weak who, given their past participation in idol worship and resulting bad consciences (8:7, 10, 12), might be tempted to return to pagan idolatry if they see other believers eating idol food in public spaces. Similarly, believers out of love for neighbor should not stumble their pagan hosts if the latter's conscience is aware of the cultic origins of the meat that they have served to their believing guests (10:28–29).[68]

Third, in the liturgical setting of 10:1–22, Paul is quite clear that no Christian should eat idol food as part of pagan veneration. At the sacrificial altar (τράπεζα), no γνῶσις can shield the believer's conscience against the dangers of idol worship (εἰδωλολατρία; 10:7). Thus, Paul explicitly warns: "You cannot participate in the table of the Lord and the table of

---

64. Waaler, *Shema and the First Commandment*, 303–43; Kim, "*Imitatio Christi* (1 Corinthians 11:1)," 199–202; Hays, *First Corinthians*, 134–46; 159–81; Lee, "Reality of Freedom," 177–81.

65. Kim, "*Imitatio Christi* (1 Corinthians 11:1)," 217–24.

66. *Pace* Horrell who thinks that Paul prioritizes Christological praxis (i.e., imitating Christ's self-giving love) over scriptural justifications ("Theological Principle or Christological Praxis," 106–7); however, these are not competitive. Paul uses both but has reinterpreted scriptural texts to put primacy on ethical concerns for the weak (Waaler, *Shema and the First Commandment*, 310–18).

67. Kim also suggests that the ransom saying of Jesus (Mark 10:45) and Jesus' warnings against stumbling others (Mark 9:42–50) forms the scriptural basis of Paul's ethical arguments in 1 Cor 8–10; see his "*Imitatio Christi* (1 Corinthians 11:1)," 197–99.

68. Fisk, "Eating Meat Offered to Idols," 63–64.

demons (οὐ δύνασθε ποτήριον κυρίου πίνειν καὶ ποτήριον δαιμονίων, οὐ δύνασθε τραπέζης κυρίου μετέχειν καὶ τραπέζης δαιμονίων; 10:21)." Even though the material idols themselves and the gods they represent are not actual deities, the unnamed demonic and spiritual forces at work in a cultic act of pagan worship are a "real presence."[69] Therefore, the believer is urged to flee every form of idolatry (φεύγετε ἀπὸ τῆς εἰδωλολατρίας; 10:14). Citing the folly of the Israelites during their wilderness journey and reflecting upon those OT texts which narrate their apostasy (Exod 32:7; Num 11:4; 21:4-9; 25:1-9), Paul warns against a communion with demons that could stumble many in the church.[70]

Here Paul's exhortations challenge the theological tenets of Epicureanism and other philosophical groups that insist δαίμονες and gods do not directly interfere with human affairs. Instead, Paul argues in the opposite direction that the God of Jesus Christ is a jealous God and would act as judge if the Corinthians continue to participate in idol feasting (10:22). This argument, I sense, would not have sat well with the Corinthian knowers who would have regarded the notion of God who can be tested (ἐκπειράζωμεν; 10:9), disturbed, and provoked to jealousy a *superstitio*. Paul's subsequent letters to the Corinthian church (especially his "tearful" one; 2 Cor 7:8) suggest that his arguments here and elsewhere in 1 Corinthians were not entirely convincing.[71]

Conclusion

I have advanced the following points in the essay. First, the way that Epicurus and his disciples restructured their knowledge of the gods so that they could participate in cultic sacrifice without problems of conscience *is analogous* to how the Corinthian γνῶσις group used their knowledge to justify the consumption of idol food in various social and religious settings. Second, Paul, in response, concedes that the Christian understanding of "one God" allows for the eating of εἰδωλόθυτα in non-cultic settings, but his theology that the God of Jesus Christ is jealous and judges the immoral behavior of believers compels him to launch an invective against participation in cultic worship. Idols are not real, but the demonic forces to which they point are. The Corinthian knowers

69. Thiselton, *First Epistle to the Corinthians*, 773-76.
70. Oropeza, *Paul and Apostasy*, 139-67; 204-6.
71. Mitchell, "Thessalonian and Corinthian Letters," 82-83.

would have found such a line of discourse disappointing and unacceptable. Third, Paul ironically faults the Corinthian knowers for not taking their γνῶσις far enough. If they really knew God and were known by God (οὗτος ἔγνωσται ὑπ' αὐτοῦ; 1 Cor 8:3), their knowledge and experience of God would have been applied in a way to love and build up their fellow believers in the Lord, not take action which would cause them to stumble.

Lastly, just as Lucretius and Philodemus individually applied Epicurus's teaching on cultic participation differently and yet were both considered adherents of the Garden, so, too, Paul's stance on εἰδωλόθυτα should be seen as a "dogmatic reformulation" that makes his reading of Israel's Scriptures both distinct among his Diaspora Jewish contemporaries and yet still *within* Judaism. Barrett's classic statement that "in matters of εἰδωλόθυτα . . . Paul was not a practicing Jew"[72] is exaggerated given the ancient context of how different adherents within the same school or philosophical movement could interpret their founder's tenets and sacred texts diversely, even competitively, and yet be considered "true believers."

---

72. Barrett, "Things Sacrificed to Idols," 50.

11

The Corporate Σῶμα in Epictetus and Paul

MICHAEL M. C. REARDON

THE RELATIONSHIP BETWEEN STOICISM and Christianity has been intensely scrutinized since the post-apostolic era. Church Fathers such as Tertullian,[1] Origen,[2] and Augustine[3] penned incisive polemics against Stoicism, yet affirmed fundamentally Stoic positions in their (meta) physical and ethical paradigms. Centuries later, John Calvin repudiated characterizations of his doctrine of providence being akin to Stoic determinism.[4] Yet when addressing identical critiques, Jonathan Edwards was far more conciliatory. In "Freedom of the Will" he states that "the Stoic philosophers, by the general agreement of Christian divines, and even Arminian divines, were the greatest, wisest, and most virtuous of all the heathen philosophers, and in their doctrine and practice came the nearest to Christianity of any of their sects."[5] More recently, Paul Tillich

---

1. "What indeed has Athens to do with Jerusalem? . . . Away with all attempts to produce a mottled Christianity of Stoic, Platonic, and dialectic composition!" (Tertullian, *Praescr.* 7; Eng. trans. by Holmes, *Ante-Nicene Fathers*, 3:246).

2. E.g., Origen, *Cels.*

3. E.g., Augustine, *Civ.* 19.4.

4. Cochran, *Protestant Virtue and Stoic Ethics*, 1; Calvin, *Institutes* I.16.8.

5. Cochran, *Protestant Virtue and Stoic Ethics*, 1; Edwards, "Freedom of the Will," 372.

proclaimed that Stoicism is "the only real alternative to Christianity in the Western world."[6]

Notwithstanding mixed sentiments, the existence of ostensible similarities between Stoicism and Christianity is undeniable. While studies utilizing methodologies reminiscent of the *Religionsgeschichtliche Schule* often foreground the resemblances or presupposed genealogical links between Stoic and Christian interlocutors,[7] some recent scholars have sought to examine the particularities of each worldview. One noteworthy project in this line of inquiry is Michelle Lee's *Paul, the Stoics, and the Body of Christ*. Lee's expansive analysis of possible parallels between Stoic and Pauline usages of a metaphorical corporate σῶμα to shape their respective ethical programs is an invaluable addition both to comparative theology and Pauline studies. However, her project prioritizes commonalities between Paul and Latin-speaking Stoics, such as Cicero and especially Seneca.[8] This approach is not entirely unreasonable since Cicero predates both figures while Seneca and Paul are contemporaries. To examine an example of contemporaneous metaphorical usage of a corporate σῶμα or speculate about Pauline "source material," these interlocutors are appropriate. Additionally, Latin-speaking Stoics have larger extant corpuses than their Greek counterparts.

Nevertheless, there is strong rationale to engage in a delimited conversation between Paul and Epictetus, a Greek Stoic who lived one generation after Paul. Firstly, according to Adolf Bonhöffer, Epictetus is "completely free from the eclecticism of Seneca and Marcus Aurelius; and, compared with his teacher Musonius Rufus . . . reveals a considerably closer connection to Stoic doctrine and terminology as developed

---

6. Tillich, *Courage to Be*, 9.

7. "Genealogical links" here is used to describe studies that argue that Paul's theology of X is drawn (or sourced) from Stoic conceptions of X as opposed to the two merely resembling one another (which, in this essay about the metaphor of a corporate body, I argue is an example of shared ethical appropriation); see, e.g., Grant, "St. Paul and Stoicism"; and Engberg-Pedersen, *Cosmology and Self in the Apostle Paul*. See also Brookins, *Corinthian Wisdom, Stoic Philosophy, and the Ancient Economy*, who sources the ethics of the Corinthian wisdom group in Stoicism.

8. To be clear, Lee examines numerous Stoa, including Epictetan passages examined in this essay; see, e.g., *Paul, the Stoics, and the Body of Christ*, 61–62; 98–100. Still, by prioritizing Latin speakers, Epictetus's voice is ultimately muted. Examples of studies adhering to this majority position include: Sevenster, *Paul and Seneca*; Berry, *Seneca and Christianity*; and the essays edited by Dodson and Briones, *Paul and Seneca in Dialogue*.

mainly by Chrysippus."[9] Thus, a better representation of how orthodox Stoicism resembles or differs from early Christianity can be ascertained by comparatively examining Epictetus and Paul.

Second, Epictetus taught in Koiné Greek[10]—a key consideration since recent scholarship suggests that Paul did not know Latin.[11] Assuming Paul's lack of Latin proficiency, it follows that all contact between Paul and Stoicism would be in Greek, as opposed to Latin, contexts.[12] Moreover, following Hans-Georg Gadamer's concept of *wirkungsgeschichtliches Bewußtsein*,[13] the overall worldview inherited through a shared sociolinguistic tradition invites comparisons between Paul and Epictetus. Of note are three recent investigations which have capitalized upon this shared tradition to compare Epictetan and Pauline conceptions of social status,[14] jurisprudence,[15] and anthropology.[16]

In this essay I examine a metaphor—the corporate σῶμα—which for reasons detailed below is further distinguished as the Epictetan cosmic σῶμα and the Pauline Christic σῶμα.[17] This endeavor necessitates methodological rigor in order to avoid three pitfalls common to comparative theological exercises. Jonathan Smith identifies the first pitfall as presupposing a "parataxis of likeness" which overemphasizes how A is "like" B to the detriment of particularities that would make such a comparison worthwhile.[18] Tied to this is a second pitfall whereby one uncritically accepts the existence of "likeness" (literary or otherwise) as unequivocal evidence for genealogical links between worldviews—a tendency of the *Religionsgeschichtliche Schule*. Samuel Sandmel defines these first two pitfalls as examples of "parallelomania"—a neologism describing "that

---

9. Bonhöffer *apud* Seddon, *Epictetus' Handbook*, 8.
10. See Dobbins, *Epictetus*.
11. Porter, "Did Paul Speak Latin?"
12. See, e.g., the Lukan witness to Paul's engagement with Greek-speaking Athenian Stoics and Epicureans in Acts 17:18–34.
13. Gadamer, *Truth and Method*.
14. Jacquette, "Paul, Epictetus, and Indifference to Status."
15. Huttunen, *Paul and Epictetus on Law*.
16. Eastman, *Paul and the Person*.
17. "Cosmic" is appropriate when referring to Epictetus's conception of a corporate σῶμα as he posits a near-equivalence of the σῶμα to the κόσμος (a flexible Epictetan term for the universe, god, or the totality of existence). For Paul, the corporate σῶμα is uniquely identified with Christ; hence, the Christic σῶμα.
18. Smith, *Drudgery Divine*, 42–43.

extravagance among scholars which first overdoes the supposed similarity in passages and then proceeds to describe source and derivation as if implying literary connection flowing in an inevitable or predetermined direction."[19]

The third pitfall is the antithesis of parallelomania—that is, the overstressing of differences between worldviews without attentiveness to their commonalities. While other reasons may exist for succumbing to this pitfall, exaggerated differentiation is often utilized as a rhetorical device to assert the superiority of A over B.[20] As with previous missteps, inordinately stressing differences between worldviews causes items of scholarly interest to be discarded when they do not fit a desired narrative. Against such errors, comparative theologian Francis Clooney calls for a nuanced approach to thematic comparison which "clarifies concepts by looking at them from different angles . . . [and] improves on them by interreligious learning."[21] Abraham Malherbe likewise suggests that successful intertextual work begins when literary similarities are affirmed, and only thereafter, conceptual dissimilarities are acknowledged.[22]

To avoid the above pitfalls, I approach the task of describing the shared metaphor of a corporate σῶμα between Stoic and Pauline discourses as follows. First, I contextualize the metaphor within Epictetan and Pauline physical presuppositions; that is, I examine how each thinker's physics inform their employment of the corporate σῶμα. Thereafter, their usage of this metaphor is examined in relation to their respective ethical frameworks, or how the metaphor shapes each thinker's paraeneses as they address their respective audiences.

Epictetus's Metaphor of a Cosmic Body

Two passages from Book II of Epictetus's *Discourses* are examined in this essay. The first describes the relationship between a human being with the wider cosmos with that of a foot and the body. It reads as follows:

19. Sandmel, "Parallelomania," 1; cf. Lee, *Paul, the Stoics, and the Body of Christ*, 12.
20. Sevenster, *Paul and Seneca*, 173.
21. Clooney, "Reading Religiously across Religious Borders," 43.
22. Malherbe, "Hellenistic Moralists and the New Testament," 276–78. Malherbe argues that the existence of borrowed terms often obscures dissimilar underlying conceptual frameworks. Rather, these borrowed terms were often modified to cohere with the particular teachings of the individual/group.

[24] How therefore is it said that some external things are natural and some are unnatural? It is because we regard ourselves as detached from the universe (κόσμος). For the foot, it is natural to be clean, but if you take it as a foot, and not as a detached thing, it will be fitting for it to walk in the mud and trample on thorns and sometimes to be cut off for the sake of the whole body. Otherwise, it will no longer be a foot. We must hold to the same view about ourselves.

[25] What are you? A person. Now if you consider yourself as a thing detached, it is natural for you to live to old age, to be rich, to enjoy health. But if you regard yourself as a person and part of some whole, on account of that whole it is fitting (καθήκει) for you now to be sick, and now to make a voyage and run risks, and now to be in want, and on occasion to die before your time. [26] Why therefore are you concerned? Do you know that as the foot, if detached, will no longer be a foot, so you too, if detached, will no longer be a person? For what is a human being? A part of a state; first of that state which is made up of gods and people, and then of that which is said to be very close to the other, the state that is a small copy of the universal state.

[27] "Now therefore must I be put on trial?" Well, would you have someone else be sick of a fever now, someone else go on a voyage, someone else die, someone else be condemned? For it is impossible in such a body (σώματι) as ours, in this [universe] that envelops us (ἐν τούτῳ [κόσμῳ] τῷ περιέχοντι), among these fellow-creatures of ours, that such things should not happen, some to one person and some to another.[23]

This extended text discusses two key concepts which inform Epictetus's metaphorical utilization of a corporate σῶμα. First, it illumines Epictetus's determination of ontological identity—that is, objects generally and humans specifically exist *as they are* by virtue of their being parts of a greater whole. For example, in line 24 Epictetus discusses the ontological identity of a πόδα (foot). Here he contends that a foot, once detached from a person's σῶμα, ceases to be a foot.

In line 26 this understanding of corporate ontological identity is extended to the human being (ἄνθρωπος) in relation to the cosmos: "Do you know that as the foot, if detached, will no longer be a foot, so you too, if detached, will no longer be a human?" The identity of the greater whole

---

23. Epictetus, *Diss.* 2.5.24–27; Eng. trans. modified from Oates, *Epictetus Discourses*, 290. The Greek text is taken from the Teubner edition edited by Schlenkl; all Eng. trans. of Epictetus are modified from Oates, *Epictetus Discourses*.

to which humans are ontologically indebted is described further in line 27 when Epictetus states that human persons are embedded "in this universe (κόσμος) that envelops us." Of import is Epictetus's identification of the σῶμα with the κόσμος—an identification which will be examined in the next section, and for now, allows for his conception to be described as a cosmic σῶμα.[24]

The second key concept in this passage is Epictetus's portrayal of a life well-lived. For Epictetus, when objects or persons are discussed in isolation of a greater whole, they possess innate or normal tendencies. For a detached foot it is "natural to be clean" (line 24) and for a detached human "it is natural for you to live to old age, to be rich, to enjoy health" (line 25). However, once a foot is rightly related to the σῶμα, considerations of what is "natural" are replaced by what is "fitting" (καθήκει), or appropriate for a given situation for the benefit of the whole. For the foot, Epictetus delineates multiple scenarios: to walk in mud, trample on thorns, or be amputated (line 24). For the human, fitting conditions may be similarly unpleasant: to be sick, encounter risky situations on journeys, or die before one's time (lines 25–27). In both cases what is important is the well-being of the greater σῶμα as opposed to its constituent parts. This focal shift—from the individual to the greater whole—is central to Epictetus's ethical outlook. Because his prioritization of the cosmic σῶμα necessitates the disregard of unpleasant circumstances (line 26), Epictetus refashions the good life as being primarily characterized by reason and virtue.[25]

Epictetan Physics and Ethics

A cursory introduction to additional aspects of Stoicism generally and Epictetan thought specifically is warranted to better understand Epictetus's use of the cosmic σῶμα. Most importantly, all Stoics are pantheists who (to varying degrees) conceptualize God as being πνεῦμα pervading the whole of cosmic existence.[26] Due to this posited immanence of πνεῦμα within the κόσμος, Epictetus's physics are akin to substance

---

24. In fact, Long notes that for the Stoics, nothing can "exist which is not a body or the state of a body" ("Soul and Body in Stoicism," 36).

25. Cooper, "Relevance of Moral Theory," 17–19.

26. Baltzly, "Stoic Pantheism," 3–5.

monism.²⁷ This close identification of πνεῦμα and the κόσμος led Stoics to conceive of the universe as a living being—that is, a living σῶμα.²⁸ Drawing these strands together, Epictetan ontology can be brought into sharper focus. In brief, because Epictetus conceives of the cosmic σῶμα as a monistic, material, inter-connected being, any object or person detached from it becomes untethered from their source of existence, and ultimately, is dispossessed of their ontological identity.

However, some Stoics—notably Epictetus—assume a different emphasis when employing πνεῦμα as opposed to κόσμος.²⁹ Rowe and Cochran make the following important observation on the technical uses of κόσμος in Stoicism:

> [N]amely, it cannot be assumed that Stoic grammar would allow us to use 'world' each and every time we wanted to say God. God, rather, is the more precise word for what is ultimately rational in what is—the order of the world, or the laws by which we are to live, or the reasoning faculty within the human being itself.³⁰

This is especially the case with Epictetus, as Long notes his proclivity for speaking of God in personal rather than pantheistic terms.³¹ By identifying the wide semantic uses of κόσμος among the Stoics, Rowe and Cochran draw attention to an important hermeneutical key informing Epictetus's particular application of the cosmic σῶμα, especially when he argues that the minds of human beings are fragments of God.³²

In *Diss.* 1.9.5 Epictetus proposes that individuals are "mingled with God through reason." Though objects are unified in the cosmic σῶμα by virtue of their ontological identity, Epictetus allows for a measure of differentiation based upon their possession and exercise of reason. He states:

---

27. I define Epictetus's physics as "akin" to substance monism instead of a more definite statement—"his physics *are* substance monism"—because for Epictetus, it is unclear to what degree πνεῦμα, κόσμος, ἄνθρωπος, and the σῶμα are interchangeable. For an introduction to substance monism, see Graham, *Explaining the Cosmos*, 50–80.

28. Lee, *Paul, the Stoics, and the Body of Christ*, 48–58.

29. Keimpe Algra argues for a subtle divergence in Epictetan thought from earlier Stoics in this regard ("Epictetus and Stoic Theology," 33–42).

30. Rowe and Cochran, "Letters, Notes, and Comments," 712.

31. Long, *Stoic and Socratic Guide to Life*, 176.

32. See, e.g., Epictetus, *Diss* 1.17.27; 2.8.11.

> [3] *Consider therefore, you are separated according to the power of reason* (κατὰ λόγον). You are separated from wild beasts; you are separated from domestic beasts. [4] On this basis you are a citizen of the world (τοῦ κόσμου) and a part of it, not one of those assigned to servitude, but one of the principal parts; for you are capable of understanding the divine administration and apprehending the connection (ἑξῆς) of things. [5] What therefore is the promise of a citizen? *To have no personal interest, never to think about anything as though one were detached, but to be like the hand or the foot, which, if they had reason and understood the order of nature, would direct every impulse and every process of the will by reference to the whole* (ἐπὶ τὸ ὅλον [= σῶμα]). [6] According to this the philosophers rightly say that "if the good person possessed foreknowledge of upcoming events, one would work towards [one's own] sickness and death and mutilation," for the good person would realize that this task is allotted to oneself by universal arrangement, and that *the whole is superior to the part* (κυριώτερον δὲ τὸ ὅλον [= σῶμα] τοῦ μέρους) and the city-state than the citizen (ἡ πόλις τοῦ πολίτου).[33]

In the above text, Epictetus asserts that the power of reason differentiates humans from animals, the latter of whom are directed by nature and impulse, not by reason. In this regard, reason plays a more formative role in the arrangement of the cosmic order than ontological identity—though to be clear, the latter is foundational to unifying the parts of the cosmic σῶμα. Indeed, it is "according the power of reason" (κατὰ λόγον) that human beings are enlightened to direct "every impulse and every process of their will by reference to the whole (ἐπὶ τὸ ὅλον [= σῶμα])."

Another important feature of the text is its assertion that the πολίτης (citizen) is never more than a part of a πόλις (city-state). In fact, Stoics often portrayed the latter as a miniature of the cosmic σῶμα.[34] Bearing this in mind, line 6 exemplifies how the cosmic σῶμα orients Epictetus's ethical outlook. Earlier, it was noted that Epictetus shifts focus from what is natural for detached and isolated humans to what was fitting for them as parts of the cosmic σῶμα. Though implied in *Diss.* 2.5.24–27, the rationale for this focal shift is explicitly stated here: "the whole [σῶμα] is superior to the part." This explicit communitarian emphasis allows Epictetus

---

33. Epictetus, *Diss.* 2.10.3–6; Eng. trans. modified from Oates, *Epictetus Discourses*, 298 (italics mine).

34. Lee, *Paul, the Stoics, and the Body of Christ*, 99–101.

to argue that those who exercise reason and truly apprehend that they are parts of the cosmic σῶμα would, if granted "foreknowledge of upcoming events," actively "work towards [their own] sickness and death and mutilation" if their present loss might benefit the cosmic σῶμα as a whole.

This prioritization of the cosmic σῶμα over its constituent parts formatively shapes a "well-lived" life or what in Hellenistic philosophy is called εὐδαιμονία ("a flourishing life" or "happiness").[35] For Epictetus, the "good life" is lived in harmony with the cosmic σῶμα. To positively account for seemingly unpleasant events (e.g., sickness, death, mutilation) experienced for the flourishing of the cosmic σῶμα, Epictetus redefined categories of "good" and "evil." Consider the following excerpts from Book II of *Discourses*:

> Of course anyone can discuss at the moment concerning what is good and what is evil in this way: Of things that are, some are good, some evil, some indifferent; the good are virtues and things that have part in virtues; the evil are the opposite; the indifferent are wealth, health, and glory.[36]

> Of things that exist, some are evil, some indifferent, and some good. The virtues and all things that share in them are good, the vices and all things that share in them are evil, and all that comes between is indifferent—wealth, health, life, death, pleasure, pain.[37]

For Epictetus, whether something is "good" or "bad" is entirely dependent upon whether it is profitable or unprofitable in *all instances*.[38] Within this delimited conception, health, wealth, or reputation are not "good," as individuals can possess them and not be benefitted by them. Rather, only ἀρετή (virtue)—which for Epictetus is inextricably linked to the power of reason, since ἀρετή is the ability to use advantages wisely—is good.[39]

The central claim of Epictetan and Stoic ethics is that there is only one good, virtue, and only one evil, vice. All other items, events, states of being—whether they be wealth, poverty, health, death, pleasure, or pain—are ἀδιάφορα (indifferents). To be sure, Epictetus acknowledges

---

35. Annas, *Morality of Happiness*, 329–33.
36. *Diss.* 2.9.15; Eng. trans. modified from Oates, *Epictetus Discourses*, 297.
37. *Diss.* 2.19.13; Eng. trans. modified from Oates, *Epictetus Discourses*, 297.
38. Seddon, *Epictetus' Handbook*, 10.
39. Stephens, *Stoic Ethics*, 113–54.

that ἀδιάφορα can be *preferred* or *dispreferred*.[40] Preferred items are those possessions or states of being which are commonly considered advantageous (e.g., children, health), whereas dispreferred ones are those generally conceived of as disadvantageous or unwanted. Nevertheless, Epictetus conceives of ἀδιάφορα in primarily instrumental terms; in other words, they lack intrinsic significance. Thus, Seddon notes that "the Stoic does not lament their absence, for their presence is not constitutive of *eudaimonia*. What is good is the virtuous use one makes of such preferred items should they be to hand, but no less good are one's virtuous dispositions in living as well as one may, even when they are lacking."[41]

As noted, these foundational categories emerge from an Epictetan physics that prioritizes the cosmic σῶμα over its constituent parts and has ethical implications, the most important of which is the equality of all humankind. Though human equality may be considered the baseline of ethical formation in a post-Enlightenment world, Greco-Roman society was largely organized according to hierarchy and status.[42] Yet for Epictetus (and most Stoics), the shared ontological identity of all humans as parts of the cosmic σῶμα meant that social relationships were exclusively understood in terms of different, yet equitable, moral obligations.[43]

For example, between a slave and a master, slaves have a duty to serve their masters, and masters have a duty to treat their slaves fairly. Yet in both cases, Epictetus argued that their unequal societal standings were not intrinsically valuable. Indeed, their respective social statuses are ἀδιάφορα. Thus, they should not be sought after for oneself; neither should they be disparaged or revered in others. Epictetus exhorts his disciples:

> Never lay claim to anything that is not yours. A platform and a prison are both places, the one high and the other low; but your moral character (προαίρεσις) can remain the same in either place if you desire to keep it that way.[44]

40. Cooper, "Relevance of Moral Theory," 12–18.

41. Seddon, *Epictetus' Handbook*, 11.

42. Koenraad, "Associative Empire," 861–63. Koenraad notes the complexity of social arrangements beyond a reductionistic patrician/plebian dichotomy to discuss multiple social spheres—cultural, economic, political—which had different qualifications determining higher or lower status.

43. Thorsteinsson, "Paul and Roman Stoicism," 153.

44. *Diss.* 2.6.25; Eng. trans. modified from Oates, *Epictetus Discourses*, 292. The term προαίρεσις denotes a central Epictetan doctrine referring to what is in one's control within a predetermined κόσμος; see Long, *Epictetus*, 210–22.

Epictetus elsewhere elucidates that:

> Because status (e.g., that of a consulship) is an external impression, and therefore, outside the province of moral control, one's attitude toward an individual who holds any position must be informed by the recognition that external impressions do not affect one's internal steadfastness.[45]

In sum, the Epictetan cosmic σῶμα engendered an ethical framework presupposing the equal worth of all human beings based on their shared ontology and corporate interconnectedness.

The Christic Σῶμα according to the Apostle Paul

Of the many passages within the Pauline corpus discussing his conception of a corporate σῶμα, "the two most important are 1 Cor 12:12–27 and Rom 12:4–21. The first of these passages reads as follows:

> [12] For, just as the body is one and has many members, and all the members of the body, though being many, are one body, so also is the Christ. [13] For also in one Spirit we all were baptized into one body, whether Jews or Greeks, whether slaves or free, and all were made to drink one Spirit. [14] For also the body is not one member but many.
>
> [15] If the foot should say, "Because I am not a hand, I am not of the body," it is not on account of this that it is not of the body; [16] and if the ear says, "Because I am not an eye, I am not of the body," it is not on account of this that it is not of the body. [17] If the whole body were an eye, where would the hearing be? If the whole body were hearing, where would smell be? [18] However, now God has placed the members, each one of them, in the body, as He willed. [19] And if all were one member, where would the body be? [20] And now, indeed there are many members and one body.
>
> [21] Now the eye is not able to say to the hand, "I have no need of you." Nor again the head to the feet, "I have no need of you." [22] But much rather the members of the body which seem to be weaker are indispensable, [23] and those that we think to be less honorable of the body, around these we bestow more abundant honor, and our disreputable members come to have more abundant repute, [24] but our reputable parts

---

45. Jaquette, "Paul, Epictetus, and Others" 74; cf. *Diss.* 3.3.18–22. See also Oates, *Epictetus Discourses*, 350–51.

have no need. But God has arranged the body and given more abundant honor to the lacking part [25] in order that there may be no division in the body but that the members may have the same care for one another. [26] So if one member suffers, all the members suffer with it; or one member is glorified, all the members rejoice with it. [27] And you are the Body of Christ and individually members.[46]

Though this passage is often examined for its sacramental implications, important to this essay is a curious turn of phrase in v. 12: οὕτως καὶ ὁ Χριστός ("so also is the Christ") instead of what a reader might reasonably expect, "so also is the church." Richard Hays notes that this term has forced interpreters to debate whether Paul presses "beyond mere analogy to make an ontological equation of the church with Christ."[47] This identification of believers as "the Christ," or later, "the Body of Christ" (v. 27) may be considered: (a) a purely rhetorical device utilized to engender an ethical outlook; (b) an analogy used to describe what the community of believers is *similar* to; or (c) a description of a realistic and concrete ontological identity which includes ethical commitments. Though modern interpreters tend to favor the first two (overlapping) designations,[48] this study assumes the latter possibility—a position held by earlier interpreters like Albert Schweitzer and John Robinson, and more recently, by Michelle Lee and Troels Engberg-Pedersen.[49]

Throughout the rest of the passage, Paul's commentary about the individuation of members (expressed by the idiom ἐκ μέρους; v. 27) is not primarily understood in terms of being autonomous selves. Rather, their differences are rooted in their distinct functionalities. By emphasizing functionality, Paul accounts for both the diversity of the members as well the ultimate aim of this discourse, which Gordon Fee rightly notes is their unity in the Christic σῶμα[50]—the individual parts possess differing functionalities (diversity), yet these functions only make sense *in*

---

46. Unless otherwise noted, all Eng. trans. from the Greek New Testament are my own.

47. Hays, *1 Corinthians*, 213.

48. E.g., Thiselton, *First Epistle to the Corinthians*, 996; Best, *One Body in Christ*, 96–104; Barrett, *First Epistle to the Corinthians*, 288.

49. Schweitzer, *Mysticism of Paul the Apostle*, 116; cf. 101–40; Robinson, *Body*, 58; cf. also 78–79; Lee, *Paul, the Stoics, and the Body of Christ*, 127–38; Engberg-Pedersen, *Cosmology and the Self in the Apostle Paul*, 174.

50. Fee, *First Epistle to the Corinthians*, 668–69.

relation to the Christic σῶμα (unity). In vv. 15–16, Paul illustrates how these diverse functions undergird their unity by utilizing four body parts as examples: the hand, foot, eye, and ear. As both Thiselton and Fee note, the fact that each part possesses a unique function not shared by other members means that each member is *necessary* for the thriving of the Christic σῶμα.[51] Conversely, the loss of any member—whether seemingly important or not—damages the Christic σῶμα.

This posited interdependence and individual valuation of each member in the Christic σῶμα allows Paul to articulate a robust ethical framework. In v. 22 he states that every member is necessary and, in fact, is included in the Christic σῶμα according to God's will (v. 19). Due to this divine placement, Paul argues that even the most disreputable or dishonorable member must be both attached *and* functioning—otherwise, the flourishing of the Christic σῶμα is at risk. Thus, while commentators are unclear what Paul means by assigning "more abundant honor" to those who lack (vv. 23–24),[52] it is evident that such activity results in the "same care" (v. 25) being afforded to all members, irrespective of social status or rank. According to Thiselton, such care extends as far as transferring one's preoccupation with their own status and gifts equally to all others of the community.[53]

Apart from locating the meaning of diversity in unity, Paul contends that the unity of the Christic σῶμα is actuated by the members' interaction with πνεῦμα. On the face of it, the inextricable link Paul posits between πνεῦμα and somatic unity is akin to Stoic conceptions. Indeed, Engberg-Pedersen enthusiastically contends that the Stoic conception of a physical πνεῦμα unifying the cosmic σῶμα is found in Paul's discourse above—notably, in v. 13 where Paul states that Christians are "in one Spirit" (ἐν ἑνὶ πνεύματι) and "baptized" (ἐβαπτίσθημεν) into the Christic σῶμα.[54] On one hand, Engberg-Pedersen draws attention to a key issue in this text—that for Paul the source of the diverse functionalities of the members is πνεῦμα.[55] However, upon closer inspection, Pauline thought disallows such easy correspondences.

---

51. Thiselton, *First Epistle to the Corinthians*, 1003; Fee, *First Epistle to the Corinthians*, 676.

52. Fee, *First Epistle to the Corinthians*, 680.

53. Thiselton, *First Epistle to the Corinthians*, 1011.

54. Engberg-Pedersen, *Cosmology and the Self in the Apostle Paul*, 69.

55. Engberg-Pedersen, *Cosmology and the Self in the Apostle Paul*, 171.

Engberg-Pedersen, I suggest, wrongly dismisses a mystical conception of the Christic σῶμα upfront without considering a key difference between the Stoics and Paul—the former asserts a fully material universe while the latter possesses an expansive non-material metaphysics.[56] Following Malherbe's method (see the first section of this essay above), the shared terminology of σῶμα should not be allowed to mask dissimilarities between how σῶμα is understood within competing philosophical frameworks. Engberg-Pedersen also argues that both the Stoics and Paul understand the role of πνεῦμα as being largely related to cognition.[57] Though there is some warrant for this relationship in Paul's writings (1 Cor 2:14–16; Rom 8:2–11), the *unifying* role of πνεῦμα for Paul is more explicitly tied to the *exercise* of diverse functionalities (i.e., spiritual gifts) than to the power of reason.[58]

Finally, Paul proposes that both the outward baptism and the inward "drinking" (ἐποτίσθημεν) of the πνεῦμα are inextricably linked not only to a member's continuous unity with, but also *initiation* into, the Christic σῶμα—the latter of which is an impossibility for the Stoic framework since all human beings already *are* constituents of the cosmic σῶμα. This link between πνεῦμα and Christian initiation creates a distinction between humans "in" and "out" of the Christic σῶμα (i.e., those baptized/drinking in the one Spirit versus those who are not). While Engberg-Pedersen rightly notes the link between Paul's conception of πνεῦμα and Christian ethics,[59] he uncritically attributes similar Stoic commitments to Paul without discussing the significant dissimilarity between them. These dissimilarities or distinctions will be expanded upon in the next section, which examines Paul's larger cosmological and ethical framework.

Paul's (Meta)physical Cosmology and Ethics

It is broadly accepted that Paul conceives of the κόσμος as being composed of two ages (or "creations") and that humans can participate in

---

56. For Stoics, the universe is entirely physical, except for four incorporeal items: place, void, time, and sayables (Vogt, "Sons of the Earth," 139).

57. Engberg-Pedersen, *Cosmology and the Self in the Apostle Paul*, 59–67.

58. Moreover, as will be discussed in the next section in Paul's somatically engendered ethics, emotions—particularly love—play a greater role than cognition.

59. Engberg-Pedersen, *Cosmology and the Self in the Apostle Paul*, 171.

either sphere of existence.⁶⁰ The first sphere, the "old creation," originated with Adam; the second sphere, the "new creation," was inaugurated by the death and resurrection of Jesus Christ (cf. 1 Cor 15:45). For Paul, all human beings by virtue of their earthly birth participate in the old creation. Yet, Christians, defined by Paul as those who are "in Christ," participate in the new creation (2 Cor 5:17). Moreover, according to Susan Eastman's recent appraisal of Pauline anthropology, it is likely that Paul conceived of Christians simultaneously participating in both the old and new creations.⁶¹

This two-"creation" cosmology undergirds the way Paul limits membership of the Christic σῶμα to Christians alone—a departure from the Stoic incorporation of all humans into the cosmic σῶμα. This is a crucial difference, as Paul's paraeneses only apply to the Christian "in-group." Nevertheless, it would be incorrect to assume that Paul's understanding of the Christic σῶμα limited the church's engagement with outsiders. Rather, it provides the basis for an ethical framework for the church's ministry to Greco-Roman society at large.⁶²

In Romans 12:4-21, Paul's rhetoric addresses the church's identity as a Christic σῶμα (vv. 4-5), the theological implications of one-body language for the pastoral care of each member (vv. 6-13), and ultimately, a wider external engagement with one's neighbor (vv. 14-21). The passage reads:

> [4] For just as in one body we have many members, and all the members do not have the same function, [5] so we who are many are one Body in Christ, and individually members one of another.
>
> [6] And having gifts that differ according to the grace given to us, if it is prophecy, let us prophesy according to the proportion of faith; [7] or if service, let us serve faithfully in that service; or the one who teaches, teach faithfully in that teaching . . .
> [10] Love one another warmly in brotherly love; show honor to

---

60. Davies, "Two Ages," 345-54; Harris, *Second Epistle to the Corinthians*, 434.

61. Eastman, "Participation in Christ," 11; see also Kruse, *2 Corinthians*, 124.

62. One must be careful when discussing "Paul's ethical framework." Victor Furnish notes that "the study of the Pauline ethic, therefore, is not the study of his ethical theory, for he had none . . . [but] the study, first of all, of the theological convictions which underlie Paul's concrete exhortations and instructions and, secondly, of those convictions [which] shape his response to practical questions of conduct" (Furnish, *Theology and Ethics in Paul*, 211-12). In other words, the Christic σῶμα is of foremost importance for Paul and ethical formation is secondary.

one another. [11] Do not be slothful in zeal, but be burning in spirit, serving the Lord. [12] Rejoice in hope; endure in tribulation; persevere in prayer. [13] Contribute to the financial needs of the saints; pursue hospitality.

[14] Bless those who persecute you; bless and do not curse. [15] Rejoice with those who rejoice; weep with those who weep . . . [19] Do not avenge yourselves, beloved, but give place to the wrath of God, for it is written, "Vengeance is mine, I will repay, says the Lord." [20] But "if your enemy is hungry, feed him; if he is thirsty, give him a drink; for in doing this you will heap coals of fire upon his head." [21] Do not be conquered by evil but conquer evil with good.

The beginning of Rom 12 corresponds with two issues discussed in 1 Cor 12: (a) members of the Christic σῶμα are identified with Christ (v. 5) yet simultaneously analogous to different members of a human body (v. 4); and (b) the differentiation of members is rooted in their respective functionalities (vv. 5–8). The rest of the passage (vv. 9–21) expands the somatically-engendered ethical framework of 1 Cor 12:22–26, including two shared exhortations: bestow honor upon other members (v. 10) and sympathize with them (v. 15).

However, beginning in v. 14 Paul urges members of the Christic σῶμα to engage with those not "in Christ"—a mode of engagement absent from 1 Cor 12. Paul contends that members of the Christic σῶμα should: bless persecutors (v. 14), live at peace with all humans (v. 18), feed their enemies (v. 20), and conquer evil with good (v. 21). Importantly, the entirety of vv. 9–21, which details much of Paul's somatically engendered ethical framework, emerges *from* his conception of the Christic σῶμα. Stated differently, these commitments are subsequent, not antecedent, to membership in the Christic σῶμα.

This begs the question: *why* does Paul deem it necessary to exhort members of the Christic σῶμα—*after* being initiated into a new age and new creation—to engage positively with those who remain in the old age and old creation? In Stoic ethics, positive engagement is based on a common identity that all human beings are part of the same body. For Paul, only believers comprise the Christic σῶμα. What, then, is the basis of Pauline ethics for those outside the body? The key is v. 14.[63] The believers' initiation into the Christic σῶμα creates controversy with the surrounding

---

63. For further reading on the relationship between persecution and the hortatory shift beginning in v. 14, see Jewett, *Romans*, 765; Longenecker, *Romans*, 938–41.

society in the form of persecution. Cognizant of this, Paul commands believers to "bless" (εὐλογεῖτε) the "out-group" who persecutes them "in a radically unnatural way."[64] Pauline ethics toward the outside is driven by what Richard Longenecker calls "the Christian love ethic."[65] Paul conceives of the Christic σῶμα as engaging in a love-filled outward witness to the non-Christic (often, anti-Christic) world.

Conclusion

Central to this essay was mapping the commonalities and particularities between Epictetus's and Paul's use of the body metaphor. At least two explicit commonalities exist: (1) a linguistic one; that is, Paul and Epictetus employ the same Greek word σῶμα which bypasses the bilingual interference of Latin if one were to compare, for example, Paul and Seneca; and (2) a conceptual and metaphorical one: both thinkers use σῶμα to portray a corporate entity where human beings are analogous to individual parts of the body.

Within this discussion of linguistic and conceptual issues, differences also exist. First, the Epictetan corporate σῶμα is (imprecisely) interchangeable with κόσμος and πνεῦμα. Paul, however, (precisely) identifies the corporate σῶμα with the person of Christ who is not identical with the κόσμος and is a distinct person from the πνεῦμα of the triune God. Second, Epictetus's cosmic σῶμα does not identify a particular "head," though his analogical relationship between the σῶμα and the city-state suggests that a governing official could be a possible analogue. However, Paul contends that the unique head of the Christic σῶμα is Jesus Christ, especially in other parts of his letter corpus (e.g., Col 1:18; Eph 4:15; 5:23; cf. Eph 1:22).

Undergirding each thinker's metaphorical corporate σῶμα are a series of (meta)physical presuppositions. For Epictetus, the cosmic σῶμα is composed of *all* human beings and is united both by πνεῦμα and their minds (indeed, minds are fragments of πνεῦμα). Any differentiation between beings is based solely upon their powers of reason (or lack thereof). Moreover, because Epictetus's cosmic σῶμα is the unique wellspring of being, human beings are inextricably tethered to their ontological embeddedness within the cosmic σῶμα. Like Paul, Epictetus analogously

---

64. Thielman, *Romans*, 592.
65. Longenecker, *Romans*, 932.

uses the parts of a human body to describe the interconnectedness of human beings in a corporate body; yet unlike for Paul, this imagery encompasses the entire human race. Epictetus also prioritizes the flourishing of the cosmic σῶμα above the parts (*Diss.* 2.10.5), even suggesting that individuals should welcome suffering and death if it benefits the cosmic σῶμα.

Paul's Christic σῶμα is narrower in scope as it only includes human beings who are "in Christ" (2 Cor 5:17). Such ones are initiated into the Christic σῶμα through an outward baptism and inward drinking of the Spirit (πνεῦμα). Unlike Epictetus, Paul conceptualizes the individuation of members as being rooted not in their power of reason, but rather in the *exercise* of their differing functionalities. Additionally, Paul assigns equal import to the flourishing of the corporate σῶμα and its constitutive members.

Turning to each thinker's somatically engendered ethical framework, Epictetus's prioritization of the cosmic σῶμα over its parts informed his conception of εὐδαιμονία. For all Stoics, εὐδαιμονία was accessible through one's exercising of wisdom to apprehend the ordering of the κόσμος and playing one's part within it. Moreover, Epictetus disregards social status and hierarchy and instead argues that all human beings are equal based upon their moral obligations to one another, and ultimately, to the cosmic σῶμα.

For Paul, the shared identity of Christians as members of the Christic σῶμα also diminishes the intrinsic value of hierarchal social status. Pauline equality requires concrete actions such as clothing dishonorable members with "more abundant honor," sympathizing with members, and financially contributing to their needs. Moreover, Paul directs the church's attention to those "outside" of the Christic σῶμα—something not compatible within an Epictetan monistic framework whereby every human being is already part of the body—and exhorts members to bless their persecutors, feed their enemies, conquer evil with good, and practice Christ-like love. Lastly, while Epictetus prioritizes the power of reason as crucial to forming (in-group) ethical commitments, Paul proposes that love is the foundation of both mutual in-group care and out-group witness.

In a recent monograph, Max Lee offers a typology of six basic interactions between Greco-Roman philosophies. Of them, Paul's and Epictetus's shared employment of a corporate σῶμα is, in my opinion, an example of a "common ethical usage" defined as "the appropriation of language and concepts that do not, or no longer, belong to any one school but are part of a larger encyclopedia of knowledge shared between all philosophical schools and moral traditions in the Greco-Roman world."[66] The metaphorical use of the body for corporate identity and ethical practice was not confined to philosophical or religious texts. Texts on political concord, for example, also employ the corporate σῶμα to emphasize both the diversity and unity of group members.[67] However successful the above comparative exercise between Epictetus and Paul may have been, it is without question that future scholarship may uncover other ancient writers who draw upon the common ethical usage of the body metaphor. This essay modestly offers a comparative analysis of Epictetan discourse alongside Paul's Christic σῶμα in the hopes of illuminating both thinkers' (meta)physical concepts and resultant ethical frameworks.

---

66. The other five are eclecticism, refutation, competitive appropriation, irenic appropriation, and concession (Lee, *Moral Transformation*, 494).

67. See, Mitchell, *Paul and the Rhetoric of Reconciliation*, 68–83; 157–64; Martin, *Corinthian Body*, 38–68; 87–103.

12

Paul: Theologian, Historian, or Something Else?

RIKK WATTS

THE DISCUSSION OF PAUL'S use of Scripture remains fraught. We have had much sound, and if not fury, at least some squalls,[1] but nothing yet signifying anything like a consensus. In this chapter, after a review of some key interpreters, I will suggest that perhaps one reason why equally well-informed and good-willed interpreters come to such divergent opinions is because we start in the wrong place. As the title indicates, the bulk of this essay begins with a general comparison of Hellenism's two main ways of knowing: philosophy/theology and history. I will suggest that Paul is far closer in his thinking to Hellenic historians than philosophers/theologians. But even then, significant differences put him more in the camp of a first-century CE Jewish understanding of Israel's prophets as inspired and far superior historians. That is, while Paul is clearly not writing history per se, his essential paradigm is history, as he understood it, in which the key "agent" is YHWH. The essay will conclude with a short examination of Rom 9 as a test case for how this approach might help us better appreciate Scriptures' normative historical status for Paul.

1. See, e.g., Watson, "Paul the Reader," 363–73; Barclay, "Faithfulness of God," 235–43.

An Overview

What follows is admittedly selective and at times almost aphoristic.[2] However, its purpose is primarily to illustrate the range of explanations covering Paul's engagement with Scripture and to note some key rising issues.

For Christopher Stanley, although Paul had a deep respect for Scripture, Paul did not derive his ideas from it. Instead, his use of Scripture was governed not by its context but his own; namely, he was asserting his authority over his immediate audience.[3] For others, such as Douglas Campbell, Paul's context is primarily christological—that is, Scripture must be read in the radically disjunctive light of Christ.[4]

While not denying that Paul, like the prophets before him, addressed his own context and at times had to assert his apostolic authority, Stanley's view of Paul's "deep respect for Scripture" strikes me as impossibly anachronistic for someone who sees Scripture as the unfailing oracles of the one true creator God (Rom 3:2; 9:6). Likewise, one can hardly overemphasize the eschatological significance of the Lord Jesus for Paul (e.g., 1 Thess 1:1; 1 Cor 8:6),[5] compelling him to reconsider his previous understanding of some (surely not all!) Scripture. Nevertheless, his pervasive use of "Lord" and "Christ," to say nothing of his arguments in Galatians and in Rom 9–11, is intelligible only on the basis of Scripture's independent and continuing authority. That Paul uses the same "word of God" terminology for Scripture (Rom 9:6) and the gospel of the Lord Jesus (e.g., 1 Cor 14:36; 1 Thess 2:13) suggests rather an inherent continuity and correlation.

Francis Watson, rejecting such dichotomous approaches, recontextualizes Paul in a three-way dialogue between Scripture, Jesus, and Paul's contemporary "non-Christian" Jewish interpreters.[6] The Lord Jesus cannot be understood apart from Scripture even while Scripture will

---

2. Unquestionably, these authors' nuanced treatments deserve far more detailed attention than I can give here. My comments, clearly, are more indicative than exhaustive.

3. Stanley, *Arguing with Scripture*.

4. Campbell, *Quest for Paul's Gospel*.

5. "Lord" here reflects Paul's apparent identification of Jesus with the Lord of the *Shema*, as per 1 Cor 8:6. The profound implications of Paul's prioritizing Jesus' identity as Israel's Lord over Christ (as per the above references, cf. also Mark 12:35–37 *par.*) have yet to be fully appreciated in discussions of Paul's engagement with Scripture.

6. Watson, *Hermeneutics of Faith*.

continue to be misinterpreted apart from him.⁷ The only caveat I would add is that the Jewish dialogue is not "equi-valent." I cannot see where Paul explicitly engages, for example, either Qumran or Philo, let alone with anywhere near the same intense attention and specificity he gives to the mutually informing and mutually endorsing "dialogue" between Scripture and the Lord Jesus.

The reason for this, I suggest, is that for Paul, what unites Scripture and the Lord Jesus is his "YHWH Christology" (e.g., 1 Cor 8:6; Deut 6:4; cf. 1 Thess 1:1). The very Lord whose oracles constitute Scripture, was also uniquely present in the Jesus who called Paul to be his apostle. Diminishing the independent and normative authority of Scripture's history only undermines the identity of the Lord Jesus whose servant and apostle he is. On the contrary, if one begins with creation and Abraham (cf. Galatians, Romans), the Scriptures and the Lord Jesus are mutually confirming. Since YHWH's words and deeds in the present must necessarily be consistent with his words and deeds in the past,⁸ Paul's hermeneutic is not a matter of deconstructively positioning Jesus (Christology) against Scripture, but correcting his own previously mistaken reading of parts of Scripture so as to honor the integrity of both. The pieces of the scriptural tapestry retain their own integrity, both individually and collectively. The change is that they are now part of that bigger picture they themselves promised and which finds fulfillment and ultimate cohesion in the Lord Jesus. Of course, the "trick" lies in our trying to understand how Paul sees this working out. Hence, others focus on his hermeneutical techniques.

Richard Hays's recent works suggest that he would now regard aspects of Paul's use of Scripture as essentially "figural."⁹ What Hays's figural

---

7. See, e.g., Ps 22, held to be written by David, must surely then be Messianic, which the Synoptics' account of Jesus' singular use presumes, even if Israel's interpretative tradition generally did not.

8. Foulkes's assessment (*Acts of God*, 9) bears quoting in full: "One of the deepest convictions that the prophets and historians of Israel had about the God in whom they trusted, and whose word they believed they were inspired to utter, was . . . that he had not left them in ignorance of his nature and purpose. Rather he had revealed himself to them, and had shown himself to be a God who acted according to principles, principles that would not change as long as sun and moon endured. They could assume, therefore, that as he had acted in the past, he could and would act in the future. By such an assumption the whole of the Old Testament is bound together and given unity."

9. Hays, *Reading Backwards*; Hays, *Echoes of Scripture in the Gospels*.

reading, Matthew Bates's "prosopological" proposal,[10] the older *sensus plenior*, and ancient allegorical approaches have in common is their attempt "technically" to "make sense" of Paul's use of Scripture where it does not fit the otherwise normal reading practices presupposed in his letters. They do this by postulating some kind of "reconciling" additional meaning to Scripture as it stands.

In terms of Paul's Hellenistic environment, allegorical interpretation historically provided Stoic and Neo-Platonist philosophers an innovative and intellectually impressive means of "saving the appearances"[11] of their foundational Hellenic myths. In a brilliant reverse engineering of already ancient allegory, they were able to impose later and more acceptable philosophical interpretations upon the original surface of Homer and Hesiod. Granted, Bates does not strictly allegorize, but he does interject the voices of persons who are not evidently in the original text;[12] *sensus plenior* does something similar by having God intend more than the original text expresses. But there is more. Since theology and physics were co-extensive for the Stoic immanentist, allegorizing became (for Chrysippus) the way to discern the eternal truth under the veil of the changeful physical, and thus (for Cleanthes) itself constitutive of theology.[13]

What infuriated Celsus and Porphyry was the incoherent and exegetically inappropriate Christian allegorizing of texts that were clearly not myths, having only a shameful, stupid, and inept literal meaning.[14] But Paul's solitary occurrence of the verb (ἀλληγορούμενα; Gal 4:24) strongly suggests his use is exceptional and, in any case, is likely not even a true allegorical reading. In this text, the formation of two families and arguably two "covenants" (Gen 21:17–21)—one by human effort and the other by God's provision and both in seeking the fulfillment of Abraham's promise—is precisely the point of the original story.

---

10. Bates, *Hermeneutics*, who cites ancient instances in Philo and even earlier in Heraclitus. Although Bates recognizes his "prosopological" solution only pertains to a tiny fraction of Paul's engagements with Scripture—Rom 10:6–8, 16; 11:9–10; 15:3, 9; and 2 Cor 4:13—he nevertheless considers it of critical hermeneutical significance.

11. Cf. Duhem, *To Save the Phenomena*, and the critique of Lloyd, "Saving the Appearances," 202–22. I use allegory here in the Stoic sense proposed by the latter.

12. Bates, *Hermeneutics*, 183.

13. Ramelli, "Philosophical Stance," 335–71. This seems to call into question Auerbach's claim that allegory belongs to the historical realm whereas *figura* connects the sacred and the secular (*Mimesis*, 74).

14. Origen, *Cels.* 4.48, 50, 51; 7.18; Eusebius, *Hist. eccl.* 6.19.4–8; see again, Ramelli, "Philosophical Stance."

Following Erich Auerbach,[15] Hays's "figural" reading is evident, for example, in Tertullian who emphatically affirms Scripture's literalness and historicity. But the problem lies in the remarkable flexibility of the word. In the writings of the Greek fathers, the most common word for prefiguration is τύπος. Rare in Paul, it seems better understood to function much more narrowly as a negative moral example.[16] Paul's use of Adam as such in Rom 5 is altogether different from Tertullian's where Eve being formed from the rib taken from a sleeping Adam's side is a figure of the church being formed out of Christ who was also wounded in his side and also slept in death (*De Anima* 43).[17] Paul's use respects Scripture's account of the universal impact of Adam's sin on all humanity.[18] But Tertullian's reading, for all his protestations, seems closer to the allegorizing imposition of an external meaning. It not only goes far beyond the original sense of both historical events but also, in deftly ignoring any discontinuities, effectively sublimates both originals to another agenda. Moreover, Tertullian's figural readings seem driven by an anxiety to shore up the importance of the Old Testament in response to pagan critics.[19] This approach seems entirely foreign to Paul for whom Scripture's authoritative history is nonpareil, regardless of what pagan philosophers might benightedly think (cf. Acts 17:18). They are, after all, in the wrong history.[20]

According to Auerbach, figural reading arises from Paul's conviction that the Old Testament—an expression Paul himself nowhere uses—was no longer for him about the law and history of Israel but "from beginning to end a promise and prefiguration of Christ, in which there is no definitive, but only a prophetic meaning."[21] Again, as argued above, this reductively dichotomous approach seems entirely foreign to Paul, not least given his opening declaration of Israel's continued priority in the one place where he gives his most extended, and scripturally dense,

15. Auerbach, "Figura," 11–76.
16. DiMattei, "Biblical Narratives," 59–93.
17. Auerbach, "Figura," 28–30.
18. Paul has no interest in philosophical/theological speculation as to the mechanics; he merely cites the uncompromising evidence—all now die.
19. A similar apologetic intention is at work in Auerbach, which apparently led to his "wrong and unwarranted" distinction between allegorical and figural; see Zakai and Weinstein, "Erich Auerbach," 320–38.
20. Rowe, "Grammar of Life," 31–50.
21. Auerbach, "Figura," 51.

understanding of the matter (Rom 9:4–6). Why not, instead, have a more nuanced "both-and" approach to history and prophecy?

Even if one silences doubts over the handful of proffered Pauline prototypes, the number and variety in the fathers' figural interpretations simply proliferates, like Nietzsche's moustache, beyond any reasonable proportion. It is hard to avoid the impression that the impetus for "figural" reading lies not with Paul but his later interpreters. First, their defending the Old Testament through figural reading already presumes an inherent devaluation of the unique status of Israel and the Scriptures, a devaluation simply not found in Paul. Second, their view that reality by its very nature needs figural unveiling seems more Stoic and Platonist than scriptural and Pauline.[22]

To return to our main concern, while it might be that Paul has a range of hermeneutical techniques upon which to draw, the question is not only whether he does (and if so which) but more importantly whether our proposals have genuine explanatory power. Do they provide a predictive account such that one can anticipate which scriptural texts, under what conditions, and in what contexts will be read in such ways? That is, do these techniques tend instead to explain away difficult readings of Paul? It may be that Paul is characteristically *ad hoc* in his treatment of Scripture. But this hardly coheres with the tenor of his argumentation overall or those numerous occasions where his use of Scripture is not problematic. Rather, Paul's choice of scriptural text—on my detailed examination over the years—could not be bettered given the argument he makes. What a satisfying explanation requires is a coherent account—that is, internally consistent with his thinking elsewhere—of why Paul applies a proposed hermeneutical "technique" to a given reading at a given point in his argument.

Finally, while I appreciate Ephraim Radner's concerns, his theological universalizing of the experience of "exile"[23] effectively elides the historical uniqueness of Israel's covenantal election—which Paul's gospel (and in terms of this paper, Rom 9–11) presuppose. Sharing a shattering sense of displacement is not the same thing as being judicially exiled by the sole creator, YHWH, for specific acts of Mosaic covenant unfaithfulness. Paul's point in Acts 17 is not an implied universalism whereby an idolatrous Athens inadvertently worships YHWH without knowing it.

22. Auerbach, "Figura," 58.
23. Radner, *Time and the Word*.

Paul's point, as noted above, is that Athens and the pagan world stand in the wrong history, that is, not Israel's. Their ignorance can only be remedied by being grafted into an Israel reconstituted around the Lord Jesus.

By way of stark contrast, the normative particularity of Israel's scriptural narrative lies at the heart of N. T. Wright's novel and equally controversial Pauline theology.[24] For Wright, because of Israel's unique status (e.g., Rom 9:4–5), their particular history of election, land, exile, and return—programmatically summarized by Deuteronomy's "song of Moses"—provides the narrative substructure of Pauline theology.[25] In its current canonical position as the conclusion to the Torah, Deut 27–30's succinct prophetic arc is so well-suited and so well-placed as to appear deliberate in preparation for the much larger trajectory of the subsequent prophets.[26]

As a footnote to this selective survey, two points should be made. First, although the concept of metanarrative was not specifically mentioned herein, it does appear scattered throughout the literature and often in critiques of positions like those of Wright. However, it is not at all clear that metanarrative is appropriate to Paul's first-century world. On the contrary, the word was coined by Jean-François Lyotard to unmask modernity's second-order, ideologically shaped, and "below-the-surface" narratives (e.g., freedom through science, education, economics, or politics) that were specifically designed to undermine traditional first-order (i.e., historical) accounts.[27] Neither Scripture nor Paul's narrative is either modern or "below-the-surface" second-order.

Second, even more common is the use of words like "story" to describe Paul's message. The problem here is that such words often connote the foregrounding of literary questions while intentionally bracketing out the historical. If so, they are equally anachronistic and unhelpful. There is nothing to suggest that Paul primarily read the Scriptures in merely literary terms, let alone that he considered them anything other than fundamentally historical, that is, reflecting what actually happened.

---

24. Wright, *Faithfulness of God*; cf. Barclay, "Faithfulness of God"; Moyise, "Wright's Understanding," 165–80.

25. See Wright's complaint: "I find Watson's account focused far too much on scripture as 'normative' and far too little on scripture as 'narrative,'" *Faithfulness of God*, 1459.

26. Cf. White, "Wright's Narrative," 181–204.

27. Lyotard, *Postmodern Condition*; see Westphal, *Overcoming Onto-theology*, xii–xv.

Paul in his Hellenistic Context: Philosophy/Theology and History

Where to from here? The purpose of this essay is not to propose a silver bullet resolution to what is clearly a complex problem. It is, however, to suggest another perspective that might enrich our understanding. Allowing the last to be first, I would like to pick up from Radner's theological approach. In spite of its near universal usage, I cannot see how Paul can be called a theologian, at least not in any sense recognizable in the first century.

In Paul's broader Hellenistic cultural environment, there were essentially two kinds of knowledge: *philosophia/theologia* and *historia*. Although both began with the senses and involved thought, the critical difference between them arose from the Hellenic conviction that the mind could only grasp that which did not change. One of the first insights of the Hellenes was that the objects of mathematics met this criterion. The mark of genuine truth was that it could be demonstrated using only the resources of the human mind.

In meeting this criterion, *philosophia*—of which *theologia* was the pinnacle (except for the skeptics)—was considered to be knowledge proper, *episteme*. Its truths were eternal precisely because they were grounded in reason and hence uniquely demonstrable through dialectical argument. Although its meaning is debated, *theologia* appears to have been developed *ad hoc* by Plato to distinguish his "rational science" of divine things from the poets' (e.g., Homer and Hesiod) often misleading myths.[28]

It should be noted that "rational science" here means demonstration by logical argument proceeding from first principles, not the explanation based on experiment and testing that "science" generally connotes today.[29] Hence, for example, in order for Aristotle rationally to demonstrate the origin of change in the universe, heavier objects had to fall faster than lighter ones.[30] Similarly, for Plato, since the divine must be perfect, the gods cannot be protean and cannot deceive as the Homeric gods do (*Resp.* Π.380D–383C).

---

28. Naddaf, "Plato's Theologia Revisited," 1–17.

29. The distinction here between demonstration and explanation is deliberate. Demonstration does not explain; it only shows that something is logically coherent.

30. Gregory, "Dynamics and Proportionality," 1–21.

But several questions arise. Since, for example, heavy objects do not fall faster than light ones, how reliable is the assumption that reality conforms to Hellenic "rational science"? In terms of persons, how does the rigid necessity of mathematical demonstration intersect, in Israel's case, with YHWH's personhood, compassion, and ability and willingness to change his mind (celebrated at Sinai; Exod 31:14; cf. Jonah 3:9) or not (leading to the exile; Jer 15:1), as expressed in the declaration that God's ways are not our ways (Isa 55:8)?

The second kind of thought was *historia*, an empirical, semi-knowledge the Hellenes called *doxa*, meaning "opinion." Based on matters of perceptual fact, which are always changing, *historia*'s truth only held good for a limited time; for example: "Today ten carts arrived in Athens, and yesterday six." Both elements are true but only for a given period. Although dismissed as mere illusion by the Eleatics for whom change was impossible, Plato later rejected their extreme position. Granted *historia* was not "rational"—there is no logical necessity that determines the number of carts in Athens on any given day—but it was at least perceptible. The Stoics were equally aware of the limitations of the senses, but held, albeit contentiously, that there were some fundamental "cognitive impressions" upon which one could rely.[31] Even so, given its changeful nature, *historia* could never be a "rational science" nor the basis of one.

Paul, the Theologian?

By the time Paul wrote, the word *theologia* had already a four hundred years-long pedigree concerning things divine.[32] Nevertheless, the word and its cognates are rare when it comes to Israel's first-century understanding of its talk about God. They are never used in the LXX while *philosophia* or its cognates (φιλόσοφος/φιλοσοφέω) are found once in the longer LXX version of Daniel and minimally in the later and highly eclectic 4 Maccabees. In the former, it describes the elite of Babylon's wise men (Dan 1:20) who pale beside the vastly superior understanding of the four observant young Jewish exiles. In the latter, it initially stands in contrast to traditional Jewish devotion (4 Macc 5:7). Although that devotion is subsequently described, first by Antiochus, as "foolish" in contrast to "true" philosophizing (5:11), and then by Eleazar as "our" philosophy

---

31. Long and Sedley, *Hellenistic Philosophers*, 1:249–53.
32. Common since Plato, *Resp.* II.379A (ca. 380 BCE).

(5:22), the entire discourse, even while arguing for some rapprochement under reason, nevertheless presumes a fundamental tension between the two.[33]

Although Josephus commonly uses *philosophia* and its cognates when affirming Jewish learning to his educated Hellenistic audience, he uses the verb θεολογέω just once, of the Essenes' "theologizing" about the soul (*J.W.* 2.158). The noun appears on only three occasions: twice of the ancient thinking behind the naming of the Hyksos Egyptian city of Avaris (*Apion* 1.78, 237), and once of Israel's superior worship compared to the folly of Egypt (*Apion* 1.225). But he never uses these terms to describe the origins or nature of Scripture or how Israel knows YHWH.

A similar reluctance is found in Philo where, in contrast to his abundant use of *philosophia* and its cognates, *theologia* and its cognates occur just five times. The nominal ὁ θεολόγος is used four times to describe Moses (*Mos.* 2.115; *Praem.* 53; *QG* 2.59; 3.21) and once adjectivally to ennoble Moses' creation narrative (*Opif.* 12), perhaps with something like Plato's critique of Hesiod's *Theogony* in mind. This probably reflects Philo's larger program of using a common term in order not only to commend Judaism to the Hellenistic world but also to justify his use of allegorical reading. Though from a traditional philosophical standpoint, his insistence on the historicity of Scripture was incoherent (see above), even so, he never uses *theologia* of Scripture or how Israel came to know YHWH.

In the New Testament, neither *theologia* nor any of its cognates are found anywhere. No one, friend or foe, ever uses them, let alone employs them to describe what the authors of Scripture or the NT writings thought they were doing. This strongly suggests that no one, whether Paul himself or, again, his friends or foes, ever understood what he was doing as in any way related to Hellenism's theological project. If Paul was a theologian, it seems that neither he nor any of his contemporaries knew it.

Philosophia does appear in the NT writings, but just once (Col 2:8). Because, as we have seen above, Josephus and especially Philo regularly deploy the word when explaining positively Judaism to "pagans," some have argued that Paul (or someone very much in the Pauline orbit) similarly means some form of Hellenistic Jewish practice. But Paul is not explaining anything, definitely not to outsider pagans, and certainly not affirming it. Indeed, if this was his meaning and given his habit of

---

33. deSilva, *4 Maccabees*, ix–xxxviii.

preaching first in Hellenistic Jewish synagogues, why does he use the word only this once and so negatively?

Paul's was a culture permeated to varying degrees by the poet Homer, the tragedians Aeschylus, Sophocles, and Euripides, and the philosophers Plato, Aristotle, and the Stoics.[34] Paul's own associations with the educationally renowned Tarsus—and the Talmudic remark that over half of Gamaliel's one thousand students were familiar with Greek wisdom (b. Sotah 49b; Acts 22:3)—suggests that he too had, if not technical expertise in, at least familiarity with, the broader tradition.[35] However, the paucity of Paul's specific appeals to either particular philosophers or their particular views—and especially when compared to the hundreds of citations and allusions to Scripture—suggests not ignorance but a considered and deliberate marginalization. The philosophers/theologians offer the occasional point of contact, but they contribute nothing substantial to his knowledge of YHWH or the Lord Jesus, nor to his exposition of their words and deeds.

The assessment is apparently mutual. The only time those who practice *philosophia/theologia* are mentioned (Acts 17), they disdainfully distance themselves and their practices from Paul and his (17:18; cf. the attitudes of Celsus and Porphyry noted above). But since the reader already knows that Paul is emphatically God's ambassador, Luke's having his critics disparage Paul as a "σπερμολόγος" neatly turns the tables on them, unmasking their *theologia* as futile superstition and ignorance (Acts 17:22), to which, with profound irony, the dedication on Athens' own altar attests (17:23).[36] In the end, Luke's brilliant literary ostracism of Paul's opponents—via his purposeful lexical ambiguities and his transvaluing Hellenic traditions within Israel's totalizing history (17:26–31)—makes very clear both the intrinsic collision between Paul's preaching and the wisdom of the philosophers/theologians and consequently their outcomes.

At issue is Paul's proclamation of Jesus' resurrection (17:18b, 31b–32a), which, if Luke is any guide, was grounded in his shattering Damascus Road *historia*, an experience of such significance as to warrant

---

34. See, e.g., Klauck, *Religious Context of Early Christianity*, 331–428.

35. See, e.g., Menander in 1 Cor 15:3; Epimenides in Titus 1:12; cf. the reported allusions to certain philosophical commonplaces in Acts 17:27b–28a, and Aratus in Acts 17:28b.

36. Rowe, "Grammar."

three tellings.³⁷ That is, the reason for Paul's marginalizing Hellenistic *philosophia* is not that he and the moral philosophers dealt with radically different questions. They did not. Even their language on such matters could at points be similar.³⁸ It is, instead, because both the Scriptures' and Paul's way of knowing YHWH were categorically not what either he or the Hellenistic world would recognize as *philosophia/theologia*.³⁹ The heart of their mutual disregard lies at a more fundamental level, namely their very different, even incommensurate, ways of knowing and their outcomes. No Hellenic *theologia* could possibly arrive at a crucified Zeus, nor Paul's vision of human life. The gospel's offer of transformation goes far beyond what the moral philosophers envisaged. Its key characteristics—trust, hope, and care—were radically other-centered. Christian life was not a matter of personal discipline, but of the indwelling Spirit.⁴⁰

As we have seen, the foundational grammar of *philosophia* and hence *theologia* was what was capable of "rational" and hence "scientific" demonstration using only the resources of the trained, elite mind. But one looks in vain for any evidence of a dialectical demonstration in Paul's letters arising from putative first principles (or fundamental cognitive impressions) as one would expect of *philosophia/theologia*. Paul begins with an unquestioned confidence in Israel's and his own *historia*. In Israel's Scriptures—especially the paradigmatic Exodus event—and in the New Testament—especially the even more paradigmatic life of the Lord Jesus—the primary appeal is to the community's shared sensory experience.⁴¹ Their *historia* is what they all saw and heard, even when their experience challenged not only gentile but even Jewish expectation. This explains, as Ian Scott has argued, the significant differences between Paul's way of thinking—reflecting on story, experience, and the work of

---

37. Cf. Barclay, "Paul's Story," 133–56.

38. See, e.g., Malherbe who notes various similarities with regard to modes of speech, topics, imagery, and shared language (*Paul and the Popular Philosophers*); Wright, *Faithfulness of God*, 206–43; 1384–85.

39. The great majority of the some 2000 or more Greek words in Talmudic materials are in "midrashic rather than legal contexts," and concern "military affairs, politics, law, administration, trade, items of food, clothing, household utensils, and building materials, and almost never ideas"; see Feldman, "Hengel's *Judaism and Hellenism*," 377.

40. Rabens, *Holy Spirit and Ethics*.

41. Avrahami, *Senses of Scripture*; cf. 1 John 1:1–3.

the Spirit—and what one would normally expect of the Hellenistic "rational science of the divine."[42]

This does not at all mean that Paul did not think. He clearly did. The profound divergence begins very early, namely, with how he responded to what his senses told him.[43] Further, this fundamental difference can only be truly appreciated within the ἐκκλησία and on the basis of an unreserved, life-long commitment.[44] Given the above, I think it wise that we refrain from describing Paul as a theologian, at least in any meaningful first-century sense.

Paul and History?

On the other hand, a long line of studies have increasingly drawn attention to the narrative character of Paul's thought,[45] and Paul himself explicitly engages with elements of Israel's history (e.g., Gal 3:6–28; 4:21–31; 1 Cor 10; 2 Cor 3; Rom 5:12–21; Rom 9–11). As to his hundreds of citations and allusions to the Scriptures, it is likely that Paul shared Josephus's conviction. The latter not only affirmed the "historiographical" character of Israel's Scriptures—even if not Hellenic *historia*—but also asserted the far superior quality of its prophets' records to anything he, and even less the Greek historians, could offer.[46] Hence, as Arnaldo Momigliano noted, "to become a Jewish or Christian proselyte meant having to learn a new history—which was an operation understandable to any educated Greek."[47] Though Paul is clearly not writing history in the Greek manner—most of Paul's writing seems propositional[48]—his underlying mode of thought appears more amenable to a first-century historian.[49]

42. Scott, *Implicit Epistemology*.
43. Cf. Wright, *Faithfulness of God*, 1355–83.
44. Rowe, *One True Life*.
45. See, e.g., Hays, *Faith of Jesus Christ*; notably Wright, *People of God*, esp. 31–144; and *Faithfulness of God*, 456–537; cf. White, "Wright's Narrative"; also Witherington, *Paul's Narrative Thought World*. On the questions that abound as to the nature, number, and coherence of that narrative(s), with regard to Galatians and Romans, see the various essays in Longenecker, *Narrative Dynamics*.
46. Mason, "Prophecy in Roman Judea," 524–56; esp. 545–50.
47. Momigliano, "Fault of the Greeks," 9–19; esp. 18.
48. Marshall, "Response to A. T. Lincoln," 213–14.
49. Cf., e.g., Collingwood, *Idea of History*, 18–19, for whom "scientific" history begins with questions, is humanistic in that it focuses on what is done by humans, is

Unfortunately, we have very little first-century material with which to compare. Nevertheless, at the very least Paul appeals to eyewitness testimony. According to 1 Cor 15, his stated interest is not the variable "oral traditions" relating tales of historical fiction, but what Jan Vansina calls the oral history concerning events that happened in living memory (e.g., 1 Cor 15:4-8; cf. also 2 Pet 1:16; 1 John 1).[50] His own Damascus Road experience, like that of Israel at Sinai, was grounded in what he saw and heard. That is, like the early Hellenic and later Hellenistic historians, and unlike the philosophers/theologians, Paul's primary concern is not the timeless past nor ahistorical abstraction but recent events within a dateable history. Hence, in the one NT occurrence of ἱστορέω, Paul himself employs it to describe his Jerusalem visit "to inquire of / become acquainted with" Peter (Gal 1:18). Even if the latter sense is in view, it is difficult to imagine that they did not discuss Peter's recollections of the events of Jesus' life.

Given, too, Paul's experience in persecuting the church, one presumes he would know, as did Herodotus five centuries earlier, something about cross-examining witnesses and thereby subjecting Christian claims to "critical" assessment. He had, presumably, also been interrogated himself by Roman authorities in his own trials (Acts 13:6-12; 16:16-40; 18:1-18; 23:24-35; 24:1-26; 25:6-12). What is more, although an older view held the historians' moralizing to be detrimental to their project, it is now recognized as fundamental and integral to ancient Greek historiography, perhaps reflecting an accepted canon of moral lessons.[51] That is, while again not writing a first-century history, at various points Paul nonetheless explains why Christians look like they do and how they came to be (e.g., 1 Thessalonians; Gal 2; 3). He also uses records from Israel's past as moral lessons, examples, and warnings for his audience (τύποι; 1 Cor 10:6).

Further, Israel's YHWH Elohim is not a concept—much less one that the philosophers/theologians rationally construct to accord with their view of what must be rational reality. God is a person, even if emphatically not human. Persons are known through their unique histories,[52] and

---

rational in that it bases its answers on evidence, and is "self-revelatory since it exists to tell humans what they are by telling them what they have done."

50. Vansina, *Oral Tradition as History*.

51. Hau, *Moral History*.

52. See, e.g., Crites, "Narrative Quality of Experience," 291–311; Young and Saver, "Neurology of Narrative," 72–84; Carter, "Telling Times," 1–27.

in this sense their actions reveal their character.[53] Since experience comes to us in often inchoate and not necessarily related fragments, the critical move in understanding and representing ourselves lies in how we make sense of those experiences by forming them into a narrative.[54] Forming "historical" narratives is how we explain ourselves to ourselves.[55] It is arguably this concern that motivated Herodotus and his successors even if the latter displayed, in their search for "social laws," a conviction that the mind could only grasp that which did not change.

In Paul's case, however, to look to various humanly constructed narratives was manifestly to start in the wrong place. The only "narrative" that provided the one truly authoritative explanation of reality was Israel's scriptural history of God's dealings with his people, and through them, other nations and all of creation. It is not primarily human action, but God's character, intention, and deeds that become the basis of human self-understanding and the most important hermeneutical key to Paul's use of Scripture.[56]

Something Else?

There are, however, very significant differences between *historia* and Paul's writings. Paul, unlike either Herodotus or Polybius, engages with the origins of the Christian story as within living memory. More importantly, *historia* could only offer *doxa*, that is, mere opinion, and draw from it some general principles by which to live. For Paul, however, scriptural history is anything but "mere opinion." Instead, being inspired by YHWH, it is normative and far more trustworthy than either philosophy's or theology's "rational" *episteme*. Along a similar vein, Josephus distinguishes Israel's prophets from himself and other Hellenic historians (cf. Philo, *Spec.*1.65) when he states:

> They [Judean historical records] are not subjective compositions produced by initiative and inquiry. They came from divine instruction through inspired prophets—qualities long since gone . . . Only inspiration could have given him [Moses] and his

---

53. Beaumont, "Modality of Narrative," 125–39.
54. Beaumont, "Modality of Narrative," esp. 134–38.
55. Collingwood, *Idea of History*.
56. Watts, "How Do You Read?" 199–220.

successors authoritative insight into the real meaning of events in their own times, which no mere participant could see.[57]

Whereas in Greco-Roman histories, the gods have no grand design—only granting success or failure to human endeavours—Paul sees history as the unfolding of God's plan. God initiates an event (e.g., the call of Abraham, the Exodus, the Lord Jesus, or the latter's call of Paul himself) or responds to human action (e.g., Israel's cry in Egypt, their golden calf idolatry, their request for a king like the nations, their rejection of Jesus, or Paul's persecution of the Way). Even in the midst of Paul's agonized discussion of Israel's present condition, his initial assumption remains firm: "It is not as if the word of God has failed" (Rom 9:6).

Unlike Livy's or Tacitus's substantialist metaphysics where one's character or nature was fixed, for Paul, believers' characters not only can—but should be—transformed.[58] As a corollary then of YHWH's agency, humans being made in his image entails a much higher view of the significance of human agency and hence of genuinely meaningful change.[59]

These fundamental differences might explain why Paul avoids using the term "*historia*." While he is certainly closer to the historians than the philosophers, he is pursuing "a third way." But this way is hardly novel. Although it cannot be argued here, the prophetic phrasing echoed in Paul's own account of his being called by Christ (e.g., Jer 1:5; Isa 49:1 in Gal 1:15–16a), suggests that he too understands himself at least in some way as standing in the same tradition as acclaimed by Josephus—that of Israel's inspired prophets.[60] The prophets had been rooted in Israel's history,[61] eyewitnesses to God's intervention in their own living memory, and on occasion had presented their cases as trials. They had also been deeply concerned with Israel's "human" actions. At the same time, they too understood that the critical issue was not how Israel and the nations explained themselves to themselves—which in Hellenic terms would be no more than mere *doxa*—but that God's words and deeds were the only

---

57. Mason, "Prophecy in Roman Judea," 546–47.
58. Collingwood, *Idea of History*, 46–52.
59. Watts, "Rethinking Context," 158–77.
60. See, e.g., Sandnes, *Paul—One of the Prophets?*; Sandnes, "Prophet-Like Apostle," 550–64; Nicklas, "Paulus—der Apostel als Prophet," 77–104; Aernie, *Is Paul Also among the Prophets?*
61. Watts, "Exodus Imagery," 205–14.

basis for any genuine human self-understanding. They likewise understood themselves to be speaking by the Spirit for the One who sent them.

The significance of this "nearer-to-history-but-something-else" approach is at least threefold. First, at the risk of anachronism, Paul's position seems much closer to the positions of Vico, Croce, Collingwood, and slightly differently, Macmurray than of Descartes, where humans are not mere thinkers but agents and in our particular histories. For Vico, this means, to paraphrase, that we really only know what we ourselves have made (*verum et factum convertuntur*); similarly, Collingwood states that the only object of which humans can have complete knowledge is themselves.[62] History has an inescapably central place. This more integrated and perhaps holistic approach to knowing and acting might help us understand why Paul writes not abstract universal treatises but letters engaging individual communities in their unique settings. This also is why it is so difficult to disentangle his *paranesis* (with a nod to the ongoing debate) from his "theology"—he simply does not share the philosophers'/theologians' views of either God or what it means to be human.

Second, there is a shift from a primarily literary exercise (framed in terms of Paul's use of Scripture) to a more personal approach that stresses the priority of God's agency. So Paul states:

> All this is *from God* (ἐκ τοῦ θεοῦ), *who reconciled* us to himself through Christ, and *has given* us the ministry of reconciliation; that is, in Christ God *was reconciling* the world to himself, *not counting* their trespasses against them, and *entrusting* the message of reconciliation to us. So we are ambassadors for Christ, *since God is making* his appeal through us; we entreat you on behalf of Christ, be reconciled *to God* (2 Cor 5:18–20).

Paul also demonstrates his own deep personal commitment to, and love for, the person of Jesus (Phil 3:8–12).[63] If so, since Scripture, as noted above, was for him the unfailing oracles of the Lord God, perhaps we ought to speak less of Paul's use of Scripture than of Scripture's "use of Paul."

This Scripture is no mere literature or document. It is the living utterance of YHWH. Paul's creativity begins less with himself than with the God who speaks to us. Oddly, while most NT scholars would affirm in Paul the priority of God's act, their basic operational framework,

---

62. Morrison, "Vico's Principle of *Verum* is *Factum*," 579–95.
63. Brown, *Introduction to the New Testament*, 446–55.

nevertheless, suggests an emphasis on Paul's own creative literary and rhetorical skills in spite of Scripture's long prophetic tradition that the agency of any prophet originates with the utterance of YHWH. I doubt very much that Paul would even comprehend the idea that his own creative originality had any crucial role to play. What he says, he gets from the Spirit (of Jesus; Phil 1:19; cf. Acts 16:7), bearing in mind the rare occasion when he offers his own opinion (e.g., 1 Cor 7:12).

Third, designers tell us that in a world gifted with the possibility of genuine agency, every "design" choice reflects the designer's character. This is simply to underline what we already know: foundational to Scripture is the revelation of YHWH's unique character which, through the authoritative prophetic records of his words and deeds, provides the "historical" basis for all human meaning. Returning to our original question—Paul's use of Scripture, but now reframed in terms of Scripture's (and YHWH's) shaping of Paul—we can now ask: what might this "agency or character" hermeneutic look like in practice?

In Practice

Here we only have space for an overview of Paul's argument in Rom 9:1–26, chosen because of the sheer volume and number of scriptural references. Given the specific aims of this section—to show how a prophetic "historical" mindset might work and make (better) sense of scriptural allusions (than a *theologia* or *historia* mindset would)—I will try to keep the argument as uncluttered as possible. For what follows, I offer not a detailed exegetical defense for a particular reading but a "thought experiment" of reading Rom 9 from the vantage point of a prophetic-historical address.

The problem in Rom 9–11 seems clear. Since Israel's identity is so entwined with Torah observance, what happens to Israel's place in God's plan, let alone God's own integrity, when his eschatological righteousness has been revealed apart from Torah, and in the Lord Jesus, whom Israel, by and large, has rejected? Paul's first and emphatic point is that Israel's priority remains (Rom 9:1–5) precisely because, as the approach here also assumes, a faithful God's word cannot fail. Hence, when Paul finally addresses gentiles in Rom 11, there is no "new" gentile church; they are all grafted into Israel, albeit reconstituted around the Lord Jesus (e.g., Rom 1:4, 7; 4:24; 5:21). This is entirely in keeping with the Torah and the prophets where gentile participation in the Lord God's people—whether in the first Exodus or the second—comes on the "coattails" of his redemption of Israel, even if only a remnant.

The problem is not with God's word—since it does not fail (9:6a)—but with "Israel" (9:6b–13). In keeping with the Scriptures' witness and a wide range of first-century Jewish opinion, not all Israel is Israel and not all of Abraham's children are his true descendants (9:6–7b). So, what makes Israel, Israel? I think the burden of Paul's argument is that the same merciful character of faithful YHWH—which directed his formation of, and subsequent dealings with, Israel in the past—has not changed. It is exactly what directs God's actions in his redemptive re-creation of his renewed Israel through the gospel of the Lord Jesus in the present.

In a concise and skillful summary of only some six verses (9:9–14), Paul arcs Israel's entire scriptural history showing that God's call from beginning to end was independent of any human claim, whether of works or bloodline. It begins in 9:9 with an account of God's promise to the first patriarch Abraham and concludes in 9:13 with the statement: "I have loved Jacob, but I have hated Esau," which draws from Mal 1:2b–3a. Malachi's final, post-exilic reference to Jacob and Esau neatly harks back to Paul's account of the patriarchal beginning of these same characters. The reference reminds his readers of the long history, from the patriarchs to the failed return, of Israel's characteristic waywardness and yet God's equally long merciful response.

Noting that Paul's text (9:13) is from Malachi is critical to the following rational complaint in 9:14a and Paul's response beginning in 9:14b. It is not, as often misread, questioning the justice of God in his arbitrary choice of one individual over the other. It is instead a very specific question arising from Israel's "historic" prophetic records. How can a just God—whose character stands at the core of everything, including Israel's very own identity—continue to show mercy to Jacob-Israel, even in the face of the returnee's post-exilic rebellion? But this is precisely the wrong question, as Paul's "you-haven't-been-listening" μὴ γένοιτο implies (9:14b). If, as Paul has just shown during the patriarchal period, Israel's call was never about "justice," why suddenly suppose that what follows with the Exodus or Christ should be any different? The foundational rubric upon which everything depends is uniquely YHWH's revealed and unchanging character.

In what comes next (9:15–18), Paul turns to perhaps the most stunning revelation of YHWH's character in Israel's history. Their outrageous golden calf apostasy was astonishingly met by YHWH's self-defining mercy and compassion. For Paul, Israel's *epistemic* (as opposed to *doxic*) "historical" account shows that the stiff-necked nation's relationship to YHWH was never about justice. What the prophetic records demonstrate is God's overwhelming predisposition to show mercy—here especially to his people—a mercy which lies at the very heart of his electing purposes. Once again we hear the near refrain: Israel's priority does not depend on either their will or exertion, but on God, as agent, whose character is revealed in his unexpected mercy (9:16).

However, returning to the justice question, this does not mean that God does not care about wickedness, or that Israel can do as it pleases. Here Paul again goes back to the Torah and the prophetic records of the foundational exodus event—God had also raised up Pharaoh (9:17a). I suspect this is a reference to his provision for Egypt through Joseph, without which Egypt would have been devastated, and by which means Pharaoh's exodus descendant came to the summit of his power. In the one pharaoh, we see God's power, first in his mercy in sustaining Pharaoh's forebears and then in his hardening Pharaoh (v.17b). Thus, the decision to show mercy or to harden lies with God (v.18).

It is the deliberate shift from justice to hardening (9:18b) that points toward the proper context for understanding the following "potter and his pot" argument (9:19–21). The key here is to recognize that the "potter/pot" language only occurs in Scripture concerning those who are already under judgment for high-handed sin against YHWH. Consequently, hardening refers to God's righteous judgment on a pharaoh who had already hardened his heart by drowning the offspring (Exod 1) of the one who, in a demonstration of God's merciful power, had earlier not only saved his kingdom but in the process increased his power. Such treatment of one's benefactor was heinous, even in terms of Egypt's own moral expectations. In this reading, there is no injustice. The time for Pharaoh's trial and sentence has come (9:20–21). Yet Pharaoh, even as an object of God's righteous wrath, received much divine patience so that God might make known both his power and mercy to Israel, whom he had earlier called (9:22–23).

For Paul this same unchanging character of YHWH is, of course, evident in the present (9:24–26). On the one hand, if God can endure with much patience an obdurate and consequently hardened Pharaoh, how can he, even in the face of Israel's present rejection of the Lord Jesus, not show the same patient endurance? After all, God's word has not and cannot fail. On the other hand, since this same merciful God had once promised a faithless "no nation" Israel that he would one day again own them as his people, why could he not offer the same for "not my people" gentiles? His character has not changed. The only change has been the breadth of, and access to, his mercy. The key to understanding the present is to understand the past. God's word, in faithfully reflecting his changeless character, has not failed but remains true.

Conclusion

Against his Hellenistic cultural background, Paul can hardly be considered a theologian, at least in any meaningful first-century sense. He thinks far more like an historian, though with significant differences. His conception of "history" is fundamentally focused on what God as agent revealed about himself in Israel's unique prophetic record. That prophetic revelation—a part of a long-standing tradition in which Paul, as an apostle of the Lord Jesus, now participates—is also the basis for his fundamental "historical" hermeneutic: that is, the acts of Israel's faithful God in the past provide the paradigmatic template for Paul's understanding of God's work in the present.

Part IV:

Practicing Intertextuality in the General Letters

13

Precedents for Prosopological Exegesis and Features of Its Use in the Epistle to the Hebrews

MADISON N. PIERCE

IN 1959, G. B. Caird changed the landscape of Hebrews studies through his article on the exegetical method. His aim is in part to show that the exegesis of Hebrews is neither (exclusively) "Alexandrian" nor "fantastic." He took important steps to show that the author of Hebrews uses Scripture to ground his overall argument using quotations to demonstrate the "confessed inadequacy" of the old covenant.[1] In the decades since Caird's article appeared, many studies examined the selection and interpretation of Scripture in the epistle to the Hebrews. This essay stands among them with a focus on a particular ancient reading strategy—prosopological exegesis. In what follows I will, first, provide some background to this reading strategy. Second, I will propose some connections between prosopological exegesis and classical rhetorical education and literary criticism. Third, I will speak generally about the use of this

1. Caird, "Exegetical Method," 47.
*Parts of this essay are taken from chapter 1 of my book *Divine Discourse in the Epistle to the Hebrews*, used here with permission from Cambridge University Press. Many thanks are due to my graduate assistant Lauren Januzik for her work on an earlier draft.

technique in Hebrews and elsewhere in the New Testament. Fourth and finally, I will offer a more detailed reading of Heb 1:10–12 in light of this phenomenon.

Hebrews' Reading Strategy for Divine Discourse

Our typical medium of intentional communication is speech. While our actions and demeanor provide additional knowledge about our character, often what we say is what we choose to reveal to the outside world. In the epistle to the Hebrews, the Father, Son, and Spirit speak to one another and to the contemporary audience, revealing themselves to any so privileged to overhear or be addressed. With this portrayal, the author of Hebrews allows them to speak for themselves. It is, after all, one thing for the author of Hebrews to say, "Jesus is God and Lord," but it is another entirely for *God the Father* to say to Jesus, "You are from the beginning, O Lord" (1:10), and "Your throne, O God, is forever" (1:8).[2] Similarly, although the author appears to have authority within the congregation to which he is writing, his exhortations cannot muster the force of the Spirit's insistence: "Today, if you hear his voice, do not harden your hearts" (3:7). While the fact that the author of Hebrews cites Scripture as speech rather than written text has often been noted, the exegetical method used by the author has not been sufficiently examined. This is particularly problematic because the method that Hebrews utilizes has its own set of underlying assumptions that have been obscured.

The ancient exegetical technique known as "prosopological exegesis"[3] interprets texts by assigning "faces" (πρόσωπα), or characters, to ambiguous or unspecified personal (or personified) entities represented in the text in question. In other words, interpreters identify new participants for clarity of understanding. While some have formulated definitions that refer explicitly to the identification of speakers (e.g., Downs),[4] it is necessary also to include the identification of addressees

---

2. All Eng. trans. from the Bible are my own unless otherwise noted.

3. Carl Andresen uses the term "prosopographic exegesis" (Andresen, "Zur Entstehung," 1–39), but Marie-Josèphe Rondeau suggests that "prosopological exegesis" should be preferred since "prosopographic" already has an established meaning. See Rondeau, *Les commentaires*, 2:8n7. Matthew Bates goes a step further by arguing that "prosopological exegesis presupposes the divine *Logos* . . . as the ultimate author" (Bates, *Hermeneutics*, 218). See also Bates, "Justin Martyr," 538–55.

4. Downs, "Prosopological Exegesis," 279.

and subjects through this technique. Prosopological exegesis does not merely disambiguate but instead views the text through the lens of a new participant. For example, Justin Martyr uses this technique to consider Jesus not only as the speaker of Ps 22:1 on the cross, as presented in the Synoptic Gospels, but also as the "I" in the entire psalm:[5]

> And when the prophetic Spirit speaks from the person of Christ [ἀπὸ προσώπου τοῦ Χριστοῦ], it is proclaimed in this way: . . . "They cast lots for my garment and pierced my hands and feet, but I lie down and sleep and rise again because the Lord has helped me." And again, when he says, "They spoke with their lips; they shook their head, saying, 'He must save himself'" (1 Apol. 38.1, 4–6).[6]

In the base text, the psalm, the "I" is unidentified, which provides Justin with the interpretive freedom to assign this text to Christ. He uses the psalm to illuminate Christ and his humanity. Marie-Josèphe Rondeau suggests that "the exegete is led to distinguish that which Christ says as a human and to analyze the elements of his personality."[7] Although the word "exegesis" implies a lengthy discussion of the text, that often is not the case, particularly in the earliest examples. An interesting aspect of this phenomenon is its relative brevity. Simply by assigning a text a new "face," a dialogical relationship is established where the text assumes previous knowledge of the character, and the character is thus illuminated further by the text. Therefore, when the author of Hebrews presents the Father saying to Jesus, "You are my Son; today, I have begotten you" (1:5), he is both illuminating Scripture and teaching his audience about Jesus—the Son of God.

The formula exhibited by the quotation above (ἀπὸ προσώπου . . .) along with the parallels in Latin and with other prepositions occurs several times in Justin's writing, as well as in other writers of this time. Although Christ is a common character in prosopological exegesis, this

---

[5]. The Gospels also portray Jesus as the "I" throughout, but through allusions—a sort of "narrative" prosopological exegesis.

[6]. Hebrews also uses this technique to interpret Ps 22:22 as spoken by Jesus. These citations of Justin are from Marcovich, *Iustini Martyris*, and all Eng. trans. are my own unless otherwise noted.

[7]. "[L]'exégète est amené à distinguer ce que le Christ dit en tant qu'homme et à analyser les éléments de sa personnalité" (Rondeau, *Les commentaires patristiques*, 2:10).

technique is by no means limited to christological readings. Justin describes several modes of "hearing" prophecy:

> But when you [plural] hear the speech of the prophets spoken as from a character [ὡς ἀπὸ προσώπου], you must not consider it to be spoken from the inspired themselves, but from the divine Word who moves them. For sometimes he declares the things that are to come as one who foretells the future; other times it is proclaimed from the person of God the Lord and Father of all; other times from the person of Christ; and other times as from the person of the people answering its Lord and Father (*1 Apol.* 36.1–2).[8]

When Justin assumes his readers will "hear" speech "from a character," he assumes that they too will see the disjunction or ambiguity in these texts. He shows that prosopological exegesis can occur with divine or human participants. These modes are intended to provide *examples* of the ways that his readers could interpret these texts—these are not the only perceivable characters. So with this statement, Justin is both reading these texts and teaching others how to read. The underlying assumption of the latter is key. If Justin thinks they will hear the words "from a character," then he assumes that prosopological exegesis is something that most of his readers will also be able to practice. But how? Some clues might be found in Greco-Roman educational practices.

Classical Precedents for Prosopological Exegesis

Prosopological exegesis, fully developed in patristic authors, likely has some parallels in classical training and literary criticism. Authors in the ancient world were expected to create characters with a unique and consistent "voice." In the rhetorical or "schoolbook" exercises (*progymnasmata*) attributed to Theon (first century CE), for instance, the author praises Homer for "his ability to attribute the right words to each of the characters he introduces" (*Prog.* 1).[9] The "right words" are those words

---

8. In *Dial.* 36.38, the Holy Spirit speaks "either from the person of His Father or from His own person (ἢ ἀπὸ προσώπου τοῦ πατρὸς ἢ ἀπὸ τοῦ ἰδίου)." This seems to counter Michael Slusser's suggestion that "the Holy Spirit does not appear as an interlocutor" (Slusser, "Exegetical Roots of Trinitarian Theology," 476).

9. Eng. trans. by Kennedy, *Progymnasmata*, 4. The consensus is that the handbook attributed to Theon is authentic to the first century, although concerns have been raised. For a comprehensive survey of the literature, see King, *Speech-in-Character, Diatribe, and Romans 3:1–9*, 38–39.

that the rhetorician judges to be appropriate based on his knowledge of the character both within and outside this composition—in the writings of others who draw upon these same "faces." Similarly, the exercises attributed to Hermogenes (second to fourth century CE) outline how one might create or imitate a known character:

> you will preserve what is distinctive and appropriate to the persons imagined as speaking and to the occasions, for the speech of a young man differs from that of an old man, and that of one who rejoices from that of one who grieves (*Prog.* 9).[10]

Based on the characters' "distinctive" and "appropriate" elements, students could practice their skills with "speech in character" exercises. Some prompts from the exercises attributed to Libanius are:

> What would Achilles say over the dead Patroclus?[11]
> What words would Odysseus say to the Cyclops when he sees him eating his comrades?[12]
> What words would a eunuch say when he falls in love?[13]

After each of these prompts, Libanius offers a short example of the sort of speech to be expected.

Although the handbooks attributed to Libanius and Hermogenes are examples after the first century, they fit (broadly) with earlier exercises and instruction. Some of the earliest evidence of this training is attested among historians.[14] For example, Lucian (second century CE) says:

> If a person has to be introduced to make a speech, above all let his language suit his person (ἐοικότα τῷ προσώπῳ) and his subject, and next let these also be as clear as possible. It is then, however, that you can play the orator and show your eloquence.[15]

While Lucian's comment acknowledges that the voice of the orator would be heard alongside the speaker, the priority is characteristic speech.[16]

---

10. Eng. trans. by Kennedy, *Progymnasmata*, 85; King, *Speech-in-Character, Diatribe, and Romans 3:1–9*, 45–46.

11. See Gibson, *Libanius's Progymnasmata*, 365–67 (Speech in Character 3).

12. See Gibson, *Libanius's Progymnasmata*, 415–16 (Speech in Character 24).

13. See Gibson, *Libanius's Progymnasmata*, 421–23 (Speech in Character 26).

14. The following examples are found in Marguerat, *First Christian Historian*, 1–25. Many thanks are due here to Max J. Lee for bringing this to my attention.

15. Lucian, *How to Write History*, 58; Eng. trans. by Kilburn, LCL, 6:70.

16. In addition to Marguerat, for more on speeches in Acts, see Padilla, *Speeches of Outsiders in Acts*.

This also reflects earlier language from Thucydides (fifth century BCE) in *History of the Peloponnesian War*:

> As to the speeches ... it has been difficult to recall with strict accuracy the words actually spoken ... Therefore the speeches are given in the language in which, as it seemed to me, the several speakers would express, on the subjects under consideration, the sentiments most befitting the occasion, though at the same time I have adhered as closely as possible to the general sense of what was actually said. (1.22.1)[17]

Historians were not expected to quote their sources verbatim, and they did not claim to. They developed material that was as accurate as it could be, while filling in the gaps with material that "fit."

In a similar way, "speech in character" exercises, such as προσωποποιΐα and ἐθοποιΐα, provide evidence that authors contemporary with early Christian writers (in the New Testament and beyond) developed characters and speeches with attention to what was appropriate for particular individuals (e.g., Achilles) or categories of characters (e.g., eunuchs) to say.[18] These practices involve the *creation* of speech in particular, by established or invented characters. Prosopological exegesis, on the other hand, does the reverse. It takes speech created by another author and identifies the character who would be the most appropriate speaker.

Other practices from the ancient world also involve identifying characters. Drawing upon the work of René Nünlist, it seems that identifying which character is speaking was a required part of engaging with dramas at this time. Ancient editions were written in a very basic form, lacking "identification of the various speakers, stage directions of all sorts, descriptions of the scenes, etc."[19] It was assumed, therefore, that the readers themselves would be able to infer this information based on the tone and content of the speech presented. Moving beyond a mere mental

---

17. Eng. trans. by Smith, LCL, 1:39.

18. Some rhetorical handbooks define προσωποποιΐα as only "personification" (e.g., those attributed to Hermogenes and Nicolaus the Sophist), while others make no distinction between ἐθοποιΐα ("making or imitating characters") and προσωποποιΐα. For more on this distinction and an evaluation of proposals that claim προσωποποιΐα occurs in the New Testament, see Dyer, "I Do Not Understand What I Do," 186–205; Peeler, *You Are My Son*, 33n67.

19. Nünlist, *Ancient Critic at Work*, 338; see also 338–43 for a more thorough discussion of this background.

note, at some point readers began to write these details "in the margins and between the lines" of their own copies to simplify use.[20]

For example, P. Oxy. XVII 2068 (c. second century CE) signifies a change in speaker with a simple horizontal line in the margin. Typically, identifying characters was straightforward, but disagreements are attested. In the *Scholia*, a later compilation of readers' notes on these texts (from σχόλιον, "comment, interpretation"), occasionally a justification for why a speaker fit a certain piece of dialogue was written next to the identification of the speaker.[21] This suggests that the reader felt obligated to justify the identification of a particular character over another (likely based upon the elements similar to those noted above in the Hermogenes handbook).[22] Although a direct line from this to prosopological exegesis cannot be drawn, it appears that ancient readers were trained to identify and resolve ambiguities regarding speakers based on their knowledge of the characters acting within the narrative.

Another relevant reading technique evidenced in the *Scholia* is called "solution from the character" (λύσις ἐκ τοῦ προσώπου).[23] When an author was perceived to contradict him/herself, the readers found it necessary to resolve the tension by looking for another speaker. Porphyry, the third-century CE philosopher, notes that he was not concerned by these so-called contradictions because he reasoned that another voice took over:

> No wonder [there are apparent discrepancies] when in Homer different things are said by different voices. Whatever is said by the poet in his own person should be consistent and not contradictory. All the words/ideas he attributes to the characters are not his, but are understood as being said by the speakers.[24]

Therefore, in addition to identifying speakers when changes were indicated (which was often supplied in the text), readers looked for other

---

20. Nünlist, *Ancient Critic at Work*, 338.

21. For example, in *Scholia vetera in Aristophanis Ranas* 1149–50; see Nünlist, *Ancient Critic at Work*, 339.

22. A further complication with regard to these ancient dramas was the absence of a cast (or *dramatis personae*). The reader, not the author, supplied this as well. See Nünlist, *Ancient Critic at Work*, 238.

23. This is also known as "solution from the poet" (λύσις ἐκ τοῦ ποιητοῦ); Nünlist, *Ancient Critic at Work*, 116.

24. Porphyry, *Homeric Questions* on *Il.* 6.265; Eng. trans. by Schrade apud Nünlist, *Ancient Critic*, 116; see also Porter, "Hermeneutic Lines and Circles," 79.

character changes as indicated by inconsistencies. If a character was speaking in an uncharacteristic way, then it seemed plausible, or perhaps even necessary, for the readers to find a more suitable speaker. These practices among the literary critics to identify ambiguities and tensions in their texts provide a useful parallel to prosopological exegesis. Christian interpreters perceived ambiguities (within a base text being quoted) and tensions (within the way it was usually interpreted) and resolved them by finding a new, more suitable speaker. While this formal training (and its terminology) might be confined to the elite in society, it is likely that these principles would dissipate to the wider public, which is why Justin can assume that his readers would also be able to use prosopological exegesis, as we have seen.

Prosopological Exegesis in the New Testament?

Despite the insistence of patristic scholars that prosopological exegesis could be traced to the New Testament,[25] most biblical scholars continue to overlook the usefulness of the technique for interpretation; however, some have begun to take note, particularly Matthew Bates. In his monograph *The Hermeneutics of the Apostolic Proclamation* (2012), Bates identifies several instances of prosopological exegesis within the New Testament. While Bates's first major work deals primarily with Paul, his second, *The Birth of the Trinity* (2015), addresses prosopological exegesis in the New Testament more broadly, with a particular focus on how this technique contributed to later Trinitarian theology.[26] For example, in Luke 4:16–21, when Jesus reads in the synagogue, he says,

---

25. For example, Andresen, "Zur Entstehung"; and esp. Rondeau, *Les commentaires patristiques*, 2:21–24.

26. This study, which appeared after the commencement of my work, also notes the use of this reading strategy in Hebrews and writes on several of the texts that I will address in this thesis; see, e.g., Bates, *Birth of the Trinity*, 69; 170 on Heb 1:5. Bates, however, by typically grouping texts as read by multiple NT authors (e.g., Ps 2:7 in Heb 1:5; Mark 1:11; Luke 3:22; Matt 3:17; Acts 13:32–35) does not address the contribution of this reading strategy to the argument of Hebrews (or any other text) as a whole. Bates and I also disagree at several points on the interpretation of the texts, in particular his denial of the Spirit's role as *prosopon* in Heb 3:7—4:11 and 10:15–18. For a more thorough review of Bates, see Pierce, "Review of *Birth of the Trinity*." Despite my focus on our differences, I want to make clear that without the work of Matthew Bates and his introduction of this method to NT studies, this thesis would be far less rich.

> The Spirit of the Lord is upon me,
>> because he has anointed me
>> to proclaim good news to the poor.
> He has sent me to preach release for the captives
>> and recovery of sight to the blind,
> To send out the oppressed with release,
>> and to preach the year of the Lord's favor.

After this, Jesus ends, "Today, this Scripture is fulfilled in your hearing." According to Jesus' reading, he is the "I" of the texts who has been anointed. Thus, as Bates notes, the fulfillment of this Scripture to which Jesus refers is not generic but specifically refers to the commencement of his ministry, the first examples of which occur shortly thereafter (4:38–44). In Luke 4, Jesus reads Isa 61:1–2 by identifying himself as the "I" in these verses.[27] With this text, Jesus asserts that he has been anointed and empowered by the Spirit of the Lord.[28] The relative lack of commentary in the New Testament in particular seems to suggest that these arguments were intuitive and accessible, again even to those who had not received a formal classical education.

Overview of the Author's Use of Prosopological Exegesis

Surveying the introductory formulas to the more than thirty citations from Scripture in Hebrews reveals that it is only the Father, the Son, and the Spirit that are named speakers who speak in a present, even occasionally timeless, way—at least until the close of the letter. In addition to the anonymous speaker in Heb 2:6–8, the only other identified speaker in Hebrews is Moses. He is quoted twice (Heb 9:20; 12:21), and in both instances, the author anchors Moses' speech to its original setting in the Pentateuch, whereas most (if not all) of the texts spoken by the divine agents do not retain their original setting.[29] Moses' speech happened once; divine discourse persists. Therefore, it seems that the author of Hebrews has set apart these divine participants to be exceptional. Only these three

---

27. Tertullian identifies Jesus as the "I" of this text also in *Prax.* 11.

28. See Bates, *Birth of the Trinity*, 94–95.

29. Some divine discourse in Hebrews is located at a certain time (e.g., 1:6; 10:5–7; cf. 4:7). In those instances, the author introduces a context for the speech to make a specific point.

continue to speak. Implicit in this portrayal by the author is the assertion that some unifying characteristic exists among them; some quality that they share makes them viable speakers. Of course, the traditional link is that they are depicted in early Christian literature as God.

The author of Hebrews uses spoken quotations of Scripture to characterize these speakers, and in many cases, also the addressees of the speech. First, while the author includes a few quotations from the Jewish Scriptures when God spoke to Abraham or another human, the Father's present speech in Hebrews typically is directed to the Son (1:5, 8–9, 10–12, 13; 5:5, 6; 7:17, 21).[30] This intra-divine discourse between the Father and the Son displays what is unique about Jesus. With these texts, the author reveals that this is the Son of God (1:5; 5:5) who is anointed (1:8–9) and worshiped by angels (1:6) and who had a role in the creation of the earth (1:10–12; cf. 1:2). This Son now sits at the right hand of the Father (1:13). He is a priest in the likeness of Melchizedek (5:6; 7:17; 7:21). With the prosopological reading strategy, the author implicitly challenges previous interpretive traditions that addressed these texts to any earlier Davidic monarch; these are texts about the Son.

Additionally, since this author is constantly comparing elements of the "old" and "new" covenants, these references often have an additional "non-addressee": in Heb 1, the angels; in Heb 5 and 7, Aaron and his lineage. This speech in Hebrews reveals the inimitability of the Son demonstrated through the superlative words of his Father. Prior to Heb 10:19, the Father speaks once more in Heb 8:8–12. Here he has no explicit conversation partner, and his speech is not about the Son per se. Instead, quoting Greek Jer 38:31–34, the Father declares that he will make a new covenant. On the heels of the author's discussion of the new covenant's "better mediator," it seems likely that the Son is not far from view.

The Son's quoted speech is exclusively directed to the Father (2:12–13; 10:5–7). The unifying characteristic of these texts is the willing

---

30. One notable exception is 13:5: "He [God] has said, 'Never will I leave you; never will I forsake you.'" Hebrews 13 revisits many main themes from the previous chapters. In his essay on the Old Testament in Heb 13:1–8 (Allen, "Constructing 'Janus-Faced' Exhortations," 401–9), David M. Allen has shown that the quotation in 13:5 recalls Joshua's entrance into the promised rest and the typological connection between Joshua (Ιησους) and Jesus (Ιησους). In addition to this implicit reference to Jesus, I think there is also an implicit reference to the Holy Spirit. As we shall see, he is the divine agent most connected with this narrative in Hebrews. Thus, in Heb 13:5, "God" (found in 13:4) could refer to the three more broadly.

submission of the Son. He presents himself as faithful (2:12–13) and obedient (10:5–7). Jesus' speech in Heb 2 also reveals his care for his "brothers and sisters" (2:12). While the Father's speech in Heb 1 shows how Jesus is unlike any other person, Jesus' speech in 2:12–13 reminds the readers of his remarkable connection with humanity. The author brackets Jesus' speech with further comments on their unity. Jesus helps Abraham's descendants (2:16) and shared in their humanity (2:14). He was made like these siblings in every way (κατὰ πάντα, 2:17), so that he might be able to help when they are tested (2:18). In Heb 10:5–7, at his entrance into the world, Christ declares his desire to do the will of the Father, speaking Greek Ps 39:7–9. In both of the Son's speeches, his solidarity with and mission to humanity is firmly in view.

Finally, the Holy Spirit's speech is exclusively directed to the community (to "you" [pl.], 3:7—4:11; to "us," 10:15–18). This clear distinction between the Father's and the Spirit's speech offers proof that the author has not merged these two agents but views them as individual participants.[31] In addition to the difference in addressees, the Spirit's speech has a different purpose and tone. He exhorts the community with a warning in Heb 3–4 and with a promise in Heb 10. The Father and the Son speak to one another, but the Spirit speaks to us. This speech by the Spirit occurs third in the pattern of divine discourse in the first two sections in Hebrews. Therefore, while readers can "hear" the conversation between Father and Son, it is only after they observe their speech that the Spirit speaks directly to them, perhaps in order to make clear its implications.

Prosopological Exegesis in Heb 1:10–12

I now would like to offer something new, though rather tentative. Among the quotations in Heb 1 stands Greek Ps 101:26–28 in Heb 1:10–12, which is also addressed to the Son. In it, he is called κύριος and praised as the one who "laid the foundations of the earth" and who claims the heavens as his handiwork (101:26). This is, as Sean McDonough says, "the boldest statement in the entire New Testament concerning Jesus' role in creation."[32] Psalm 102 (Ψ 101) stands within Book IV of the Psalter (Pss 90–106). This collection of psalms moves from a focus on the Davidic monarchy and covenant to a reflection on YHWH as king as

---

31. For some examples of this claim, see Pierce, *Divine Discourse*, ch. 4, esp. n95.
32. McDonough, *Christ as Creator*, 205.

well as the Mosaic covenant. The psalms look backward—"reminiscing" about the earlier covenants and institutions.³³ The superscription of this psalm in the Greek Psalter reads: "A prayer for the one who is poor (MT: 'afflicted' [עָנִי]) whenever he is in anguish and pouring out his prayer before the Lord" (Ψ 101:1). The first part of the psalm is an individual lament, calling out to God for help in the future (101:2–4) and recalling a state (or states) of despair (101:5–12). The psalmist then transitions into a description of the corporate need for rescue (101:14, 21) and praise, looking forward to a day when he along with all YHWH's servants and all the nations will fear the name of the Lord (101:13–23, esp. 101:16). This psalm is a prayer to YHWH, which begins with petition and lament but ends with sincere praise and worship (101:26–29).

Elsewhere in Hebrews, Jesus is identified with the psalmist (2:12; 10:5–7), but here the quotation of Greek Ps 101 is not spoken by Jesus in Hebrews. Instead, the speaker is YHWH himself—the original addressee of the quotation. Various explanations have been offered for why the author identifies Jesus as a character within the psalm. One potential explanation comes in the Greek translations.³⁴ In verse 24, they translate the root ענה with the Greek word for "answer" instead of "afflict," understanding this to be one Hebrew root with those radicals rather than another.³⁵ This introduces additional dialogue to the psalm. For many, this allows the author of Hebrews to identify YHWH as the speaker who addresses the psalmist³⁶ or an exalted figure (e.g., the messiah, Wisdom, the Logos);³⁷ however, this might not be the best explanation. One reason is the point of view. The psalmist speaks of himself in the first person at the outset of the psalm (Ψ 101:1–12). First-person language is absent from 101:13–23, and no shift in person is indicated. Therefore, it would be unlikely in Greek Ps 101:24 for either of the people in view to be the psalmist since they are both referred to in the third person:

> He answered him on the way to his strength.
> ἀπεκρίθη αὐτῷ ἐν ὁδῷ ἰσχύος αὐτοῦ

---

33. Ndoga, "Revisiting the Theocratic Agenda," 151. In a similar way, the author of Hebrews will look backward to the worship in the tabernacle, rather than the temple.

34. The Göttingen edition does not attest to any relevant variations in Ψ 101:24.

35. Many call attention to this, such as: Bacon, "Heb. 1,10–12," 280–85; Guthrie, "Hebrews," 940; Ellingworth, *Epistle to the Hebrews*, 126; Lane, *Hebrews 1–8*, 30.

36. Bruce, *Epistle to the Hebrews*, 61–63.

37. Guthrie, "Hebrews," 940; Lane, *Hebrews 1–8*, 30.

This means not one, but two additional participants are in view—participants that the author of Hebrews identifies as the Father and the Son.

As mentioned above, the interpretations of Ps 110 and Deut 32 likely rely upon ambiguities in the text about the speakers and/or an implicit dialogue between two figures identified as κύριος. Other early Christian interpretations identify two κύριοι also, but in texts where the figures are not involved in a dialogue. For example, in Gen 18–19, Jesus is identified as one of the "characters" because Genesis seems to allow for two "Lords"—one in heaven and one on earth:

> And the Lord rained down sulfur on Sodom and Gomorrah and fire from the Lord from heaven.
> καὶ κύριος ἔβρεξεν ἐπὶ Σοδομα καὶ Γομορρα θεῖον καὶ πῦρ παρὰ κυρίου ἐκ τοῦ οὐρανοῦ

This is not the only ambiguity in this passage in Genesis (see, e.g., the three men in 18:1–15), but for Justin, Irenaeus, and Augustine (among others), this serves as a prooftext for the presence of two lords—and more specifically for the authority of Jesus.[38] Greek Ps 101 might also allow for this type of reading. In the verses leading up to the portion quoted by Hebrews, the psalm says:

19 This is to be written for another generation,	19 γραφήτω αὕτη εἰς γενεὰν ἑτέραν,
and a people, which is being created, will praise <u>the Lord</u>	καὶ λαὸς ὁ κτιζόμενος αἰνέσει <u>τὸν κύριον,</u>
20 Because he looked out from the heights of his holy place;	20 ὅτι ἐξέκυψεν ἐξ ὕψους ἁγίου αὐτοῦ,
<u>the Lord looked down on the earth from heaven</u>	<u>κύριος ἐξ οὐρανοῦ ἐπὶ τὴν γῆν ἐπέβλεψεν</u>

---

38. Some have argued that Justin influenced Irenaeus. For this and a discussion of this reading in Eusebius, see Rondeau, *Les commentaires patristiques*, 2:29, as well as ch. 3. Slusser also discusses Justin's reading; see Slusser, "Exegetical Roots of Trinitarian Theology," 266–67.

21 To hear the groaning of those who are bound fast	21 τοῦ ἀκοῦσαι τὸν στεναγμὸν τῶν πεπεδημένων,
To set free the children of those who have been put to death	τοῦ λῦσαι τοὺς υἱοὺς τῶν τεθανατωμένων,
22 <u>To proclaim in Zion the name of the Lord</u>	22 <u>τοῦ ἀναγγεῖλαι ἐν Σιων τὸ ὄνομα κυρίου</u>
and his praise in Jerusalem,	καὶ τὴν αἴνεσιν αὐτοῦ ἐν Ιερουσαλημ
23 While peoples gather over it, as well as kingdoms,	23 ἐν τῷ συναχθῆναι λαοὺς ἐπὶ τὸ αὐτὸ καὶ βασιλείας
To serve <u>the Lord</u>.	τοῦ δουλεύειν <u>τῷ κυρίῳ</u>

Examining the occurrences of κύριος reveals that here again, we see that YHWH looks down from heaven with set purposes, which are outlined through the use of a series of three parallel articular infinitives. If they are read in true parallel with one another, each modifying ἐπέβλεψεν, then the Lord's third purpose is to "proclaim in Zion the name of the Lord" (Ψ 101:22).[39] Elsewhere in the Psalms, God's people communicate his name through songs, proclamations, and even blessings (e.g., 7:18; 22:23; 29:2; 34:4), but in all of biblical literature YHWH rarely proclaims his own name.[40] Is it possible that the Lord in heaven proclaims the name of another "Lord" and that they are the two entities of Greek Ps 101:24? If so, then the passage could be interpreted as:

> the Lord [1] looked down on the earth from heaven . . .
> 22 To proclaim in Zion the name of the Lord [2]
>   and his praise in Jerusalem,
> 23 While peoples gather over it, as well as kingdoms,
>   To serve the Lord [2?].[41]
> He [Lord 1?] answered him [Lord 2?] on the way to his strength.

Given traditional associations between the Father and heaven, it is safe to assume that "Lord 1" is the Father and then that "Lord 2" is the Son.

---

39. For a similar proposal, see Glasson, "Plurality of Divine Persons," 270–72. Glasson and I reached these conclusions independently.

40. The only parallel for this language appears in Exod 33:19, where Moses sees the glory of God. YHWH says: "I will pass by in front of you in my glory, and I will call upon my name—the Lord—before you (Ἐγὼ παρελεύσομαι πρότερός σου τῇ δόξῃ μου καὶ καλέσω ἐπὶ τῷ ὀνόματί μου Κύριος ἐναντίον σου)."

41. For those who identify κύριος in verse 23 (and not 22) as the Davidic king, see Motyer, "Psalm Quotations of Hebrews 1," 20; Compton, *Psalm 110*, 32.

This would result in the Father speaking the words of the quotation in Hebrews to the Son. But some of the language of the speech presents a challenge:

> [The Father] answered [the Son] in the way of his strength,
> Declare to me the fewness of my days.
> Do not bring me back in the middle of my days.

This language does not appear to be "characteristic" of the Father. So how do we explain this language?

A proposal for evaluation is that this is a true dialogue between the Father and the Son. Looking again to Greek Ps 101:24, if we work backward, then we see that the most proximate participant is "Lord 2" (101:22, as the object of the verb) and "Lord 1" is the last to communicate when he "proclaims [Lord 2's] name" (101:22). Thus, verse 24 could also be interpreted as: "[The Son] answered [the Father] in the way of his strength." Since the author of Hebrews interprets verses 26–28 as the words of the Father, then the Son would speak verses 24–25. While there is not an abrupt shift or an indication of another speaker between those two sections, there is a shift in the pronouns from first to second person. As we have seen, readers were encouraged to "hear" shifts in voices and also to find "solutions" when tensions in speech arose. This offers the possibility that this psalm was interpreted with dialogue, but is it fitting for these words to be spoken to the Father by the Son?

In Greek Ps 101:25, the speaker says, "Do not bring me back [ἀναγάγῃς] at the midpoint of my days." This lexeme is also used in Heb 13:20, where the God of peace is described as the "one who brought back from the dead [ὁ ἀναγαγὼν ἐκ νεκρῶν] Jesus our Lord." Likewise, in Greek Ps 39:3, just verses before the text spoken by the Christ in Heb 10:5–7, the speaker asks God to raise [ἀνάγω] him from the pit of distress.[42] In these texts, Jesus is the one who is "brought back" or "raised," and YHWH (or "the Father")[43] is the one who raises. Likewise, in 1 Kingdoms 2:6 (or 1 Sam 2:6), YHWH is described as the one who "puts to death and makes alive, leads down to Hades and brings back [ἀνάγει]." Also, countless

---

42. Throughout his monograph, David M. Moffitt develops a case that these verses in Hebrews refer to the resurrection. See Moffitt, *Atonement and the Logic of Resurrection*.

43. I recognize that "father" and "son" language is foreign to the psalm; however, this language (chosen due to its use in Hebrews) is used for the sake of clarity throughout.

times in Scripture, this lexical form is used to describe YHWH raising the people up out of Egypt (e.g., Lev 11:45; Num 14:13; Josh 24:17; Judg 6:13). Therefore, interpreting Greek Ps 101:25 as the Son's speech to the Father fits not only for the speaker but also for the addressee. The Son, as he does elsewhere in Hebrews, accepts his mission on behalf of humanity and asks that he not be "brought back" before it is completed; the Father commends the Son and highlights his exalted status.

Conclusion

The author of Hebrews introduces his quotations from Scripture as divine speech. The speeches of the Father, Son, and Spirit each serve a particular purpose in the argument of Hebrews. In each instance of divine speech, the author of Hebrews recontextualizes the quotation he cites by identifying the Father, Son, or Spirit as the speaker, subject, or addressee. This reading strategy has been identified as "prosopological exegesis," a technique that has parallel features in classical education and historiography. After introducing this feature and offering a summary of its use in Hebrews more broadly, this chapter examined the use of prosopological exegesis in Heb 1:10–12. Here the author of Hebrews introduces a quotation of Greek Ps 101:26–28, which confounds interpreters. I propose that the author of Hebrews builds upon tensions already present in the Greek versions of this text in his interpretation of these verses as the Father's commendation of the Son. Though this reading of Ps 101 is not found elsewhere in early Jewish and Christian literature, the possible assumptions behind it are similar to other textual traditions.

14

Humor in Hebrews

Rhetoric of the *Ridiculus* in the Example of Esau

JASON A. WHITLARK AND JON-MICHAEL CARMAN

THIS ESSAY APPROACHES INTERTEXTUALITY and Hebrews with a primary focus on texts from the Greco-Roman context and its cultural scripts through the construct of the authorial audience. This approach is what Vernon Robbins labels as the "cultural intertexture" of the New Testament.[1] We are concerned with which potential cultural, rhetorical, ethical, and literary expectations were activated by the audience to whom the author imagines that he is writing.[2] Christ-followers, whether Jews or gentiles, did not exist in isolation from the pagan imperial society in which they lived. Thus, as Paul Foster notes, an intertextuality that

---

1. Robbins, *Early Christian Discourse*, 108–15.

*We would like to thank Kelly Iverson for his helpful feedback on an earlier version of this essay, as well as B. J. Oropeza for the insights from his response paper at the joint session of the Intertextuality in the New Testament and Hebrews sections at SBL San Diego 2019.

2. Chatman, *Story and Discourse*, 50; Jauss, "Literary History," 7–37; Rabinowitz, *Before Reading*; Rabinowitz, "Truth in Fiction," 126. The author will be referred to throughout with masculine pronouns, as the case made by some commentators for female authorship of the letter (e.g., Hoppin, *Priscilla's Letter*) has not won widespread support; for further discussion of this question, see also, e.g., Attridge, *Hebrews*, 1–6.

ignores this context of early Christianity may fail to recognize innovative ideas in the NT text or those ideas adapted from, or in conversation with, the pagan milieu.³ Moreover, communities of Christ-followers sat at the intersection of emerging Christian traditions, a variegated Jewish heritage, and a pervasive pagan culture all under the rule of Rome. This essay looks at one cultural-rhetorical intertext of the Greco-Roman milieu through expectations associated with humor.

There were significant discussions about humor in the ancient world. In particular, rhetorical theorists explored this topic in some depth. The influence of the classical rhetorical tradition was pervasive in the ancient Mediterranean world, whether it was experienced secondhand through public speeches and private discourses, or whether it was studied in the classroom. It also left its distinctive mark on Jewish writers such as Philo and Josephus, in rabbinic exegetical methods, in Melito of Sardis's *Peri Pascha* sermon, and on Augustine who adapts Cicero for Christian rhetoric in *De doctrina christiana*.⁴

Despite these realities, humor has gone unexplored in Hebrews, though the author's rhetorical sophistication has long been recognized. This is partly due to a long-held assumption that the Scriptures are humorless.⁵ Stephen Halliwell in his definitive tome *Greek Laughter: A Study of Cultural Psychology from Homer to Early Christianity* comments that second- and third-century Christians exhibited a reticence against laughter, and thus he muses that humor did not have "any worthwhile place" among Christians. Moreover, Halliwell believes this characteristic can be traced back to the New Testament itself.⁶ A cursory reading of Hebrews might find some sympathy with the assessment of Scripture as humorless texts. The author exhorts his audience repeatedly with the utmost urgency against apostasy with some of the most fear-inducing warnings in the New Testament. In this essay, however, we propose that

---

3. Foster, "Echoes without Resonance," 98–99.

4. Cf. the recent monograph by Alexandre, *Rhetorical Argumentation*; Kennedy, *Classical Rhetoric*, 156–57; Neyrey, "Josephus' *Vita*," 177–206; Stewart-Sykes, *Lamb's High Feast*, 72–92; 113–39 (esp. 114).

5. Cf. Iverson, "Incongruity," 2–3.

6. Halliwell, *Greek Laughter*, 475; 478; 512; 518. See also examples cited from the patristic period in Bussie, "Laughter," 172–73. This assessment has been effectively challenged in Gospels studies, e.g., Bednarz, *Humor in the Gospels*; Iverson, "Incongruity," 2–19. Indeed, Bednarz's entire project is ample evidence that the problem is not so much whether the Gospels are humorous as much as it is the fact that scholars generally ignore this particular stream of Jesus studies.

the author does portray the example of Esau in Heb 12:16 as humorous to further his deliberative aims.

Though the analysis of humor is not particularly humorous (cf. Cicero, *De or.* 2.217), we will show that the example of Esau in Hebrews fulfills certain expectations that would characterize it as potentially humorous from the perspective of the author's audience in the first century CE. Moreover, we will examine what rhetorical effect the author might have hoped this instance of humor would have on his audience. First, we will point to a meta-analysis of humor, laughter, and wit in the ancient Mediterranean world. This meta-analysis demonstrates that there were efforts to make sense of the common phenomena of laughter and humor. Second, we will focus on relevant aspects of discussion regarding the rhetoric of the *ridiculus* among the rhetorical theorists—itself an artifact of this ancient humor meta-analysis. Third, we will look at examples of a particular cause for humor in the absurd, especially in ill-conceived, incongruous exchanges. Fourth, we will apply these observations to Heb 12:16, arguing that the author's strategic use of humor bolsters his exhortations to remain faithful and not to apostatize.

Humor in the Ancient Mediterranean World

In the ancient Mediterranean world, in addition to the pervasive traditions of Greek comedy that made their way into the Roman world, there were numerous rhetorical analyses of humor, many of which are no longer extant. Among these, there are the lost works Περὶ γελοίου by Theophrastus and Περὶ ἀστεϊσμός by Neoptolemus of Parium.[7] Aristotle discusses humor and jests in parts of his various works. He succinctly addresses the topic in *Ars rhetorica* 3.18.7 (περὶ τῶν γελοίων). In this analysis, Aristotle refers to an earlier discussion in *Poetica* that is no longer extant (cf. 1449a1–5; 1449b20–22). Possibly this is a reference to a lost second volume of *Poetica* where Aristotle takes up the discussion of comedy. Some have contended that this lost volume is represented in brief by *Tractatus Coislinianus*.[8]

By the first century BCE, Cicero acknowledges that there were many Greek books on the laughable bearing the title Περὶ γελοίου or its Latin

---

7. Rabbie, "Wit and Humor," 213.

8. Watson, *Lost Second Book*, 1–9, esp. 8: "Tractatus . . . is a straightforward and reliable summary in Aristotle's own words of the lost second book of the *Poetics*."

translation, *De ridiculis* (*De or.* 2.217; cf. Quintilian, *Inst.* 6.3.22). Cicero himself was known for his wit and had three collections of witticisms or joke books attributed to him (Cicero, *Fam.* 7.32; Quintilian, *Inst.* 6.3.5; Plutarch, *Cic.* 26–27 and *Comp. Dem. Cic.* 1). The fourth- or fifth-century CE joke book, *Philogelos*, is still read today.[9] Quintilian, at the end of the first century CE, acknowledges other witticisms that were in general circulation as well as the scholarly work on urbanity by Domitius Marsus, an Augustan contemporary (*Inst.* 6.3.5; 102). Both Cicero and Quintilian devote significant space to a rhetorical analysis of humor in their rhetorical handbooks.

Also, in the first and second centuries CE, Pliny the Elder, Plutarch, and Galen take up an investigation of laughter. Pliny discusses laughter in various parts of his *Naturalis historia*, including where laughter originates in the body, tales about laughter, and plants that cause laughter (cf. 7.2; 7.72; 7.79–80; 24.164). Plutarch discusses laughter and humor at dinner (cf. *Quaest. conviv.* 2.1.11–12). Galen reflects on the comic nature of apes (cf. *De usu part.* 1.22).[10]

Taken together, all these select examples indicate that the topic of humor was analyzed extensively in antiquity. Whether represented by Greek comic traditions in playwrights such as Aristophanes and Menander or Latin comedic writers such as Plautus and Terence, philosophized upon by Aristotle and Plato; analyzed by naturalists and physicians; or considered for its place in public deliberation by rhetoricians, humor was treated quite seriously. This points us to important meta-analyses of humor and laughter in the context of Hebrews. The rhetorical analysis especially helps us to understand not only what ancients considered ridiculous or laughable and why, but also what they considered its function to be in declamation.

Rhetoric of the *Ridiculus*

The rhetorical theorists discuss forms, topics, aims, and causes of humor in a speech. We will examine each of these in turn.

---

9. Beard, *Laughter*, 186–201.

10. See Beard, *Laughter*, 160–67, for a discussion of humor surrounding primates in ancient Rome.

Forms of the *Ridiculus*

In form, humor could pervade the whole speech or be a brief remark, a "shaft of wit" (cf. Cicero, *De or.* 2.218-19; Quintilian, *Inst* 6.3.37). Humor could also take the form of gestures and props, though rhetorical discussions were weary that the use of such visual humor could turn the orator into a mimic actor (cf. Cicero, *De or.* 2.251). This is humor that is seen instead of being heard (cf. Quintilian, *Inst.* 6.3.37-38).

Topics of the *Ridiculus*

Regarding topics, Cicero and Quintilian acknowledge that topics for humor are the same as those for serious speech (cf. Cicero, *De or.* 2.248; Quintilian, *Inst.* 6.3.101). Those who discuss humor typically broke humor into two broad divisions—words and facts/deeds (cf. *Tractatus Coislinianus*; Cicero, *De or.* 2.240; 248; Quintilian, *Inst.* 6.3.23). Aristotle also included persons in his analysis (ἄνθρωποι, λόγοι, ἔργα; *Rhet.* 1.11.35). Aristotle's category of persons includes topical divisions based on physical appearance, mental attitude, and external circumstances—these three areas were common *topoi* for the encomium and invective of persons in rhetoric (e.g., Theon 109; *Inst.* 3.7.12). When discussing arousing laughter, Quintilian notes that these three areas relate also to all forms of invective, even the humorous sort (*Inst.* 6.3.37).

Quintilian acknowledges that any topic related to arguments, tropes, or figures of thought could be employed for humor (cf. *Inst.* 6.3.65-70). Topics such as comparison and analogy are explicitly cited in the discussions of humor (cf. Cicero, *De. or.* 2.265; Quintilian, *Inst.* 6.3.66; 68-69). Quintilian also lists ambiguity as a method of humor stating that "indeed, the whole principle of witty speech is expressing things in a way other than the direct and truthful one."[11] Comparison, analogy, and even ambiguity will be relevant to our analysis of the example of Esau in Hebrews below.

Rhetorical Aims of the *Ridiculus*

There are three rhetorical functions of humor discussed by the theorists that are relevant to this study: (1) stirring the emotions, (2) avoiding folly,

---

11. Quintilian, *Inst.* 6.3.89; Eng. trans. by Russell, LCL, 3:109-10.

and (3) deriding an opponent. These rhetorical aims distinguish the orator who attempts to gain some benefit in his or her jest from a buffoon who merely wants to be funny or is excessively so (cf. Cicero, *De or.* 2.247; cf. Aristotle, *Eth. nic.* 4.8.3).

Concerning the first aim, the theorists primarily discuss humor in relation to stirring the emotions. Cicero and Quintilian follow their discussion of *ethos* and *pathos* with an excursus on humor (*De or.* 2.178–216; 2.216–90; *Inst.* 6.2.1–36; 6.3.1–112). When discussing the fitness of humor, Cicero notes that humor wins the goodwill of the audience, wins admiration for the orator, and relieves dullness and austerity in a speech (*De or.* 2.236; cf. Quintilian, *Inst.* 6.3.1). Quintilian states that the effect of a jest depends upon emotion and not reason (*Inst.* 6.3.6). Elsewhere, he declares that wit and pity are the most powerful elements in emotional writing (*Inst.* 10.1.107). Anonymous Seguerianus observes that wit or humor creates delight in the audience (99).[12]

With regard to the second aim, one target of humor is folly, especially moral vices or failings. Socrates in the *Republic* explicitly states that only baseness (κακόν) is laughable (γελοῖον), and one should only make a joke at the foolish (ἄφρων). The fool (μάταιος), however, does not think this (Plato, *Rep.* 452D). Cicero lists ridiculing foolishness as among the subjects of humor (*De. or.* 2.289). Quintilian states that "it is very easy to take folly (*stultus*) to task because folly itself is ridiculous (*ridicula*)."[13] Cicero and Quintilian, however, discuss limits to ridiculing folly. One such limit is that an orator should not target outstanding wickedness as this is likely to elicit strong disgust from the audience and not a laugh. In the same way, outstanding wretchedness should also not be targeted as this will elicit the deepest sympathies of the audience (cf. *De or.* 2.237–38; Quintilian, *Inst.* 6.3.31; 33).

---

12. In the exordium, where emotions are commonly stirred, Cicero states that one might begin with a laughable incident since laughter refreshes the audience (*Inv.* 1.25). Likewise, *Rhetorica ad Herennium* discusses an introduction with a subtle approach where the orator might provoke laughter if the audience appears fatigued (1.10).

13. Quintilian, *Inst.* 6.3.71; Eng. trans. by Russell, LCL, 3:99; cf. 6.3.7. In the epistolary novella allegedly written by Hippocrates but likely from the first century CE, the citizens of Abdera ask Hippocrates to come and cure Democritus, the uncontrollably laughing philosopher (*Ep.* 10.1). Hippocrates finds that Democritus is not ill or out of his mind, but that he laughs appropriately at the foolishness of humanity (*Ep.* 17.4–5). For introduction, text, and translation, see Smith, *Hippocrates*. See also the discussion by Beard, *Laughter*, 92–93.

Taking folly to task also falls under the category of humorous invective (cf. Cicero, *De or.* 2.222).[14] In a deliberative speech, humor then can function as a type of reproach so that one will avoid a foolish course of action. This is the goal of much invective generally. For example, Cicero states that the principles of awarding praise and blame "have value not only for good oratory but also for right conduct."[15] *Rhetorica ad Herennium* comments that epideictic material most often serves judicial and deliberative aims (3.15). Pseudo-Dionysius observes that Pericles's funeral oration—the most quintessential encomiastic exercise—did not only praise the dead but exhorted the living to take up arms ([*Rhet.*] 8.9). The common goal of imitation suggested by praise and the opposite by vituperation is echoed in a proverbial statement that Quintilian writes: "Virtue brings praise, so it should be pursued."[16]

The third aim is to deride an opponent. Aristotle comments that "raillery is a sort of vilification."[17] Cicero notes that humor makes light of an opponent (*De or.* 2.236). As already discussed, ridiculing character is a particular object of rhetorical humor (cf. *De or.* 2.289). Quintilian, when listing various words for humor, names *dicacitas* or "shafts of wit" as useful for attacking people in a laughable manner (*Inst.* 6.3.21). Elsewhere, he states that laughter can come at the expense of others, which can be especially useful in a judicial setting (*Inst.* 6.3.23; 27–28).

Related to this third aim is the notion that humor is one way of resisting authority by diminishing its self-importance. One example is illustrative. Dio Cassius recounts an incident from 192 CE where Emperor Commodus's threats became an object of laughter. Commodus had just decapitated an ostrich in the amphitheater after which he held up the head and bloody sword before the seated senators, which Dio reports was a threat that "gave us every reason to look for our death."[18] Dio, however, states that the response of the senators was to laugh at the ridiculous display, though the senators had to chew on laurel leaves in order to conceal their mirth.

There are at least three observations from Dio's account that are significant:

14. Cf. Arena, "Roman Oratorical Invective," 150–51.
15. Cicero, *Part. or.* 71; Eng. trans. by Rackham, LCL, 2:363.
16. Quintilian, *Inst.* 5.10.83; Eng. trans. by Russell, LCL, 2:409.
17. Aristotle, *Eth. nic.* 4.8.9; Eng. trans. by Rackham, LCL, 247.
18. Dio Cassius, *Hist. rom.*, 73.21.1; Eng. trans. by Cary, LCL, 9:113.

(1) Power is met and challenged by laughter or humor.[19] As Mary Beard notes about this episode: "One response by the disaffected was violence, conspiracy, or rebellion, another was to refuse to take it seriously."[20] The shared humor and laughter makes Commodus look ridiculous and "cuts him down to size."[21] This is often the goal of opening monologues of American late-night shows in the current political context.[22]

(2) We note that humor and laughter can emerge as a response to serious, even grave or menacing, situations, such as when derided authorities hold the power of death.[23] In fact, Cicero comments that humor can be cleverly deployed even if the underlying thought is serious (*De or.* 2.262). Quintilian asserts that humor "often turns the scale in very important matters."[24] Quintilian also observes that humorous actions could include an element of seriousness (*Inst.* 6.3.25). For example, Quintilian recounts that Caelius quarreled with the consul, Isauricus. Isauricus barred Caelius from the Senate, assigned his duties to another praetor, and broke his curule chair. Caelius subsequently had his curule chair repaired with leather straps to recall the flogging Isauricus had allegedly received at the hands of his father (cf. Dio Cassius, *Hist. rom.* 42.23–25). Such a precarious response is tinged with humor.[25]

---

19. Beard (*Laughter*, 136–37) notes that in Ovid's *Metamorphoses*, human laughter aimed at deities is a display of human defiance and is often punished by the offended deity. Cf. Schutz, "Cryptic Humor," 51–64.

20. Beard, *Laughter*, 3.

21. Beard, *Laughter*, 5. Also, from the visual culture of Pompeii, there are paintings of Aeneas and Romulus as dog-headed apes with human bodies, tales, and long phalli, which may represent a comic resistance to Roman power (see Clarke, *Looking at Laughter*, 151–54).

22. Cf. Kersten, "Laugh Resistance," 299–316.

23. Cf. Bussie, "Laughter," 169–82.

24. Quintilian, *Inst.* 6.3.10; Eng. trans. by Russell, LCL, 3:69.

25. Laughter can emerge in the context of a life-death situation. For example, in Homer, *Il.* 466–85, Hector and Andromache share a laugh over the reaction of their infant son, Astyanax, though Andromache has been pleading with Hector to stay behind the walls and not go out to battle where he might die. Also see Prudentius's portrayal of humor in the martyrdom of Lawrence (*Peristephanon* 2.313–29; 409–12; cf. Beard, *Laughter*, 154–55).

(3) Humor against oppressive authority is often ambiguous, deflected, or concealed so that those under threat of the authorities are the only ones "in on the joke."[26]

Causes of the *Ridiculus*

Rhetorical theorists acknowledge that there are several causes of humor. These causes may also be considered as special *topoi* for humor. One of the most common causes of humor is the unexpected turn or deceiving expectations; as Demetrius states, "there is a sort of charm in the unexpected (παρά προσδοκίαν)."[27] *Tractatus Coislinianus* list things that are contrary to expectation as giving rise to laughter.[28] Aristotle notes that the wittiest (ἀστεῖα) sayings derive from the deception of the audience's expectations (cf. *Rhet.* 3.11.6).[29] Cicero states that the unexpected is the most familiar category of humor, such as when "one expects to hear a particular phrase, and something different is uttered."[30] Cicero also points to unexpected turns (*discrepantia*) in a speech as a source of humor (*De or.* 2.281–85; cf. *Rhet. Her.* 1.10). The theorists' discussion of the unexpected has similarities to what modern humor theory labels as incongruity.[31]

The *subabsurda* was also a cause of humor identified by Cicero and Quintilian. Cicero states that *subabsurda* is appropriate to actors of a farce, but can also be usefully executed by an orator. Quintilian narrows this category to pretended foolishness or stupidity on the part of the speaker (*stulti simulation*; *Inst.* 6.3.99). In the example that Cicero gives, however, the *subabsurda* is demonstrated by folly:

---

26. Figured speech, even in the form of humor, was the anticipated form of communication when criticizing authority in the Roman Empire. See Whitlark, *Resisting Empire*, 21–48. See also Schutz, "Cryptic Humor," 51–64.

27. Demetrius, *Eloc.* 152; Eng. trans. by Innes and Roberts, LCL, 441; cf. Quintilian, *Inst.* 6.3.23–24; 64; 84.

28. Janko, *Aristotle*, 37.

29. Cf. Ps.-Longinus, [*Subl.*] 34.2, and Anonymous Seguerianus, 99 where ἀστεϊμός means wit.

30. Cicero, *De or.* 2.255; Eng. trans. by Sutton and Rackham, LCL, 1:389; cf. *De or.* 2.289.

31. E.g., Attardo, "Cognitive Theories of Humor," 396–97.

The foolish (*fatuus*) man as soon as he was growing rich he died.[32]

The aphorism recalls the parable of the rich fool (ἄφρων) in the Gospel of Luke who stores up his wealth only to die before he can enjoy it (cf. Luke 12:16–20). This example of the absurd retains an element of the unexpected because we anticipate that the man, once he has come into wealth, will enjoy it. It also highlights the illogical foolishness of a person who pursues wealth unmindful of his or her own mortality or lack of control over one's fate (or in the case of Jesus' parable, God's judgment). Quintilian notes that "the combination of various kinds of humorous points is very common."[33]

Indeed, absurdity is part of the semantic range of γελοῖα and *ridiculus*. The absurd often defies customs or expectations and, in this way, exhibits something of the humor of the unexpected. The absurd is also disproportionate or even illogical. Two examples helpfully illustrate these points. First, humorous absurdity could take the form of defying the expectations of customs. Plato provides an apt example. In the *Republic*, Socrates discusses whether men and women should be given the same upbringing and nurture in order to do the same tasks, such as guardians of the polis. Socrates acknowledges that what he is discussing—contrary to tradition—looks "absurd or laughable (γελοῖα)" with men and women, both young and old, exercising together naked in the gymnasium. He acknowledges that would be "most ridiculous (γελοιότατον)" (451A–452B). The translations of γελοῖα and γελοιότατον as "absurd" and "most ridiculous" in the sense of defying custom are certainly suitable to Socrates's example.

Second, humorous absurdity could also take the form of disproportion or caricature. Aristotle states that the further the resemblance of something is from the ideal, even a caricature of it, the more ridiculous or laughable or absurd (γελοίτερον) it is. Thus, it is ridiculous or laughable to compare a monkey to a man. Galen found much humor in this comparison, as was mentioned earlier (cf. *Top.* 3.2.1077; cf. Cicero, *De or.* 2.266). We are familiar with this type of absurd humor in distortion and disproportion that is done by caricature artists in theme parks.

---

32. Cicero, *De or.* 2.274; Eng. trans. by Sutton and Rackham, LCL, 1:407.

33. Quintilian, *Inst.* 6.3.63; Eng. trans. by Russell, LCL, 3:95; cf. Cicero, *De or.* 2.254–55.

Examples of the Absurd in Ancient Humor

There are specific humorous examples of absurdity related to disproportion and incongruous exchanges that may be illustrated outside the rhetorical handbooks. First, we will consider the humorous disproportion that strains custom in incongruous reciprocity and then the humorous disproportion and illogical foolishness in exchanging one's patrimony for something worthless.

Humor of Incongruous Reciprocity

Disproportion could be depicted in distortions of reciprocal exchanges that defy customs. One of the most common ancient relationships held together by reciprocity was friendship. In Greco-Roman ethical thought, the ideal friendship is one that confers mutual benefit. "A friend is one who is loved and loves in return (ἀντιφιλούμενος)."[34] More specifically, Plutarch writes that "grace and usefulness (ἡ χάρις καὶ ἡ χρεία) go with friendship" (*Adul. amic.* 51b). Elsewhere, Plutarch notes that the essential qualities of friendship are virtue, intimacy, and usefulness (*Amic. mult.* 94b).

In the *Iliad*, the disproportionate exchange between two guest-friends becomes an occasion for humor. Diomedes and Glaucas face off in a battle scene from Book 6 (119–236). The rather lengthy (and thus possibly humorous) opening family history of Glaucus as a prelude to their contest reveals that he shares ties of χενία with Diomedes. In an effort to reaffirm this tie, they exchange armor. Glaucus gives his gold armor in exchange for Diomedes's bronze armor. The incongruity is not lost on the narrator who comments that "then from Glaucus did Zeus, son of Cronos, take away his senses, in that he made an exchange (ἄμειβε) of armor ... giving gold for bronze."[35]

In the second century CE, Lucian humorously riffs on friendship by distorting the traditional expectations of friendship, especially straining the ideal of reciprocity. In *Toxaris*, Lucian recounts humorous exchanges among friends in a debate over whether Scythians or Greeks are better friends. The Greek, Mnesippus, recounts Greek friends who give

---

34. Aristotle, *Rhet.* 2.4.2; Eng. trans. by Freese and Striker, LCL, 191; cf. Gill, "Altruism and Reciprocity," 303–28; Konstan, "Reciprocity and Friendship," 279–301.

35. Homer, *Il.* 6.234–36; Eng. trans. by Murray, LCL, 1:291; cf. Meltzer, "Homer's Tragic Vision," 265–80, esp. 266.

unilateral *and* extraordinary benefits to another, whereas the Scythian, Toxaris, recounts tales of Scythian friends who bestow useless benefits on one another. Based upon the expectations associated with friendship, the humor of defied expectations or the absurd in these stories is apparent.

The Greek examples especially highlight, in a humorous manner, a notion of exaggerated or disproportionate reciprocity, even to the point where giving and usefulness are completely one-sided and disadvantageous. One example is illustrative in Lucian's dialogue. Eudamidas, an extremely poor person, was said to have two wealthy friends, Aretaeus and Charixenus. There is no account of Eudamidas's usefulness to his friends. In fact, Mnessipus's account begins with Eudamidas's death after which his will is read. In his will, he leaves to Aretaeus the care of his aging mother, and he gives to Charixenus his daughter of marital age the responsibility of bestowing a sizeable dowry for her marriage. Moreover, if anything should happen to either Aretaeus or Charixenus, the other would take over the unfulfilled charge stipulated in the will. Indeed, Mnessipus states that Eudamidas's will appeared "absurd" (γελοῖος) to others (*Tox.* 22). All who heard it considered it a "joke" (γελῶν) and amidst laughing said: "What a fine fortune Aretaeus and Charixenus . . . are coming into . . . if they must pay out money to Eudamidas and have the dead man inherit from them while they themselves are still alive!"[36] Again, here we are dealing with humor of the absurd through defying customary expectations because of the disproportion in incongruous reciprocity. The rich friends may also be targeted as fools for taking up the absurd demands of a dead man.

Humor of Exchanging One's Patrimony

Another subject of humorous or disproportionate exchanges that is particularly relevant to this study involves the illogical foolishness of squandering one's patrimony. In fact, squandering one's patrimony is a special topic of foolishness and the object of much rhetorical humor. Cicero made common use of this topic against Antony in his *Second Philippic* (42; 44; 50; cf. Quintilian, *Inst.* 6.3.74).[37] Quintilian cites a humorous anecdote when Crassus cleverly ridiculed Brutus for losing much of his "paternal estates" (*Inst.* 6.3.44; cf. Cicero, *De or.* 2.226–27). The

---

36. Lucian, *Tox.* 22; Eng. trans. by Harmon, LCL, 141.
37. Cf. Craig, "Audience Expectations," 190–92.

squandering of one's patrimony is in line with the what *Tractatus Coislinianus* describes for actions that elicit laughter, namely, *neglecting the greatest things to take the most worthless*.[38]

The most relevant example of comic foolishness where a person exchanges his or her patrimony for something worthless is found in Aristophanes's comedy *Aves*. In the play, birds have set up a kingdom between the realm of the gods and earth. Because of this blockade, the gods are no longer receiving sacrifices and thus are starving. The gods, eager to resolve this dilemma, send an embassy of Poseidon, Heracles, and a Triballian god to meet with the leader of the birds, Peisetaerus (*Aves* 1565). Upon their arrival, Peisetaerus is cooking a savory meal of birds who recently rebelled against the bird polis. A starving Heracles is particularly interested in this meal upon his arrival. Peisetaerus makes his demand, namely that Zeus return the scepter to the birds and that Zeus makes Sovereignty (Βασίλεια) Peisetaerus's wife. If the embassy can agree to these terms, then they are invited to the meal that is being prepared.

Upon hearing the invitation to lunch, Heracles immediately votes for Peisetaerus's demands so that he can go straight to the meal. Poseidon is astonished and rebukes Heracles calling him "possessed of an evil spirit (κᾰκοδαιμον)" and "an idiotic glutton (ἠλίθιος καὶ γάστρις)" who is robbing Zeus, his father, of his rule (1604–5). Moreover, Poseidon argues that Heracles, as a son of Zeus, is harming himself: "Look if Zeus surrenders his rule to these birds, you will be left a pauper when he dies, because now you stand to get the whole estate that he leaves behind at his death."[39] Of course, it is absurd to think that deathless Zeus would die, but, just as absurd, Heracles, who is ruled by his belly, goes ahead and trades his inheritance for a single meal.[40]

Summary of the Absurd

Taken together, these examples illustrate the humor of absurdity through disproportion, especially disproportion that defies customary

---

38. Janko, *Aristotle*, 37. The common use of this cultural intertext speaks to the issue of "volume" and "historical plausibility" or the likelihood that squandering one's patrimony would be heard as a humorous trope by the audience of Hebrews (cf. Hays, *Echoes*, 30).

39. Aristophanes, *Aves* 141–45; Eng. trans. by Henderson, LCL, 237.

40. This portrayal of Heracles as gluttonous fool is a common trope in Greek comedy. Cf. Stafford, *Herakles*, 105–17.

expectations in incongruous exchanges. Moreover, foolishness has been made the target of humor with regard to incongruous reciprocity and especially in the case of squandering one's patrimony. In Cicero's speech, squandering one's patrimony functions as a humorous invective against his opponent, Antony, while in Aristophanes's play, the humor, in part, diminishes one of the chief Greek heroes by portraying him as an idiotic glutton. Such examples raise the possibility of interpreting incongruous exchange, particularly as it regards patrimony, as comical for ancient audiences—a fact which is critical in assessing Esau's actions as characterized by the author of Hebrews.

The Humorous Example of Esau in Heb 12:16

In turning to Heb 12:16, the question is not whether we personally find the example of Esau humorous, but whether or not the example fits the expectations associated with humor from the ancient Mediterranean world.[41] Moreover, if this example fits these expectations, what function might it have in the discourse? First, we will consider the elements of humor present in the example of Esau. Second, we will look at the function of humor in this example.

Identifying the Elements of Humor in Esau's Example

The example of Esau satisfies several points of rhetorical humor discussed above.

First, the form of humor we are dealing with is obviously not the continuous sort that runs through a whole speech. Instead, the example of Esau is a brief "shaft of wit." As Cicero notes, these short witticisms or "shafts of wit" can be inserted "with no palpable pause for thought," which the author of Hebrews has apparently done.[42]

In fact, we have a shaft of wit that is integrated into a serious discourse. The point of the humor is serious, as Quintilian recognizes and the senators' disguised laughter at Commodus illustrates. "With no palpable pause for thought," the author reminds his audience of the seriousness of the circumstances in 12:17. Especially for those who might not

---

41. Cicero acknowledges that intended humor was not always "gotten" by everyone (cf. *Fam.* 207[XV.21].2).

42. Cicero, *De or.* 2.218–20; Eng. trans. by Sutton and Rackham, LCL, 1:359.

feel the humor in the example of Esau, the author reminds the audience that Esau's actions have irrevocable consequences. Esau was rejected and found no place for repentance though he sought the return of his birthright with tears.

Second, rhetorical theorists, as previously mentioned, divided humor into two large topical categories of words and things/deeds. Some topics related to words from which humor arises are homonyms, synonyms, repetition, paronyms, diminutives, alteration by sound or by genus, and parody (*Tractatus Coislinianus*; cf. Cicero, *De or.* 2.250-63; Quintilian, *Inst.* 6.3.96-98).[43] While possibly not particularly humorous, the author of Hebrews seems to have carefully chosen his words to create a sense of delight when heard. He states that Esau "for one meal gave up his own birthright." The central phrase in 12:16 "one meal gave up the birthright" in Greek is:

βρώσεως μιᾶς
ἀπέδετο τὰ
πρωτοτόκια.

Here the author has employed the "Gorgianic" figures of *homoeokatarkton* (βρω/πρω), *homoeoteleuton* (μιας/κια), and parisosis (βρώσεως μιᾶς = 5 syllables / πρωτοτόκια = 5 syllables). These are elements which he has already used in the opening exordium.[44] The phrase in 12:16 is then one that would likely stick in the minds of the audience and possibly create awareness for potential humor when hearing it.

Third, there are a few other topical categories and causes of humor that can be identified in the example of Esau. Again, Quintilian notes that several points of humor may converge in one instance. Regarding special topics discussed with humor, the author has employed a historical example. As an instance of humor, the example is what the rhetorical theorists might label "a joke from history." Quintilian particularly notes that a joke from history shows the orator's erudition (*Inst.* 6.3.98; cf. Cicero, *De or.* 2.264).

The author of Hebrews has also drawn upon one of the most common causes of humor, the unexpected. The author opens his description of Esau as one who is sexually immoral and profane. After such a description, the audience (or those in the audience who knew the fuller story of Esau) might expect the author to say something about Esau's marriage to

43. Janko, *Aristotle*, 29-35.
44. Martin and Whitlark, *Inventing Hebrews*, 202-9.

Hittite women, which was a source of vexation and bitterness for his parents.[45] Instead, the author turns to the instance of the story where Esau gives Jacob his birthright for a bowl of lentil soup. Such an unexpected turn also alerts the audience to think of πόρνος and βέβηλος in more figural terms where sexual immorality and godlessness are associated with covenant unfaithfulness by turning to idols (e.g., Hos 1–4; Rev 2:14, 20).

The example of Esau falls under the topic of absurdity, especially in the form of disproportionate and incongruous exchanges. In particular, the author draws upon the common trope of squandering one's patrimony or—as *Tractatus Coislinianus* more broadly categorizes the topic—exchanging the better for the worse. Like Heracles in *Aves*, Esau, who is starving, happens upon Jacob while he is preparing a meal of lentil soup. Like Heracles, Esau gives no thought to the value of his birthright but only to the immediate demands of his empty stomach. The exchange is absurd, ridiculous, even laughable because it is disproportionate and incongruous. Such exchanges are a common source of humor as previously discussed.

Lastly, the author of Hebrews is clearly targeting foolishness, a common object of humor, with the example of Esau. The author leaves no question about this by beginning his characterization of Esau as πόρνος and βέβηλος. In fact, in line with Cicero's and Quintilian's instructions, the author has not targeted extreme wickedness or wretchedness in the episode he highlights from Esau's life. He has fittingly chosen an instance of humor that would not illicit the audience's deepest sympathies or strongest disgust.

Identifying the Function of Humor in Esau's Example

If the example of Esau fulfills standard rhetorical and cultural expectations for humor in form, object, and topics, what then is the function of the humorous example in Hebrews? There are three potential considerations here. Before discussing these functions, it should be noted that the invective against Esau is analogously related to the audience. Esau exchanging his birthright as the firstborn son of Isaac for a single meal parallels the choice that the audience faces regarding their own birthright as children of God. The author has just affirmed the audience's filial

---

45. Cf. Gen. 26:34–35; Jub. 25:1. For a discussion of Esau in Second Temple Jewish texts, see Löhr, *Umkehr*, 123–39.

relationship to God as father in the previous verses of Heb 12:4–11, has stated that they have received the promise of an eternal inheritance in 9:15, and will refer in the forthcoming verses to the redeemed faithful as the "assembly of the firstborn" (12:23). Esau, then, is a fittingly chosen analogy for the audience. He belongs to the patriarchal period that predominates the previous list of exemplars in Heb 11. He has a birthright as a firstborn son, which he gives up. Moreover, he is unable to recover it once it is given up, even though he expresses regret—an example that recalls the stern warnings of Heb 6:4–6 and 10:26–31 from the two preceding deliberative sections (5:11—6:20 and 10:19—12:13).

Regarding the first function of the humorous example of Esau in Hebrews 12:16, we should recognize that it belongs to 12:14–17, which is a secondary *peroratio* (13:1–25 being the primary). In line with the expectations associated with a *peroratio*, it is brief. It comes at the end of the lengthy central sections that span from 4:14—12:17. It exhibits the typical function of recapitulation, as in the example of Esau noted above. The other typical function of a *peroratio* is to stir the emotions of the audience. Quintilian acknowledges the pervasive assessment of rhetorical theorists that the *exordium* and the *peroratio* are the most common places for engaging the emotions (*Inst.* 6.1.51–52). There are a couple of ways that the author stirs the emotions. Heb 12:14–17 uses cryptic, figured language which is recognized as a forceful and emotional way of speaking (cf. Demetrius, *Eloc.* 243). It also uses the stylistic feature of asyndeton commonly recommended for *perorationes* in order to heighten the emotions (e.g., Apsines, *Rhet.* 10.55). Thus, an appeal to humor would be appropriate here in Hebrews since the rhetorical theorists commonly associated humor with the emotions.[46]

Second, Esau's exchanging his birthright for a single meal is analogous to apostasy. Apostasy is the danger to the community. To quit the community, to reject God's promise in Jesus Christ, and to return to their former lives are the pressures that the members of the community face (e.g., 3:12–14; 6:4–6, 11–12; 10:25, 35–36; 12:25). The author returns again and again to encourage his audience to remain faithful and to warn them against committing apostasy.[47] With the comical example of Esau,

46. Further arguments for identifying Heb 12:14–17 as a secondary *peroratio* are found in Martin and Whitlark, *Inventing Hebrews*, 222–49.

47. This is the whole argument of the five deliberative sections 2:1–18; 3:7—4:13; 5:11—6:20; 10:19—12:13; 12:25–29; cf. Martin and Whitlark, *Inventing Hebrews*, 86–128. On apostasy in general in Hebrews, see Oropeza, *Churches under Siege*, 3–70.

the author shows his audience the absurdity of apostasy. It is not only foolish, but also ridiculous. It is a shortsighted, incongruous exchange, giving up the better for the worse. Any in the audience who can see or, better yet, feel the humor in this analogous example has appropriately valued the "great salvation" he or she has been promised by God.[48]

Third, attacking an opponent is particularly recommended for a *peroratio* and is the goal of much humorous invective (cf. Aristotle, *Rhet.* 3.19.1; Cicero, *Inv.* 1.98–105; *Rhet. Her.* 2.47–49) and "shafts of wit" as noted by Quintilian. In deliberative cases, like Hebrews, the opponent may be the one recommending the alternative course of action that should be avoided or, more figural, the opponent may be the alternative course of action itself.[49] But what opponent or alternative course of action does the situation of Esau recall for the audience?

We are given a clue as to the type of apostasy that the choice of Esau analogously warns against. In the previous verse of 12:16, the author had just warned against "a root of bitterness." The imagery is taken from Deut 29:17 (LXX) where the people are warned not to turn away from God and serve the gods of the nations. Such apostasy will lead to "a root which grows in gall and bitterness" among the Israelite community. Moreover, these apostates will be blotted out from under heaven. This warning against idolatry provides potent imagery from the Old Testament, and the author finds it particularly fitting for any members of the audience who might be considering identifying with their former pagan lives and with the hopes promised by Rome and its rule. Indeed, the author consistently draws his imagery and references for his warning against apostasy from OT texts whose contexts warn against idolatry and compromise with pagan nations.[50] This is demonstrated poignantly in Heb 11 wherein we find the author drawing upon such examples as Moses and Rahab to support his exhortations to endure and not to apostatize to pagan society and the promises of imperial power.

---

48. Of course, we cannot avoid the conclusion here that any actual apostate is portrayed as foolish.

49. For a defense of the overall deliberative purpose of Hebrews, see Martin and Whitlark, *Inventing Hebrews*, 250–59.

50. This observation arises from the idea of *metalepsis* in intertextual studies that quotations and allusions often assume an understanding of the broader literary context from which they are taken (cf. Hollander, *Figure of Echo*, 115). For further discussion of the function of idol polemic and the warning against idolatry in Hebrews, see Whitlark, *Resisting Empire*, 49–76.

The opponent, then, is not specifically Esau, Jacob, or even the apostates that Esau might represent. The opponent is more broadly defined. It is the pagan imperial culture experienced through those who represent its agenda and are pressuring the audience to forsake its commitment to God and his Son.[51] More apocalyptically, the opponent could be the devil "who holds the power of death" and stands behind the pagan imperial culture that seeks to dislodge the community from its hope in God's promise (cf. 2:14).[52] In fact, in his example of Esau, the author employs a measure of ambiguity, a characteristic of rhetorical humor and of figured speech when authorities or authoritarian power is ridiculed. He does not name his opponent but instead allows members of his audience to make the analogous connection to their own lives.

As the author points out, the community has already experienced and continues to undergo humiliation, privation, imprisonment, and torture. The choice they face is like that of Moses: they may continue to suffer with the people of God living in the hope of God's promise, or they can return to the pleasure of Egypt, a life marked by idolatry and the pleasures promised by Roman rule. The humor in Esau's example cuts Rome and its gods down to size, thereby diminishing the arrogant boasts of Rome. They are nothing more than a single meal of lentil soup, a momentary salve for the pain of suffering, but a loss of something more precious and lasting—an eternal inheritance and rule with Jesus in the world to come (Heb 2:5-9).

In this humor, the audience is able to form resistance and a defense against the mocking and denigration they are experiencing in a way similar to the response of the senators to Commodus's ridiculous display that was meant as a serious threat against them. Recognizing humor here in the discourse of Hebrews also shows that the world as lived under Roman rule is not inevitable. The audience can see the absurdity of apostasy because only God's promise is inevitable. The humor is not cynical but hopeful. Or, more accurately, for one to feel the humor in the example of Esau, there is a "holding to the confidence and boasting of hope" that

---

51 Moreover, the object of the humor is not Judaism or the Jews, a common supposition of traditional relapse theories. The author, in fact, employs the old covenant to encourage faithfulness to God. The exhortation under the new covenant and old covenant is fundamentally the same: "[C]hoose for yourselves this day whom you will serve, whether the gods your ancestors served beyond the Euphrates, or the gods of the Amorites, in whose land you are living. But as for me and my household, we will serve the LORD" (Josh 24:15). Cf. Martin and Whitlark, *Inventing Hebrews*, 265-70.

52. Cf. Whitlark, *Resisting Empire*, 122-41.

is grounded on God's promise (Heb 3:6). Only then is the absurdity of apostasy recognized.

Conclusion

While this study limited its examination of humor in Heb 12:16 to expectations related to humor in the milieu of the audience of Hebrews, studies of humor in the modern era also enhance our understanding of the various functions of humor. First, studies by Paul McGhee have shown that the active use of humor provides powerful tools to cope with and recover from adverse situations.[53] Gaining through humor a different perspective on stressful situations can make those circumstances seem less anxiety-ridden and threatening.[54] Certainly the author consistently works to shift the audience's perspective to the unseen realities of the world to come, which is their inheritance.

Second, modern studies affirm that humor has powerful community-forming effects.[55] The ability to share in the humor of a group signals a willingness to belong because of a shared perspective represented by the humor. Shared humor makes a group more cohesive.[56] If the audience even shares a gesture or mutually recognizes the *ridiculus* in the example of Esau, they are affirming not only shared experiences but also a shared reality—a reality of things hoped for through Jesus Christ (cf. Heb 11:1).[57]

Hopefully, this study continues to invite investigation of humor and intertextuality in the New Testament, especially in non-Gospel texts.[58] As Mary Beard notes, "It almost goes without saying that we could write a better and 'thicker' description of any historical society if we understood the protocols and practice of its laughter."[59] Additionally, this study raises

53. McGhee, *Humor*.
54. Papousek, "Humor," 313; 316.
55. Cf. Beard, *Laughter*, 106–7.
56. Gockel and Kerr, "Cohesion in Groups," 207–8.
57. Beard hypothesizes that Romans did not smile as we do, though possibly other silent gestures communicated the range of meaning we associate with a smile (*Laughter*, 73–76).
58. E.g., see Oropeza, *Exploring*, 645; 653; 669; 678; 682–87 (esp. 685), where, in Paul's Fool's Discourse (1 Cor 11:21—12:13), Paul's "paradoxical *encomium*" potentially points to humor and his "comic relief" explicitly does so.
59. Beard, *Laughter*, 51.

questions as to whether the earliest Christians developed their own "sense of humor" that arose from their gospel-shaped perspective. Sub-groups within larger cultural matrices often develop identifiable humor, even a humor of resistance that negotiated the experience of oppressive power.[60] Finally, the presence of humor among early Christians invites theological reflection on humor as a creational aspect of human life under God.

---

60. Cf. Cowan, "Plantation Comic Modes," 1–24, esp. 8–12.

15

Intertextuality beyond Echoes

Cain and Abel in the Second Temple Jewish Cultural Context

Ryder A. Wishart

REFERENCES TO CAIN AND Abel in the New Testament exemplify the problematic nature of trying to identify direct connections between texts.[1] Sometimes a reference lacks key words from the supposed reference text.[2] At other times, a single lexeme in context indicates an entire thematic structure.[3] Rather than seeing such references as allusions, echoes, or any other kind of document-to-document connection, these may reflect text-to-culture-to-text connections.[4] Where scholars in the

---

1. *Reference* denotes all of the myriad intertextual phenomena that are formally distinguished in the field, such as quotation/citation, allusion, paraphrase, echo, etc.; one might also use an umbrella term such as *similarity, point of contact,* or *connection*—but *reference,* here meaning "any of the above," will do just as well. Cf. Stamps "Use of the Old Testament," 11.

2. Cf. Lucas, "Paul and the Calf," 111. Mason ("Traces of the Golden Calf," 142) likewise notes that, for example, "the author of Hebrews uses texts from elsewhere in the Jewish Scriptures to discuss events or figures from the Pentateuch rather than from the books of the Pentateuch themselves."

3. Cf. Frey, "Notion of the Spirit."

4. Foster ("Echoes without Resonance," 98) notes, "This approach . . . has been especially generative for doctoral topics . . . and has become more than a 'cottage

field trace *direct* connections between texts, these should be reconsidered as *indirect* connections, connections by way of shared cultural meanings.[5] The NT references to Cain and Abel, though following the Septuagintal tradition in some respects, nevertheless evidence engagement with the Masoretic tradition as well. These references engage both traditions simultaneously because they engage neither directly.[6] It is my contention that Hebrews answers a question the MT raises and that many different Jewish communities over the centuries sought to answer: namely, what kind of sacrifice pleases God?

One particular line of discussion in the secondary literature on Cain and Abel examines the relationship between construals of the brothers in the MT, LXX, and NT. Using Jay Lemke's model of heteroglossic intertextual relations, I bring these "canonical"[7] text traditions into dialogue with other non-canonical primary sources, illustrating the broad cultural conversation on Cain and Abel within Second Temple Judaism.[8] Finally, I demonstrate how faith, as the disposition acceptable to God in Heb 11:4

---

industry' . . . more akin to a mechanized production line, with its own methodology and theological agendas." Hays's "seven tests" for identifying/interpreting echoes or allusions remain standard criteria for many, despite challenges outlined by Allen, "Study of the Use of the Old Testament," 11.

5. For an example of how this direct dependence is traced between NT documents and specific OT documents, see Hilhorst, "Abel's Speaking," 120.

6. For a similar argument, see Byron, "Slaughter, Fratricide and Sacrilege."

7. Canonical texts played a decisive role in Second Temple Jewish culture, nevertheless, as Krentz (*Historical-Critical Method*, 48) says: "Restrict yourself to the canon and you will not understand the canon." The assumption, cf. Moyise (*Old Testament in the New*, 186), is that a reference is a reference to a canonical OT text unless the referent cannot be found, in which case one may go beyond the boundaries of the Catholic canon in search of the referent. In fact, this line of reasoning inverts the order. References refer to cultural formulations of meaning, concepts, themes, or topics. Some of these refer to a particular thematic formation in a specific text, as when a reference is introduced with γεγράπται ("it is written")—these are the "quotations." Even in these cases, however, the significance of the later text's reference goes beyond the content of the referent text, since the later text does not make references in a cultural (nor a canonical) vacuum. Later references must be located against the backdrop of their cultural context, its texts and social groupings, and the social values they realize.

8. For a "historically plausible" outline of the skeleton of a shared, late Second Temple, Jerusalemite Judaic cultural system," see Lightstone, "Late Second Temple Judaism," 89–90. Lightstone describes five "thematic categories" that are referenced throughout the Hebrew Bible, the Gospels, Acts, the NT epistles, Josephus, and the Dead Sea Scrolls, and also in the Mishnah and Tosefta.

(and 12:24), both supports and opposes other uses of the Cain and Abel tradition in Second Temple culture.

Cain and Abel in the "Canonical" Sources

The Cain and Abel tradition occurs more than once in the New Testament. While in each case readers recognize the same core tradition of the story, all of these references appear to expand on the story itself without offering any clear indication of how that original story (in Hebrew) gives rise to NT embellishments. These NT passages are listed as follows:[9]

- In order that all the just blood poured out upon the earth might come upon you, from the blood of righteous Abel to the blood of Zachariah son of Barachiah, whom you murdered between the temple and the altar. (Matt 23:35 // Luke 11:51)

- By faith Abel offered a better sacrifice to God than Cain, through which he was testified to be righteous (God testifying on the basis of his gifts), and through which he, despite being dead, still speaks. (Heb 11:4)

- And to Jesus, mediator of the new covenant, and to the sprinkling blood, to the one who speaks stronger than Abel.[10] (Heb 12:24)

- Woe to them, because they have gone in the way of Cain, and they were poured out for wages in the error of Balaam, and in the rebellion of Korah they destroyed themselves. (Jude 11)

- Not as Cain was from the evil one and murdered his brother. And for what did he murder him? Because his works were evil, and those of his brother were righteous. (1 John 3:12)

Each of these passages makes reference to the story of Cain and Abel, and as each seems to be doing something different with the story, they have occasioned various scholarly analyses. Here I outline one thread of discussion, namely, the way NT texts expand upon (or do not expand upon) Gen 4 (MT).

Bruce Waltke has offered a reading in Gen 4 that is highly congruent with the NT above passages. He points out how Abel's sacrifice in the MT

---

9. All Greek and Hebrew translations given in this paper are my own.
10. For justification of this particular reading, see Smillie, "One Who Is Speaking," 282.

is qualified by "firstborn," whereas Cain's sacrifice lacks the corresponding "firstfruits" that would be expected, and Cain's also lacks a parallel to the "fat" of Abel's sacrifice.[11] "Cain's flawed character," Waltke says, "led to his feigned worship."[12] These and other arguments lead Waltke to conclude that "Abel's sacrifice represents acceptable, heartfelt worship; Cain's represents unacceptable tokenism."[13] Waltke claims: "The NT validates our conclusions drawn from the text."[14] One interesting assumption implied in Waltke's comparison is that the NT writers apparently drew their own interpretations from the MT, not LXX.

By contrast, Joel Lohr argues that the MT's Cain and Abel tradition is ambiguous on a number of points, whereas the LXX decidedly slants the narrative against Cain.[15] Lohr delineates the differences between the MT and LXX, pointing out the effects of these interpretive changes introduced by the LXX translators who, by implication, denigrate Cain and exalt Abel (see Table 1 below).[16]

TABLE 1. LXX ELABORATIONS ON THE MT ACCOUNT

Verse	MT	LXX	(Potential) Effect
2	ו	δέ	The brothers' vocations are contrasted.
4	מנחה	δῶρον	Abel offers a superior "gift."
5	מנחה	θυσία	Cain offers a lesser "sacrifice."
4	שעה	ἐφοράω	Abel is "looked upon with favor."
5	שעה	προσέχω	Cain is rejected or "forsaken."
7	enigmatic Hebrew	suggests a ritual error in Cain's way of offering	Cain's actions become clearly responsible for his previous lack of divine favor.
8	no speech	Cain says: διέλθωμεν εἰς τὸ πεδίον	Cain invites Abel to the field, suggesting a plotted, premeditated murder.

11. Waltke, "Cain and His Offering," 368.
12. Waltke, "Cain and His Offering," 371.
13. Waltke, "Cain and His Offering," 369.
14. Waltke, "Cain and His Offering," 371.
15. Lohr, "Righteous Abel, Wicked Cain," 485.
16. Lohr, "Righteous Abel, Wicked Cain," 491.

Lohr argues that the NT authors uncritically adopt the LXX view, such that the NT represents an unjustly critical construal of Cain. "The reasons for YHWH's choice of Abel," he says, "are not to be readily found in the Hebrew text," and, "Cain, despite killing his brother, is left in a relatively positive light when compared to the LXX."[17] "To be sure," Lohr clarifies, "he is cursed for his action of murder, but it is not made explicit, prior to this act, whether he is guilty of any sin in his offering or if his actions constitute the reason for his lack of favor."[18] This ambiguity has led interpreters to offer a number of more concrete reasons for God's rejection of Cain's sacrifice. Lohr states:

> God prefers shepherds over farmers, animal over grain offerings, or a sacrifice of blood over one without. Others suggest that it is because the אדמה ("ground") was cursed in the previous chapter (3:17), and Cain should have known better than to bring an offering from it. Still others point to the idea that Abel offers from the best sheep and their fat portions while Cain, it is said, offers only some of the fruit, likely bad fruit. This is but a partial list.[19]

All of these possible explanations, says Lohr, share the common failure of going beyond the original MT, offering explanations for Cain's personal and ritual inadequacy without textual grounds for doing so. He argues such explanations are guilty of "microscopic over-reading," and this same technique can be used to argue for the precise opposite points.[20] For example, Waltke states: "In such a laconic story the interpreter may not ignore that whereas Abel's gift is qualified by 'firstborn,' the parallel 'firstfruits' does not modify Cain's." But Lohr points out that Cain is said to offer "to YHWH," something not said of Abel's sacrifice; can this omission be ignored by Waltke?[21] Lohr evaluates this state of affairs, saying:

> The problem here seems to stem from a determination on the part of interpreters to explain the divine choice and excise any hint that it is arbitrary or unjustified. Surely Abel's favor must have been with reason; surely Cain must have deserved his lack

---

17. Lohr, "Righteous Abel, Wicked Cain," 491–92. For an even stronger positive interpretation of Cain as a "culture hero," see McNutt, "In the Shadow of Cain," 60.
18. Lohr, "Righteous Abel, Wicked Cain," 492.
19. Lohr, "Righteous Abel, Wicked Cain," 492 with n25–30.
20. Lohr, "Righteous Abel, Wicked Cain," 492–93; cf. Levenson, *Death and Resurrection*, 72.
21. Waltke, "Cain and His Offering," 368.

of favor in some way. As I have observed, the MT text does not make this explicit; the interpreter must make a conscious decision to fill these details in.[22]

Lohr's intuition on this point appears to be correct, but such interpretive determination is very ancient indeed. He does not pursue this line of reasoning, but instead concludes that Gen 4 recounts a common trope of God's favouring the younger son without cause.[23]

Tom Thatcher accepts Lohr's basic premise that the LXX and the New Testament have extrapolated from an inherently ambiguous MT tradition.[24] Thatcher, however, argues:

> Lohr stops short just at the point where his observations might have yielded the most interesting interpretive fruit. Specifically, although Lohr traces the contours of the LXX and NT readings of Cain … he does not venture an answer to the obvious question, Why did the LXX translators and the NT authors interpret the Genesis account in the particular ways in which they did?[25]

To be fair, Lohr does offer something of an explanation for the NT interpretation, namely that the NT authors were simply adopting the LXX uncritically. Thatcher, however, is interested in two more important questions: "What factors shaped early Christian memory of these tragic figures from the ancient past, and what rhetorical purposes did the evocation of Cain and Abel serve?"[26]

Thatcher also points out that Lohr's treatment does not explain why these ancient figures would be evoked in the first place.[27] Using social/collective memory theory, Thatcher argues that the memory of Cain and Abel among early Christians served two major functions. First, it helped rationalize experiences of group-external persecution, as Christians saw their own experiences as a reenactment of innocent Abel's suffering at the hands of wicked Cain. Second, this memory provided a means for dichotomizing group-internal conflict, as those on the wrong side of the debate were rescripted in the present situation as those who willfully rejected God's warnings and proceeded to turn against their righteous

22. Lohr, "Righteous Abel, Wicked Cain," 493.
23. Lohr, "Righteous Abel, Wicked Cain," 495.
24. Thatcher, "Cain and Abel," 736.
25. Thatcher, "Cain and Abel," 733.
26. Thatcher, "Cain and Abel," 733.
27. Thatcher, "Cain and Abel," 736.

brother.[28] The reason Cain and Abel were evoked at all is that elements of their story "could be readily keyed to the dynamics of situations where Christian identity was at risk."[29]

Thatcher's argument clarifies two pressing methodological issues in the study of the use of the Old Testament in the New Testament. First, Thatcher adopts a social focus in his study, providing the right contextual lens for adopting a functional focus. Typically, studies in this field focus on the formal alignments or lack thereof between a NT text and an OT intertext.[30] Thatcher adopts a better, functional emphasis with his focus on how "communities shape recollections of the past in service of present social needs."[31]

Second, and closely related to the first point, Thatcher advocates a cultural rather than documentary focus.[32] Thatcher advocates that intertextual references operate not on a documentary level, as if every reference directly depends on a specific document. Rather, references operate on a cultural level drawing on, for Thatcher, "collective memory." This distinction between a documentary and cultural focus is precisely where Hays's notion of echo falls short. The literary echo evokes for readers, according to Hays, the textual context of the echoed material. The problem with this view sometimes is that it focuses on the wrong context, namely the textual rather than the cultural. For Thatcher, thinking solely in terms of text-dependencies (whether exact wordings or content) misses the larger picture of how intertextual references function.[33]

Where Thatcher's study itself stops short is in generating a description not only of the rhetorical functions of certain recollections, but also what these functions imply about the underlying social values being negotiated in the culture—and more specifically—the ways in which particular configurations of meaning in the discourses of different groups realize those social values. An interpretation of one group's texts actually requires that we situate them against a backdrop of a broader cultural

28. Thatcher, "Cain and Abel," 749.

29. Thatcher, "Cain and Abel," 749.

30. Even Hays's introduction of literary "echo" as a classification of non-formal connections is still placed on a scale of most-to-least-explicit intertextual relationship. See Hays, *Echoes of Scripture in the Gospels*, 10; Porter, "Further Comments"; Porter, "Brief Comment."

31. Thatcher, "Cain and Abel," 736.

32. Thatcher, "Cain and Abel," 749.

33. Thatcher, "Cain and Abel," 740–41n26.

conversation. In short, further consideration is required of the intertextual setting of the NT writings. Bringing the discussion back to the textual and intertextual level allows one to describe not only the content of a text, but also its value(s) relative to other texts. This is an especially important part of the interpretive task for which Thatcher has laid the groundwork, but which requires a model of how distinct voices interact both within texts and also within a broader culture by means of texts.

In summary, Waltke's analysis of Cain and Abel in the MT is exemplary of the possibility for generating explanatory readings that comport with the New Testament's own interpretive traditions. Lohr demonstrates in turn that these interpretive traditions, both in the primary and secondary literature, are a reflex of the ambiguities in the MT, which leave readers with unanswered questions that continue to motivate responses. Finally, Thatcher pushes toward a social and functional understanding of the NT texts, arguing that these texts "keyed" Cain and Abel as "landmarks," that is, as part of a normative past that existed in collective memory, to the present experience of the community as a way for it to structure that experience and reinforce group identity. In the next section, I outline Lemke's model of intertextual thematic formations in order to situate an intertextual analysis of NT Cain and Abel material.

Methodology: Heteroglossia and Intertextuality

The term *intertextuality* has been variously understood in biblical studies,[34] but here I adopt the understanding put forward by Jay Lemke: "The meaning of a text depends directly on the kinds of connections made in a particular community between it and other texts."[35] In other words, neglecting to take stock of the intertextual nature of texts or discourses, which always exist within a cultural context that includes other discourses, results in an inadequate account of textual meaning. Lemke argues: "Meanings are made between texts and between parts of a text that are not made in words, clauses, or clause complexes taken in isolation," and therefore, "a complete account of textual meaning must describe how the sense we make with words depends, not just on their grammatical and situational contexts, but on the intertextual contexts in which we place

---

34. Emadi, "Intertextuality in New Testament," 8–9, 21.
35. Lemke, "Intertextuality and Text Semantics," 85.

them."[36] Lemke therefore offers the following definition of intertextuality: "Intertextuality is concerned with the recurrent discourse and activity patterns of the community and how they are constituted by, instanced in, and interconnected or disjoined through particular texts."[37]

For Lemke, there are three components to text analysis: thematics, genre, and word choice.[38] These three components have been essential to the field of biblical studies all along—scholars have always studied the Bible in terms of its themes and genres, and any text-based discipline engages in responsible exegesis or analysis of wordings. In this essay, the focus is on thematics, which involves the *thematic formations* in a text. A thematic formation is "a recurrent pattern of semantic relations used in talking about a specific topic from text to text."[39] A thematic formation can be represented as a set of thematic *items* connected by thematic *relations*.[40] An *intertextual* thematic formation can be understood as a generalized thematic formation that is abstracted from numerous texts instantiating a similar or the same thematic formation.[41] Below I argue that Second Temple Jewish culture realizes a [Cain and Abel] intertextual thematic formation.[42]

While these three components are in principle independent—for example, selection of theme does not determine genre or word choice—certain combinations become conventional in a social system. When one generalized combination of thematics, genre, and wording becomes conventional and recognizable, that combination can be called a *discourse formation*. A given discourse formation, such as *prophecies and warnings about the future* (thematics) in a *sermon* (genre) using *wordings drawn from well-recognized, authoritative OT texts* (word choice), will be realized in a social group in many different actual texts, or *instances*. It is here that intertextuality enters the picture, since any text of a given discourse formation (i.e., the combination of the three components) is a potentially relevant intertext essential for interpreting all other instances

---

36. Lemke, "Intertextuality and Text Semantics," 85.
37. Lemke, "Intertextuality and Text Semantics," 86.
38. Lemke, "Intertextuality and Text Semantics," 90; Lemke, *Talking Science*, 203.
39. Lemke, "Intertextuality and Text Semantics," 91.
40. For examples of graphic representation, see Lemke, "Intertextuality and Text Semantics"; Xue, "Intertextual Discourse Analysis," 94.
41. Lemke, "Intertextuality and the Project," 223.
42. I follow Lemke in using square brackets to designate thematic items, and square brackets with capitalized words to designate thematic formations.

of that discourse formation.[43] "The *intertexts* of a text," Lemke explains, "are all the other texts that we use to make sense of it."[44] These intertexts will either be (1) cothematic, sharing the same thematic patterns or parts thereof; (2) coactional, as two different elements in the same activity, such as the opening and closing of a letter; or else (3) cogeneric, sharing the same genre structure.[45]

Where intertextual relations become most interesting is in the ways that texts differ from one another, both in terms of content and in terms of evaluative stance. Different groups within a society will use language in different ways, and the way someone speaks about a given issue, particularly when it is a source of tension within a society, will indicate the group(s) they belong to.[46] Groups will thus tend to use (1) different thematic formations (even when different formations fall within the same "umbrella" formation), and (2) different evaluative stances, particularly *positive* or *negative* stances to the same thematic formations. Heteroglossia means "different ways of speaking" and it "covers the differences of thematic formations and the different value orientations of each group to those formations."[47] The ways in which groups differ relate systematically within the total possibilities of their shared cultural/societal context. Thus, two thematic formations that are regarded as being "about the same thing" will relate based on "thematic-semantic" differences or similarities and also based on axiological relations (i.e., value orientation or stance).[48]

In summary, the notion of thematic formations enables one to identify potentially relevant intertexts for any given text, for two texts that share the same intertextual thematic formation or similar thematic formations are "talking about the same thing," and thus may be important for mutual interpretation. Heteroglossic intertextual relations in turn offer a principled means by which intertexts can be examined for their allied or opposed value orientations. Together, these two notions enable one to speak about the systematically related ideas (thematic formations) and values (alliances or oppositions) operative within a given set of intertexts

43. Lemke, *Talking Science*, 204.
44. Lemke, *Talking Science*, 204.
45. In actuality, texts will not be "pure" instances, but will mix multiple thematic formations and genres and will realize these in multiple ways (Lemke, *Talking Science*, 205).
46. Lemke, *Talking Science*, 206–7.
47. Lemke, *Talking Science*, 207.
48. Lemke, *Talking Science*, 208.

in a culture. These tools allow us to examine in a principled manner "the actual social construction of ideological oppositions, alliances, and co-optations" within a culture.[49]

It is worth pointing out that biblical scholars have been doing this sort of analysis for generations. Sandmel's timeless warning about "parallelomania," for example, can be reframed in this way: formal similarities between texts do not necessarily entail that the texts are co-discursive, since their thematics may be entirely different despite similarities in their wordings.[50] Intertexts relate by virtue of their meanings, not their forms, and they relate insofar as they participate in cultural conceptions of particular themes or topics.[51]

Cain and Abel in Second Temple Culture

Here I analyze a number of primary sources which instantiate the [Cain and Abel] intertextual thematic formation. I attempt through this analysis to examine the breadth of the cultural conversation on Cain and Abel within Second Temple Judaism. John Byron, in *Cain and Abel in Text and Tradition*, offers a catalogue of the various interpretive traditions surrounding this formation.[52] He convincingly demonstrates that the MT is ambiguous on a number of points where the LXX and New Testament are more explicit, but he also examines a number of other Second Temple interpretive traditions. His monograph moves through the text of the MT of Gen 4, showing the way its ambiguities shape the resulting traditions.

According to Byron, "ambiguities in the Hebrew represented both a challenge and an opportunity to early translators and exegetes."[53] He explains:

---

49. Lemke, "Discourses in Conflict," 31.

50. Sandmel, "Parallelomania."

51. Allegories and typologies, in some circles being proposed as the "premodern" cure to postmodern madness, are generally unconvincing, but if considered in terms of their heteroglossic intertextual meanings, they might be found to be much more interesting. For a recent proposal that is more promising, see Huizenga's ("Old Testament in the New," 25–30) analysis of Stefan Alkier's semiotic model.

52. In fact, Byron notes that in some ways he has only scratched the surface in terms of numerical quantity. He points out, however, that "many of the traditions are repeated numerous times by a variety of interpreters over the centuries. It simply becomes impossible to register them all" (*Cain and Abel*, 8).

53. Byron, *Cain and Abel*, 19.

The exegetical traditions that developed around Gen 4 . . . provide far more detail than is contained in the canonical [MT] version. The presence of linguistic and grammatical ambiguities coupled with the lack of specific details provided translators and interpreters with a number of exegetical pegs on which they could expand the story. The focus of these expansions is to respond to a number of questions that the story left unanswered.[54]

Without simply reproducing Byron's masterful treatment of the ancient reception history of the Cain and Abel formation in all of its complexity, I point to several key sources that illustrate what I see as the core topics of discussion in the intertextual thematic formation. First, I consider Greek instances, and then I examine some evidence from non-Greek texts.[55] Finally, I offer a synthesis of several heteroglossic relations that can be observed, and describe their significance for understanding the Cain and Abel formation as it is instantiated in the New Testament.

Text Traditions in Jewish Greek and non-Greek Texts

The following fifteen excerpts come from the LXX and OT Pseudepigrapha. Following these excerpts, I briefly mention some contributions from Philo and Josephus since—for Philo in particular—the relevant material is too voluminous to reproduce here.

- And the Lord God said to Cain: "To what end are you so distraught? And to what end has your face fallen? Is it not true that you have sinned if you offer correctly but do not divide correctly? Be silent. He will turn back to you [lit: his turning back is to you] and you will rule over him" . . . (Gen 4:1–17 LXX)

- And repudiating her [i.e., wisdom], an unrighteous man in his anger, destroyed himself as he destroyed[56] in fratricidal rage. When

---

54. Byron, *Cain and Abel*, 36.

55. Although I recognize the multilingual nature of Second Temple Judaism, and the role Greek played as a prestige language, I nevertheless maintain that drawing distinctions between sets of texts for heuristic purposes on the basis of language is a workable and reasonable way to distinguish between traditions broadly conceived. Cf. Ong, "Language of the New Testament"; Porter, "Introduction: Diglossia"; Porter, "Sociolinguistics."

56. The verb here indicates codestroying, in this case in the middle voice indicating the destroyer is himself killed in a frenzied act.

- the world was washed away on his account, wisdom again saved the righteous man, steering his shabby [wooden boat]. (Wis 10:3–4)
- He read to you the slaying of Abel by Cain . . . (4 Macc 18:11a)
- And he answered me saying: "This spirit is the one who has gone out from Abel, whom Cain his brother murdered, and Abel petitions about him for the destruction of his seed from the face of the land, that his seed might vanish from the seed of men." (1 En. 22:7)
- This [love] provoked in the heart of Abel; this [love] worked together [with?] the patriarchs; this [love] kept Moses; this one made David a dwelling of the holy spirit; this [love] strengthened Joseph. (Apoc. Sedr. 1:18)
- That the Lord will bless you with the first-fruits of the land, just as he blessed all the holy ones from Abel until now. (T. Iss. 5:4)
- Cain was rendered seven vengeances by God, for each year the Lord brought one plague upon him. Two hundred years old, he began to suffer, and in the nine-hundredth year he was destroyed by the flood on account of his righteous brother Abel. With seven evils Cain was judged . . . Forevermore those who are like Cain in envy unto hatred of their brothers will be judged with the same punishment. (T. Benj. 7:3–5)
- And the chief commander said: "You see, all-holy Abraham, the fearful man who is sitting on the throne? This is the son of Adam the first-formed, the one called Abel, whom Cain the wicked killed." (T. Ab.[A] 13:2)
- And Michael said to Abraham: "You see the judge? This is Abel, who in the very beginning testified, and God brought him here to judge." (T. Ab.[B] 11:2)
- In the seventieth year a firstborn son, Cain, was born to them. In the seventy-seventh year Abel the righteous came to be . . . Cain brought an offering . . . Abel offered up a sacrifice to God . . . Cain a fruit-bearing sacrifice . . . in the same ninety-ninth year Cain put Abel to death, and the first-formed [pl.] mourned him four sevens, that is, twenty-eight years. (Jub. 4:1–2)
- But Seth the third son after Abel was born [was given] to his sister, the one called Azoura. (Jub. 4:11)

- In his 930th year Cain also died when his house fell on top of him. For it was with stones that he killed Abel . . . (Jub. 4:31)

- Eve conceived and gave birth to two sons, Diaphotos, who is called Cain, and Amilabes, who is called Abel . . . Then Adam said to Eve: "Let's get up and go, and we will see what is going on with them in case some enemy is attacking them." So, going, they came together upon Abel, who had been murdered by the hand of his brother Cain. And God told Michael the archangel: "Tell to Adam, 'You should not tell Cain your son the secret you have discovered, because he is a son of rage . . .'" (Apoc. Mos. 1:3—3:3)

- Abel, whom Cain killed (Apoc. Mos. 4:2)

- Then the Lord said, "Let the body of Abel also be brought." And bringing other linens, they buried him also, for he was unburied since the day Cain his brother murdered him. For many times the wicked Cain intended to hide him [in the ground], but he couldn't, for the land would not accept this body, saying, "I will not accept a fellow body, until the dirt which was taken and shaped upon me returns to me." . . . (Apoc. Mos. 40:3–5)

What all of these instances have in common is a thematic formation, in which [Cain], because he was [evil], [murdered] his [brother] [Abel], who was [righteous] and whose [blood] [cries] to [God] for [vengeance].[57] In the examples given above, one notices that some references to Cain and Abel are long and elaborate, while others are short and terse. In actual fact, sometimes a single word, such as ἀνθρωποκτόνος ("murderer") or ἀδελφοκτόνος ("fratricide") is used to instantiate this thematic formation.[58] In these cases, the longer texts comprise intertexts relevant for understanding the shorter texts.

Philo's writings include numerous instances of this thematic formation, detailed in almost every chapter of Byron's work. Something Philo and Josephus both include, which is absent from the Greek traditions cited above, is play off of the pun in Cain's name, קנה ('gain'). Philo (*Sacr.* 1:2) states: "For the first symbol is *Cain*, which is called 'possession,' on account of his thinking he possessed all things." Josephus, for his part, presents Cain as being spared the death penalty for murder on account of

---

57. A reminder to the reader that brackets with lower case letters indicate themes, while brackets with capitalized letters designate thematic formations.

58. Byron, *Cain and Abel*, 209-10.

his sacrifice, though God was less pleased with Cain's sacrifice than Abel's. Cain was, for Josephus, wholly selfish and wicked, and even his offering of produce was an exhibit of Cain's ecological rapine (*Ant.* 1:53–61).

What is most notable for comparative purposes is that Cain is described fundamentally as unjust or evil. As Byron says: "Cain's crime became the archetype of all wrongdoing and thus earned him an extraordinary name"—i.e., "unrighteous" (ἄδικος; Wis 10:3).[59] In this formation, Cain's evil designation is fundamentally related to his evil deed, he is the "guilty" one. This semantic relation—that [Cain] is the carrier of an attribute [evil]—can probably be traced genealogically to the LXX translation, and thus Lohr's contention that the LXX translators have had a hand in turning Cain's reception history against him appears well-founded in that respect.

The evidence of the Aramaic Targums introduces a new dimension into its thematic formations, namely the demonic or even satanic origin of Cain.[60] Targum Pseudo-Jonathan, for example, notes in 4:1 and 5:3:

> Adam knew his wife Eve *who* had conceived *from Sammael, the angel of the Lord.* Then, *from Adam her husband* she bore *his twin sister* and Abel . . . When Adam had lived a hundred and thirty years, he begot *Seth, who resembled* his image and likeness. *For before that, Eve had borne Cain, who was not from him and who did not resemble him. Abel was killed by Cain . . . But afterwards he begot one who resembled him* and he called his name Seth.[61]

Similarly, in Pirqe Rabbi Eliezer, we read:

> He [i.e., Sammael] riding on the serpent came to her, and she conceived; afterwards Adam came to her, and she conceived Abel, as it is said, "And Adam knew Eve his wife." . . . And she saw his likeness that it was not of the earthly beings, but of the heavenly beings, and she prophesied and said: "I have gotten a man with the Lord."[62]

---

59. Byron, *Cain and Abel*, 207.

60. Later Nag Hammadi texts, such as *The Hypostasis of the Archons* and *The Apocryphon of John* render these human–angel encounters more graphically (*Hyp. Arch.* 19–31 [NHC II, 89; Layton's translation]; *Apoc. John* 22 [NHC II, 1]).

61. Maher, *Targum Pseudo-Jonathan: Genesis*, 36. In the translations cited here italics indicate "pluses" to the Hebrew original.

62. Pirqe R. El. 21 (Friedlander trans.).

One of the most interesting distinctions in the Aramaic texts is the fuller description of the dispute between Cain and Abel that precipitated Abel's murder. In Tg. Neof. 4:8, it says:

> Cain answered and said to Abel: . . . Why was your offering received favorably and my offering was not received favorably from me?" Abel answered and said to Cain: ". . . because my works were better than yours, my offering was received from me favorably and yours was not received favorably from you." Cain answered and said to Abel: "There is no judgment, and there is no judge and there is no other world. There is no giving of good reward to the just nor is vengeance exacted of the wicked." . . . Concerning this matter the two of them were disputing in the open field. And Cain rose up against Abel his brother and killed him.[63]

Thus, the explanation for why Cain's sacrifice was rejected looms large in these texts, much more than we observed in the Greek instances. Targum Neofiti can be seen to offer answers to the question about what pleases God raised by the MT, namely good works.[64]

What these non-Greek instances have in common is a thematic formation where [Cain], because he was the [offspring] of a [demon], [murdered] his [brother] [Abel], who was [righteous] because he practices [good works],[65] and whose [blood] [cries] to [God] for [vengeance]. Texts that have Cain and Abel arguing about the reason for Cain's rejected sacrifice introduce a text-specific heteroglossic relation of opposition between two distinct thematic formations, which have been noted for their similarities to the typical positions of the Pharisees and Sadducees in the first century.[66]

All that remains is to examine the most obvious instance of this thematic formation, the MT of Gen 4. This text exhibits the following, more complex thematic formation:[67]

63. McNamara, *Targum Neofiti 1: Genesis*, 64–67.
64. Cf. Jackson, "Legalism and Spirituality"; Wishart, "Emerging Account," 183–84.
65. Here I am taking "good words" as having a thematic meaning that makes it hyponymic to "good works."
66. "Many scholars think that the dispute may reflect the controversy between the Sadducees and the Pharisees concerning the world to come" (McNamara, *Targum Neofiti 1: Genesis*, 32n17).
67. "The Hebrew is more ambiguous and difficult to translate than is sometimes appreciated . . . Such ambiguities in the Hebrew represented both a challenge and an opportunity to early translators and exegetes" (Byron, *Cain and Abel*, 12).

> [Cain] was born to [Eve], who [received] him—and this has something to do with [YHWH]—and [Adam] and was a [tiller of the ground] <u>unlike [Abel] who was a [shepherd of sheep]</u> or <u>[Seth] who was the image and likeness of [Adam]</u>. [Cain] brought an [offering] from the [produce of the field] to [YHWH] <u>unlike [Abel] who brought an [offering] of [livestock and fat]</u>. [YHWH] did not [regard] the [offering] of [Cain] <u>but did [regard] the [offering] of [Abel]</u> causing the [face] of [Cain] to [fall] in [fury]. [Cain] <u>could do what is [right] in order to be [lifted up]</u>, but he could do what is [wrong]. [Cain] could [master] the [sin] that is [crouching at the door] with [desire] for [Cain]. [Cain] [spoke] to [Abel] his [brother] in the [field] and [murdered] him. [YHWH] [asked] [Cain] where [Abel] his [brother] was, and [Cain] [asked] whether he was his [brother's] [keeper]. [YHWH] [asked] [Cain] what he had done and told him the [blood] of his [brother] [cried] from the [ground].[68]

In this thematic formation we can perceive, perhaps, the origin of the intertextual thematic formation observed in the Greek texts, which is distinguished by its construal of Cain as an unrighteous person. The MT provided the opportunity for the LXX to elaborate on an ambiguity in the original story. The MT does not tell us why Cain murdered Abel, and so the LXX does. At the same time, we can also see how the MT's thematic formation gave rise to the tradition observed in the non-Greek texts, that Cain's evil can be explained by the discrepancies in the description of how he is conceived as opposed to both Abel and Seth, besides his inability ultimately to master sin. While the Greek-text formation consistently represents Abel as righteous or just, the non-Greek-text formation introduces the notion of Abel's good works as meriting the acceptance of his sacrifice, which is not explicitly discussed in the Greek-text formation observed above.

Thematic Formulations in Second Temple Jewish Literature and the New Testament

Returning to NT instances of [CAIN AND ABEL], the various texts realize the following thematic formations:[69]

---

68. Heteroglossic relations are underlined.

69. Text-specific heteroglossic relations are underlined; see above for the MT thematic formation. I have examined numerous texts as if they all contribute to an abstracted thematic formation, but I am now introducing individual texts as if they

- Matt 23:35: [Abel] is [just] and his [blood] was [poured out] upon the [earth] and is ultimately [requited]
- Heb 11:4; 12:24: [Slain] [Abel] offered to [God] by [faith] [a better sacrifice] than [Cain] and is testified to be [righteous] by [God] on the basis of his [gifts] that serve as his ongoing [speech], which is less [strong] than [Jesus']
- Jude 11: The [way] of [Cain] is aligned with the [error] of [Balaam] for [wages] and the [rebellion] of [Korah]
- 1 John 3:12: [Cain] was from [the evil one] and [murdered] his [brother] because [his works] were [evil] while the [works] of his [brother] were [righteous]

The thematic formations for the Greek texts are:

- [Cain], because he was [evil], [murdered] his [brother] [Abel], who was [righteous] and whose [blood] [cries] to [God] for [vengeance]

For the non-Greek texts, they are:

- [Cain], because he was the [offspring] of a [demon], [murdered] his [brother] [Abel], who was [righteous] because he practiced [good works]

What is striking in this synoptic view is the fact that the NT instances do not appear to follow exclusively and uniformly any of the thematic formations examined in the Jewish Greek and non-Greek texts. The Hebrews instances of this thematic formation are indicative of both kinds of value-orientation in text-specific and intertextual heteroglossic relations.

Abel's actions are allied to Jesus as examples of faith, by virtue of which his sacrifices are acceptable to God. Abel is also opposed to Cain, whose sacrifice was not acceptable to God, implicitly because he did not have faith like Abel. While Cain is not actually mentioned in the text, we have seen how references to Abel exploit the cultural-level (i.e., intertextual) thematic formation of [Abel] the [righteous] [brother] whom [Cain] [killed]. This thematic formation in turn is intertextually related as being a constituent part of the [CAIN AND ABEL] formation, and even though no explicit linkage is made in this instance, the explicit

---

have their own unique formations. This difference in depth of analysis is due to space constraints. See Lemke, "Intertextuality and Text Semantics," 93.

linkage is commonly found in other texts within the discourse of Second Temple Judaism. Looking specifically at the Hebrews instances, we see that the author of Hebrews has introduced the notion of faith to explain why Abel's sacrifice was accepted. Hebrews also presents Abel's ongoing speech—something all the other formations include—as being a positive testimony about his faith or gifts. Faith, then, is construed as the disposition required for a sacrifice and sacrificer to be acceptable to God.

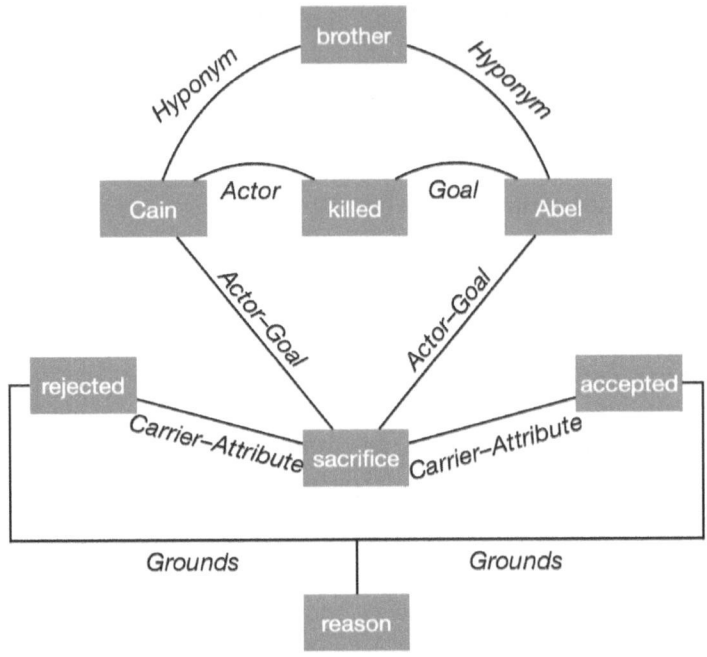

Figure 1: Intertextual thematic formation for [CAIN AND ABEL]

Faith, in this thematic context, allies and opposes other uses of the Cain and Abel tradition in Second Temple culture within the same thematic context (i.e., Cain and Abel), but in order to see how this is the case, it is necessary to interpret a generalized intertextual thematic formation to describe the core thematic formation [CAIN AND ABEL] that existed intertextually within Second Temple Jewish culture (see Figure 1 above).[70] What is key to this diagram is the bottom thematic item [reason], which grounds [acceptance] or [rejection] of the offered [sacrifice].

70. The semantic labels come from abstracted semantic classes (i.e., the thematic items), and the thematic relations are lexicogrammatical labels drawn from Halliday and Matthiessen (*Halliday's Introduction*, 219).

The thematic formation drawn from the Greek texts grounded God's rejection of Cain's sacrifice in his essential character flaw—he was "evil." In comparison, the non-Greek thematic formation grounded God's rejection of Cain's sacrifice in a similar flaw, but this one tended to be related instead to his demonic lineage. Acceptance of Abel's sacrifice, in turn, was grounded in the Greek thematic formation by a general but almost always explicit notion of Abel's righteousness. In the non-Greek thematic formation, by contrast, Abel's good works qualified his sacrifice for acceptance.

The MT's thematic formation does not explain why God rejects Cain's sacrifice, or accepts Abel's, but the author of Hebrews grounds the acceptance in Abel's faith. Thus we can see that an ambiguity in the MT tradition led to a sustained cultural conversation on the same inquiry—namely how to please God—because of shared social values within Jewish culture. At the same time, the ambiguity led to conflicting and diverse answers.

Conclusion

The fundamental questions that later texts and traditions sought to answer are driven primarily by the ambiguities or "gaps" in the [CAIN AND ABEL] thematic formation in the MT tradition. The question I have focused on is: What makes a sacrifice pleasing to God? Jewish communities before, during, and after the Second Temple Period found it important to situate themselves relative to other communities, and one way they accomplished this was by allying or opposing existing thematic formations. It is likely that the intertextual thematic formations that had their genesis in the MT tradition, particularly the Torah, served as the discursive locations for negotiating many of the most important social values in Jewish culture.[71]

Second, Lemke's model describes how meanings are made "between" texts that are not made within texts using clauses or words. Something interesting I have begun to explore here is the way theological values can be derived from texts within a cultural and communal context. At stake is not simply what a text says, but also the questions it raises that give rise to later theological interpretation. The author of Hebrews interprets Abel's acceptance theologically because (1) larger patterns of social activity and

---

71. Lightstone, "Late Second Temple Judaism," 78.

value—including Israel's history of interaction with YHWH and the concrete societal values and practices arising from that history—have given rise to certain pressing questions, such as how one might please God; and (2) Jewish reception history opens up the possibility for answering those questions since the MT does not. Textual traditions of this sort invite expansive interpretation.

Finally, questions about intertextual meaning cannot be resolved simply on the basis of traditional distinctions such as quotation, paraphrase, allusion, echo, and so on. These categories reflect similarities of *wordings*. It hardly matters how many words two texts have in common if it can be established that they are talking about the same thing. *It is more important to figure out how what is said in one text compares and contrasts with the other texts in the culture that also talk about the same thing.* Where do they differ, and where are they in agreement? These are the questions that make intertextuality the important subject that it is. Many studies of "intertextuality" turn out instead to be examinations of how a NT author "invokes" or "imports" or "draws upon" theological arguments from a previous text. Such studies are at their best when what is said is compared with what else might have been said or was in fact said in the cultural context. Without this critical context, an observed similarity between texts functions like a line on a graph without axes. The phenomenon is there, but its meaning is not obvious.

I have shown how intertextual meaning involves shared patterns and configurations of *meanings* that realize indirect—instead of direct—intertextual connections. Such connections have potential for illuminating not only the function of ancient citations of various kinds, but also subsequent interpretation of these passages in the millennia since their writing.

16

Intertextual Echoes in Ephesus

"From the Beginning" in the City of Ephesus and the Letters of John

Paul Trebilco

In the Johannine Epistles, the phrase, ἀπ' ἀρχῆς—"from the beginning"—is used ten times, a uniquely high prominence compared with the rest of the New Testament. The phrase points to a certain understanding of the past, and of tradition, on which this essay will focus.

In my view, strong arguments can be mounted that Johannine literature was written in Ephesus, although this issue is much debated.[1] This raises the possibility that there might be something to be learned from reading the Johannine Epistles against the background of the city of Ephesus. In particular, are there intertextual links between the phrase "from the beginning" and life in the city of Ephesus?

We know that the Artemis cult was a very important part of life in the city of Ephesus for many centuries. Artemis's first temple was

---

1. See Trebilco, *Early Christians*, 241–63.
*This is a revised version of an essay previously published as "'From the Beginning' in the Ancient City of Ephesus and in the Letters of John," in *Internationalising Higher Education from South Africa to England via New Zealand: Essays in Honour of Professor Gerald Pillay*, used here with permission from Mediakor Press.

probably constructed in the second half of the eighth century BCE,[2] and although the final temple on the site was plundered by the Goths in 262 CE, it was partially rebuilt and probably continued to be used throughout the fourth century CE.[3] Artemis was clearly the most important deity in Ephesus. She was regarded as the "ancestral goddess" and the "founder" of the city, with whom Ephesus claimed a special relationship.[4]

Here I will argue that the phrase ἀπ' ἀρχῆς can be seen to resonate with the emphasis in Ephesus on the foundation myth of the Artemis cult and other foundation stories of the city; the phrase resonates with the vivid sense in Ephesus that what was "from the beginning" remains "present" and vitally important in the city. By making this intertextual connection between a broad and significant cultural theme in Ephesus and the NT text, I think significant light can be shed on the Johannine Epistles. Even if one is not convinced that the Epistles were written in Ephesus, the characteristics of the ancient city that I will discuss here are not unique to the city. I hope that looking at these letters in the context of some key characteristics of the Greco-Roman city is of value.

Ἀπ' ἀρχῆς in the Johannine Letters

The expression ἀπ' ἀρχῆς is found eight times in 1 John and twice in 2 John.[5] This usage is striking, given the small size of these two books. It is used in three main ways.

Firstly, the phrase is used to refer to an absolute beginning on two occasions. In 1 John 2:13–14 we read:

> **13** I am writing to you, fathers, because you know him who is *from the beginning* (ὅτι ἐγνώκατε τὸν ἀπ' ἀρχῆς). I am writing to you, young people, because you have conquered the evil one. **14** I write to you, children, because you know the Father. I write to you, fathers, because you know him who is *from the beginning* (ὅτι ἐγνώκατε τὸν ἀπ' ἀρχῆς). I write to you, young people,

---

2. Bammer, "Peripteros," 142.
3. See Foss, *Ephesus*, 86.
4. See details and references in Rogers, *Mysteries*, 6.
5. See 1 John 1:1; 2:7, 13, 14, 24 (twice); 3:8, 11; 2 John 5–6. It is also found in Matt 19:4, 8; 24:21; Mark 13:19; Luke 1:2; John 8:44; 15:27; Acts 26:4; 2 Pet 3:4; see also Mark 10:6.

because you are strong and the word of God abides in you, and you have overcome the evil one.[6]

Although the reference in 1 John 2:14 to "him who is *from the beginning*," whom the addressees now "know," could be to God, it is almost certainly a reference to the Son for three reasons.[7] Firstly, the previous verse (2:12) speaks of your sins being "forgiven on account of *his* name (διὰ τὸ ὄνομα αὐτοῦ)," which is a reference to Jesus.[8] This makes it very likely that the next clause—"because you know him who is *from the beginning*"—also refers to the Son. Secondly, this is followed in 2:13 by a clause saying that young people have "conquered the evil one"; in 5:5 conquering is associated with Jesus. Thirdly, the next clause in 2:14 reads: "because you know the Father." That the Father is explicitly named here suggests a change of referent at this point, and hence that the previous clauses concern the Son.

Accordingly, I suggest that ἀπ᾽ ἀρχῆς in 1 John 2:13–14 is used with reference to the Son, and so refers to his eternity. Marshall notes that the reference is "to the beginning of time and not to the beginning of the Christian era or the readers' Christian experience."[9] John wishes to underline that the Son has been "from the beginning," which is in keeping with what is said in the Gospel of John (1:1–2). Both 1 John 2:13–14 and John 1:1–2 underline the eternity and pre-existence of the Son, who can also be called the Word.

A second usage of ἀπ᾽ ἀρχῆς is found in 1 John 3:8: "Everyone who commits sin is a child of the devil; for the devil has been sinning *from the beginning* (ὅτι ἀπ᾽ ἀρχῆς ὁ διάβολος ἁμαρτάνει)." That the devil "has been sinning *from the beginning*" is not to say that the devil is eternal in the way that the Father or the Son are, since the reference here is clearly to the Garden of Eden story of Gen 3.[10] That this is the case is reinforced by 1 John 3:12, just a few verses later, which is the only overt reference to the

---

6. All Eng. trans. of scriptural texts are from the NRSV unless otherwise noted.

7. Stott (*Epistles*, 97) argues for a reference to God; Brown (*Epistles*, 303) notes Stott "is almost alone" in arguing for this.

8. He is said to be "the atoning sacrifice for our sins" in 1 John 2:2 and 4:10.

9. Marshall, *Epistles*, 139. Others who argue that the reference is to the Son include Wendt, "Anfang," 40; Conzelmann, "Anfang," 195; Schnackenburg, *Johannine*, 117; Strecker, *Johannine*, 57 (who thinks the reference is "probably" to Jesus); Painter, *1, 2, and 3 John*, 120.

10. Strecker, *Johannine*, 100; see also de la Potterie, "La notion," 399.

Old Testament in 1 John,[11] and it clearly has Gen 4 and the Cain and Abel story in view. This makes it very likely that 1 John 3:8 is a reference to Gen 3 and the story of the serpent's deception and the Fall. In addition, 1 John clearly reads Gen 3 and Gen 4 together, since in 1 John 3:12 the author can associate Cain of Gen 4 with "the evil one" (Cain was "from the evil one"), who features in Gen 3. Indeed, Brown suggests that the author of 1 John is reading all of Gen 1–4 together,[12] and so ἐν ἀρχῇ of Gen 1:1 may be the inspiration for the use of the phrase ἀπ' ἀρχῆς here in 1 John 3:8. Finally, Philo in *On Rewards* XII writes: "At the very beginning (κατ' ἀρχάς) . . . there was a fratricide," showing that the Cain-Abel narrative can be regarded as a "beginning."[13] Accordingly, in 1 John 3:8 the author emphasizes that "the devil has been sinning *from the beginning*." This is, then, a reference to the Fall.

The third usage of ἀπ' ἀρχῆς is with reference to "the beginning of Jesus' ministry" or what we might call "the beginning of the Johannine tradition," which includes stories about Jesus found in John's Gospel. It is used six times with this meaning.[14] Thus, in 1 John 2:7, the commandment or the message is *not* new; rather, it is something the addressees have had, or have heard, "from the beginning." The reference is to the teaching of Jesus, or, as Brown puts it, to "the person, words, and deeds of Jesus as this complexus reflects his self-revelation . . . to his disciples after his baptism."[15] But of course this is also the start of the traditions about Jesus and so of the Johannine tradition, which has continued into the present and about which the author writes in his letters. The assurance is that as John writes 1 John, perhaps in the 90s CE, what he says is not novel but rather goes back many years in the history of the group of which the addressees are a part.[16]

It is important to note the language used about "you" in 1 John 2:7: "Beloved, I am writing *you* [pl.] no new commandment, but an old commandment that *you* [pl.] have had from the beginning; the old commandment is the word that *you* [pl.] have heard." When John, writing in the 90s CE, speaks of "you" here, he is not referring to individuals but

---

11. Brown, *Epistles*, 406.
12. Brown, *Epistles*, 406.
13. Philo, *Praem.* 68; Eng. trans. by Colson, LCL, 353; Brown, *Epistles*, 406.
14. It is used with this sense in 1 John 2:7, 24 (twice); 3:11; 2 John 5, 6.
15. Brown, *Epistles*, 158; see also Conzelmann, "'Anfang,'" 196.
16. Lieu, "Us or You?" 805–19; see also Nienhuis, "Beginning," 71–85.

rather is thinking about the group. All of those addressed by John were not *there* when Jesus was teaching his disciples around 30 CE or even at the foundation of the Johannine school and tradition, perhaps shortly after.[17] Those who were part of "John's school" when the Johannine tradition first took decisive shape and were also still alive when the Johannine Epistles were written would have been a very small group.

The author's point in these verses is that there is *continuity* between those first "receivers" and contemporary members of the group, such that what these first receivers heard "back then" can be said to have been heard by "you readers." This points to a vivid sense of the vitality of tradition—those currently addressed stand in continuity with those who have gone before. The tradition is sufficiently "alive," so that to have received the tradition from those who have handed it on means one can affirm that *we* have had this commandment, or *we* have heard this word "from the beginning." That they have had the commandment "from the beginning" reassures the readers that what they have believed all along has been true. The emphasis, then, is on encouragement and assurance.

John has this emphasis on "what you have heard from the beginning," in part, because of the disruption to the community caused by the departure of a group mentioned in 1 John 2:19. The departure of the group (commonly called the secessionists) has caused much difficulty for those who remained. "Are we right?" has become a key question. The use of ἀπ' ἀρχῆς with reference to Jesus' ministry and to Johannine tradition has this need for reassurance in mind. Readers can be confident because John is writing about the message "you" heard from the beginning (1 John 3:11). "Be reassured," says John. But there is more to the use of the phrase "from the beginning" than reassurance, as I hope to show.

As I have noted, John uses the expression ἀπ' ἀρχῆς in three main ways. However, 1 John 1:1 is rather ambiguous, perhaps intentionally so. What was "from the beginning" in 1:1 is clearly a reference to the ministry of the earthly Jesus, yet the reference to "the word of life" that was revealed has overtones of the preexistent Son. As Yarbrough notes: "Without minimizing the historicity of Jesus's existence, John evokes the horizon of eternity past as he opens his epistle."[18] John goes on to say that we "declare to you the *eternal life that was with the Father* and was revealed to us" (1 John 1:2). Again, there are overtones of the eternal Son

---

17. We may wonder if any of Jesus' first disciples were still alive when 1–2 John were written, but this depends in part on the identity of John the author.

18. Yarbrough, *1–3 John*, 34.

here, which suggests that "what was *from the beginning*" in 1 John 1:1 is not simply a reference to the ministry of the earthly Jesus, even though this is clearly in view. It is no surprise that in 1 John 2:13–14 ἀπ' ἀρχῆς is used explicitly to refer to eternity before time, that is, the eternity of the Son.

In 1–2 John, then, the phrase "from the beginning" refers to the Son's eternity, to the work of the evil one and to the beginning of Jesus' ministry and the traditions about Jesus. In each case, the stress is on "antiquity," on foundations.

Why is there this very strong interest in and emphasis on "from the beginning" in 1–2 John? At least in part, this has the secessionists in view. But is that all? Further, how would this phrase "from the beginning" have sounded in Ephesus? How would it have been heard? Before I turn to this I must note the two most proximate sources of this language—the LXX and other NT books. I will then go on to discuss the phrase's resonances in Ephesus.

Ἀπ' ἀρχῆς in the LXX and the Rest of the New Testament

In the LXX, ἀπ' ἀρχῆς is found a number of times; it is used with reference to the time of creation,[19] and to a temporal beginning which can be recent or further back in the past.[20] In each case, the emphasis is on "the situation in ancient times." There is nothing in the LXX that is comparable to the third usage found in 1 John 3:8 where ἀπ' ἀρχῆς relates to the evil one. In the rest of the New Testament apart from 1–2 John, ἀπ' ἀρχῆς is used with reference to creation,[21] to refer to an event of a comparatively recent time,[22] and in relation to the evil one.[23]

First and Second John thus share this expression with both the LXX and the rest of the New Testament, and since 1–2 John is almost certainly later than these other texts, there is a range of possible sources

---

19. See, e.g., Isa 22:11; Sir 16:26; 24:9; Hab 1:12; Wis 14:13; Eccl 3:11; Sir 51:20; see Muraoka, s.v. ἀρχή, ῆς, in *GELS*, 94–95; Yarbrough, *1–3 John*, 34.

20. See, e.g., Ezek 16:55; Sir 36:13, 16; Wis 12:11; Sol 17:30; Isa 2:6; Ezek 48:1; see also Delling, "ἄρχω, ἀρχή, κτλ.," in *TDNT* 1.481.

21. See Matt 19:4, 8; Mark 10:6; see also Matt 24:21; Mark 13:9; 2 Pet 3:4.

22. See Luke 1:2; John 15:27; on this usage, see Conzelmann, "Anfang," 197.

23. John 8:44, which is the most proximate source for this usage in 1 John.

for Johannine usage.²⁴ But in this essay, I am not mounting an argument about the origin of ἀπ' ἀρχῆς as a phrase. That would be very difficult to sustain, since we are dealing with such a common expression and 1-2 John could simply be reflecting contemporary Greek usage. I am not arguing that the origin of the usage of 1-2 John is the LXX, or the historical Jesus, or other NT books (such as John's Gospel, although 1-3 John clearly shares much with John's Gospel).

My argument here is about how this language *resonates* in Ephesus. How would it have sounded there? I will argue here that the strong interest in and emphasis on "from the beginning" in 1-2 John is *also* related to the stress on "antiquity" and on foundations in Ephesus. I am asking how this phrase "from the beginning" would have been heard in Ephesus. Here I am concerned not with the origin of the phrase, but with its *impact and resonance*, and hence with its *intertexts*, in Ephesus. What intertextual echoes does it set off? Does this explain the striking number of times it is used in 1-2 John (ten times) and so why it is quite so prominent in these very brief letters?

Reading the Johannine Letters in Ephesus

What would Ephesian readers associate with ἀπ' ἀρχῆς as a phrase and, more importantly, as a concept? I will now turn to Artemis and discuss the ongoing significance of the birth story of Artemis in the city. I will then discuss another foundation story.

An additional point is important here. I am not suggesting that the sense of vitality of myths and foundation stories that I will present here was *unique* to Ephesus. Such stories were found throughout the ancient world.²⁵ But they *are* found in Ephesus, and we have strong evidence for how vitally "alive" ancient stories were there. While there is nothing unique to Ephesus in what I will go on to discuss, that we can document this sense of lively foundation stories is, in my view, significant when it comes to readers of 1-2 John in the city.

---

24. It is often noted that the Johannine Letters never quote the LXX. Lieu, however, has convincingly shown the impact of the LXX on the Johannine Letters, and so it is quite possible that this was the source of the language; see Lieu, "What was from the Beginning," 458-77.

25. Rogers, *Sacred*, 139. On foundation stories in the cities of Asia Minor, see, e.g., Linant de Bellefonds, "Pictorial," 26-46.

Artemis's Birth and Its Annual Celebration

In Greek myth, the birthplace of Artemis, the daughter of Zeus and Leto and the twin sister of Apollo, was generally said to be a grove known as Ortygia. It was usually located on the island of Delos or of Rhenaea.[26] But Strabo tells us that according to the Ephesians, there was a place known as Ortygia in the region of Ephesus and the Ephesians identified this grove with the nativity site of Artemis of Ephesus.[27] The site of Ortygia is thought to be about five miles southeast of the center of Ephesus in a place now called Arvalya.[28] Clearly, then, by the time of the early empire, the Ephesians had transferred the nativity myth of the Greek Artemis to Artemis of Ephesus.

Writing in 29 BCE,[29] in his account of the Ionians and others, and in relation to Ephesus in particular, Strabo writes:

> On the same coast, slightly above the sea, is also Ortygia, which is a magnificent grove of all kinds of trees, of the cypress most of all. It is crossed by the Cenchrius River, where Leto *is said* (φασί) to have bathed herself after her travail [in giving birth to Artemis and Apollo]. For here is the mythical scene of the birth, and of the nurse Ortygia, and of the holy place where the birth took place, and of the olive tree near by, where the goddess *is said* (φασί) first to have taken a rest after she was relieved from her travail. Above the grove lies Mt. Solmissus, where, *it is said* (φασί), the Curetes stationed themselves, and with the din of their arms frightened Hera out of her wits when she was jealously spying on Leto, and when they helped Leto to conceal from Hera the birth of her children. There are several temples in the place, some ancient and others built in later times; and in the ancient temples are many ancient wooden images, but in those of later times there are works of Skopas; for example, Leto holding a sceptre and Ortygia standing beside her with a child in each arm. A general festival is held there annually; and by a certain custom the youths vie for honour, particularly in the splendour of their banquets there. At that time, also, a special

---

26. See LSJ, s.v. Ὀρτυγία, 1257. Murphy-O'Connor (*Ephesus*, 16) notes that the Homeric Hymn to Apollo locates the birth story in Delos; this was clearly a competing story which the Ephesians vigorously denied; see Tacitus, *Ann.* 3.61.

27. Strabo, *Geogr.* 14.1.20; Tacitus, *Ann.* 3.61.1.

28. See the discussion in Rogers, *Mysteries*, 36–38, esp. Map 2 (xiv).

29. Date in Rogers, *Mysteries*, 9. Strabo lived from 64 BCE to 21 CE.

college of the Curetes holds symposiums and performs certain mystic sacrifices.[30]

The background to this story is that Leto had been made pregnant by Zeus. But Zeus was married to Hera, and so Hera resented Zeus's unfaithfulness. She persecuted Leto and attempted to kill both her and her children.

We learn a number of important things from this account. Firstly, in Strabo's time the site at which the myth of Artemis's birth was physically located was well-known and regularly visited. Secondly, in this account Strabo reports that "it is said" (φημί) three times. He emphasizes that he is drawing on contemporary Ephesian voices as he writes. We can be reasonably confident about his evidence, then, and that he is writing of the present-day significance of the myth. Thirdly, he mentions a contemporary annual festival that is held at the site and so in connection with a celebration of Artemis's birth and also the association of the Kuretes (an association of males in Ephesus), who also held contemporary symposia and sacrifices at the time of the festival. We know a great deal about the association of the Kuretes from Ephesian inscriptions,[31] and this corroborates what Strabo says.

That in Strabo's time there was an annual festival shows us that the story of Artemis's birth was not just of "historical interest" in 29 BCE but was "re-presented" every year. We know that the celebration of the nativity of Artemis of Ephesus was held annually on the sixth of Thargelion (late April / early May) at the grove of trees that was called Ortygia, where Strabo says there were several temples. From other evidence, we know that the annual celebration of the nativity of Artemis was conducted in Ephesus until well into the third century CE.[32] Predominantly using inscriptions, Rogers has reconstructed some of the things that happened during this festival celebrating Artemis's birth. A pipe was played while

30. Strabo, *Geogr.* 14.1.20; Eng. trans. by Jones, LCL, 6:223–25 (italics mine). The Kuretes were a special group of Artemis's priests. On the annual celebration of Artemis's mysteries and the role of the Kuretes, see Knibbe, *Staatsmarkt*, 70–73; IEph 26; Rogers, "Mysteries," 241–50; Portefaix, "Image," 611–17; see also Horsley, "Mysteries," 141–46. Note that from the time of the early empire there was probably a transfer of responsibility for the celebrations of the mysteries of Artemis from the temple of Artemis to the Prytaneion, through the direction of the prytanis; see Rogers, *Sacred*, 44; "Mysteries," 245. However, Salutaris associated his benefactions (on which see below) with the Temple of Artemis, not the Prytaneion.

31. Rogers, *Mysteries*, 122–204.
32. Murphy-O'Connor, *Ephesus*, 16.

libations were poured and incense burned on an altar, a trumpet was blown, and then an acrobatic dance was performed. A diviner then inspected the livers of sacrificial victims. There were banquets for wealthy young Ephesians, and then members of the Gerousia, the council of elders, would make sacrifices to Artemis and, from the first century CE, to the emperor. Then the Gerousia held their own banquet.[33]

We do not know whether the story of Artemis's birth was actually physically reenacted at the celebration of the mysteries, but we do know from what Strabo says that this story of her birth was associated with the mysteries of Artemis from 29 BCE.[34] If they did act the story out, then while someone who was acting the part of Hera was attempting to spy on Leto giving birth to Artemis and Apollo, the Kuretes would have frightened Hera by clashing their spears against their shields. Then a herald would have made the announcement that, with the help of Ortygia the nurse and the Kuretes who had hidden the births from Hera, Leto had given birth to Artemis and Apollo. Leto would then have rested and bathed in the Kenchrios River, while Ortygia held the babies.[35] Onlookers would have celebrated that Artemis and Apollo had again been safely brought into the world.

But whether there was such a reenactment or not, the important point here is that the story of Artemis's birth was the center of an annual festival, and of mystic sacrifices.[36] To quote Rogers: "The birth of Artemis was not just a story told to Ephesian children by their parents; it was the event of the Ephesian year, performed by generations of Ephesians, at the most important religious festival in the city."[37] This was not just a story for the elite; all sectors of society were caught up in the festival celebrating Artemis's birth. In this way the ancient story of the birth of the most important goddess of Ephesus was "made alive" annually. The "foundation myth" was annually represented. Thus, "the Ephesians' re-creation of the past was founded upon one non-human event, the birth of the goddess Artemis at Ephesos."[38] Although these are my words, the story "from the

---

33. Rogers, *Mysteries*, 3–4; also Rogers, *Sacred*, 150n15.
34. Rogers, *Mysteries*, 31; 315n2.
35. For this re-creation, see Rogers, *Mysteries*, 3.
36. Rogers (*Mysteries*, 8) argues that the mysteries were first celebrated before the end of the fourth century BCE.
37. Rogers, *Sacred*, 145.
38. Rogers, *Sacred*, 138.

beginning" was retold again and again and was as lively and as powerful as ever in Strabo's time.

The Kuretes were highly significant here. In mythology, they were young divine warriors from Crete, who were the male equivalent of Nymphs. In the Ephesian story about Artemis's birth, by taking up arms they played the key role in ensuring that Artemis was born near Ephesus. Rogers writes that the myth of Artemis's birth provided:

> a model for the creation of a city unified behind a sacred event. In Strabo's account of the myth at least, only the willingness of the Kuretes to take up arms and then conceal the birth of Leto's children from Hera ensured the successful birth of Artemis (and Apollo). Since there could be no Greek city at the site of Ephesos without the prior condition of Artemis' birth in the grove of Ortygia, and there could be no birth of Artemis without the Kuretes, the Kuretes could reasonably claim that, without them, the Greek city of Ephesos would not exist. In other words, when the Ephesians, dressed as Kuretes each year at the celebration of the mysteries, re-enacted their role in the birth of Artemis, they did far more than take part in the biggest birthday party of the city; rather, they reaffirmed their vital contribution not only to Artemis' birth, but to the very existence of the Greek city itself ... Thus Artemis gave the city its sacred identity as the birthplace of one of the original Olympian deities; but the Ephesians themselves, as the Kuretes, also had a major role in creating that sacred identity, a corporate role which defined the Ephesians for all time as Artemis' protectors and defenders against hostile and jealous deities.[39]

In addition, Tacitus provides helpful information here. During the early empire, there had been widespread abuses of the rights of temples to grant asylum. Tiberius wanted to make reforms in this area, and so required Greek cities to ask the Roman Senate for the continuation of this privilege. Cities were required to authenticate the antiquity of their own asylum privileges, and so of their temples. Tacitus writes of the claim made by the people of Ephesus that, according to local legend, Artemis (called Diana by Tacitus) and Apollo were born near the city.[40] Tacitus writes:

---

39. Rogers, *Sacred*, 145–46.
40. See Oster, "Ephesus," 1707.

> The Ephesians were the first to appear [before the Senate]. "Apollo and Diana," they stated, "were not, as commonly supposed, born at Delos. In Ephesus there was a river Cenchrius, with a grove Ortygia; where Latona [that is, Leto], heavy-wombed and supporting herself by an olive-tree which remained to that day, gave birth to the heavenly twins. The grove had been hallowed by divine injunction; and there Apollo himself, after slaying the Cyclopes, had evaded the anger of Jove. Afterwards, Father Liber, victor in war, had pardoned the suppliant Amazons who had seated themselves at the altar. Then the sanctity of the temple had been enhanced, with the permission of Hercules, while he held the crown of Lydia; its privileges had not been diminished under the Persian empire; later, they had been preserved by the Macedonians—last by ourselves."[41]

Clearly, this relates the ancient past to present structures—an olive tree, a sacred grove, and a temple. This story from the past lived on in present celebrations, at the time about which Tacitus writes during the time of Tiberius.[42] In addition, as Rogers notes: "From Tacitus' account [in *Ann.* 3.60–63] we may infer that the story of Artemis' birth in the grove of Ortygia was known to everyone, from Ephesian slaves to the most powerful men in the Roman world, including the Roman emperor himself."[43]

We conclude, then, that the story of Artemis's birth was well-known and was commemorated and represented to the city in the first century CE. What was "from the beginning," in relation to Artemis's birth, was "alive."

We also know of the Ἀρτεμίσια, which was a second major festival held in honor of Artemis in the first century CE. This was held annually in the month of Artemision (March–April), with both the name of the festival and the name of the month in which it was held being derived from Artemis. The Artemisia probably included athletic, theatrical, and musical competitions.[44] One of the reasons for the popularity of the Artemisia may have been the custom described by Xenophon of Ephesus in his (probably) first-century CE romance *Anthia and Habrocomes*,[45] where he said that it had become traditional for young women to select

41. Tacitus, *Ann.* 3.61; Eng. trans. by Jackson, LCL, 619–21.
42. Tacitus lived from c. 56–after 117 CE.
43. Rogers, *Mysteries*, 11.
44. See Oster, "Ephesus," 1708–9; Strabo, *Geogr.* 14.1.20; Dionysius of Halicarnassus, *Antiq. rom.* 4.25.4; IEph 1606.15; 1615.11; 4114.4.
45. On the date, see Hoag, *Wealth*, 14–15.

their fiancés, and young men their brides at this festival. As a result, according to Xenophon, at the time of the festival the city was full of local citizens as well as many visitors.[46] It was clearly a major festival in honor of the goddess.

Brought Alive in the Procession of Salutaris

A very long inscription set up in the Great Theatre in Ephesus in 104 CE as a result of the foundation of C. Vibius Salutaris and now known as the Salutaris inscription is also significant for our study. From the inscription we learn that on procession day, thirty-one gold and silver type-statues and images, nine of which were of Artemis,[47] were carried from the pronaos of the temple of Artemis outside the city wall, to the Magnesian Gate, which was the main entrance to the city from the south, where the procession was joined by the ephebes. The procession then went to the theater, to the Koressos Gate and back to the Artemisium.[48] Artemis was the "dominant symbolic representation"[49] in the procession, although other figures, such as Androklos, Lysimachos, Augustus, Trajan, "the Roman Senate and People" (SPQR), and the Ephesian Gerousia were also represented.[50] Of the nine statues of Artemis, five "contained strong allusions to the celebration of the mysteries of Artemis."[51]

The procession occurred on the days the Ephesian assembly met, on important festivals such as the nativity of Artemis, and on a number of other occasions. Rogers estimated that the procession would have occurred at least once every two weeks throughout the year,[52] and that the whole procession would have lasted at least 90 minutes on each occasion.[53] It is clear that Salutaris intended the procession to be a sig-

---

46. See Xenophon of Ephesus, *Anthia and Habrocomes* 1.2.2–4. It is also called the *Ephesiaca*.

47. See the list of type-statues and images in Rogers, *Sacred*, 84–5; 110. For a helpful discussion of the inscription in relation to "the past" in Ephesus see Carter, *John*, 94–97.

48. For the route, see Rogers, *Sacred*, 85–107.

49. Rogers, *Sacred*, 110.

50. See Table 9 in Rogers, *Sacred*, 84–85.

51. Rogers, *Sacred*, 110.

52. Rogers, *Sacred*, 83.

53. Rogers, *Sacred*, 110.

nificant event in the city each time it occurred.[54] Further, since at least 260 individuals were involved in the procession through the streets, it would have almost certainly halted traffic in the city when the procession took place.[55] Rogers suggests that "except for slaves and foreigners, virtually the whole adult male population of Ephesos either took part in or watched these public rituals."[56] The procession was designed as a public spectacle, a performance that spoke of the identity of the city.[57]

As I will show, the inscription shows the vitality of the cult of Artemis and of her birth stories in Ephesus in 104 CE. Clearly, at this time, perhaps only a few years after 1–3 John were written in the city,[58] the Artemis cult continued to flourish.

The way Artemis was presented in Salutaris's procession is important. One gold statue of Artemis symbolized her immortality.[59] Artemis carrying a torch was also mentioned at least five times in the inscription, and was the procession's dominant representation.[60] As Rogers notes: "Such a representation would immediately evoke the spectacle of the celebration of her mysteries, which were probably performed at night."[61] The connection with the mysteries is important. The procession, held every two weeks or so as we have noted, would recall and reinforce the annual celebration of the mysteries, serving to keep the story of Artemis's birth, which was at the center of the mysteries, alive in the city's memory and imagination. Clearly this was intended by Salutaris, who strongly associated his endowment with the celebration of these mysteries of Artemis.

Further, Rogers has shown how Salutaris's foundation caused the people involved "to look (metaphorically) to the institutional structure of their city, to its Ionian foundation, and to the birth of the goddess Artemis, for their sense of social and historical identity in the complex and changing Roman world."[62] Salutaris's foundation, through focusing on the birth of the goddess, taught the people to look "to the birth of

54. The statues were to be carried "before everyone (πρὸ κοιν[οῦ])"; see IEph 27.91.
55. Rogers, *Sacred*, 86; at least 250 ephebes were involved in the procession.
56. Rogers, *Sacred*, 136.
57. Rogers, *Sacred*, 111.
58. Trebilco, *Early Christians*, 271–73.
59. Rogers, *Sacred*, 111.
60. Rogers, *Sacred*, 111; Artemis is called "the Torchbearer" in the Salutaris inscription in IEph 27.164–5, 168, 173 (restored), 186–87, 196 (restored).
61. Rogers, *Sacred*, 111.
62. Rogers, *Sacred*, 41.

the goddess Artemis at Ephesos, for a theological sense of how Ephesian social and historical identity was grounded in a 'sacred' reality, which was impervious to all humanly wrought challenges."[63] We can see again, then, how central the goddess was to the identity of the city in 104 CE, and the intimate connection that existed between the city and her goddess.[64]

The inscription that relates to Salutaris's foundation not only established the procession, but also sought to ensure that it continued unchanged. One part of the inscription records a decree by Aquillius Proculus, the proconsul, which confirms the foundation and congratulates Salutaris and the city. Towards the end it reads:

> I wish no one now in any way, or under any pretext, to alter or to change any of the things arranged by him [Salutaris]. And if anyone attempts either to rescind or change any of the things ratified by you [the archons, boule, and demos of Ephesus] through this decree, or tries to introduce any such thing, let him be liable for 25,000 denarii toward the further adornment of lady Artemis, and another 25,000 denarii to the most holy fiscus, and every act contrary to the dedication will be nonetheless invalid.[65]

Clearly, this is to be for all time. The sense of continuity, and that what had been established should continue, is very evident. What Salutaris established related to "what was from the beginning"—the story of Artemis—and it was to continue to be retold in the same way into the future.

We conclude that the Salutaris foundation shows again that the story of the birth of Artemis continued to be a living myth in 104 CE. What was "from the beginning" continued to be alive. As Rogers writes: "At Ephesos in AD 104, the boule and demos did not merely pretend that the past was the present. The past, in certain ways, *was* the present."[66]

---

63. Rogers, *Sacred*, 69; see also 112–15; 145–47. The arrangements made by Salutaris were approved by the demos as a whole, so the foundation ultimately represented the attitude of the demos of Ephesus. It was also confirmed by Roman proconsuls.

64. The Salutaris inscription is dated 104 CE, but it is likely that the practice of carrying the images of Artemis in procession on the festival of the goddess existed prior to this.

65. IEph 27.358–65; Eng. trans. by Rogers, *Sacred*, 173.

66. Rogers, *Sacred*, 2 (author's own italics).

Androklos and the Foundation of the City

Yet there was more to Ephesus than Artemis. Here I want to note the Ionian foundation myth of the city. This is given by Athenaeus and reads:

> Creophylus, in his *Chronicles of the Ephesians,* says that the founders of Ephesos, after suffering many hardships because of the difficulties of the region, finally sent to the oracle of the god [Apollo of Delphi] and asked where they should place their city. And he declared to them that they should build a city "wheresoe'r a fish shall show them and a wild boar shall lead the way." It is said, accordingly, that some fishermen were eating their noonday meal in the place where are the spring today called Oily and the sacred lake. One of the fish popped out with a live coal and fell into some straw, and a thicket in which a wild boar happened to be was set on fire by the fish. The boar, frightened by the fire, ran up a great distance on the mountain which is called Trecheia, and when brought down by a javelin, fell where today stands the temple of Athena. So the Ephesians crossed over from the island after living there twenty years, and for the second time settled Trecheia and the regions on the slopes of Coressus; they also built a temple of Artemis overlooking the marketplace, and a temple of the Pythian Apollo at the harbour.[67]

Strabo and Pausanias also identify these original settlers of Ephesus as Ionians and say that they were under the leadership of Androklos. Strabo writes: "Pherecydes ... says that Androclus, legitimate son of Codrus the king of Athens, was the leader of the Ionian colonisation, which was later than the Aeolian, and that he became the founder of Ephesus."[68]

The important point to note here is that in the first century CE, Androklos, the founder of the city, continued to be "present" in Ephesus in many ways. This is shown by a number of points. One of the gates of the city was called the Koressian Gate, with the name commemorating this foundation story, which is associated with "the slopes of Koressos."[69] The name given to this gate recalled the story of Androklos and the boar,

---

67. Athenaeus, *Deipn.*, 8.361D, Eng. trans. by Gulick, LCL, 4:135–37.

68. Strabo, *Geogr.* 14.1.3; Eng. trans. by Jones, LCL, 6:197–99; Murphy-O'Connor, *Ephesus*, 9. See also Pausanias, *Descr.* 7.2.8.

69. Rogers, *Sacred*, 106.

and hence the foundation of the city itself.[70] It was the Greek foundation legend's architectural focal point in the city.

Rogers also notes that "the image of the city founder was present throughout the city during the imperial period. Ephesians saw Androklos represented in statuary form, with his hunting dog, in armor and in scenes with the boar, and on coins carrying a spear or charging the boar. Around the middle of the second century, a large statue of Androklos (196 cm) was perhaps placed in the Vedius gymnasium, the head of which probably was a portrait of Antinoos, the favorite of Hadrian."[71]

Inscriptions also tell us that the image of Androklos was part of a mosaic in the south side of the agora, and was on a relief in the theater.[72] Each year, a special day was celebrated in honor of Androklos.[73] Further, an image of Androklos was almost certainly included in Salutarius's procession,[74] which meant that one focus of the procession was on the Ionian founder of the city. The processional route decided upon by Salutarius also incorporated sites that honored Androklos, such as the heroön of Androklos.[75]

Thus, in addition to Artemis's birth story and festivals, much else in the city focused it backward, on what was "from the beginning" or "at the beginning."

Reading the Johannine Letters in this Ephesian Context

How does this background help us to interpret the Johannine Letters? I am suggesting that the striking frequency of ten occurrences of the phrase ἀπ' ἀρχῆς in these letters can be seen against the background of "foundation stories" in Ephesus.

I suggest that when original readers of 1-2 John (whether Jew or Gentile) kept coming across the phrase ἀπ' ἀρχῆς in these letters, the phrase would have resonated with their sense of the importance of foundation stories. Perhaps they would have been reminded of the frequency

70. Rogers, *Sacred*, 106-7.

71. Rogers, *Sacred*, 107. For a full discussion of this evidence, see Rathmayr, "Präsenz," 19-60.

72. Rogers, *Sacred*, 107, IEph 501A, 557A; Rathmayr, "Präsenz," 37.

73. IEph 644.12; see also Rogers, *Sacred*, 108.

74. Rogers, *Sacred*, 107; he notes that Merkelbach restored this name in a lacuna in IEph 27.183 and that no one has disputed this reading.

75. Thür, "Processional," 158-82; Harrison, "Epigraphic," 3-7.

with which stories about "beginnings" and what was "from the beginning" were current in their environment. Of course, given this frequency, their attention may not have been drawn to it. Perhaps they would only have noticed if there had been no such phrases. But certainly "from the beginning" as a concept represents and encapsulates the pervasive worldview and mindset of the period—that such "foundation stories" were vital. This emphasis on "from the beginning" in 1–2 John springs from, and gives testimony to, the same idea and the same sense of antiquity that we find in Ephesus in relation to Artemis and to Androklos.

Such contemporary readers would probably also see that what was asserted in 1–2 John about what was "from the beginning" was *different* in a number of ways from concepts and ideas they encountered in Ephesus. Firstly, the claim that "the Son" is "from the beginning," that is, that the phrase refers to an "absolute beginning," or better, to eternity before time, would have contrasted strongly with their myths of Artemis and Androklos, which belong in the past—admittedly the very ancient past—but *not* in eternity before time. The Son trumps Artemis and Androklos.

Secondly, we have noted that "from the beginning" can relate to the life of Jesus, and the beginning of Johannine tradition about him. The claim in this usage of the phrase that the origin of what was "from the beginning" is the life, teaching, death, and resurrection of a person who lived recently as a Jew—Jesus—would be quite startling. It was *this person* who was vital for the ongoing identity and life of the listening community, just as such foundation stories were vital for the ongoing identity and life of the city.

What can we say about John as an author in this regard? I suggest it was entirely natural and understandable for John to "think backward." As one who was familiar with both Jewish and Greco-Roman thought,[76] it was natural within both (overlapping) worlds to speak of "what was from the beginning." As I have noted, "going back to the beginning" is evident in 1 John 2:13–14, where we are told twice that fathers "know him who is *from the beginning* (ἀπ' ἀρχῆς)," that is, the eternal Son. "Going back to the beginning" is most obvious in John's Gospel with regard to the Logos in John 1:1–3. John's theological thinking in the Gospel has extended backward, as it were. In contrast to Mark, who begins with the adult ministry of Jesus, and Matthew and Luke who start with birth

---

76. A view that cannot be defended here, but see further Trebilco, *Early Christians*, 384–93.

stories (although they also have genealogies), John begins with "in the beginning" as a reference to before creation.[77]

We can suggest that one of the reasons that John's theological thinking has developed or extended backward—in both the Gospel and 1–2 John—was because it was entirely natural to do so in Ephesus. Here, the sights one saw (the Salutaris procession), the monuments one encountered (Androklos's tomb and so on), the very air that one breathed, proclaimed that "from the beginning" was vitally important. In the ancient city, one was like a rower—you went forward by looking backward. Of course, this is true elsewhere, but it is strongly true in Ephesus.[78] Perhaps John was open to such developments and expanded on them in his Gospel and in 1–2 John, not only as a result of his own theological thought, but at least in part because of his context and because of how vital "from the beginning" was in Ephesus, as well as for intrinsic theological reasons.

It seems likely, too, that in his use of "from the beginning," John is responding to the charge of "newness" and "innovation." This of course was a problem for early Christians. In the dominant Greco-Roman culture, what was old was tried and true. To be new was to be wrong. This is all of a piece with an emphasis on what was "from the beginning." Against this background, John states: "I am writing you *no new commandment*, but *an old commandment that you have had from the beginning*; the old commandment is the word that you have heard. Yet I am writing you a *new commandment* that is true in him" (1 John 2:7–8; italics added; cf. 2 John 5). One dimension of what John wants to say is that in one way, what he writes is not a *new* commandment, but is old; it is "from the beginning." The apparent countering of the charge of being simply "new" here makes us suspect that John has been accused of being novel, and that this is a damning charge that he wants to counter. In this context we can suggest he is aware of the importance of foundation stories. Certainly, placing such emphasis on "not new but old" suggests this.[79] The charge of "being new" makes perfect sense against the background of Ephesian foundation stories.

---

77. See further Carter, *John*, 93–122, who explores this theme in John's Gospel.

78. Of course, Paul "goes backward" in speaking of the preexistence of the Son; see, e.g., Phil 2:6–11; Col 1:15–20.

79. Lieu, *Second*, 74, notes that the love command in John's Gospel is a "new" command (John 13:34), but in 1 John 2:7–8 it is said to be "no new commandment" but rather an old one that the readers have had from the beginning, although it is *also* new because it belongs to the new age (1 John 2:8; 2 John 5).

In using the phrase "from the beginning," did John *intentionally* polemicize against Artemis and Androklos? Did he *intend* to contrast his faith with what others claimed of Artemis? Recall Acts 19, with its record of the clash between the worshipers of Artemis (the silversmiths, in particular) and Paul's preaching that led to the riot and the demonstration against Paul and for Artemis in the Ephesian theater (cf. Acts 19:21–41). Here was a strong and direct polemic *against* Paul and his preaching by worshipers of Artemis. Could John be responding to a similar polemic addressed to him by Artemis's worshipers?

The mid-second-century Acts of John also has John address worshipers in the temple of Artemis in Ephesus, and then John prays to God and the altar and the temple itself are destroyed (Acts John 37–44). Here is evidence for Christian confrontation with the Artemis cult in the form of a strong and head-on polemic against Artemis.[80] Does 1 John do so, but more subtly? Perhaps.

So John *may* have been consciously thinking: "I want to emphasize that *not Artemis but the one I call the Son* is from the very beginning, and the vital tradition, the vital foundation story about Jesus that I am passing on to my readers is 'from the beginning', that is, it has its origins in the one whom we have heard and seen, and that tradition has been consistently passed on from that vital fountain head."

There is one other piece of evidence that I have not yet discussed that suggests 1 John might intentionally be polemical against Artemis and that John might be led, at least in part, to "think backward" because of Artemis. The ending of 1 John is puzzling. It reads:

> And we know that the Son of God has come and has given us understanding so that we may know him who is true; and we are in him who is true, in his Son Jesus Christ. He is the true God and eternal life. Little children, keep yourselves from idols (Τεκνία, φυλάξατε ἑαυτὰ ἀπὸ τῶν εἰδώλων; 1 John 5:20–21).

Why does the author suddenly, abruptly, speak of idols at the end of the letter? They have not been mentioned until now. Commentators debate this at length.[81] Is the "idol" a false view of God, as is commonly argued, and therefore is this a reference to the secessionists? Perhaps.

---

80. For further discussion of the Acts of John in this regard, see Trebilco, "Acts of John."

81. See for example Brown, *Epistles*, 627–29 (who gives ten possible explanations of "idols"); Kruse, *Letters*, 200–202; Griffith, *Keep*.

But it could be that John means this: "I know there are plenty of *real* idols in the city where you live—Artemis comes to mind, and Apollo too. And I know they are competing for the loyalties of the followers of the Son. But 'keep yourselves from these idols.' They are not 'the true God' and they do not bring 'eternal life.'"

If this is a possible interpretation of what John means (and some have argued that real idols are in view here),[82] then perhaps this increases the likelihood of an intended polemical edge to John's use of "from the beginning." Others in the city speak of this, but John insists that what he is saying is the true "foundation story." This increases the likelihood that—what I have said was an entirely natural development of John's thought "backward"—also had in view a polemic against "false gods," false myths of what was "from the beginning"—and that his theological "thinking backward" was influenced by his context.

Conclusions

John's tenfold use of the phrase ἀπ' ἀρχῆς is startling. It has a threefold usage—to refer to the Son's eternity, to the work of the evil one, and to the tradition about Jesus that became the Johannine tradition. In each case, the stress is on "antiquity," that is, on foundations. This usage has a context in the LXX and in the usage of other NT authors, including the Gospel of John.

However, the emphasis on "foundations" also has a strong intertextual resonance with the foundation stories of Artemis and Androklos, and so with myths in the city of Ephesus, with what was "from the beginning" in the city. This sense of the liveliness of tradition, of "looking back" to foundations, of what was told about the past, was a vital part of the city of Ephesus and of Ephesian identity.

John's emphasis in 1–2 John on what was "from the beginning" resonates in this urban context with a key theme in wider Greco-Roman culture—that "what was from the beginning" plays a crucial role in identity. This is an example of common usage of a theme or ethical idea[83] between

---

82. See for example Hills, "Little Children," 285–310; Strecker, *Johannine*, 214.

83. Lee, *Moral Transformation*, 494. Oakes has also very helpfully outlined what he calls the "four basic interpretative options" we can adopt when we notice a parallel between Roman and Christian discourse; see Oakes, "Re-mapping," 301–22. Oakes notes that Christians and non-Christians in the Greco-Roman city can "follow common models," which I think is the case regarding the significance of foundation stories.

a NT author and the wider culture, since the importance of foundations can be seen to be part of the "larger encyclopedia of knowledge"[84] that many groups or people shared. As a result of John's use of this common theme, the first readers of the letters may well have been led to ponder that, not Artemis, but the Son was the one who was "from the beginning," in fact from eternity. The *true* "foundation story," the true past, was what they had heard "from the beginning," that is the story about the eternal Son, and about the life, death, and resurrection of Jesus.

It might even be—though it can only be a suggestion—that John intended a polemical contrast and so was involved in the polemical refutation of the claims of the wider culture about "beginnings." [85] The true foundation story—what was true "from the beginning"—is found *only* in the Son, the eternal Word, and not in any other such story. As John ends his letter: "He is the true God and eternal life. Little children, keep yourselves from idols" (1 John 5:20b–21).

---

84. Lee, *Moral Transformation*, 494.
85. Lee, *Moral Transformation*, 494.

Bibliography

Aasgaard, Reidar. "Like a Child: Paul's Rhetorical Uses of Childhood." In *The Child in the Bible*, edited by Marcia L. Bunge et al., 249–77. Grand Rapids: Eerdmans, 2008.
———. *My Beloved Brothers and Sisters! Christian Siblingship in Paul*. LNTS 265. London: T. & T. Clark, 2004.
———. "Paul as a Child: Children and Childhood in the Letters of the Apostle." *JBL* 126 (2007) 129–59.
Abasciano, Brian J. "Diamonds in the Rough: A Reply to Christopher Stanley Concerning the Reader Competency of Paul's Original Audiences." *NovT* 49 (2007) 153–83.
Abogunrin, Samuel O. "Jesus' Sevenfold Programmatic Declaration at Nazareth: An Exegesis of Luke 4:15–30 from an African Perspective." *Black Theology* 1 (2003) 225–49.
Adams, Sean A., and Seth M. Ehorn. "Composite Citations in Antiquity: A Conclusion." In *New Testament Uses of Composite Citations in Antiquity*, edited by Sean A. Adams and Seth M. Ehorn, 2:209–49. LNTS 593. London: Bloomsbury, 2018.
———, eds. *Composite Citations in Antiquity. Vol. 1, Jewish, Graeco-Roman, and Early Christian Uses*. LNTS 525. London: Bloomsbury, 2016.
Adewuya, J. Ayodeji. *Holiness and Community in 2 Cor 6:14—7:1: Paul's View of Communal Holiness in the Corinthian Correspondence*. StBibLit 40. New York: Peter Lang, 2001.
Ådna, Jostein. *Jesu Stellung zum Tempel: Die Tempelaktion und das Tempelwort als Ausdruck seiner messianischen Sendung*. WUNT 2/119. Tubingen: Mohr Siebeck, 2000.
Aernie, Jeffrey W. *Is Paul Also Among the Prophets? An Examination of the Relationship Between Paul and the Old Testament Prophetic Tradition in 2 Corinthians*. LNTS 467. London: Bloomsbury, 2013.
Albl, Martin C. *"And Scripture Cannot be Broken": The Form and Function of the Early Christian Testimonia Collections*. NovTSup 96. Leiden: Brill, 1999.
Alexander, Loveday. "*IPSE DIXIT*: Citation of Authority in Paul and in Jewish and Hellenistic Schools." In *Paul Beyond the Judaism/Hellenism Divide*, edited by Troels Engberg-Pedersen, 103–27. Louisville: Westminster John Knox, 2001.
Alexandre, Manuel, Jr. *Rhetorical Argumentation in Philo of Alexandria*. BJS 322. SPhiloM 2. Atlanta: Scholars, 1999.
Algra, Keimpe. "Epictetus and Stoic Theology." In *The Philosophy of Epictetus*, edited by Theodore Scaltsas and Andrew S. Mason, 33–56. Oxford: Oxford University Press, 2007.

Allen, Amy Lindeman. *For Theirs Is the Kingdom: Inclusion and Participation of Children in the Gospel according to Luke*. Lanham, MD: Lexington / Fortress Academic, 2019.

———. "'Theirs Is the Kingdom': Children as Proprietors of the Kingdom of God in Luke 18:15–17." In *T. & T. Clark Handbook of Children in the Bible and the Biblical World*, edited by Julie Faith Parker and Sharon Betsworth, 265–89. London: T. & T. Clark, 2019.

Allen, David M. "Constructing 'Janus-Faced' Exhortations: The Use of Old Testament Narratives in Heb 13:1–8." *Bib* 89 (2008) 401–9.

———. *Deuteronomy and Exhortation in Hebrews: A Study in Narrative Re-presentation*. WUNT II/238. Tübingen: Mohr Siebeck, 2008.

———. "Introduction: The Study of the Use of the Old Testament in the New." *JSNT* 38 (2015) 3–16.

Allen, Graham. *Intertextuality*. 2nd ed. London: Routledge, 2011.

Allison, Dale C. *The Intertextual Jesus: Scripture in Q*. Harrisburg: Trinity Press International, 2000.

Allison, Justin Reid. *Saving One Another: Philodemus and Paul on Moral Formation in Community*. Ancient Philosophy and Religion 3. Leiden: Brill, 2020.

Andresen, Carl. "Zur Entstehung und Geschichte des trinitarischen Personbegriffes." *ZNW* 52 (1961) 1–39.

Annas, Julia. *The Morality of Happiness*. Oxford: Oxford University Press, 1993.

Arena, Valentina. "Roman Oratorical Invective." In *A Companion to Roman Rhetoric*, edited by William Dominik and Jon Hall, 149–60. Blackwell Companions to the Ancient World. Oxford: Blackwell, 2007.

Arnold, Irene R. "Festivals of Ephesus." *AJA* 76 (1972) 17–22.

Arrighetti, Graziano, ed. and trans. *Epicuro: Opere*. 2nd ed. Biblioteca di cultura filosofica 41. Torino: Giulio Einaudi, 1973.

Asmis, Elizabeth. "Psychology." In *The Oxford Handbook of Epicurus and Epicureanism*, edited by Phillip Mitsis, 189–220. Oxford/New York: Oxford University Press, 2020.

Attardo, Salvatore. "The Semantic Foundations of Cognitive Theories of Humor." *Humor* 10 (1997) 395–420.

Attridge, Harold W. *The Epistle to the Hebrews*. Hermeneia. Philadelphia: Fortress, 1989.

Auerbach, Erich. "Figura." In *Scenes from the Drama of European Literature*, 11–76. Theory and History of Literature 9. Minneapolis: University of Minnesota Press, 1984.

———. *Mimesis: The Representation of Reality in Western Literature*. Translated by William R. Trask. Princeton: Princeton University Press, 2003.

Autero, Esa. "Social Status in Luke's Infancy Narrative: Zechariah the Priest." *Biblical Theology Bulletin* 41 (2011) 36–45.

Avrahami, Yael. *The Senses of Scripture: Sensory Perception in the Hebrew Bible*. New York: T. & T. Clark, 2012.

Babbit, Frank C., et al., eds. and trans. *Plutarch: Moralia*. 16 vols. LCL. Cambridge, MA: Harvard University Press / London: William Heinemann, 1927–2004.

Back, Frances. *Verwandlung durch Offenbarung bei Paulus: Eine religionsgeschichtlich-exegetische Untersuchung zu 2 Kor 2,14—4,6*. WUNT II/153. Tübingen: Mohr Siebeck, 2002.

Bacon, Benjamin W. "Heb. 1:10–12 and the Septuagint Rendering of Ps. 102:23." *ZNW* 3 (1902) 280–85.

Bailey, D. R. Shackleton, ed. and trans. *Valerius Maximus: Memorable Doings and Sayings.* 2 vols. LCL. Cambridge, MA: Harvard University Press, 2000.

Bailey, K. E. "The Song of Mary: Vision of a New Exodus." *Near East School of Theology Theological Review* 2 (1979) 29–35.

Baird, William. *History of New Testament Research. Vol. 2: From Jonathan Edwards to Rudolf Bultmann.* Minneapolis: Fortress, 2003.

Balla, Peter. *The Child-Parent Relationship in the New Testament and Its Environment.* WUNT 155. Tübingen: Mohr Siebeck, 2003.

Baltzly, Dirk. "Stoic Pantheism." *Sophia* 42 (2003) 3–33.

Bammer, Anton. "A Peripteros of the Geometric Period in the Artemision of Ephesus." *AnSt* 40 (1990) 137–60.

Barber, Michael P. "Jesus as the Davidic Temple Builder and Peter's Priestly Role in Matthew 16:16–19." *JBL* 132 (2013) 935–53.

Barclay, John M. G. "'O wad som Pow'r the giftie gie us, To see oursels as other see us!': Method and Purpose in Comparing the New Testament." In *The New Testament in Comparison: Validity, Method, and Purpose in Comparing Traditions*, edited by John M. G. Barclay and Benjamin G. White, 9–22. LNTS 600. London/New York: T. & T. Clark, 2020.

———. "Paul and the Faithfulness of God." *SJT* 68 (2015) 235–43.

———. "Paul's Story: Theology as Testimony." In *Narrative Dynamics in Paul: A Critical Assessment*, edited by Bruce W. Longenecker, 133–56. Louisville: Westminster John Knox, 2002.

———. "There Is Neither Old nor Young? Early Christianity and Ancient Ideologies of Age." *NTS* 53 (2007) 225–41.

———. "Why the Roman Empire Was Insignificant to Paul." In *Pauline Churches and Diaspora Jews*, 363–87. WUNT II/275. Tübingen: Mohr Siebeck, 2011.

Barclay, John M. G., and Benjamin G. White, eds. *The New Testament in Comparison: Validity, Method, and Purpose in Comparing Traditions.* LNTS 600. London: T. & T. Clark, 2020.

Barker, Margaret. "The Time is Fulfilled: Jesus and the Jubilee." *SJT* 53 (2000) 22–32.

Barr, David R. "John's Ironic Empire." *Int* 63 (2009) 20–30.

Barrett, C. K. *A Commentary on the First Epistle to the Corinthians.* HNTC. Repr. London: Continuum, 2004.

———. "Things Sacrificed to Idols." In *Essays on Paul*, 40–59. Philadelphia: Westminster Press, 1982.

Barth, Markus. "The Old Testament in Hebrews: An Essay in Biblical Hermeneutics." In *Current Issues in New Testament Interpretation: Essays in Honour of Otto A. Piper*, edited by William Klassen and Grayden F. Snyder, 53–78. London: SCM, 1962.

Bartholomew, Craig G., et al., eds. *Reading Luke: Interpretation, Reflection, Formation.* Scripture and Hermeneutics 6. Grand Rapids: Zondervan, 2005.

Bateman, Herbert W. *Early Jewish Hermeneutics and Hebrews 1:5–13: The Impact of Early Jewish Exegesis on the Interpretation of a Significant New Testament Passage.* AUS 7/193. New York: Lang, 1997.

Bates, Matthew W. *The Birth of the Trinity: Jesus, God, and Spirit in New Testament and Early Christian Interpretations of the Old Testament.* Oxford: Oxford University Press, 2015.

———. *The Hermeneutics of the Apostolic Proclamation: The Center of Paul's Method of Scriptural Interpretation*. Waco, TX: Baylor University Press, 2012.

———. "Justin Martyr's Logocentric Hermeneutical Transformation of Isaiah's Vision of the Nations." *JTS* 60 (2009) 538–55.

Bauckham, Richard J. *2 Peter, Jude*. WBC 50. Dallas: Word, 1983.

Beale, Gregory K. *Handbook on the New Testament Use of the Old Testament: Exegesis and Interpretation*. Grand Rapids: Baker Academic, 2012.

———. *The Temple and the Church's Mission: A Biblical Theology of the Dwelling Place of God*. Downers Grove, IL: IVP Academic, 2014.

Beale, Gregory K., and Sean M. McDonough. "Revelation." In *Commentary of the New Testament Use of the Old Testament*, edited by G. K. Beale and D. A. Carson, 1081–161. Grand Rapids: Baker Academic, 2007.

Beard, Mary. *Laughter in Ancient Rome: On Joking, Tickling, and Cracking Up*. Berkeley: University of California Press, 2014.

Beasley-Murray, George. *Baptism in the New Testament*. London: Macmillan / New York: St. Martin's, 1962.

Beaumont, Daniel. "The Modality of Narrative: A Critique of Some Recent Views of Narrative in Theology." *JAAR* 65 (1997) 125–39.

Becker, Eve-Marie. *Schreiben und Verstehen: Paulinische Briefhermeneutik im Zweiten Korintherbrief*. Neutestamentliche Entwürfe zur Theologie 4. Tübingen: Francke, 2002.

Becker, Matthias. *Lukas und Dion von Prusa: das lukanische Doppelwerk im Kontext paganer Bildungsdiskurse*. Studies in Cultural Contexts of the Bible 3. Paderborn: Schöningh, 2020.

Bednarz, Terri. *Humor in the Gospels: A Sourcebook for the Study of Humor in the New Testament, 1863–2014*. New York: Lexington, 2015.

Beetham, Christopher A. *Echoes of Scripture in the Letter of Paul to the Colossians*. Atlanta: SBL, 2010.

Belleville, Linda L. *Reflections of Glory: Paul's Polemical Use of the Moses-Doxa Tradition in 2 Corinthians 3.1–18*. JSNTSup 52. London: T. & T. Clark, 1991.

Bennema, Cornelius. *A Theory of Character in New Testament Narrative*. Minneapolis: Fortress, 2014.

Ben-Porat, Ziva. "The Poetics of Literary Allusion." *PTL: A Journal for Descriptive Poetics and Theory of Literature* 1 (1976) 105–28.

Berry, Paul. *The Encounter between Seneca and Christianity*. Lewiston: Edwin Mellen, 2002.

Best, Ernest. "1 Corinthians 7:14 and Children in the Church." *IBS* 12 (1990) 158–66.

———. *One Body in Christ*. London: SPCK, 1955.

Betsworth, Sharon. *Children in Early Christian Narratives*. London: T. & T. Clark, 2015.

———. "Children Playing in the Marketplaces." In *T. & T. Clark Handbook of Children in the Bible and the Biblical World*, edited by Julie Faith Parker and Sharon Betsworth, 245–63. London: T. & T. Clark, 2019.

Billings, Bradly S. "'At the Age of 12': The Boy Jesus in the Temple (Luke 2:41–52), the Emperor Augustus, and the Social Setting of the Third Gospel." *JTS* 60 (2009) 70–89.

Block, Daniel I. "The Prophet of the Spirit: The Use of RWH in the Book of Ezekiel." *JETS* 32 (1989) 27–49.

Blomberg, Craig L. *Matthew*. NAC. Nashville: Broadman & Holman, 1992.

———. "Reflections on Jesus' View of the Old Testament." In *The Enduring Authority of the Christian Scriptures*, edited by D. A. Carson, 669–701. Grand Rapids: Eerdmans, 2016.
Blumhofer, C. M. "Luke's Alteration of Joel 3.1–5 in Acts 2.17–21." *NTS* 62 (2016) 499–516.
Bock, Darrell L. *A Theology of Luke and Acts*. Biblical Theology of the New Testament. Grand Rapids: Zondervan, 2012.
Boda, Mark J. *The Book of Zechariah*. NICOT. Grand Rapids: Eerdmans, 2016.
Bovon, François. *Luke 1: A Commentary on the Gospel of Luke 1:1—9:50*. Translated by Christine M. Thomas. Hermeneia. Minneapolis: Fortress, 2002.
Boyarin, Daniel. "Midrash in Hebrews / Hebrews as Midrash." In *Hebrews in Context*, edited by Gabriella Gelardini and Harry W. Attridge, 15–30. Ancient Judaism and Early Christianity 91. Leiden: Brill, 2016.
Brawley, Robert. *Luke-Acts and the Jews: Conflict, Apology and Conciliation*. Atlanta: Scholars, 1987.
Brookins, Timothy A. *Corinthian Wisdom, Stoic Philosophy, and the Ancient Economy*. SNTSMS 159. Cambridge: Cambridge University Press, 2014.
Brown, Jeannine. "Metalepsis." In *Exploring Intertextuality: Diverse Strategies for New Testament Interpretations of Texts*, edited by B. J. Oropeza and Steve Moyise, 29–41. Eugene, OR: Cascade, 2016.
Brown, Raymond E. "The Annunciation to Zechariah, the Birth of the Baptist, and the Benedictus (Luke 1:5–25, 57–80)." *Worship* 62 (1988) 482–96.
———. *The Birth of the Messiah: A Commentary on the Infancy Narratives in Matthew and Luke*. Updated ed. ABRL. New York: Doubleday, 1993.
———. *The Epistles of John: Translated with Introduction, Notes and Commentary*. AB 30. Garden City, NY: Doubleday, 1982.
———. *An Introduction to the New Testament*. ABRL. New York: Doubleday, 1997.
Bruce, F. F. *The Epistle to the Hebrews*. NICNT. Grand Rapids: Eerdmans, 1964.
Brueggemann, Walter. *First and Second Samuel*. IBC. Louisville: John Knox, 1990.
Bruno, Christopher R. "'Jesus Is Our Jubilee' . . . But How? The OT Background and Lukan Fulfillment of the Ethics of Jubilee." *JETS* 53 (2010) 81–101.
Bunge, Marcia J., et al., eds. *The Child in the Bible*. Grand Rapids: Eerdmans, 2008.
Bussie, Jacqueline A. "Laughter as Ethical and Theological Resistance: Leymah Gbowee, Sarah, and the Hidden Transcript." *Int* 69 (2015) 169–82.
Butler, H. E., ed. and trans. *The Institutio Oratoria of Quintilian*. 4 vols. LCL. London: William Heinemann, 1920–1922.
Butterworth, Alex, and Ray Laurence. *Pompeii, The Living City*. London: Phoenix, 2006.
Byron, John. *Cain and Abel in Text and Tradition: Jewish and Christian Interpretations of the First Sibling Rivalry*. Themes in Biblical Narrative Jewish and Christian Traditions 14. Leiden: Brill, 2011.
———. "Slaughter, Fratricide and Sacrilege: Cain and Abel Traditions in 1 John 3." *Bib* 88 (2007) 526–35.
Cadbury, Henry J. "The Marcellum of Corinth." *JBL* 53, no. 2 (1934) 134–41.
Cagusi, P. "Spunti di polemica politica in alcuni graffiti di Pompei e di Terracina." *ZPE* 61 (1985) 23–29.
Cahill, Michael. "Not a Cornerstone! Translating Ps 118,22 in the Jewish and Christian Scriptures." *RB* 106 (1999) 345–57.

Caird, George B. "The Exegetical Method of the Epistle to the Hebrews." *CJT* 5 (1959) 44–51.
Callahan, Allen Dwight. "Babylon Boycott." *Int* 63 (2009) 48–54.
Calvin, John. *Commentary on a Harmony of the Evangelists Matthew, Mark, and Luke*. Translated by William Pringle. Bellingham: Logos Bible Software, 2010.
Campbell, Douglas C. *The Quest for Paul's Gospel: A Suggested Strategy*. London: T. & T. Clark, 2005.
Campbell, R. Alastair. *The Elder: Seniority within Earliest Christianity*. Studies of the New Testament and Its World. Edinburgh: T. & T. Clark, 1994.
———. "The Elders of the Jerusalem Church." *JTS* 44 (1993) 511–28.
Caragounis, Chrys C. *Peter and the Rock*. Berlin: De Gruyter, 1990.
Carey, Greg. "The Book of Revelation as Counter-Imperial Script." In *In the Shadow of Empire: Reclaiming the Bible as a History of Faithful Resistance*, edited by Richard A. Horsley, 157–76. Louisville: Westminster John Knox, 2008.
Carroll, John T. *Luke: A Commentary*. NTL. Louisville: Westminster John Knox, 2012.
———. "'What Then Will This Child Become?' Perspectives on Children in the Gospel of Luke." In *The Child in the Bible*, edited by Marcia J. Bunge et al., 177–94. Grand Rapids: Eerdmans, 2008.
Carter, Jonathan A. "Telling Times: History, Emplotment, and Truth." *History and Theory* 42 (2003) 1–27.
Carter, Warren. "Accommodating 'Jezebel' and Withdrawing John." *Int* 63 (2009) 32–47.
———. *John and Empire: Initial Explorations*. London: T. & T. Clark, 2008.
Cary, Earnest, ed. and trans. *Dio Cassius: Roman History*. Vol. 9: *Books 71–80*. LCL. Cambridge, MA: Harvard University Press, 1927.
Chatman, Seymour. *Story and Discourse: Narrative Structure in Fiction and Film*. Ithaca: Cornell University Press, 1978.
Chen, Diane G. *Luke: A New Covenant Commentary*. New Covenant Commentary Series. Eugene, OR: Cascade, 2017.
Chester, Andrew J. *Messiah and Exultation: Jewish Messianic and Visionary Traditions and New Testament Christology*. WUNT 207. Tübingen: Mohr Siebeck.
Cheung, Alex T. *Idol Food in Corinth: Jewish Background and Pauline Legacy*. JSNTSup 176. Sheffield: Sheffield Academic, 1999.
Ciampa, Roy E., and Brian S. Rosner. *The First Letter to the Corinthians*. PNTC. Grand Rapids: Eerdmans, 2010.
Clarke, John R. *Looking at Laughter: Humor, Power, and Transgression in Roman Visual Culture, 100 B.C.–A.D. 250*. Berkeley: University of California Press, 2007.
Clay, Diskin. "Diogenes and His Gods." In *Epikureismus in der späten Republik und der Kaiserzeit*, edited by Michael Erler, 76–92. Philosophie der Antike 11. Stuttgart: Franz Steiner, 2000.
Clooney, Francis X. "Reading Religiously across Religious Borders: A Method for Comparative Study." *Religions* 9 (2018) 42–54.
Cochran, Elizabeth Agnew. *Protestant Virtue and Stoic Ethics*. London: Bloomsbury T. & T. Clark, 2018.
Cockerill, Gareth L. *The Epistle to the Hebrews*. NICNT. Grand Rapids: Eerdmans, 2012.
Cokayne, Karen. *Experiencing Old Age in Ancient Rome*. London: Routledge, 2003.
Collingwood, R. G. *The Idea of History*. Oxford: Clarendon, 1967.
Collins, Raymond F. *Divorce in the New Testament*. Collegeville, MN: Liturgical, 1992.

———. *First Corinthians* SP 7. Collegeville, MN: Liturgical, 1999.
Colson, Francis H., et al., eds. and trans. *Philo*. 10 vols. LCL. Cambridge, MA: Harvard University Press / London: William Heinemann, 1929–1962.
Compton, Jared. *Psalm 110 and the Logic of Hebrews*. LNTS 537. New York: T. & T. Clark, 2015.
Conzelmann, Hans. *A Commentary on the First Epistle to the Corinthians*. Translated by J. W. Leitch. Hermeneia. Minneapolis: Fortress, 1976.
———. *The Theology of St. Luke*. Translated by Geoffrey Buswell. London: Faber and Faber, 1960.
———. "'Was von Anfang war.'" In *Neutestamentliche Studien für Rudolf Biltmann zu seinem siebzigsten Geburtstag am 20. August 1954*, edited by Walther Eltester, 194–201. BZNW 21. Berlin: Alfred Töpelmann, 1954.
Cooley, Alison, and M. G. L. Cooley. *Pompeii and Herculaneum: A Sourcebook*. New York: Routledge, 2014.
Cooper, John M. "The Relevance of Moral Theory to Moral Improvement in Epictetus." In *The Philosophy of Epictetus*, edited by Theodore Scaltsas and Andrew S. Mason, 9–19. Oxford: Oxford University Press, 2007.
Cover, Michael. *Lifting the Veil: 2 Corinthians 3:7-18 in Light of Jewish Homiletic and Commentary Traditions*. BZNW 210. Berlin: De Gruyter, 2015.
Cowan, William Tynes. "Plantation Comic Modes." *Humor* 14 (2001) 1–24.
Coxhead, Steven R. "The Cardionomographic Work of the Spirit in the Old Testament." *WTJ* 79 (2017) 77–95.
Craddock, Fred B. *Luke*. IBC: A Bible Commentary for Teaching and Preaching. Louisville: John Knox, 1990.
Craig, Christopher. "Audience Expectations, Invective, and Proof." In *Cicero the Advocate*, edited by Jonathan Powell and Jeremy Paterson, 187–213. Oxford: Oxford University Press, 2004.
Cranfield, C. E. B. *Romans 1-8*. ICC. Repr. London: T. & T. Clark, 2010.
Crites, Stephen. "The Narrative Quality of Experience." *JAAR* 39 (1971) 291–311.
Culpepper, R. Allan. "Luke." In *NIB: Luke-John*, edited by Leander Keck, 9:1–490. Nashville: Abingdon, 1995.
Dahl, Nils A. "The Story of Abraham in Luke-Acts." In *Studies in Luke-Acts: Essays Presented in Honor of Paul Schubert*, edited by Leander E. Keck and J. Louis Martyn, 139–58. Philadelphia: Fortress, 1966.
D'Angelo, Mary R. *Moses in the Letter to the Hebrews*. SBLDS 42. Missoula: Scholars, 1979.
Danker, Frederick W. "Hardness of Heart: A Study in Biblical Thematic." *CTM* 44 (1973) 89–100.
Das, A. Andrew. *Paul and the Stories of Israel: Grand Thematic Narratives in Galatians*. Minneapolis: Fortress, 2016.
Davies, J. P. "The Two Ages and Salvation History in Paul's Apocalyptic Imagination." In *Paul and the Apocalyptic Imagination*, edited by Ben C. Blackwell et al., 339–59. Minneapolis: Fortress, 2016.
Davies, W. D., and Dale C. Allison. *Matthew*. ICC. New York: Bloomsbury, 1999.
de la Potterie, Ignace. "La notion de 'commencement' dans les écrits johanniques." In *Die Kirche des Anfangs. Festschrift für Heinz Schürmann zum 65. Gerburstag*, edited by R. Schnackenburg et al., 379–403. Leipzig: Benno, 1977.
de Jonge, Henk J. "Sonship, Wisdom, Infancy: Luke II. 41–51a." *NTS* 24 (1978) 317–54.

De Long, Kindalee Pfremmer. *Surprised by God: Praise Responses in the Narrative of Luke-Acts*. Beiheft zur Zeitschrift für die neutestamentliche Wissenschaft und die Kunde der älteren Kirche 166. Berlin: De Gruyter, 2009.

Delling, Gerhard. "ἄρχω, ἀρχή, κτλ." In *TDNT* 1, edited by Gerhard Kittel et al., 478–89. Grand Rapids: Eerdmans, 1964.

———. "Nun aber sind sie Heilig." In *Gott und die Götter: Festgabe für Erich Fascher zum 60. Geburtstag*, edited by Hans Bardtke, 84-93. Berlin: Evangelische Verlangsanstalt, 1958.

Derret, J. D. M. "Thou art the Stone, and Upon This Stone . . ." *DRev* 106 (1988) 276–85.

deSilva, David A. *4 Maccabees: Introduction and Commentary on the Greek Text in Codex Sinaiticus*. Septuagint Commentary Series. Leiden: Brill, 2006.

DiMattei, Steven. "Biblical Narratives." In *As it is Written: Studying Paul's Use of Scripture*, edited by Stanley E. Porter and Christopher D. Stanley, 59–93. SymS 50. Atlanta: SBL, 2008.

Dobbin, Robert F., trans. *Epictetus: Discourses and Selected Writings*. London: Penguin, 2008.

Docherty, Susan E. "Composite Citations and Conflation of Scriptural Narratives in Hebrews." In *New Testament Uses of Composite Citations in Antiquity*, edited by Sean A. Adams and Seth M. Ehorn, 2:190–208. LNTS 593. London: Bloomsbury, 2018.

———. "Exegetical Techniques in the New Testament and 'Rewritten Bible': A Comparative Analysis." In *Ancient Readers and Their Scriptures: Engaging the Hebrew Bible in Early Judaism and Christianity*, edited by Garrick V. Allen and John A. Dunne, 77–97. Leiden: Brill, 2018.

———. "Genesis in Hebrews." In *Genesis in the New Testament*, edited by Steve Moyise and Maarten J. J. Menken, 124–48. LNTS 466. London: T. & T. Clark, 2012.

———. "How Hebrews Reads Scripture." In *The Oxford Handbook of Hebrews and the Catholic Epistles*, edited by Patrick Gray. Oxford: Oxford University Press, forthcoming.

———. "New Testament Scriptural Interpretation in Its Early Jewish Context: Reflections on the *Status Quaestionis* and Future Directions." *NovT* 57 (2015) 1–19.

———. "The Text Form of the Old Testament Citations in Hebrews Chapter 1 and the Implications for the Study of the Septuagint." *NTS* 55 (2009) 355–65.

———. *The Use of the Old Testament in Hebrews: A Case Study in Early Jewish Bible Interpretation*. WUNT II/260. Tübingen: Mohr Siebeck, 2009.

———. "Why So Much Talk? Direct Speech as a Literary and Exegetical Device in Rewritten Bible with Special Reference to Pseudo-Philo's *Biblical Antiquities*." *SEÅ* 82 (2017) 52–75.

Dodson, Joseph R., and David E. Briones, eds. *Paul and Seneca in Dialogue*. Ancient Philosophy and Religion 2. Leiden: Brill, 2017.

Doohan, Leonard. "Zechariah, Elizabeth, and John: Heralds of a New Age." *TBT* 47 (2009) 382–88.

Dorandi, Tiziano. "The School and Texts of Epicurus in the Early Centuries of the Roman Empire." In *Plotinus and Epicurus: Matter, Perception, Pleasure*, edited by Angela Longo and Daniela Patrizia Taormina, 29–48. Cambridge/New York: Cambridge University Press, 2016.

Downs, David J. *The Offering of the Gentiles: Paul's Collection for Jerusalem in Its Chronological, Cultural, and Cultic Contexts.* WUNT II/248. Tübingen: Mohr Siebeck, 2008.

———. "Prosopological Exegesis in Cyprian's *De opere et eleemosynis.*" *Journal of Theological Interpretation* 6 (2012) 279-93.

Duff, Paul B. *Moses in Corinth: The Apologetic Context of 2 Corinthians 3.* NovTSup 159. Leiden: Brill, 2015.

Duhem, Pierre. *To Save the Phenomena: An Essay on the Idea of Physical Theory from Plato to Galileo.* Translated by Edmund Doland and Chaninah Maschler. Chicago: University of Chicago Press, 1969.

Dunn, James D. G. *Did the First Christians Worship Jesus? The New Testament Evidence.* London: SPCK, 2010.

———. *Romans 9-16.* WBC 38A. Waco, TX: Word, 1988.

Dupont, Jacques. "Vin vieux, vin nouveau (Lc 5:39)." *CBQ* 25 (1963) 286-304.

Dyer, Bryan R. "'I Do Not Understand What I Do': A Challenge to Understanding Romans 7 as *Prosopopoeia.*" In *Paul and Ancient Rhetoric: Theory and Practice in the Hellenistic Context,* edited by Stanley E. Porter and Bryan R. Dyer, 186-205. Cambridge: Cambridge University Press, 2016.

Eastman, Susan. "Participation in Christ." In *The Oxford Handbook of Pauline Studies,* edited by Matthew V. Novenson and R. Barry Matlock. Oxford: Oxford University Press, 2014. https://www.oxfordhandbooks.com/view/10.1093/oxfordhb/9780199600489.001.0001/oxfordhb-9780199600489.

———. *Paul and the Person: Reframing Paul's Anthropology.* Grand Rapids: Eerdmans, 2017.

Edenburg, Cynthia. "Intertextuality, Literary Competence and the Question of Readership: Some Preliminary Observations." *JSOT* 32 (2010) 131-48.

Edwards, Jonathan. "The Freedom of the Will." In *The Works of Jonathan Edwards,* edited by Paul Ramsey, 1:175-470. New Haven, CT: Yale University Press, 1957.

Eisenbaum, Pamela M. *The Jewish Heroes of Christian History: Hebrews 11 in Literary Context.* SBLDS 156. Atlanta: Scholars, 1997.

Eliav, Yaron A. "The Temple Mount in Jewish and Early Christian Traditions: A New Look." In *Jerusalem: Idea and Reality,* edited by Tamar Mayer and Suleiman A. Mourad, 65-84. London: Routledge, 2008.

Ellingworth, Paul. *The Epistle to the Hebrews. A Commentary on the Greek Text.* NIGTC. Grand Rapids: Eerdmans, 1993.

Elliot, John H. "Elders as Leaders in 1 Peter and the Early Church." *CurTM* 28 (2001) 549-50.

Elliott, J. K. "Anna's Age (Luke 2:36-37)." *NovT* 30 (1988) 100-102.

Ellis, E. Earle. *Paul's Use of the Old Testament.* Repr. Eugene, OR: Wipf & Stock, 2003.

Elvey, Anne. "A Hermeneutics of Retrieval: Breath and Earth Voice in Luke's Magnificat—Does Earth Care for the Poor?" *ABR* 63 (2015) 67-83.

Emadi, Samuel. "Intertextuality in New Testament Scholarship: Significance, Criteria, and the Art of Intertextual Reading." *CurBR* 14 (2015) 8-23.

Engberg-Pedersen, Troels. *Cosmology and the Self in the Apostle Paul: The Material Spirit.* Oxford: Oxford University Press, 2010.

———. "Introduction: A Historiographical Essay." In *From Stoicism to Platonism: The Development of Philosophy, 100 BCE-100 CE,* edited by Troels Engberg-Pedersen, 1-26. Cambridge: Cambridge University Press, 2017.

———. "Introduction: Paul Beyond the Judaism/Hellenism Divide." In *Paul Beyond the Judaism/Hellenism Divide*, edited by Troels Engberg-Pedersen, 1–16. Louisville: Westminster John Knox, 2001.

———. "The Past Is a Foreign Country." In *The New Testament in Comparison: Validity, Method, and Purpose in Comparing Traditions*, edited by John M. G. Barclay and Benjamin G. White, 41–61. LNTS 600. London: T. & T. Clark, 2020.

Engels, Donald. *Roman Corinth: An Alternative Model for the Classical City*. Chicago: University of Chicago Press, 1990.

Enns, Peter E. "Creation and Re-Creation: Psalm 95 and Its Interpretation in Hebrews 3:1—4:13." *WTJ* 55 (1993) 255–80.

Eriksson, Anders. "The Old Is Good: Parables of Patched Garment and Wineskins as Elaboration of a Chreia in Luke 5:33–39 about Feasting with Jesus." In *Rhetoric, Ethic, and Moral Persuasion in Biblical Discourse: Essays from the 2002 Heidelberg Conference*, edited by Thomas H. Olbricht and Anders Eriksson, 52–72. London: T. & T. Clark, 2005.

Erler, Michael. *Epicurus: An Introduction to His Practical Ethics and Politics*. Basel: Schwabe, 2020.

———. "Epicurus as Deus Mortalis: Homoiosis Theoi and Epicurean Self-Cultivation." In *Traditions of Theology: Studies in Hellenistic Theology, Its Background, and Aftermath*, edited by Dorothea Frede and André Laks, 159–81. Leiden: Brill, 2002.

Evans, Craig A. *Matthew*. NCBC. Cambridge: Cambridge University Press, 2012.

———. "Why Did the New Testament Writers Appeal to the Old Testament?" *JSNT* 38 (2015) 36–48.

Fee, Gordon D. "Εἰδωλόθυτα Once Again: An Interpretation of 1 Corinthians 8–10." *Bib* 61, no. 2 (1980) 172–97.

———. *The First Epistle to the Corinthians*. NICNT. Rev. ed. Grand Rapids: Eerdmans, 2014.

Feldman, Louis H. "Hengel's *Judaism and Hellenism* in Retrospect." *JBL* 96 (1977) 371–82.

Festugière, A. J. *Epicurus and His Gods*. Translated by C. W. Chilton. Cambridge, MA: Harvard University Press, 1955.

Figueras, Pau. "Syméon et Anne, ou le Témoignage de la Loi et des Prophètes." *NovT* 20 (1978) 84–99.

Fish, Jeffrey, and Kirk R. Sanders. "Introduction." In *Epicurus and the Epicurean Tradition*, edited by Jeffrey Fish and Kirk R. Sanders, 1–8. Cambridge/New York: Cambridge University Press, 2011.

Fisk, Bruce N. "Eating Meat Offered to Idols: Corinthian Behavior and Pauline Response in 1 Corinthians 8–10 (A Response to Gordon Fee)." *TJ* 10 (1989) 49–70.

Fitzgerald, John, et al., eds. *Philodemus and the New Testament World*. NovTSup 111. Leiden: Brill, 2004.

Fitzmyer, Joseph A. *The Gospel according to Luke I–IX: Introduction, Translation, and Notes*. AB 28A. Garden City, NY: Doubleday, 1981.

———. *The One Who Is To Come*. Grand Rapids: Eerdmans, 2008.

Fletcher-Louis, Crispin. "Revelation of the Sacral Son of Man: The Genre, History of Religions Context and the Meaning of the Transfiguration." In *Auferstehung—Resurrection*, edited by Friedrich Avemarie and Hermann Lichtenberger, 247–98. Tübingen: Mohr Siebeck, 2001.

Ford, J. Massyngberde. "'Hast Thou Tithed Thy Meal' and 'Is Thy Child Kosher?'" *JTS* 17 (1966) 71–79.
Foss, Clive. *Ephesus after Antiquity: A Late Antique, Byzantine and Turkish City*. Cambridge: Cambridge University Press, 1979.
Foster, Paul. "Echoes without Resonance: Critiquing Certain Aspects of Recent Scholarly Trends in the Study of the Jewish Scriptures in the New Testament." *JSNT* 38 (2015) 96–111.
Foulkes, Francis. *The Acts of God*. London: Tyndale, 1958.
Fotopolous, John. *Food Offered to Idols in Roman Corinth: A Social-Rhetorical Reconsideration of 1 Corinthians 8:1–11:1*. WUNT II/151. Tübingen: Mohr Siebeck, 2003.
France, Richard T. *The Gospel of Matthew*. NICNT. Grand Rapids: Eerdmans, 2007.
———. "The Writer of Hebrews as a Biblical Expositor." *TynBul* 47 (1996) 245–76.
Franklin, James L., Jr. *Pompeis Difficile Est: Studies in the Political Life of Imperial Pompeii*. Ann Arbor: University of Michigan Press, 2001.
Freese, J. H., and Gesila Striker, eds. and trans. *Aristotle: Art of Rhetoric*. LCL 22. Cambridge, MA: Harvard University Press, 2020.
Frey, Jörg. "The Notion of the Spirit in the Dead Sea Scrolls and in Texts of the Early Jesus Movement." In *The Religious Worldviews Reflected in the Dead Sea Scrolls: Proceedings of the Fourteenth International Symposium of the Orion Center for the Study of the Dead Sea Scrolls and Associated Literature, 28-30 May, 2013*, edited by Ruth Clements et al., 83–102. STDJ 127. Leiden: Brill, 2018.
Furnish, Victor Paul. *II Corinthians*. AB 32A. New York: Doubleday, 1985.
———. *Theology and Ethics in Paul*. Nashville: Abingdon, 1968.
Gadamer, Hans-Georg. *Truth and Method*. Translated by Joel Weinsheimer and Donald G. Marshall. London: Bloomsbury, 2004.
Garani, Myrto, et al. *Intertextuality in Seneca's Philosophical Writings*. New York: Routledge, 2020.
García Serrano, Andrés. "Anna's Characterization in Luke 2:36–38: A Case of Conceptual Allusion?" *CBQ* 76 (2014) 464–80.
Garland, David E. *Luke*. Zondervan Exegetical Commentary on the New Testament. Grand Rapids: Zondervan, 2011.
Gaventa, Beverly Roberts. "Finding a Place for Children in the Letters of Paul." In *The Child in the Bible*, edited by Marcia L. Bunge et al., 233–48. Grand Rapids: Eerdmans, 2008.
———. *Our Mother St. Paul*. Louisville: Westminster John Knox, 2007.
———. *When in Romans: An Invitation to Linger with the Gospel according to Paul*. Grand Rapids: Baker Academic, 2016.
Gerber, Christine. *Paulus und seine "Kinder": Studien zur Beziehungsmetaphorik der paulinischen Briefe*. BZNW 136. Berlin: De Gruyter, 2005.
Gheorghita, Radu. *The Role of the Septuagint in Hebrews: An Investigation of Its Influence with Special Consideration to the Use of Hab 2:3-4 in Heb 10:37-38*. WUNT II/160. Tübingen: Mohr Siebeck, 2003.
Ghisalberti, Giosuè. *Soteriology and the End of Animal Sacrifice*. Eugene, OR: Wipf & Stock, 2018.
Gibson, Craig A., ed. *Libanius's Progymnasmata: Model Exercises in Greek Prose Composition and Rhetoric*. WGRW 27. Leiden: Brill, 2008.

Gill, Christopher. "Altruism and Reciprocity in Greek Ethical Philosophy." In *Reciprocity in Ancient Greece*, edited by Christopher Gill et al., 303–28. Oxford: Oxford University Press, 1998.

Gillihan, Yonder Moynihan. "Jewish Laws on Illicit Marriage, the Defilement of Offspring, and the Holiness of the Temple: A New Halakhic Interpretation of 1 Corinthians 7:14." *JBL* 121 (2002) 711–44.

Gillmayr-Bucher, Susanne. "Intertextuality: Between Literary Theory and Text Analysis." In *The Intertextuality of the Epistles: Explorations of Theory and Practice*, edited by Thomas L. Brodie et al., 13–23. New Testament Monographs 16. Sheffield: Sheffield Phoenix, 2006.

Glad, Clarence E. *Paul and Philodemus: Adaptability in Epicurean and Early Christian Psychagogy*. NovTSup 81. Leiden: Brill, 1995.

Glasson, Thomas Francis. "Plurality of Divine Persons and the Quotations in Hebrews 1:6ff." *NTS* 12 (1966) 270–72.

Gockel, Christin, and Norbert L. Kerr. "Put-Down Humor Directed at Outgroup Members Increases Perceived—but Not Experienced—Cohesion in Groups." *Humor* 28 (2015) 205–28.

González, Justo L. *Luke*. Belief: A Theological Commentary on the Bible. Louisville: Westminster John Knox, 2010.

Gooch, Peter D. *Dangerous Food: 1 Corinthians 8–10 in Its Context*. Studies in Christianity and Judaism 5. Waterloo: Wilfrid Laurier University Press, 1993.

Goodacre, Mark. "The Protoevangelium of James and the Creative Rewriting of Matthew and Luke." In *Connecting Gospels: Beyond the Canonical/Non-Canonical Divide*, edited by Francis Watson and Sarah Parkhouse, 57–76. Oxford: Oxford University Press, 2018.

Goodwin, Mark J. *Paul, Apostle of the Living God: Kerygma and Conversion in 2 Corinthians*. Harrisburg: Trinity Press, 2001.

Gowler, David. "Socio-Rhetorical Interpretation: Textures of a Text and Its Reception." *JSNT* 33 (2010) 191–206.

Graham, Daniel W. *Explaining the Cosmos: The Ionian Tradition of Scientific Philosophy*. Princeton: Princeton University Press, 2006.

Grant, Frederick Clifton. "St. Paul and Stoicism." *The Biblical World* 45 (1915) 268–81.

Grant, Michael. *Cities of Vesuvius: Pompeii and Herculaneum*. New York: Macmillan, 1971.

Graverini, Luca. "Ovidian Graffiti: Love, Genre and Gender on a Wall in Pompeii." *Incontri di filologia classica* 12 (2012–2013) 1–28.

Gregory, Andrew. "Dynamics and Proportionality." *Early Science and Medicine* 6 (2001) 1–21.

Green, Joel B. *The Gospel of Luke*. NICNT. Grand Rapids: Eerdmans, 1997.

———. "The Problem of a Beginning: Israel's Scriptures in Luke 1–2." *BBR* 4 (1994) 61–86.

———. "The Social Status of Mary in Luke 1:5—2:52: A Plea for Methodological Integration." *Bib* 73 (1992) 457–72.

———. "'Tell Me a Story': Perspectives on Children from the Acts of the Apostles." In *The Child in the Bible*, edited by Marcia J. Bunge et al., 215–32. Grand Rapids: Eerdmans, 2008.

———. *The Theology of the Gospel of Luke*. New Testament Theology. Cambridge: Cambridge University Press, 1995.

Griffith, Terry. *Keep Yourselves from Idols: A New Look at 1 John*. JSNTSup 233. Sheffield: Sheffield Academic, 2002.
Guelich, Robert A. *Mark 1—8:26*. WBC 34A. Grand Rapids: Zondervan, 1989.
Guite, Malcolm. "The Visitation." *Malcolm Guite* (2012). https://malcolmguite.wordpress.com/2012/05/31/a-sonnet-for-the-feast-of-the-visitation/.
Gulick, Charles Burton, ed. and trans. *Athenaeus: The Deipnosophists VIII-X*. LCL 4. Repr. Cambridge, MA: Harvard University Press, 1961.
Gundry, Robert H. *Peter—False Disciple and Apostate according to St. Matthew*. Grand Rapids: Eerdmans, 2015.
Gundry-Volf, Judith M. "The Least and the Greatest: Children in the New Testament." In *The Child in Christian Thought*, edited by Marcia L. Bunge, 29–60. Grand Rapids: Eerdmans, 2001.
Gupta, Nijay K. "The Thessalonian Believers, Formerly 'Pagans' or 'God-Fearers'?: Challenging a Stubborn Consensus." *Neot* 52 (2018) 91–113.
Guthrie, George H. "Hebrews." In *Commentary on the New Testament Use of the Old Testament*, edited by G. K. Beale and D. A. Carson, 919–96. Grand Rapids: Baker Academic, 2007.
———. "Hebrews' Use of the Old Testament: Recent Trends in Research." *CurBS* 1 (2003) 271–94.
Hafemann, Scott J. *Paul, Moses, and the History of Israel: The Letter/Spirit Contrast and the Argument from Scripture in 2 Corinthians 3*. WUNT 81. Tübingen: Mohr Siebeck, 1995.
———. *Suffering and the Spirit: An Exegetical Study of II Cor. 2:14—3:3 within the Context of the Corinthian Correspondence*. WUNT II/19. Tübingen: Mohr Siebeck, 1986.
Halliday, M. A. K., and Christian M. I. M. Matthiessen. *Halliday's Introduction to Functional Grammar*. 4th ed. London: Routledge, 2014.
Halliwell, Stephen. *Greek Laughter: A Study of Cultural Psychology from Homer to Early Christianity*. Cambridge: Cambridge University Press, 2008.
Hanson, Anthony T. "Christ in the Old Testament According to Hebrews." *SE* II (1964) 393–407.
Harmon, A. M., and M. D. MacLoed, eds. and trans. *Lucian*. 8 vols. LCL. Cambridge, MA: Harvard University Press, 1921–61.
Harris, Murray J. *The Second Epistle to the Corinthians: A Commentary on the Greek Text*. NIGTC. Grand Rapids: Eerdmans, 2005.
Harrison, James R. "An Epigraphic Portrait of Ephesus and Its Villages." In *The First Urban Churches 3: Ephesus*, edited by James R. Harrison and L. L. Welborn, 1–67. WGRWSup 7. Atlanta: SBL, 2018.
———. "Paul and the Gymnasiarchs: Two Approaches to Pastoral Formation in Antiquity." In *Paul: Jew, Greek, and Roman*, edited by Stanley E. Porter, 141–77. Leiden: Brill, 2008.
Hartnett, Jeremy. *The Roman Street: Urban Life and Society in Pompeii, Herculaneum, and Rome*. New York: Cambridge University Press, 2017.
Harvey, A. E. "Elders." *JTS* 25 (1974) 318–22.
Hau, Lisa Irene. *Moral History from Herodotus to Diodorus Siculus*. Edinburgh: Edinburgh University Press, 2016.
Hayes, Christine E. *Gentile Impurities and Jewish Identities: Intermarriage and Conversion from the Bible to the Talmud*. Oxford: Oxford University Press, 2002.

Hays, Richard B. *The Conversion of the Imagination*. Grand Rapids: Eerdmans, 2005.
———. *Echoes of Scripture in the Gospels*. Waco, TX: Baylor University Press, 2016.
———. *Echoes of Scripture in the Letters of Paul*. New Haven, CT: Yale University Press, 1989.
———. *The Faith of Jesus Christ: An Investigation of the Narrative Substructure of Galatians 3:1—4:11*. SBLDS 56. Chico: Scholars, 1983.
———. *First Corinthians*. Interpretation. Louisville: John Knox, 1997.
———. "On the Rebound: A Response to Critiques of *Echoes of Scripture in the Letters of Paul*." In *Paul and the Scriptures of Israel*, edited by Craig A. Evans and James A. Sanders, 72–96. Sheffield: JSOT, 1993.
———. *Reading Backwards: Figural Christology and the Fourfold Gospel Witness*. Waco, TX: Baylor University Press, 2014.
———. *Reading with the Grain of Scripture*. Grand Rapids: Eerdmans, 2020.
Hays, Richard B., and Judith C. Hays. "The Christian Practice of Growing Old: The Witness of Scripture." In *Growing Old in Christ*, edited by Stanley Hauerwas et al., 3–18. Grand Rapids: Eerdmans, 2003.
Hedrick, Charles. "Literature and Communication." In *The Oxford Handbook of Social Relations in the Roman World*, edited by M. Peachin, 167–90. Oxford: Oxford University Press, 2011.
Heilig, Christoph. *Hidden Criticism? The Methodology and Plausibility of the Search for a Counter-Imperial Subtext in Paul*. WUNT II/392. Tübingen: Mohr Siebeck, 2015.
Hellholm, David. "Moses as διάκονος of the παλαιά διαθήκη — Paul as διάκονος of the καινή διαθήκη. *Argumenta amplificationis* in 2 Cor 2,14—4,6." *ZNW* 99 (2008) 247–89.
Helyer, Larry R. "What about Anna?" *Priscilla Papers* 23 (2009) 5–6.
Henderson, Jeffery, ed. and trans. *Aristophanes: Birds*. LCL 3. Cambridge, MA: Harvard University Press, 2000.
Henning, Bruce. *Matthew's Non-Messianic Mapping of Messianic Texts: Evidences of a Broadly Eschatological Hermeneutic*. BibInt 188. Leiden: Brill, 2020.
Hicks, Robert D., ed. and trans. *Diogenes Laertius: Lives of Eminent Philosophers*. 2 vols. LCL. Cambridge, MA: Harvard University Press / London: William Heinemann, 1925. Repr. 1991.
Hilhorst, Anthony. "Abel's Speaking in Hebrews 11.4 and 12.24." In *Eve's Children: The Biblical Stories Retold and Interpreted in Jewish and Christian Traditions*, edited by Gerard P. Luttikhuizen, 119–27. Leiden: Brill, 2003.
Hills, Julian. "'Little Children, Keep Yourselves from Idols'. 1 John 5,21 Reconsidered." *CBQ* 51 (1989) 285–310.
Hillyer, C. N. "'Rock-Stone' Imagery in I Peter." *TynBul* 22 (1971) 58–81.
Hoag, Gary G. *Wealth in Ancient Ephesus and the First Letter to Timothy: Fresh Insights from* Ephesiaca *by Xenophon of Ephesus*. BBRSup 11. Winona Lake, IN: Eisenbrauns, 2015.
Hofius, Otfried. "'Einer ist Gott—Einer ist Herr': Erwagungen zu Struktur und Aussage des Bekenntnisses 1 Kor 8,6." In *Paulusstudien II*, 167–80. WUNT 143. Tubingen: Mohr Siebeck, 2002.
———. "Glaube und Taufe nach dem Zeugnis des Neuen Testaments." In *Neutestamentliche Studien*, 253–75. WUNT 132. Tubingen: Mohr Siebeck, 2000.
Hollander, John. *The Figure of Echo: A Mode of Allusion in Milton and After*. Berkeley: University of California Press, 1981.

Hoppin, Ruth. *Priscilla's Letter: Finding the Author of the Epistle to the Hebrews.* Repr. Fort Bragg: Lost Coast, 2009.

Horn, C. B., and J. W. Martens. *"Let the Little Children Come to Me": Childhood and Children in Early Christianity.* Washington, DC: Catholic University of America Press, 2009.

Horrell, David G. "Ethnicisation, Marriage and Early Christian Identity: Critical Reflections on 1 Corinthians 7, 1 Peter 3 and Modern New Testament Scholarship." *NTS* 62 (2016) 439–60.

———. "Theological Principle or Christological Praxis? Pauline Ethics in 1 Corinthians 8:1–11:1." *JSNT* 67 (1997) 83–114.

Horsley, Greg H. R. "The Mysteries of Artemis Ephesia in Pisidia: A New Inscribed Relief." *AnSt* 42 (1992) 119–50.

Hübner, Hans. *Vetus Testamentum in Novo. Vol. 2: Corpus Paulinum.* Göttingen: Vandenhoeck & Ruprecht, 1997.

Hughes, Graham. *Hebrews and Hermeneutics: The Epistle to the Hebrews as a New Testament Example of Biblical Interpretation.* SNTSMS 36. Cambridge: Cambridge University Press, 1979.

Huizenga, Leroy A. "The Old Testament in the New, Intertextuality and Allegory." *JSNT* 38 (2015) 17–35.

Hurd, John C., Jr. *The Origin of 1 Corinthians.* Macon: Mercer University Press, 1983.

Huttunen, Niko. *Paul and Epictetus on Law: A Comparison.* London: T. & T. Clark, 2009.

Hylen, Susan E. *Women in the New Testament World.* Oxford: Oxford University Press, 2019.

Ibita, Marilou, and Reimund Bieringer. "The Beloved Child: The Presentation of Jesus as a Child in the Second Testament." In *Children's Voices: Children's Perspectives in Ethics, Theology, and Religious Education,* edited by Annemie Dillen and Didier Pollefeyt, 117–36. Leuven: Peeters, 2010.

Innes, Doreen C., and W. Rhys Roberts, eds. and trans. *Aristotle: Poetics, Longinus: On the Sublime, Demetrius: On Style.* LCL 23. Cambridge, MA: Harvard University Press, 1995.

Inselmann, Anke. "Emotions and Passions in the New Testament: Methodological Issues." *BibInt* 24 (2006) 536–54.

———. *Die Freude im Lukasevangelium: Ein Beitrag zur psychologischen Exegese.* WUNT II/322. Tübingen: Mohr Siebeck, 2012.

Iverson, Kelly R. "Incongruity, Humor, and Mark: Performance and the Use of Laughter in the Second Gospel (Mark 8.14–21)." *NTS* 59 (2013) 2–19.

Jackson, Bernard S. "Legalism and Spirituality: Historical, Philosophical, and Semiotic Notes on Legislators, Adjudicators, and Subjects." In *Religion and Law: Biblical-Judaic and Islamic Perspectives,* edited by Edwin B. Firmage et al., 243–61. Winona Lake, IN: Eisenbrauns, 1990.

Janko, Richard. *Aristotle on Comedy: Towards a Reconstruction of Poetics II.* Berkeley: University of California Press, 1984.

Jaquette, James L. "Paul, Epictetus, and Others on Indifference to Status." *CBQ* 56 (1994) 68–80.

Jauhiainen, Marko. *The Use of Zechariah in Revelation.* WUNT II/199. Tübingen: Mohr Siebeck, 2005.

Jauss, Hans Robert. "Literary History as a Challenge to Literary Theory." *New Literary History* 2 (1970) 7–37.
Jeremias, Joachim. *Infant Baptism in the First Four Centuries*. London: SCM, 1960.
———. "Λίθος, Λίθινος." In *TDNT* 3, edited by Gerhard Kittel et al., 272–83. Grand Rapids: Eerdmans, 1965.
Jewett, Robert. *Romans*. Hermenia. Minneapolis: Fortress, 2007.
Jobes, Karen H. "The Function of Paronomasia in Hebrews 10:5–7." *TJ* 13 (1992) 181–91.
———. "Rhetorical Achievement in the Hebrews 10 'Misquote' of Ps 40." *Bib* 72 (1991) 387–96.
Johnson Hodge, Caroline. "Married to an Unbeliever: Households, Hierarchies, and Holiness in 1 Corinthians 7:12–16." *HTR* 103 (2010) 1–25.
Joshel, Sandra R., and Lauren Hackworth Petersen. *The Material Life of Roman Slaves*. Cambridge: Cambridge University Press, 2014.
Juel, Donald. *Messiah and Temple: The Trial of Jesus in the Gospel of Mark*. SBLDS. Missoula: Scholars, 1977.
Just, Arthur A. *Luke*. ACCS 3. Downers Grove, IL: IVP Academic, 2006.
Karrer, Martin. "LXX Psalm 39:7–10 in Hebrews 10:5–7." In *Psalms and Hebrews: Studies in Reception*, edited by Dirk Human and Gert J. Steyn, 126–46. New York: T. & T. Clark, 2010.
———. "Die Schriften Israels im Hebräerbrief." *TLZ* 11 (2013) 1181–96.
Käsemann, Ernst. *Commentary on Romans*. Translated by G. W. Bromiley. Grand Rapids: Eerdmans, 1980.
Kee, Alastair. "Old Coat and the New Wine: A Parable of Repentance." *NovT* 12 (1970) 13–21.
Keegan, Peter. *Graffiti in Antiquity*. London: Routledge, 2015.
Keener, Craig S. *Acts: An Exegetical Commentary. Vol. 1: Introduction and Acts 1:1—2:47*. Grand Rapids: Baker Academic, 2012.
———. *A Commentary on the Gospel of Matthew*. Grand Rapids: Eerdmans, 1999.
Keesmaat, Sylvia C. *Paul and His Story: (Re)Interpreting the Exodus Tradition*. JSNTSup 181. Sheffield: Sheffield Academic, 1999.
Kennedy, George A. *Classical Rhetoric and Its Christian and Secular Tradition from Ancient to Modern Times*. Chapel Hill: University of North Carolina Press, 1980.
———, ed. *Progymnasmata: Greek Textbooks of Prose Composition and Rhetoric*. WGRW 10. Leiden: Brill, 2003.
Kersten, Holger. "America's Faith in the Laugh Resistance—Popular Beliefs about Political Humor in the 2016 Presidential Elections." *Humor* 32 (2019) 299–316.
Kilburn, K., ed. and trans. *Lucian. Vol. 6*. LCL. Cambridge, MA: Harvard University Press, 1959.
Kim, Seyoon. *Christ and Caesar: The Gospel and the Roman Empire in the Writings of Paul and Luke*. Grand Rapids: Eerdmans, 2008.
———. "*Imitatio Christi* (1 Corinthians 11:1): How Paul Imitates Jesus Christ in Dealing with Idol Food (1 Corinthians 8–10)." *BBR* 13, no. 2 (2003) 193–226.
———. "Jesus—The Son of God, the Stone, the Son of Man, and the Servant: The Role of Zechariah in the Self-Identification of Jesus." In *Tradition and Interpretation in the New Testament: Essays in Honor of E. Earle Ellis*, edited by Gerald F. Hawthorne and Otto Betz, 134–48. Tübingen: Mohr Siebeck, 1987.

———. "Die Vollmacht Jesu und der Tempel—Der geschichtliche Zusammenhang und der theologische Sinn der 'Tempelreinigung' Jesu." In *ANRW* 2.26.6, edited by W. Haase, Berlin: De Gruyter, 1987.

King, Justin. *Speech-in-Character, Diatribe, and Romans 3:1-9: Who's Speaking When and Why It Matters*. BibInt 163. Leiden: Brill, 2018.

Kirk, J. R. Daniel. "Narrative Transformation." In *Exploring Intertextuality: Diverse Strategies for New Testament Interpretations of Texts*, edited by B. J. Oropeza and Steve Moyise, 165–75. Eugene, OR: Cascade, 2016.

Kistemaker, Simon. *Psalm Citations in the Epistle to the Hebrews*. Amsterdam: Van Soest, 1961.

Klauck, Hans-Josef. *Die antike Briefliteratur und das Neue Testament: Ein Lehr- und Arbeitsbuch*. Uni-Taschenbücher 2022. Paderborn: Schöningh, 1998.

———. *The Religious Context of Early Christianity*. Translated by Brian McNeil. Minneapolis: Fortress, 2003.

Klein, Ralph W. *1 Samuel*. WBC 10. 2nd ed. Nashville: Thomas Nelson, 2008.

Knibbe, Dieter. *Der Staatsmarkt. Die Inschriften des Prytaneions*. Forschungen in Ephesos 9.1.1. Wien: Österreichischen Akademie der Wissenschaften, 1981.

Knox, Peter E. "Ovidian Myths on Pompeian Walls." In *A Handbook to the Reception of Ovid*, edited by John F. Miller and Carole E. Newlands, 36–54. Hoboken: Wiley Blackwell, 2014.

Knox, Peter E., and J. C. McKeown, eds. *The Oxford Anthology of Roman Literature*. Oxford: Oxford University Press, 2013.

Koch, Dietrich-Alex. *Die Schrift als Zeuge des Evangeliums: Untersuchungen zur Verwendung und zum Verständnis der Schrift bei Paulus*. BHT 69. Tübingen: Mohr Siebeck, 1986.

Koch Piettre, Renée. "Paul and the Athens Epicureans: Between Polytheisms, Atheisms, and Monotheisms." *Diogenes* 205 (2018) 47–60.

Kodell, J. "Luke's Gospel in a Nutshell (Lk 4:16–30)." *BTB* 13 (1983) 16–18.

Koenraad, Verboven. "The Associative Empire: Status and Ethos among Roman Businessmen in Late Republic and Early Empire." *Athenaeum* 95 (2007) 861–93.

Koester, Craig R. "Revelation's Visionary Challenge to Ordinary Empire." *Int* 63 (2009) 5–18.

Konstan, David. "Reciprocity and Friendship." In *Reciprocity in Ancient Greece*, edited by Christopher Gill et al., 279–301. Oxford: Oxford University Press, 1998.

Koskenniemi, Heikki. *Studien zur Idee und Phraseologie des griechischen Briefes bis 400 n. Chr*. Suomalaisen Tiedeakatemian toimituksia Series B 102,2. Helsinki: Suomalainen Tiedeakatemia, 1956.

Kovacs, David, ed. and trans. *Euripides: Helen, Phoenician Women, Orestes*. LCL. Cambridge, MA: Harvard University Press, 2002.

Krentz, Edgar. *The Historical-Critical Method*. GBS. Philadelphia: Fortress, 1975.

Krückemeier, Nils. "Der zwölfjärige Jesus im Tempel (Lk 2.40–52) und die biographische Literatur der hellenistichen Antike." *NTS* 50 (2004) 307–19.

Kruse, Colin G. *The Letters of John*. PNTC. Grand Rapids: Eerdmans, 2000.

———. *2 Corinthians: An Introduction and Commentary*. TNTC. Downers Grove, IL: IVP, 1987.

Kujanpää, Katja. *The Rhetorical Functions of Scriptural Quotations in Romans: Paul's Argumentation by Quotations*. NovTSup 172. Leiden: Brill, 2019.

Kuschnerus, Bernd. *Die Gemeinde als Brief Christi: Die kommunikative Funktion der Metapher bei Paulus am Beispiel von 2 Kor 2–5.* FRLANT 197. Göttingen: Vandenhoeck & Ruprecht, 2002.

Kwon, Oh-Young. "A Critical Review of Recent Scholarship on the Pauline Opposition and the Nature of Its Wisdom (σοφία) in 1 Corinthians 1–4." *CurBR* 8, no. 3 (2010) 386–427.

LaFosse, Mona Tokaret. "Age Matters: Age, Aging and Intergenerational Relationships in Early Christian Communities, with a Focus on 1 Timothy 5." PhD thesis. Centre for the Study of Religion, University of Toronto, 2011.

Lampe, Peter. "Quintilian's Psychological Insights in His Institutio Oratoria." In *Paul and Rhetoric*, edited by J. P. Sampley and Peter Lampe, 180–99. London: Continuum, 2009.

Land, Christopher D. *The Integrity of 2 Corinthians and Paul's Aggravating Absence.* New Testament Monographs 36. Sheffield: Phoenix, 2015.

Lane, William L. *Hebrews 1–8.* WBC 47A. Dallas, TX: Word, 1991.

Lee, Max J. "Ancient Mentors and Moral Progress according to Galen and Paul." In *Doing Theology for the Church: Essays in Honor of Klyne Snodgrass*, edited by Rebekah A. Eklund and John E. Phelan Jr., 55–70. Eugene, OR: Wipf and Stock / Chicago: Covenant, 2014.

———. *Moral Transformation in Greco-Roman Philosophy of Mind: Mapping the Moral Milieu of Apostle Paul and his Diaspora Jewish Contemporaries.* WUNT II/515. Tübingen: Mohr Siebeck, 2020.

———. "The Reality of Freedom in Christ: Theological Reflection." In *Living Faith: Reflections on Covenant Affirmations*, edited by James K. Bruckner, et al., 170–89. Chicago: Covenant Publications, 2009.

———. "Review of *Christ and Caesar: The Gospel and the Roman Empire in the Writings of Paul and Luke* by Seyoon Kim." *Horizons in Biblical Theology* 33 (2011), 92–94.

Lee, Michelle V. *Paul, the Stoics, and the Body of Christ.* SNTSMS 137. Cambridge: Cambridge University Press, 2006.

Lemke, Jay L. "Discourses in Conflict: Heteroglossia and Text Semantics." In *Systemic Functional Approaches to Discourse: Selected Papers from the 12th International Systemic Workshop*, edited by James D. Benson and William S. Greaves, 29–50. Norwood: Ablex, 1988.

———. "Intertextuality and Text Semantics." In *Discourse in Society: Functional Perspectives*, edited by Michael Gregory and Peter H. Fries, 85–114. Advances in Discourse Processes. Norwood: Ablex, 1995.

———. "Intertextuality and the Project of Text Linguistics: A Response to de Beaugrande." *Text* 20 (2000) 221–25.

———. *Talking Science: Language, Learning, and Values.* Language and Educational Processes. Norwood: Ablex, 1990.

Lenski, R. C. H. *The Interpretation of St. Matthew's Gospel.* Minneapolis: Augsburg, 1961.

Leonard, Jeffery M. "Identifying Inner-Biblical Allusions: Psalm 78 as a Test Case." *JBL* 127 (2008) 241–65.

Lessing, Erich, and Antonio Varone. *Pompeii.* Paris: Éditions Pierre Terrail, 1995.

Levenson, Jon D. *The Death and Resurrection of the Beloved Son: The Transformation of Child Sacrifice in Judaism and Christianity.* New Haven, CT: Yale University Press, 1993.

Levin-Richardson, Sarah. *The Brothel of Pompeii: Sex, Class, and Gender at the Margins of Roman Society*. Cambridge: Cambridge University Press, 2019.
Levine, Amy-Jill, and Ben Witherington III. *The Gospel of Luke*. Cambridge: Cambridge University Press, 2018.
Liddell, Henry G., et al. *A Greek-English Lexicon*. 9th ed. Repr. Oxford: Clarendon, 1996.
Lieu, Judith. *The Gospel of Luke*. Peterborough: Epworth, 1997.
———. *The Second and Third Epistles of John: History and Background*. SNTW. Edinburgh: T. & T. Clark, 1986
———. "Us or You? Persuasion and Identity in 1 John." *JBL* 127 (2008) 805–19.
———. "What Was from the Beginning: Scripture and Tradition in the Johannine Epistles." *NTS* 39 (1993) 458–477.
Lightfoot, Joseph B. *The Apostolic Fathers, Part II: S. Ignatius, S. Polycarp*. 2 vols. London: Macmillan, 1889.
Lightstone, Jack N. "Late Second Temple Judaism: A Reconstruction and Re-Description as a Religio-Cultural System." In *Religions and Education in Antiquity: Studies in Honour of Michel Desjardins*, edited by Alex Damm, 76–106. SHR 160. Leiden: Brill, 2019.
Lim, Timothy H. *Pesharim*. London: Continuum, 2002.
Linant de Bellefonds, Pascale. "Pictorial Foundation Myths in Roman Asia Minor." In *Cultural Identity in the Ancient Mediterranean*, edited by Erich S. Gruen, 26–46. Getty Research Institute Issues & Debates. Los Angeles: Getty Research Institute, 2011.
Lindemann, Andreas. *Der erste Korintherbrief*. HNT 9/1. Tübingen: Mohr Siebeck, 2000.
Linell, Per. "Discourse across Boundaries: On Recontextualizations and the Blending of Voices in Professional Discourse." *Text* 18 (1998) 143–57.
Litwa, M. David. "Transformation through a Mirror: Moses in 2 Cor. 3.18." *JSNT* 34 (2012) 286–97.
Lloyd, G. E. R. "Saving the Appearances." *The Classical Quarterly* 28 (1978) 202–22.
Loader, William. *The New Testament on Sexuality*. Grand Rapids: Eerdmans, 2012.
Löhr, Hermut. *Umkehr und Sünde im Hebräerbrief*. BZNW 73. Berlin: De Gruyter, 1994.
Lohr, Joel N. "Righteous Abel, Wicked Cain: Genesis 4:1–16 in the Masoretic Text, the Septuagint, and the New Testament." *CBQ* 71 (2009) 485–96.
Long, Anthony A. *Epictetus: A Stoic and Socratic Guide to Life*. Oxford: Oxford University Press, 2002.
———. "Soul and Body in Stoicism." *Phronesis* 27 (1982) 34–57.
Long, Anthony A., and David N. Sedley. *The Hellenistic Philosophers*. 2 vols. Cambridge: Cambridge University Press, 1987. Reprint 1998–99.
Longenecker, Bruce W. *In Stone and Story: Early Christianity in the Roman World*. Grand Rapids: Baker Academic, 2020.
———, ed. *Narrative Dynamics in Paul: A Critical Assessment*. Louisville: Westminster John Knox, 2002.
Longenecker, Richard N. *The Epistle to the Romans: A Commentary on the Greek Text*. NIGTC. Grand Rapids: Eerdmans, 2016.
López Mauleón, Jesús María. "Τὸ Πνεῦμα (τὸ) ἅγιον en san Lucas." *Mayéutica* 31.72 (2005) 273–370.

Lucas, Alec J. "Assessing Stanley E. Porter's Objections to Richard B. Hays's Notion of Metalepsis." *CBQ* 76 (2014) 93–111.

———. "Paul and the Calf: Texts, Tendencies, and Traditions." In *Golden Calf Traditions in Early Judaism, Christianity, and Islam*, edited by Eric F. Mason and Edmondo Lupieri, 110–31. TBN 23. Leiden: Brill, 2018.

Lutz, Cora E., ed. and trans. "Musonius Rufus: 'The Roman Socrates.'" In *Yale Classical Studies* 10, edited by Alfred R. Bellinger, 3–147. New Haven, CT: Yale University Press, 1947.

Lyotard, Jean-François. *The Postmodern Condition: A Report on Knowledge.* Minneapolis: University of Minnesota Press, 1984.

Macaskill, Grant. *Union with Christ in the New Testament*. Oxford: Oxford University Press, 2013.

MacDonald, Dennis R. *The Gospels and Homer: Imitations of Greek Epic in Mark and Luke-Acts. Vol. 1: The New Testament and Greek Literature.* London: Rowman & Littlefield, 2015.

MacDonald, Margaret Y. *Early Christian Women and Pagan Opinion: The Power of the Hysterical Woman*. Cambridge: Cambridge University Press, 1996.

———. "A Place of Belonging: Perspectives on Children from Colossians and Ephesians." In *The Child in the Bible*, edited by Marcia L. Bunge et al., 278–304. Grand Rapids: Eerdmans, 2008.

———. *The Power of Children: The Construction of Christian Families in the Greco-Roman World*. Waco, TX: Baylor University Press, 2014.

———. "Reading the New Testament Household Codes in Light of New Research on Children and Childhood in the Roman World." *SR* 41 (2012) 376–87.

MacDonald, Margaret Y., and Leife E. Vaage, "Unclean but Holy Children: Paul's Everyday Quandary in 1 Corinthians 7:14." *CBQ* 73 (2011) 526–46.

MacGillivray, Erlend D. "The Popularity of Epicureanism in Elite Late-Republic Roman Society." *The Ancient World* 43 (2012) 151–72.

Maher, Michael, ed. *Targum Pseudo-Jonathan: Genesis, Translated with Introduction and Notes*. ArBib 1B. Collegeville, MN: Liturgical, 1992.

Malherbe, Abraham J. "Hellenistic Moralists and the New Testament." *ANRW* 2.26.1, edited by Wolfgang Haase, 267–333. Berlin: De Gruyter, 1992.

———. *Moral Exhortation: A Greco-Roman Sourcebook*. Philadelphia: Westminster, 1986.

———. *Paul and the Popular Philosophers*. Minneapolis: Fortress, 1989.

———. *Paul and the Thessalonians: The Philosophic Tradition of Pastoral Care.* Philadelphia: Fortress, 1987.

Marcovich, Miroslav, ed. *Iustini Martyris Apologiae pro Christianis*. Patristische Texte und Studien 38. Berlin: De Gruyter, 1994.

Marcus, Joel. "The Gates of Hades and the Keys of the Kingdom (Matt 16:18–19)" *CBQ* 15 (1988) 443–55.

Marguerat, Daniel. *The First Christian Historian: Writing the "Acts of the Apostles."* SNTSMS 121. Cambridge: Cambridge University Press, 2002.

Marshall, I. Howard. *The Epistles of John*. NICNT. Grand Rapids: Eerdmans, 1978.

———. *The Gospel of Luke: A Commentary on the Greek Text*. NIGTC. Grand Rapids: Eerdmans, 1978.

———. "Response to A. T. Lincoln: The Stories of Predecessors and Inheritors of Galatians and Romans." In *Narrative Dynamics in Paul: A Critical Assessment,*

edited by Bruce W. Longenecker, 204-14. Louisville: Westminster John Knox, 2002.
Martin, Dale B. *The Corinthian Body*. New Haven, CT: Yale University Press, 1999.
Martin, Michael Wade, and Jason A. Whitlark. *Inventing Hebrews: Design and Purpose in Ancient Rhetoric*. SNTSMS 171. Cambridge: Cambridge University Press, 2018.
Mason, Eric F. "Traces of the Golden Calf in the Epistle to the Hebrews." In *Golden Calf Traditions in Early Judaism, Christianity, and Islam*, edited by Eric F. Mason and Edmondo Lupieri, 142-56. TBN 23. Leiden: Brill, 2018.
Mason, Steve. "Prophecy in Roman Judea: Did Josephus Report the Failure of an 'Exact Succession of the Prophets' (*Against Apion* 1.41)?" *JSJ* 50 (2019) 524-56.
McAuley, David. *Paul's Covert Use of Scripture: Intertextuality and Rhetorical Situation in Philippians 2:10-16*. Eugene, OR: Pickwick, 2015.
McCullough, J. Cecil. "The Old Testament Quotations in Hebrews." *NTS* 26 (1980) 363-79.
———. "Some Recent Developments in Research on the Epistle to the Hebrews." *IBS* 3 (1981) 28-45.
McDonough, Sean M. *Christ as Creator: Origins of a New Testament Doctrine*. Oxford: Oxford University Press, 2010.
McGhee, Paul. *Humor: The Lighter Path to Resilience and Health*. Bloomington: Author House, 2010.
McGowan, Andrew B. *Ascetic Eucharists: Food and Drink in Early Christian Ritual Meals*. Oxford: Clarendon, 1999.
McKelvey, R. J. "Christ the Cornerstone." *NTS* 8 (1961-62) 352-59.
———. *The New Temple: The Church in the New Testament*. Oxford Theological Monographs. London: Oxford University Press, 1969.
McKnight, Scott, and Joseph B. Modica, eds. *Jesus Is Lord, Caesar Is Not: Evaluating Empire in the New Testament Studies*. Downers Grove, IL: IVP Academic, 2013.
McNamara, Martin, ed. *Targum Neofiti 1: Genesis, Translated, with Apparatus and Notes*. ArBib 1A. Collegeville, MN: Liturgical, 1992.
McNeile, Alan Hugh. *The Gospel according to St. Matthew: The Greek Text with Introduction, Notes and Indices*. London: MacMillan, 1915.
McNutt, Paula M. "In the Shadow of Cain." *Semeia* 87 (1999) 45-64.
Meeks, Wayne A. *The First Urban Christians: The Social World of the Apostle Paul*. New Haven, CT: Yale University Press, 1983.
———. "Judaism, Hellenism, and the Birth of Christianity." In *Paul Beyond the Judaism/Hellenism Divide*, edited by Troels Engberg-Pedersen, 17-27. Louisville: Westminster John Knox, 2001.
Meltzer, Gary S. "The Role of Comic Perspectives in Shaping Homer's Tragic Vision." *Classical World* 83 (1990) 265-80.
Méndez, Hugo. "Semitic Poetic Techniques in the Magnificat: Luke 1:46-47, 55." *JBL* 135 (2016) 557-74.
Merkle, Benjamin L. *The Elder and Overseer: One Office in the Early Church*. StBibLit 57. New York: Peter Lang, 2003.
Meyer, Ben F. *The Aims of Jesus*. London: SCM, 1979.
Mikalson, Jon D. *Greek Popular Religion in Greek Philosophy*. Oxford/New York: Oxford University Press, 2010.
Miller, Geoffrey D. "Intertextuality in Old Testament Research." *CurBR* 9 (2010) 283-309.

Miller-McLemore, Bonnie. "Jesus Loves the Little Children? An Exercise in the Use of Scripture." *Journal of Childhood and Religion* 1 (2010) 1–35.

Milnor, Kristina. *Graffiti and the Literary Landscape in Roman Pompeii*. Oxford: Oxford University Press, 2014.

———. "Literary Literacy in Roman Pompeii: The Case of Virgil's *Aeneid*." In *Ancient Literacies: The Culture of Reading in Greece and Rome*, edited by W. A. Johnson and H. N. Parker, 288–319. New York: Oxford University Press, 2009.

Minear, Paul S. "Luke's Use of the Birth Stories." In *Studies in Luke-Acts: Essays Presented in Honor of Paul Schubert*, edited by Leander E. Keck and J. Louis Martyn, 111–30. Philadelphia: Fortress, 1966.

Mitchell, Margaret M. "On Comparing, and Calling the Question." In *The New Testament in Comparison: Validity, Method, and Purpose in Comparing Traditions*, edited by John M. G. Barclay and Benjamin G. White, 95–124. LNTS 600. London: T. & T. Clark, 2020.

———. *Paul and the Rhetoric of Reconciliation: An Exegetical Investigation of the Language and Composition of 1 Corinthians*. HUT 28. Tübingen: Mohr Siebeck / Louisville: Westminster John Knox, 1991.

———. "The Thessalonian and Corinthian Letters." In *The New Cambridge Companion to St. Paul*, edited by Bruce W. Longenecker, 69–91. Cambridge/New York: Cambridge University Press, 2020.

Moessner, David P., ed. *Jesus and the Heritage of Israel: Luke's Narrative Claim upon Israel's Legacy*. Harrisburg: Trinity Press International, 1999.

Moffitt, David M. *Atonement and the Logic of Resurrection in the Epistle to the Hebrews*. NovTSup 141. Leiden: Brill, 2011.

Momigliano, Arnaldo. "The Fault of the Greeks." *Daedalus* 104 (1975) 9–19.

Moo, Douglas J. *The Letter to the Romans*. NICNT. 2nd ed. Grand Rapids: Eerdmans, 2018.

Moor, Johannes C. de. "The Targumic Background of Mark 12:1–12: The Parable of the Wicked Tenants." *JSJ* 29 (1998) 63–80.

Morales, Rodrigo J. *The Spirit and the Restoration of Israel: New Exodus and New Creation Motifs in Galatians*. WUNT II/282. Tübingen: Mohr Siebeck, 2010.

Morrison, James C. "Vico's Principle of *Verum* is *Factum* and the Problem of Historicism." *Journal of the History of Ideas* 39 (1978) 579–95.

Motyer, Stephen. "The Psalm Quotations of Hebrews 1: A Hermeneutic-Free Zone?" *TynBul* 50 (1999) 3–22.

Moxnes, Halvor, ed. *Constructing Early Christian Families: Family as Social Reality and Metaphor*. London: Routledge, 1997.

Moyise, Steve. "Intertextuality and Biblical Studies: A Review." *Verbum et Ecclesia* (2002) 418–31.

———. "Intertextuality and Historical Approaches to the Use of Scripture in the New Testament." In *Reading the Bible Intertextually*, edited by Richard B. Hays et al., 23–32. Waco, TX: Baylor University Press, 2009.

———. *The Old Testament in the New: An Introduction*. 2nd ed. T. & T. Clark Approaches to Biblical Studies. London: Bloomsbury T. & T. Clark, 2015.

———. "Quotations." In *As it is Written: Studying Paul's Use of Scripture*, edited by Stanley E. Porter and Christopher D. Stanley, 5–28. SymS 50. Atlanta: SBL, 2008.

———. "Wright's Understanding of Paul's Use of Scripture." In *God and the Faithfulness of Paul: A Critical Examination of the Pauline Theology of N. T. Wright*, edited by Christoph Heilig et al., 165–80. WUNT II/413. Tübingen: Mohr Siebeck, 2016.
Müller, Peter. *In der Mitte der Gemeinde: Kinder im Neuen Testament*. Neukirchen-Vluyn: Neukirchener Verlag, 1992.
Muraoka, Takamitsu. *A Greek-English Lexicon of the Septuagint*. Louvain: Peeters, 2009.
Murphy, A. James. *Kids and the Kingdom: The Precarious Presence of Children in the Synoptic Gospels*. Eugene, OR: Pickwick, 2013.
Murphy-O'Connor, Jerome. *St. Paul's Corinth: Texts and Archaeology*. 3rd rev. ed. Collegeville: Liturgical, 1983. Repr. 2002.
———. *St. Paul's Ephesus*. Collegeville, MN: Liturgical, 2008.
———. "Works without Faith in 1 Corinthians 7:14." *RB* 84 (1977) 349–61.
Naddaf, Gerard. "Plato's Theologia Revisited." *The Society for Ancient Greek Philosophy Newsletter* 198 (1995) 1–17.
Nanos, Mark D. "The *Polytheist* Identity of the 'Weak,' and Paul's Strategy to 'Gain' Them: A New Reading of 1 Corinthians 8:1—11:1." In *Paul: Jew, Greek, and Roman*, edited by Stanley E. Porter, 179–210. Leiden: Brill, 2008.
Nasrallah, Laura Salah. *Archaeology and the Letters of Paul*. Oxford: Oxford University Press, 2019.
Ndoga, Sampson S. "Revisiting the Theocratic Agenda of Book 4 of the Psalter for Interpretive Premise." In *The Shape and Shaping of the Book of Psalms: The Current State of Scholarship*, edited by Nancy L. DeClaissé-Walford, 147–59. SBL Ancient Israel and Its Literature 20. Atlanta: SBL, 2014.
Newberry, Julie Nicole. "You Will Have Joy and Gladness: A Narrative Analysis of the Conditions that Lead to Lukan Joy." PhD diss., Graduate Program in Religion, Duke University, 2020.
Neyrey, Jerome H. "Josephus' *Vita* and the Encomium: A Native Model of Personality." *JSJ* 25 (1994) 177–206.
Nicklas, Tobias. "Paulus—der Apostel als Prophet." In *Prophets and Prophecy in Jewish and Early Christian Literature*, edited by Josef Verheyden et al., 77–104. WUNT II/286. Tübingen: Mohr Siebeck, 2010.
Nienhuis, David R. "'From the Beginning': The Formation of an Apostolic Christian Identity in 2 Peter and 1–3 John." In *Muted Voices of the New Testament: Readings in the Catholic Epistles and Hebrews*, edited by Katherine M. Hockey, et al., 71–85. London: Bloomsbury, 2017.
Nolan, Mary Catherine. "The Magnificat: A Hermeneutical Study of Luke 1:45–55." *Marian Studies* 61 (2010) 1–28.
Nolland, John. *The Gospel of Matthew: A Commentary on the Greek Text*. NIGTC. Grand Rapids: Eerdmans, 2005.
Norton, Jonathan D. H. *Contours in the Text: Textual Variation in the Writings of Paul, Josephus, and the Yaḥad*. LNTS 430. London: T. & T. Clark, 2011.
Nünlist, René. *The Ancient Critic at Work: Terms and Concepts of Literary Criticism in Greek Scholia*. Cambridge: Cambridge University Press, 2011.
Oakes, Peter. "Re-Mapping the Universe: Paul and the Emperor in 1 Thessalonians and Philippians." *JSNT* 27 (2005) 301–22.
Oates, Whitney Jennings, ed. *The Stoic and Epicurean Philosophers: The Complete Extant Writings of Epicurus, Epictetus, Lucretius Marcus Aurelius*. New York: Modern Library, 1940.

Obbink, Dirk. "The Atheism of Epicurus." *GRBS* 30 (1989) 187–223.
———, ed. and trans. *Philodemus: On Piety, Part 1: Critical Text with Commentary*. Vol. 1 of 2. Oxford: Clarendon, 1996.
———. "Sulla religiosità e il culto popolare (POxy 215)." In *Corpus dei papiri filosofici greci e latini. Testi e lessico nei papiri di cultura greca e latina*, 167–91. Parte I: Autori Noti, Vol. 1. Firenze: Olschki, 1992.
O'Day, Gail. "Singing Woman's Song: A Hermeneutic of Liberation." *CurTM* 12 (1985) 205–27.
O'Keefe, Tim. *Epicureanism*. Ancient Philosophies 7. Berkeley/Los Angeles: University of California Press, 2010.
Oliver, H. H. "The Lucan Birth Stories and the Purpose of Luke-Acts." *NTS* 10 (1964) 202–26.
Oliver, James H. *The Sacred Gerusia*. Hesperia Supplement 6. Athens: American School of Classical Studies at Athens, 1941.
O'Neil, J. C. "1 Corinthians 7.14 and Infant Baptism." In *L'Apôtre Paul: Personnalité, Style, et Conception du Ministère*, edited by Albert Vanhoye, 358–59. Leuven: Leuven University Press, 1986.
Ong, Hughson T. "The Language of the New Testament from a Sociolinguistic Perspective." *JGRChJ* 12 (2016) 163–90.
Oropeza, B. J. "Ancient Midrash in the Age of Intertextuality." In *New Studies in Textual Interplay*, edited by Craig A. Evans et al., 9–28. SSEJC 20/LNTS 632. London: T. & T. Clark, 2020.
———. *Churches under Siege of Persecution and Assimilation: The General Epistles and Revelation*. Apostasy in the New Testament Communities 3. Eugene, OR: Cascade, 2012.
———. *Exploring Second Corinthians: Death and Life, Hardship, and Rivalry*. Rhetoric of Religious Antiquity 3. Atlanta: SBL, 2016.
———. *1 Corinthians*. New Covenant Commentary Series. Eugene, OR: Cascade, 2017.
———. "1 Corinthians 10:1–22 in Light of the Corinthians' Knowledge of Scripture." In *Paul and Moses: The Exodus and Sinai Traditions in the Letters of Paul*, edited by Florian Wilk, 121–37. Studies in Education and Religion in Ancient and Pre-Modern History in the Mediterranean and Its Environs 11. Tübingen: Mohr Siebeck, 2021.
———. "Intertextuality." In *The Oxford Encyclopedia of Biblical Interpretation*, edited by Steven L. McKenzie, 1.453–63. Oxford: Oxford University Press, 2013.
———. "New Studies in Textual Interplay: An Introduction." In *New Studies in Textual Interplay*, edited by Craig Evans et al., 3–7. SSEJC 20/LNTS 632. London: T. & T. Clark, 2020.
———. *Paul and Apostasy: Eschatology, Perseverance, and Falling Away in the Corinthian Congregation*, WUNT II/115. Tübingen: Mohr Siebeck, 2000.
Oropeza, B. J., and Steve Moyise, eds. *Exploring Intertextuality: Diverse Strategies for New Testament Interpretation of Texts*. Eugene, OR: Cascade, 2016.
Osborne, Robin. "Sacrificial Theologies." In *Theologies of Ancient Greek Religion*, edited by Esther Eidinow, et al., 233–48. Cambridge/New York: Cambridge University Press, 2016.
Osiek, Carolyn, and David L. Balch. *Families in the New Testament World: Households and House Churches*. Louisville: Westminster John Knox, 1997.

Osiek, Carolyn, and Margaret Y. MacDonald with Janet H. Tulloch. *A Woman's Place: House Churches in Earliest Christianity.* Minneapolis: Fortress, 2006.
Oster, Richard E., Jr. "Ephesus as a Religious Center under the Principate, I. Paganism before Constantine." In *ANRW* 2.18.3, edited by Wolfgang Haase, 1661–728. Berlin: De Gruyter, 1990.
———. "Use, Misuse, and Neglect of Archaeological Evidence in Some Modern Works on 1 Corinthians (1 Cor 7:1–5; 8:10; 11:2–16; 12:14–26)." *ZNW* 83, no. 1–2 (2009) 52–73.
Otto, Konrad. "Zwischen den Welten. Rezeption und Verarbeitung der Mose-Exodus-Tradition in 1 Kor 10 und 2 Kor 3." PhD diss., Georg-August-Universität Göttingen, 2020. Tübingen: Mohr Siebeck, forthcoming.
Ounsworth, Richard. *Joshua Typology in the New Testament.* WUNT II/328. Tübingen: Mohr Siebeck, 2012.
Overland, Paul B. "Chiasm." In *Dictionary of the Old Testament: Wisdom, Poetry and Writings,* edited by Tremper Longman III and Peter Enns, 54–57. Downers Grove, IL: IVP Academic, 2008.
Padilla, Osvaldo. *The Speeches of Outsiders in Acts: Poetics, Theology and Historiography.* SNTSMS 144. Cambridge: Cambridge University Press, 2008.
Painter, John. *1, 2, and 3 John.* SP 18. Collegeville, MN: Liturgical, 2002.
Papousek, Ilona. "Humor and Well-Being: A Little Less Is Quite Enough." *Humor* 31 (2018) 311–27.
Parker, Julie Faith, and Sharon Betsworth, eds. *T. & T. Clark Handbook of Children in the Bible and the Biblical World.* London: T. & T. Clark, 2019.
Parsons, Mikael C. *Luke: Storyteller, Interpreter, Evangelist.* Peabody, MA: Hendrickson, 2007.
Peeler, Amy L. B. *You Are My Son: The Family of God in the Epistle to the Hebrews.* LNTS 486. London: T. & T. Clark, 2014.
Perrin, Nicholas. *Jesus and the Temple.* Grand Rapids: Baker, 2010.
Perry, Ben Edwin, ed. and trans. *Babrius and Phaedrus: Fables.* LCL. Cambridge, MA: Harvard University Press, 1965.
Petterson, Anthony R. *Haggai, Zechariah and Malachi.* AOTC. Downers Grove, IL: IVP, 2015.
Pfister, Manfred. "Konzepte der Intertextualität." In *Intertextualität: Formen, Funktionen, anglistische Fallstudien,* edited by Ulrich Broich and Manfred Pfister, 1–30. Berlin: De Gruyter, 1985.
Phillips, Elaine A. "Peter's Declaration at Caesarea Philippi." In *Lexham Geographic Commentary on the Gospels,* edited by Barry J. Beitzel, 286–97. Bellingham: Lexham, 2017.
Pierce, Madison N. *Divine Discourse in the Epistle to the Hebrews: The Recontextualization of Spoken Quotations of Scripture.* SNTSMS 178. Cambridge: Cambridge University Press, 2020.
———. "Review of *Birth of the Trinity,* by Matthew W. Bates." *Reviews of Biblical and Early Christian Studies* (2015). https://rbecs.org/2015/10/17/bt/.
Piotrowski, Nicholas G. "'Whatever You Ask' for the Missionary Purposes of the Eschatological Temple: Quotation and Typology in Mark 11–12." *The Southern Baptist Journal of Theology* 21 (2017) 97–121.
Plett, Heinrich F. "Intertextualities." In *Intertextuality,* edited by Heinrich F. Plett, 3–29. Research in Text Theory 15. Berlin: De Gruyter, 1991.

Pomeroy, Sarah B. *Xenophon, Oeconomicus: A Social and Historical Commentary.* Oxford: Clarendon, 1994.
Portefaix, Lilian. "The Image of Artemis Ephesia—A Symbolic Configuration Related to Her Mysteries?" In *100 Jahre Österreichische Forschungen in Ephesos. Akten des Symposions Wien 1995*, edited by Herwig Friesinger and Fritz Krinzinger, 611–17. Wien: Verlag der Österreichischen Akademie der Wissenschaften, 1999.
Porter, James I. "Hermeneutic Lines and Circles: Aristarchus and Crates on the Exegesis of Homer." In *Homer's Ancient Readers*, edited by Robert Lamberton and John J. Keaney, 67–115. Princeton, NJ: Princeton University Press, 1992.
Porter, Stanley E. "Allusions and Echoes." In *As it is Written: Studying Paul's Use of Scripture*, edited by Stanley E. Porter and Christopher D. Stanley, 29–40. SymS 50. Atlanta: SBL, 2008.
———. "Did Paul Speak Latin?" In *Paul: Jew, Greek, and Roman*, edited by Stanley E. Porter, 289–308. Pauline Studies 5. Leiden: Brill, 2008.
———. "Further Comments on the Use of the Old Testament in the New Testament." In *The Intertextuality of the Epistles: Explorations of Theory and Practice*, edited by Thomas L. Brodie et al., 98–110. New Testament Monographs 16. Sheffield: Sheffield Phoenix, 2006.
———. "Introduction: Diglossia and Other Topics in New Testament Linguistics." In *Diglossia and Other Topics in New Testament Linguistics*, edited by Stanley E. Porter, 13–16. JSNTSup 193. Studies in New Testament Greek 6. Sheffield: Sheffield Academic, 2000.
———. "Pauline Techniques of Interweaving Scripture into His Letters." In *Paulinische Schriftrezeption: Grundlagen—Ausprägungen—Wirkungen—Wertungen*, edited by Florian Wilk and Markus Öhler, 23–55. FRLANT 268. Göttingen: Vandenhoeck & Ruprecht, 2017.
———. "Sociolinguistics and New Testament Study." In *Linguistic Analysis of the Greek New Testament: Studies in Tools, Methods, and Practice*, 113–31. Grand Rapids: Baker Academic, 2015.
———. "The Use of the Old Testament in the New Testament: A Brief Comment on Method and Terminology." In *Early Christian Interpretation of the Scriptures of Israel: Investigations and Proposals,* edited by Craig A. Evans and James A. Sanders, 79–96. JSNTSup 148. Sheffield: Sheffield Academic, 1997.
Porter, Stanley E., and Andrew W. Pitts. "Greco-Roman Culture in the History of New Testament Interpretation: An Introductory Essay." In *Christian Origins and Greco-Roman Culture: Social and Literary Contexts for the New Testament*, edited by Stanley E. Porter and Andrew W. Pitts, 1–12. TENTS 9. Early Christianity in Its Hellenistic Context 1. Leiden: Brill, 2013.
Price, Simon. *Religion of the Ancient Greeks.* Cambridge/New York: Cambridge University Press, 1999.
Punt, Jeremy. "Not Child's Play: Paul and Children." *Neot* 51 (2017) 255–59.
Quarles, Charles L. *Matthew.* Exegetical Guide to the Greek New Testament. Nashville: B&H Academic, 2017.
Rabbie, Edwin. "Wit and Humor in Roman Rhetoric." In *A Companion to Roman Rhetoric*, edited by William Dominik and Jon Hall, 207–17. Blackwell Companions to the Ancient World. Oxford: Blackwell, 2007.
Rabens, Volker. *The Holy Spirit and Ethics in Paul.* WUNT II/238. Tübingen: Mohr Siebeck, 2010.

Rabinowitz, Peter J. *Before Reading: Narrative Conventions and the Politics of Interpretation*. Ithaca: Cornell University Press, 1987.

———. "Truth in Fiction: A Reexamination of Audiences." *Critical Inquiry* 4 (1977) 121–41.

Rackham, Harris, ed. and trans. *Aristotle: Nicomachean Ethics*. LCL 19. Cambridge, MA: Harvard University Press, 1926.

———, ed. and trans. *Cicero: De Natura Deorum [et] Academica*. LCL. Cambridge, MA: Harvard University Press / London: William Heinemann, 1933. Repr. 1951.

———, ed. and trans. *Cicero: Divisions of Oratory*. LCL 4. Cambridge, MA: Harvard University Press, 1942.

Radner, Ephraim. *Time and the Word: Figural Reading of the Christian Scriptures*. Grand Rapids: Eerdmans, 2016.

Ramelli, Ilaria. *Hierocles the Stoic: Elements of Ethics, Fragments and Excerpts*. Translated by David Konstan. Leiden: Brill, 2009.

———. "The Philosophical Stance of Allegory in Stoicism and its Reception in Platonism, Pagan and Christian: Origen in Dialogue with the Stoics and Plato." *IJCT* 18 (2011) 335–71.

Rasco, Emilio. "Hans Conzelmann y la 'historia salutis': a propósito de *Die Mitte der Zeit* y *Die Apostelgeschichte*." *Greg* 46 (1965) 286–319.

Rathmayr, Elisabeth. "Die Präsenz des Ktistes Androklos in Ephesos." *Anzeiger der philosophisch-historischen Klasse* 145 (2010) 19–60.

Rawson, Beryl. *Children and Childhood in Roman Italy*. Oxford: Oxford University Press, 2006.

———. "'The Roman Family' in Recent Research: State of the Questions." *BibInt* 11 (2003) 119–38.

Reinmuth, Eckart. "Das Alter würdigen: Antike Anerkennungsdiskruse und Neues Testament." In *Jenseits von Indikativ und Imperativ: Kontexte und Normen neutestamentlicher / Contexts and Norms of New Testament Ethics*, edited by Friedrich W. Horn and Ruben Zimmermann, 1:97–116. WUNT I/238. Tübingen: Mohr Siebeck, 2009.

Robbins, Vernon. K. *Exploring the Texture of Texts: A Guide to Socio-Rhetorical Interpretation*. Valley Forge: Trinity Press International, 1996.

———. *The Tapestry of Early Christian Discourse: Rhetoric, Society and Ideology*. New York: Routledge, 1996.

Roberts, Alexander, and James Donaldson, eds. *The Ante-Nicene Fathers. Vol. 3*. Translated by Peter Holmes. Grand Rapids: Eerdmans, 1978.

Robinson, John. *The Body: A Study in Pauline Theology*. London: SCM, 1952.

Robinson, Laura. "Hidden Transcripts? The Supposedly Self-Censoring Paul and Rome as Surveillance State in Modern Pauline Scholarship." *NTS* 67 (2021) 55–72.

Robson, James E. *Word and Spirit in Ezekiel*. LHBOTS 447. London: T. & T. Clark, 2006.

Rodriguez, Rafael, and Matthew Thiessen, eds. *The So-Called Jew in Paul's Letter to the Romans*. Minneapolis: Fortress, 2016.

Rogers, Guy M. "The Mysteries of Artemis at Ephesos." In *100 Jahre Österreichische Forschungen in Ephesos. Akten des Symposions Wien 1995*, edited by Herwig Friesinger and Fritz Krinzinger, 241–50. Wien: Verlag der Österreichischen Akademie der Wissenschaften, 1999.

———. *The Mysteries of Artemis of Ephesos: Cult, Polis, and Change in the Graeco-Roman World*. Synkrisis: Comparative Approaches to Early Christianity in Greco-Roman Culture. New Haven, CT: Yale University Press, 2012.

———. *The Sacred Identity of Ephesos: Foundation Myths of a Roman City*. London: Routledge, 1991.

Rondeau, Marie-Josèphe. *Les commentaires patristiques du Psautier (IIIe–Ve siècles)*. Vol. 2. Exégèse prosopologique et théologie. Rome: Institutum Studiorum Orientalium, 1985.

Rosenberg, Gil. "Hypertextuality." In *Exploring Intertextuality: Diverse Strategies for New Testament Interpretations of Texts*, edited by B. J. Oropeza and Steve Moyise, 16–28. Eugene, OR: Cascade, 2016.

Rosner, Brian S. *Paul, Scripture and Ethics: A Study of 1 Corinthians 5–7*. Repr. Grand Rapids: Baker, 1999.

Rowe, C. Kavin "The Grammar of Life: The Areopagus Speech and Pagan Tradition." *NTS* 57 (2010) 31–50.

———. "Making Friends and Comparing Lives." In *The New Testament in Comparison: Validity, Method, and Purpose in Comparing Traditions*, edited by John M. G. Barclay and Benjamin G. White, 23–40. LNTS 600. London: T. & T. Clark, 2020.

———. *One True Life: The Stoics and Early Christians as Rival Traditions*. New Haven, CT: Yale University Press, 2016.

———. "A Response to Friend-Critics." In *The New Testament in Comparison: Validity, Method, and Purpose in Comparing Traditions*, edited by John M. G. Barclay and Benjamin G. White, 125–41. LNTS 600. London: T. & T. Clark, 2020.

Rowe, C. Kavin, and Elizabeth Agnew Cochran. "Letters, Notes, and Comments." *The Journal of Religious Ethics* 40 (2012) 705–29.

Runge, Steven E. "Joel 2.28–32a in Acts 2.17–21: The Discourse and Text-Critical Implications of Variation from the LXX." In *Early Christian Literature and Intertextuality*, edited by Craig A. Evans and H. Daniel Zacharias, 103–13. London: T. & T. Clark, 2009.

Rüpke, Jörg. *Religion of the Romans*. Cambridge: Polity, 2007.

Russell, Donald A., ed. and trans. *Quintilian: The Orator's Education*. 5 vols. LCL. Cambridge, MA: Harvard University Press, 2002.

Samely, Alexander. *The Interpretation of Speech in the Pentateuch Targums: A Study of Method and Presentation in Targumic Exegesis*. TSAJ 27. Tübingen: Mohr Siebeck, 1992.

———. *Rabbinic Interpretation of Scripture*. Oxford: Oxford University Press, 2002.

Sanders, E. P. *Paul and Palestinian Judaism: A Comparison of Patterns of Religion*. Philadelphia: Fortress, 1977.

Sandmel, Samuel. "Parallelomania." *JBL* 81 (1962) 1–13.

Sandnes, Karl Olav. *Paul—One of the Prophets? A Contribution to the Apostle's Self-Understanding*. WUNT II/43. Tubingen: Mohr Siebeck, 1991.

———. "Prophet-Like Apostle: A Note on the 'Radical New Perspective.'" *Bib* 96 (2015) 550–64.

Schafroth, Verena. "An Exegetical Exploration of 'Spirit' References in Ezekiel 36 and 37." *Journal of the European Theological Association* 29 (2009) 61–77.

Schenkl, Heinrich, ed. *Epicteti Dissertationes ab Arriano digestae*. Leipzig: Teubner, 1916.

Schnabel, Eckhard J. *Der Brief des Paulus an die Römer: Kapitel 6–16*. Historisch Theologische Auslegung. Witten: Brockhaus / Giessen: Brunnen, 2016.

Schnackenburg, Rudolf. *The Johannine Epistles. Introduction and Commentary*. New York: Crossroad, 1992.

Schnelle, Udo, et al., eds. *Neuer Wettstein: Texte zum Neuen Testament aus Griechentum und Hellenismus*. Vols. 1–3. Göttingen: De Gruyter, 1996–2012.

Schrage, Wolfgang. *Der erste Brief an die Korinther I–III*. EKK 7. Düsseldorf: Neukirchen-Vluyn, 1991–2001.

Schreiner, Patrick. "Peter, the Rock: Matthew 16 in Light of Daniel 2." *CTR* 13 (2016) 99–117.

Schrenk, Gottlob. "γράφω, γραφή, κτλ." In *TWNT* 1, edited by Gerhard Kittel, 742–73. Stuttgart: Kohlhammer, 1933.

Schutz, Charles E. "Cryptic Humor: The Subversive Message of Political Jokes." *Humor* 8 (1995) 51–64.

Schweitzer, Albert. *The Mysticism of Paul the Apostle*. London: Black, 1931.

Schweizer, Eduard. *Das Evangelium nach Matthaus*. NTD 2. 3rd ed. Gottingen: Vandenhoeck & Tuprecht, 1981.

Scott, Ian W. *Implicit Epistemology in the Letters of Paul: Story, Experience, and the Spirit*. WUNT II/205. Tübingen: Mohr Siebeck, 2006.

Scott, James C. *Domination and the Art of Resistance: Hidden Transcripts*. New Haven, CT: Yale University Press, 1990.

Seddon, Keith. *Epictetus' Handbook and the Tablet of Cebes: Guides to Stoic Living*. London: Routledge, 2005.

Seim, Turid Karlsen. *The Double Message: Patterns of Gender in Luke and Acts*. Nashville: Abingdon, 1994.

———. "The Gospel of Luke." In *Searching the Scriptures*, edited by Elisabeth Schüssler Fiorenza, 2:728–62. New York: Crossroad, 1998.

———. "The Virgin Mother: Mary and Ascetic Discipleship in Luke." In *A Feminist Companion to Luke*, edited by Amy-Jill Levine, 89–105. Cleveland: T. & T. Clark, 2001.

Seitz, Oscar J. F. "Upon This Rock: A Critical Re-Examination of Matt 16:17–19" *JBL* 69 (1950) 329–40.

Sell, Nancy A. "The Magnificat as a Model for Ministry: Proclaiming Justice, Shifting Paradigms, Transforming Lives." *Liturgical Ministry* 10 (2001) 31–40.

Sevenster, J. N. *Paul and Seneca*. NovTSup 4. Leiden: Brill, 1961.

Shäfer, Peter. "Tempel und Schopfung: Zur Interpretation einiger Heiligtumstraditionen in der rabbischen Literature." In *Studien zur geschichte und Theologie des rabbinischen Judentums*, 122–33. AGJU 15. Leiden: Brill, 1978.

Shakhnovich, Marianna. "Theological Paradox in Epicurus." In *Epicurus: His Continuing Influence and Contemporary Relevance*, edited by Dane R. Gordon and David B. Suits, 157–66. Rochester: RIT Cary Graphic Arts, 2003.

Shaw, David A. "Converted Imaginations? The Reception of Richard Hays's Intertextual Method." *CurBR* 11 (2013) 234–45.

Shepherd, David. "When He Comes, Will He Build It? Temple, Messiah and Targum Jonathan." *AS* 12 (2014) 89–107.

Shum, Shiu-Lun. *Paul's Use of Isaiah in Romans: A Comparative Study of Paul's Letter to the Romans and the Sibylline and Qumran Sectarian Texts*. WUNT II/156. Tübingen: Mohr Siebeck, 2002.

Silva, Moisés, ed. *New International Dictionary of New Testament Theology and Exegesis*. 5 vols. Grand Rapids: Zondervan, 2014.

———. "Old Testament in Paul." In *Dictionary of Paul and His Letters*, edited by Gerald F. Hawthorne et al., 630–42. Downers Grove, IL: IVP, 1993.

Simons, Robert. "The Magnificat: Cento, Psalm or Imitatio?" *TynBul* 60 (2009) 25–46.

Simpson, Adelaide D. "Epicureans, Christians, Atheists in the Second Century." *TAPA* 72 (1941) 372–81.

Sloan, Robert B. *The Favorable Year of the Lord: A Study of Jubilary Theology in the Gospel of Luke*. Austin: Schola, 1977.

Slusser, Michael. "The Exegetical Roots of Trinitarian Theology." *TS* 49 (1988) 461–76.

Smillie, Gene. "'The One Who Is Speaking' in Hebrews 12:25." *TynBul* 55 (2004) 275–94.

Smith, C. F., ed. and trans. *Thucydides: History of the Peloponnesian War*. Vol. 1 of 4. LCL. Rev. ed. Cambridge, MA: Harvard University Press, 1928.

Smith, Dennis E. *From Symposium to Eucharist: The Banquet in the Early Christian World*. Minneapolis: Fortress, 2003.

Smith, Jonathan Z. *Drudgery Divine: On the Comparison of Early Christianities and the Religions of Late Antiquity*. Chicago: University of Chicago Press, 1990.

Smith, Martin Ferguson, ed. and trans. *Diogenes of Oinoanda: The Epicurean Inscription*. La Scuola di Epicuro, Supplemento 1. Naples: Bibliopolis, 1993.

Smith, Martin Ferguson, and William H. D. Rouse, eds. and trans. *Lucretius: De rerum natura*. LCL. 2nd ed. Cambridge, MA: Harvard University Press, 1992.

Smith, Wesley D., ed. and trans. *Hippocrates: Pseudepigraphic Writings*. Studies in Ancient Medicine 2. Leiden: Brill, 1990.

Snodgrass, Klyne. "The Christological Stone Testimonia in the New Testament." PhD diss., University of St. Andrews, 1973.

Solin, Heikki. "Die herkulanensischen Wandinschriften. Ein soziologischer Versuch." *CErc* 3 (1973) 97–103.

Spencer, F. Scott. "The Ethiopian Eunuch and His Bible: A Social-Science Analysis." *BTB* 22 (1992) 155–65.

———. "Wise Up, Young Man: The Moral Vision of Saul and Other νεανίσκοι in Acts." In *Acts and Ethics*, edited by Thomas E. Phillips, 34–48. Sheffield: Sheffield Phoenix, 2005.

Spicq, Celsas. "La place ou le rôle des jeunes dans certaines communautés néotestamentaires." *RB* 76 (1969) 508–27.

Spinelli, Emidio, and Francesco Verde. "Theology." In *The Oxford Handbook of Epicurus and Epicureanism*, edited by Phillip Mitsis, 94–117. Oxford/New York: Oxford University Press, 2020.

Spivak, Gayatri Chakravorty. "Can the Subaltern Speak?" In *Marxism and the Interpretation of Culture*, edited by Cary Nelson and Lawrence Grossberg, 271–313. Urbana: University of Illinois Press, 1988.

———. "Gayatri Spivak on the Politics of the Subaltern: Interview with H. Winant." *Socialist Review* 20 (1990) 85–97.

Stafford, Emma. *Herakles*. Gods of the Ancient World. New York: Routledge, 2012.

Stamps, Dennis L. "The Use of the Old Testament in the New Testament as a Rhetorical Device: A Methodological Proposal." In *Hearing the Old Testament in the New Testament*, edited by Stanley E. Porter, 9–37. McMaster New Testament Studies. Grand Rapids: Eerdmans, 2006.

Stanley, Christopher D. *Arguing with Scripture: The Rhetoric of Quotations in the Letters of Paul*. London: T. & T. Clark, 2004.

———. *Paul and the Language of Scripture: Citation Technique in the Pauline Epistles and Contemporary Literature*. SNTSMS 74. Cambridge: Cambridge University Press, 1992.

———. "'Pearls before Swine': Did Paul's Audiences Understand His Biblical Quotations?" *NovT* 41 (1999) 124–44.

———. "Scripture in 1 Corinthians: Assessing the *Status Quaestionis*." In *Scripture, Texts, and Tracings in 1 Corinthians*, edited by Linda L. Belleville and B. J. Oropeza, 249–57. Lanham, MD: Lexington / Fortress Academic, 2019.

———. "What We Learned—And What We Didn't." In *Paul and Scripture: Extending the Conversation*, edited by Christopher D. Stanley, 321–30. ECL 9. Atlanta: SBL, 2012.

Stephens, William O. *Stoic Ethics: Epictetus and Happiness as Freedom*. London: Bloomsbury, 2007.

Stewart-Sykes, Alistair. *The Lamb's High Feast: Melito, Peri Pascha and the Quartodeciman Paschal Liturgy at Sardis*. Supplements to Vigiliae Christianae 42. Leiden: Brill, 1998.

Steyn, Gert J. *A Quest for the Assumed LXX Vorlage of the Explicit Quotations in Hebrews*. FRLANT 235. Göttingen: Vandenhoeck & Ruprecht, 2011.

Still, E. Coye. "Paul's Aims Regarding ΕΙΔΩΛΟΘΥΤΑ: A New Proposal for Interpreting 1 Corinthians 8:1–11:1." *NovT* 44, no. 4 (2002) 334–41.

Stockhausen, Carol K. *Moses' Veil and the Glory of the New Covenant: The Exegetical Substructure of II Cor. 3,1—4,6*. AnBib 116. Rome: Pontificio Istituto Biblico, 1989.

Stott, John R. W. *The Epistles of John*. TNTC. Grand Rapids: Eerdmans, 1964.

Strecker, Georg. *The Johannine Letters. A Commentary on 1, 2, and 3 John*. Hermeneia. Minneapolis: Fortress, 1996.

Summers, Kirk. "Lucretius and the Epicurean Tradition of Piety," *CP* 90, no. 1 (1995) 32–57.

Sutton, E. W., and Harris Rackham, eds. and trans. *Cicero: On the Orator*. LCL 3. Cambridge, MA: Harvard University Press, 1942.

Swetnam-Burland, Molly. "Encountering Ovid's Phaedra in House V.2.10–11, Pompeii." *American Journal of Archaeology* 119 (2015) 217–32.

Talbert, Charles H. *Reading Acts: A Literary and Theological Commentary on the Acts of the Apostles*. New York: Crossroad Publishing, 1997.

———. *Reading Luke: A Literary and Theological Commentary on the Third Gospel*. Macon: Smyth and Helwys, 2002.

———. "Shifting Sands: The Recent Study of the Gospel of Luke." *Int* 30 (1976) 381–95.

Tannehill, Robert C. *The Narrative Unity of Luke-Acts: A Literary Interpretation*. 2 vols. Philadelphia: Fortress, 1986–90.

Tatum, W. Barnes. "Epoch of Israel: Luke 1–2 and the Theological Plan of Luke-Acts." *NTS* 13 (1967) 184–95.

Thackery, Henry St. John, et al., eds. and trans. *Josephus*. 9 vols. LCL. Cambridge, MA: Harvard University Press / London: William Heinemann, 1926–1965.

Thatcher, Tom. "Cain and Abel in Early Christian Memory: A Case Study in 'The Use of the Old Testament in the New.'" *CBQ* 72 (2010) 732–51.

Theobald, Michael. *Die überströmende Gnade: Studien zu einem paulinischen Motivfeld*. Forschung zur Bibel 22. Würzburg: Echter, 1982.

Thielman, Frank. *Romans*. BECNT. Grand Rapids: Baker Academic, 2018.
Thiessen, Matthew. *Jesus and the Forces of Death: The Gospels' Portrayal of Ritual Impurity within First-Century Judaism*. Grand Rapids: Baker Academic, 2020.
Thiselton, Anthony C. *The First Epistle to the Corinthians: A Commentary on the Greek Text*. NIGTC. Grand Rapids: Eerdmans, 2000.
Thom, Johan C. "The Mind Is Its Own Place: Defining the *Topos*." In *Early Christianity and Classical Culture: Comparative Studies in Honor of Abraham J. Malherbe*, edited by John T. Fitzgerald et al., 555–73. NovTSup 110. Leiden: Brill, 2003.
———. "Popular Philosophy in the Hellenistic-Roman World." *Early Christianity* 3 (2012) 279–95.
Thomas, Kenneth J. "The Old Testament Citations in Hebrews." *NTS* 11 (1964–1965) 303–25.
Thompson, Michael. *Clothed with Christ: The Example and Teachings of Jesus in Romans 12.1—15.13*. JSNTSup 59. Sheffield: JSOT, 1991.
Thorsteinsson, Runar. "Paul and Roman Stoicism: Romans 12 and Contemporary Stoic Ethics." *JSNT* 29 (2006) 139–61.
Thraede, Klaus. *Grundzüge griechisch-römischer Brieftopik*. Zetemata 48. München: Beck, 1970.
Thrall, Margaret E. *A Critical and Exegetical Commentary on the Second Epistle to the Corinthians: Introduction and Commentary on II Corinthians I–VII*. Vol. 1 of 2. Edinburgh: T. & T. Clark, 1994.
Thür, Hilke. "The Processional Way in Ephesos as a Place of Cult and Burial." In *Ephesos: Metropolis of Asia. An Interdisciplinary Approach to its Archaeology, Religion, and Culture*, edited by Helmut Koester, 157–99. Valley Forge: Trinity Press International, 1995.
Thurston, Bonnie Bowman. "Who Was Anna? Luke 2:36–38." *PRSt* 28 (2001) 47–55.
Tillich, Paul. *The Courage to Be*. New Haven, CT: Yale University Press, 1952.
Tite, Philip L. "Roman Diet and Meat Consumption: Reassessing Elite Access to Meat in 1 Corinthians 8 and 10." *JSNT* 42, no. 2 (2019) 185–222.
Tomlin, Graham. "Christians and Epicureans in 1 Corinthians." *JSNT* 68 (1997) 51–72.
Tomson, Peter. *Paul and the Jewish Law*. Minneapolis: Fortress, 1990.
Tooman, William A. *Gog of Magog: Re-Use of Scripture and Compositional Technique in Ezekiel 38–39*. FAT II/52. Tübingen: Mohr Siebeck, 2011.
Toussaint, Stanley D. *Behold the King: A Study of Matthew*. Grand Rapids: Kregel, 1980.
Trebilco, Paul R. "The Acts of John and Christian Communities in Ephesus in the Mid-Second Century CE." In *Authority and Identity in Emerging Christianities in Asia Minor and Greece*, edited by Cilliers Breytenbach and Julien M. Ogereau, 33–61. Ancient Judaism and Early Christianity 103. Leiden: Brill, 2018.
———. *The Early Christians in Ephesus from Paul to Ignatius*. WUNT 166. Tübingen: Mohr Siebeck, 2004.
———. "'From the Beginning' in the Ancient City of Ephesus and in the Letters of John." In *Internationalising Higher Education from South Africa to England via New Zealand: Essays in Honour of Professor Gerald Pillay*, edited by Hoffie (J. W.) Hofmeyr and John Stenhouse, 59–82. Highveld Park: Mediakor, 2018.
———. *Self-Designations and Group Identity in the New Testament*. Cambridge: Cambridge University Press, 2012.
Trinacty, Christopher. *Senecan Tragedy and the Reception of Augustan Poetry*. Oxford: Oxford University Press, 2014.

Tsumura, David Toshio. *The First Book of Samuel*. NICOT. Grand Rapids: Eerdmans, 2007.
Tuck, Steven L. *A History of Roman Art*. Hoboken: Wiley Blackwell, 2015.
———. *Pompeii: Daily Life in an Ancient Roman City*. The Great Courses. 24 Lectures. Chantilly: The Teaching Company, 2010.
Turner, David L. *Matthew*. BECNT. Grand Rapids: Baker Academic, 2008.
———. "*Primus inter pares*? Peter in the Gospel of Matthew." In *New Testament Essays in Honor of Homer A. Kent Jr.*, edited by G. T. Meadors, 179–201. Winona Lake, IN: BMH, 1991.
Tyson, Joseph B. *Luke, Judaism, and the Scholars: Critical Approaches to Luke-Acts*. Columbia: University of South Carolina Press, 1999.
Usener, Hermann, ed. *Epicurea*. Leipzig: Teubner, 1887.
Vaage, Leif E. "The Translation of 1 Cor 7:14c and the Labile Social Body of the Pauline Church." *RB* 116 (2009) 557–71.
van Maaren, John. "Does Mark's Jesus Abrogate Torah? Jesus' Purity Logion and Its Illustration in Mark 7:15–23." *Journal of the Jesus Movement in Its Jewish Setting* 4 (2017) 21–41.
Vansina, Jan. *Oral Tradition as History*. Madison: University of Wisconsin Press, 1985.
Varela, Alfredo Tepox. "Luke 2.36–37: Is Anna's Age Really the Focus?" *BT* 27 (1976) 446.
Vegge, Tor. "Sacred Scripture in the Letters of Paul." In *Paulusperspektiven: Dieter Sänger zum 65. Geburtstag*, edited by Matthias R. Hoffmann et al., 1–32. BThSt 145. Neukirchen-Vluyn: Neukirchener, 2014.
Veyne, Paul. "Inviter les dieux, sacrificer, banqueter. Quelques nuances de la religiosité gréco-romaine." *Annales: Histoire, Sciences Sociales* 55, no. 1 (2000) 3–42.
Viviano, Benedict T. "The Gospel according to Matthew." In *The New Jerome Biblical Commentary*, edited by Raymond Brown et al., 630–74. Englewood Cliffs, NJ: Prentice Hall, 1990.
Vogt, Katja Maria. "Sons of the Earth: Are the Stoics Metaphysical Brutes?" *Phronesis* 54 (2009) 136–54.
von Campenhausen, Hans. *Ecclesiastical Authority and Spiritual Power in the Church of the First Three Centuries*. Translated by J. A. Baker. Peabody, MA: Hendrickson, 1997.
von Harnack, Adolf. "Der Spruch über Petrus als den Felsen der Kirche." In *Sitzungsberichte der Königlich Preussischen Akademie der Wissenschaften zu Berlin*, 637–54. Berlin: Jahrgang, 1918.
Waaler, Erik. *The Shema and the First Commandment in First Corinthians: An Intertextual Approach to Paul's Re-reading of Deuteronomy*. WUNT II/253. Tübingen: Mohr Siebeck, 2008.
Wagner, J. Ross. "Epilogue." In *Paulinische Schriftrezeption: Grundlagen—Ausprägungen—Wirkungen—Wertungen*, edited by Florian Wilk and Markus Öhler, 297–305. FRLANT 268. Göttingen: Vandenhoeck & Ruprecht, 2017.
———. *Heralds of the Good News: Isaiah and Paul in Concert in the Letter to the Romans*. Leiden: Brill, 2003.
———. "Paul and Scripture." In *The Blackwell Companion to Paul*, edited by Stephen Westerholm, 154–71. Repr. Oxford: Wiley-Blackwell, 2014.
Walker, Alexander, trans. *Protoevangelium of James*. Vol. 8 of the *Ante-Nicene Fathers*, edited by Alexander Roberts et al., 361–67. Rev. ed. by Kevin Knight. Buffalo:

Christian Literature Publishing, 1886. http://www.newadvent.org/fathers/0847.htm.
Waltke, Bruce K. "Cain and His Offering." *WTJ* 48 (1986) 363–72.
Walvoord, John F., and Charles H. Dyer. *Matthew*. Chicago: Moody, 2013.
Wankel, Hermann, et al., eds. *Die Inschriften von Ephesos*. 8 vols. in 11. Inschriften grieschischer Städte aus Kleinasien 11–17. Bonn: Habelt, 1979–84.
Watson, Duane F. "1 Corinthians 10:23—11:1 in the Light of Greco-Roman Rhetoric: The Role of Rhetorical Questions." *JBL* 108 (1989) 301–18.
Watson, Edward W., and Martin M. Culy. *Quoting Corinthians: Identifying Slogans and Quotations in 1 Corinthians*. Eugene, OR: Pickwick, 2018.
Watson, Francis. "Paul the Reader: An Authorial Apologia." *JSNT* 28 (2006) 363–73.
———. *Paul and the Hermeneutics of Faith*. London: T. & T. Clark, 2004.
Watson, Walter. *The Lost Second Book of Aristotle Poetics*. Chicago: University of Chicago Press, 2012.
Watts, Rikk E. "Exodus Imagery." In *Dictionary of the Old Testament Prophets*, edited by M. J. Boda & J. G. McConville, 205–14. Downers Grove, IL: IVP, 2012.
———. "How Do You Read? God's Faithful Character as the Primary Lens for the NT Use of the OT." In *From Creation to New Creation—Biblical Theology and Exegesis: Essays in Honor of Greg Beale*, edited by Daniel M. Gurtner and Benjamin L. Gladd, 199–220. Peabody, MA: Hendrickson, 2013.
———. "Rethinking Context in the Relationship of Israel's Scriptures to the NT: Character, Agency, and the Possibility of Genuine Change." In *Methodology in the Use of the Old Testament in the New*, edited by David Allen and Steve Smith, 158–77. LNTS 579. London: T. & T. Clark, 2019.
Weissenrieder, Annette. "Der Blick in den Spiegel: II Kor 3,18 vor dem Hintergrund Antiker Spiegeltheorien und ikonographischer Abbildungen." In *Picturing the New Testament: Studies in Ancient Visual Images*, edited by Annette Weissenrieder et al., 312–43. WUNT II/193. Tübingen: Mohr Siebeck, 2005.
Wendt, H. H. "Der 'Anfang' am Beginne des I Johannesbriefes." *ZNW* 21 (1922) 38–42.
Wenkel, David. *Joy in Luke-Acts: The Intersection of Rhetoric, Narrative, and Emotion*. Paternoster Biblical Monographs. Carlisle: Paternoster, 2015.
Westphal, Merold. *Overcoming Onto-theology: Toward a Postmodern Christian Faith*. New York: Fordham University Press, 2001.
White, Joel R. *Die Erstlingsgabe im Neuen Testament*. TANZ 45. Tübingen: Francke, 2007.
———. "Identifying Intertextual Exegesis in Paul: Methodological Considerations and a Test Case (1 Corinthians 6:5)." In *The Crucified Apostle: Essays on Peter and Paul*, edited by Todd A. Wilson and Paul R. House, 167–88. WUNT II/450. Tübingen: Mohr Siebeck, 2017.
———. "N. T. Wright's Narrative Approach." In *God and the Faithfulness of Paul: A Critical Examination of the Pauline Theology of N.T. Wright*, edited by Christoph Heilig et al., 181–204. WUNT II/413. Tübingen: Mohr Siebeck, 2016.
White, L. Michael, and John T. Fitzgerald. "*Quod est comparandum*: The Problem of Parallels." In *Early Christianity and Classical Culture: Comparative Studies in Honor of Abraham J. Malherbe*, edited by John T. Fitzgerald et al., 13–39. NovTSup 110. Leiden: Brill, 2003.
Whitlark, Jason A. *Resisting Empire: Rethinking the Purpose of the Letter to "the Hebrews."* LNTS 484. London: T. & T. Clark, 2014.

Wilcox, Max. "Peter and the Rock: A Fresh Look at Matthew XVI.17–19." *NTS* 22 (1975) 73–88.
Wilder, Terry L., ed. *Perspectives on Our Struggle with Sin: 3 Views of Romans 7.* Nashville: B&H Academic, 2011.
Wilk, Florian. "Durch Schriftkenntnis Zur Vollkommenheit: Zur Funktion des vielgestaltigen Schriftgebrauchs in 1Kor 2,6–16 und 14,20–25." *ZNW* 110 (2019) 21–41.
———, ed. *Paul and Moses: The Exodus and Sinai Traditions in the Letters of Paul.* Studies in Education and Religion in Ancient and Pre-Modern History in the Mediterranean and Its Environs 11. Tübingen: Mohr Siebeck, 2021.
———. "Schriftauslegung als Bildungsvorgang im ersten Korintherbrief des Paulus— untersucht ausgehend von 1Kor 4,6." In *Scriptural Interpretation at the Interface between Education and Religion: In Memory of Hans Conzelmann*, edited by Florian Wilk, 88–111. TBN 22. Leiden: Brill, 2018.
———. "Zur Funktion von 2Kor 3,4–18 in seinem literarischen Zusammenhang." In *Paul and Moses: The Exodus and Sinai Traditions in the Letters of Paul*, edited by Florian Wilk, 139–154. SERAPHIM 11. Tübingen: Mohr Siebeck, 2020.
Wilk, Florian, and Markus Öhler, eds. *Paulinische Schriftrezeption: Grundlagen— Ausprägungen—Wirkungen—Wertungen.* FRLANT 268. Göttingen: Vandenhoeck & Ruprecht, 2017.
Williams, Demetrius K. "The Acts of the Apostles." In *True to Our Native Land: An African American New Testament Commentary*, edited by Brian K. Blount et al., 213–48. Minneapolis: Fortress, 2007.
———. "'Upon All Flesh': Acts 2, African Americans, and Intersectional Realities." In *They Were All Together in One Place? Toward Minority Biblical Criticism*, edited by Randall C. Bailey et al., 289–310. Atlanta: SBL, 2009.
Williams, H. H. Drake. "From the Perspective of the Writer or the Perspective of the Reader: Coming to Grips with a Starting Point for Analyzing the Use of Scripture in 1 Corinthians." In *Paul and Scripture*, edited by Stanley E. Porter and Christopher D. Land, 153–72. Leiden: Brill, 2019.
Willis, Wendell Lee. *Idol Meat in Corinth: The Pauline Argument in 1 Corinthians 8 and 10.* SBLDS 68. Chico: Scholars, 1985.
Wilson, Brittany E. *Unmanly Men: Refigurations of Masculinity in Luke-Acts.* Oxford: Oxford University Press, 2015.
Wilson, John Francis. *Caesarea Philippi: Banias, the Lost City of Pan.* London: I. B. Taurus, 2004.
Wilson, S. G. "Lukan Eschatology." *NTS* 16 (1970) 330–47.
Winn, Adam. "Striking Back at the Empire: Empire Theory and Response to Empire in the New Testament." In *An Introduction to Empire in the New Testament*, edited by Adam Winn, 1–14. RBS 84. Atlanta: SBL, 2016.
———, ed. *An Introduction to Empire in the New Testament.* RBS 84. Atlanta: SBL, 2016.
Wise, Michael O., et al., eds. and trans. *The Dead Sea Scrolls: A New Translation.* New York: HarperOne, 2005.
Wishart, Ryder A. "An Emerging Account of Biblical Law: Common-Law Tradition in the Old and New Testaments." *McMaster Journal of Theology and Ministry* 18 (2017) 160–92.

Witherington, Ben, III. *Jesus, Paul and the End of the World: A Comparative Study in New Testament Eschatology*. Downers Grove, IL: IVP, 1999.
———. *Matthew*. Macon: Smyth & Helwys, 2006.
———. "Not So Idle Thoughts about *Eidolothuton*." *TynBul* 42, no. 2 (1993) 237–54.
———. *Paul's Narrative Thought World: The Tapestry of Tragedy and Triumph*. Louisville: Westminster John Knox; 1994.
———. *What Have They Done with Jesus? Beyond Strange Theories and Bad History—Why We Can Trust the Bible*. New York: Harper Collins, 2006.
Wolter, Michael. *Luke 1—9:50*. Vol. 1 of *The Gospel according to Luke*. Translated by Wayne Coppins and Christoph Heilig. Baylor-Mohr Siebeck Studies in Early Christianity. Waco, TX: Baylor University Press, 2016.
Wright, N. T. "Jerusalem in the New Testament." In *Jerusalem, Past and Present in the Purposes of God*, edited by Peter W. L. Walker, 53–77. Grand Rapids: Baker, 1994.
———. *Jesus and the Victory of God*. London: SPCK, 1996.
———. "New Exodus, New Inheritance: The Narrative Structure of Romans 3–8." In *Romans and the People of God: Essays in Honor of Gordon D. Fee on the Occasion of His 65th Birthday*, edited by Sven Soderlund and N. T. Wright, 26–35. Grand Rapids: Eerdmans, 1999.
———. *The New Testament and the People of God*. Minneapolis: Fortress, 1992.
———. *Paul and the Faithfulness of God*. Minneapolis: Fortress, 2013.
Wurster, Sonya. "Changing Perceptions: Philodemus and Epicurean Philosophy." *Iris: Journal of the Classical Association of Victoria* 29 (2015) 13–28.
Wynne, J. P. F. *Cicero on the Philosophy of Religion*. Cambridge/New York: Cambridge University Press, 2019.
Xue, Xiaxia E. "An Intertextual Discourse Analysis of Romans 9:30—10:13." In *Modeling Biblical Language*, edited by Stanley E. Porter et al., 277–308. Linguistic Biblical Studies 13. Leiden: Brill, 2016.
Yarbrough, O. Larry. "Parents and Children in the Letters of Paul." In *The Social World of the First Christians: Essays in Honor of Wayne A. Meeks*, edited by L. Michael White and O. Larry Yarbrough, 126–41. Minneapolis: Fortress, 1995.
Yarbrough, Robert W. *1–3 John*. BECNT. Grand Rapids: Baker Academic, 2008.
York, John. *The Last Shall Be First: The Rhetoric of Reversal in Luke*. LNTS 29. London: Bloomsbury Academic, 2015.
Young, Kay, and Jeffrey L. Saver. "The Neurology of Narrative." *SubStance* 30 (2001) 72–84.
Zadorojnyi, Alexei V. "Transcripts of Dissent? Political Graffiti and Elite Ideology under the Principate." In *Ancient Graffiti in Contexts*, edited by Jennifer Baird and Claire Taylor, 110–32. New York: Routledge, 2010.
Zakai, Avihu, and David Weinstein. "Erich Auerbach and His 'Figura': An Apology for the Old Testament in an Age of Aryan Philology." *Religions* 3 (2012) 320–38.
Zangemeister, Carolus, et al., eds. *Corpus Inscriptionum Latinarum*. Vol. 4 and Supplements 1–2. Berlin: George Reimer, 1871–1909.
Zanker, Paul. *Pompeii: Public and Private Life*. Cambridge, MA: Harvard University Press, 1998.
Zeller, Dieter. *Der erste Brief an die Korinther*. KEK 5. Göttingen: Vandenhoeck & Ruprecht, 2010.

Index of Subjects

Abel, 13, 246–54, 256–65, 270
Aeneas/*Aeneid*, 31–35, 38, 232n21
allegory/allegorical, 189–90,
    190n19, 195
allusion, xvi, 8–9, 11, 13, 17–25,
    27–28, 34, 41n35, 44–46,
    50–51, 53–58, 61, 69–74, 78,
    80–81, 83–84, 88–91, 92n5,
    95, 98, 101, 132n3, 163–64,
    196, 198, 203, 211n5,
    242n50, 246, 247n4, 266,
    279; *see* also Echo
analogy, 14, 20, 31, 100n47, 140–41,
    159, 178, 183, 229, 241
angel, 70, 95, 101, 103, 218, 260
apocalyptic, 72, 125, 243
argumentation, *see* Rhetoric
Artemis, 15–16, 267–68, 273–84,
    286–88
audience competency, 9, 22, 25,
    44–47, 50, 54–55, 57–58
—competent audience, 9, 25,
    50–53, 55–56
—informed audience, 9, 25,
    50–53, 55–57
—minimal audience, 9, 25,
    44–45, 50–58

body / σῶμα, 12–13, 63, 65, 69,
    110, 135n14, 139, 140n39,
    167–85

Cain 13, 246–54, 256–65, 270
chiasm, 104n68, 111n1, 118

Christology / Christological, 15, 57,
    66, 80, 84, 164n66, 187–88,
    212
citation, *see* quotation
common ethical usage, 5, 7, 184–85
competitive appropriation, 5–6,
    15–16, 185n66
composite texts, 9, 70–72, 74
concession, 5, 16, 163, 185n66
conversion, 55, 133, 140

doctrinal reformulation, 5, 8–12, 16,
    153, 156, 162, 166

echo, xvi, 8–9, 13, 15, 17–18, 20–21,
    23–25, 27, 43–44, 52, 56,
    71–72, 78, 80, 88n36, 97–98,
    112, 114, 126n26, 127,
    163n62, 201, 226, 231, 237,
    242n50, 246–47, 252, 266–
    67, 273; *see* also allusion,
    metalepsis
eclecticism, 5, 16, 168, 185n66, 194
Elizabeth, 11, 93–99, 100n42,
    105–7, 120
empire / imperial, xvi, 4, 6–7, 13, 31,
    33n14, 34n16, 38n27, 40n30,
    41, 225, 233n26, 242–43,
    274, 275n30, 277–78, 283
encomium, 37, 229, 231, 244n58
encyclopedia (of knowledge), 5, 7–8,
    12–13, 22, 57, 185, 288
endogamy, 12, 131, 143, 145–47
Ephesus / Ephesian, xvi, 15, 133,
    145n60, 267–68, 272–87

INDEX OF SUBJECTS

Epicurus / Epicurean(ism), 6n6, 10, 12, 35–38, 148–62, 165–66, 169n12
Esau, 14, 204, 225, 227, 229, 238–43
eschatology, 55, 65, 78, 82, 88n39, 89, 94n13, 103–4, 187, 203
ethics / ethical, 5, 7, 12, 15–16, 73, 152–53, 162n58, 164, 167–68, 170, 172, 174–85, 225, 235, 287

figurative / figural language, 11, 80, 83, 188, 189n13, 190–91, 240, 242, 252, 266

genre, 9, 14, 16, 254–55, 255n45
Gezerah shawa, 9, 68
graffiti, 8, 13, 25n27, 29–42, 32n11, 32n13, 33n14, 34n16, 35n21, 39n28, 40n30

Halakha, 135–36
Hannah, 11, 109–12, 111n1, 114–17, 123–27
heteroglossia, 253, 255
holiness, *see* sanctified
Holy Spirit, 66, 103, 105–107, 139, 139n35, 140n39, 212n8, 218n30, 219, 258
household(s), 12, 40n30, 102n51, 133, 140, 143–47, 144n54, 145n60, 197n39, 243n51
humor, 13–14, 34–35, 35n20, 226–45, 228n10, 232n25, 233n26, 238n41, 243n51, 244n58
hypertextuality, 35, 39

idol food, 10, 147, 153, 159–61, 159n44, 162n58, 163–65
illiteracy, *see* literacy
imitatio / imitation, 7, 153, 231
infancy narrative, 11, 92–96, 98–101, 99n39, 103, 106–8, 106n80
inspiration, 70, 200, 270
interaction types, xvi, 4n5, 5–9, 13–16, 73, 150, 156n31

intertextuality, xv, xvii, 8–10, 13, 16, 17–18, 17n1, 28, 30, 34–35, 38–39, 41n35, 43, 45–46, 50, 57–58, 59, 92n5, 93, 103n61, 127, 225, 244, 253–54, 266; *see also* Allusion, Echo, Quotation
intertexture, 111n1, 225
irenic appropriation, 5, 14, 16, 185n66
irony, 36n24, 196

law, *see* Torah
literacy, 8, 13n18, 25n27, 31n9, 34n16
—illiteracy, 25
Logos, 20, 210, 220, 284

Mary's song / *Magnificat*, 11, 104n68, 109–10, 116–18, 117n10, 121, 123, 125–27, 126n26
metalepsis, 8, 13, 32, 127, 242n50
metaphor, 5, 12, 39, 47, 53–54, 84, 90n40, 122, 168n7, 169–70, 183, 185
midrash, 82
multi-layered reading, 51, 57–58

new covenant, 9, 48–49, 53–55, 62, 218, 243, 248
new creation, 52n32, 181–82

parallelomania, 44n8, 169–70, 256
paronomasia, 63
pathos, 20, 40n31, 230
personification, *see* speech-in-character, προσωποποιΐα
philosophy / *philosophia*, 175, 186, 193–97
Plato(nism), 193–94, 196, 228, 234, 191
pluriformity (textual), 9, 60–61, 64
Pompeii, 8, 29–35, 31n10, 32n11, 32n13, 37–38, 38n27, 39, 41–42, 232
prayer, 72, 144, 151, 154, 158, 182, 220

prefiguration, 190; *see* also foreshadow, typology
pretext, 21, 21n13, 23–24, 281
Progymnasmata, 212
prophecy, 20, 105, 126, 181, 191, 212, 254
prosopological, *see* speech-in-character / προσωποποιΐα

quotation, 5, 8–9, 13, 15, 18–20, 18n3, 20n10, 21n13, 25, 27, 30, 44, 50, 60–65, 69, 71, 73, 92, 101, 105, 153n15, 209, 218–20, 223–24, 242n50, 246, 247n7, 266

reader competency, *see* audience competency
refutation, 5–6, 14, 16, 185, 288
Religionsgeschichtliche Schule, 3, 16, 168–69
resurrection, 181, 196, 223n42, 284, 288
rhetoric / rhetorician, 14–15, 20, 37, 63, 181, 213, 225–29
ridiculus, 225, 227–29, 233–34, 244
rock, 11, 79, 83–89, 84n21, 87n33, 88n36, 88n37

sacrifices, 65, 144, 146, 149, 155, 157–58, 160, 237, 263, 275–76
sanctified / sanctification (holiness), 121, 123, 132n3, 133–34, 135n14, 136, 139–42, 139n35, 141n44, 138
salvation, 55, 92–94, 103, 107, 132, 135, 141–42, 146, 242
Satan, devil, 243, 260, 269–70
Second Temple Judaism, 4, 10, 13, 60, 247–48, 247n7, 254, 256, 257n55, 264
social justice, 109–10, 112, 115, 117, 121–27
Socrates / Socratic, 12, 144, 230, 234
speech-in-character / προσωποποιΐα, 15, 22, 214, 214n18
Stoicism, 161, 167–69, 168n7, 172–73
stone, *see* rock

taxonomy
—of interactions, xv–xvi, 5, 7–8, 16
—of readers, 9, 50
temple imagery, 78, 78n1, 80n7, 81, 84, 88n36, 89
topos / topoi, 12–13, 52n29, 54, 54n40, 229, 233
Torah (law), 6, 48, 65, 69–70, 82, 98n32, 141, 190, 192, 197n39, 203, 205, 265
typology, 184, 256n51

woman / women, 33n14, 109, 125, 135, 136n22, 140n39, 144–45, 145n58, 234, 240, 278
worldview, 38, 168–70, 284

Index of Modern Authors

Aasgaard, Reidar, 132
Abasciano, Brian J., 25, 28
Abogunrin, Samuel O., 126
Adams, Sean A., 71
Adewuya, J. Ayodeji, 132
Ådna, Jostein, 81
Aernie, Jeffrey W., 51, 52n30, 201
Albl, Martin C., 68
Alexander, Loveday, 6
Alexandre, Manuel, Jr., 226
Algra, Keimpe, 173n29
Allen, Amy Lindeman, 91, 99–100, 102n52
Allen, David M., 40, 218n30, 247
Allen, Graham, 18n3
Allison, Dale C., 24, 78, 80, 162
Allison, Justin Reid, 162
Andresen, Carl, 210n3, 216
Annas, Julia, 175
Arena, Valentina, 231
Arrighetti, Graziano, 158, 160
Asmis, Elizabeth, 157
Attardo, Salvatore, 233
Attridge, Harold W., 60, 225
Auerbach, Erich, 189n13, 190–91, 190n19
Autero, Esa, 91
Avrahami, Yael, 197
Back, Frances, 50
Bacon, Benjamin W., 220
Bailey, D. R. Shackleton, 40
Bailey, K. E., 117
Baird, William, 3
Baltzly, Dirk, 172
Bammer, Anton, 268

Barber, Michael P., 78
Barclay, John M. G., 4, 6, 91, 162, 186, 192, 197
Barker, Margaret, 126
Barr, David R., 7
Barrett, C. K., 162, 166, 178
Barth, Markus, 67
Bateman, Herbert W., 61
Bates, Matthew W., 66, 189, 189n10, 210, 216–17, 216n26
Bauckham, Richard J., 20n9
Beale, Gregory K., 19, 22–23, 78
Beard, Mary, 228, 230, 232, 232n19, 244, 244n57
Beasley-Murray, George, 132n3, 141
Beaumont, Daniel, 200
Becker, Eve-Marie, 54
Becker, Matthias, 49
Bednarz, Terri, 226
Beetham, Christopher A., 24n24
Belleville, Linda L., 45–46, 56
Bennema, Cornelius, 73
Ben-Porat, Ziva, 23
Berry, Paul, 168
Best, Ernest, 132, 178
Betsworth, Sharon, 91, 99–100
Bieringer, Reimund, 100
Billings, Bradly S., 91, 100
Block, Daniel I., 54n37
Blomberg, Craig L., 85, 85n25
Blumhofer, C. M., 102–103, 105
Bock, Darrell L., 120n14, 126
Boda, Mark J., 81
Bovon, François, 119
Boyarin, Daniel, 68

INDEX OF MODERN AUTHORS 329

Brawley, Robert, 126
Briones, David E., 168n8
Brookins, Timothy A., 159, 161, 168n7
Brown, Jeannine, 8, 32
Brown, Raymond E., 93n10, 94, 97–99, 101, 104n63, 105n74, 106, 202, 269n7, 270, 286
Bruce, F. F., 220
Brueggemann, Walter, 115, 125
Bruno, Christopher R., 126
Bunge, Marcia J., 91
Bussie, Jacqueline A., 226n6, 232
Butler, H. E., 35
Butterworth, Alex, 36n24
Byron, John, 247, 256–57, 256n52, 259–60, 261
Cadbury, Henry J., 59
Cagusi, P., 28
Cahill, Michael, 85n25
Caird, George B., 59, 209
Callahan, Allen Dwight, 7
Calvin, John, 86, 167
Campbell, Douglas C., 187
Campbell, R. Alastair, 101
Caragounis, Chrys C., 86–87
Carey, Greg, 7
Carroll, John T., 100–102, 101n51, 104, 119
Carter, Jonathan A., 199
Carter, Warren, 7, 279, 285
Cary, Earnest, 231
Chatman, Seymour, 225
Chen, Diane G., 95, 97, 101, 106
Chester, Andrew J., 81
Cheung, Alex T., 162–63
Ciampa, Roy E., 138
Clarke, John R., 232
Clay, Diskin, 149
Clooney, Francis X., 170
Cochran, Elizabeth Agnew, 167, 173
Cockerill, Gareth L., 60
Cokayne, Karen, 96n21
Collingwood, R. G., 198n49, 200–202
Collins, Raymond F., 131n1, 132, 141n44, 142–43
Colson, Francis H., 270

Compton, Jared, 222
Conzelmann, Hans, 93–94, 94n13, 104n63, 138, 269–70, 272
Cooley, Alison, 29, 34
Cooley, M. G. L., 29, 34
Cooper, John M., 172, 176
Cover, Michael, 45–46, 56
Cowan, William Tynes, 245
Coxhead, Steven R., 53
Craddock, Fred B., 98n34
Craig, Christopher, 236
Cranfield, C. E. B., 6
Crites, Stephen, 199
Culpepper, R. Allan, 101, 106
Culy, Martin M., 159
Dahl, Nils A., 98
D'Angelo, Mary R., 73
Danker, Frederick W., 52n31
Das, A. Andrew, 44
Davies, J. P., 181
Davies, W. D., 78, 80
de la Potterie, Ignace, 269
de Jonge, Henk J., 91
De Long, Kindalee Pfremmer, 98, 103, 120
Delling, Gerhard, 132, 272
Derret, J. D. M., 80n7
deSilva, David A., 163, 195
DiMattei, Steven, 90
Dobbin, Robert F., 169
Docherty, Susan E., 60n4, 61, 65, 67–68, 70–71, 73
Dodson, Joseph R., 168
Doohan, Leonard, 104
Dorandi, Tiziano, 156
Downs, David J., 140, 210
Duff, Paul B., 45, 47, 49
Duhem, Pierre, 189
Dunn, James D. G., 67, 134, 141, 141n42
Dupont, Jacques, 100
Dyer, Bryan R., 214
Dyer, Charles H., 86, 88
Eastman, Susan, 169, 181
Edenburg, Cynthia, 23
Edwards, Jonathan, 167
Ehorn, Seth M., 71
Eisenbaum, Pamela M., 73

Eliav, Yaron A., 79
Ellingworth, Paul, 72, 220
Elliot, John H., 101
Elliott, J. K., 95, 98
Ellis, E. Earle, 20
Emadi, Samuel, 253
Engberg-Pedersen, Troels, 4, 168, 178–80
Engels, Donald, 50
Enns, Peter E., 64–65
Eriksson, Anders, 100
Erler, Michael, 149, 151, 153, 155n27, 159
Evans, Craig A., 72, 80n11
Fee, Gordon D., 140–42, 162, 178–79
Feldman, Louis H., 197
Festugière, A. J., 149, 151, 153
Figueras, Pau, 98n32, 100, 104
Fish, Jeffrey, 156
Fisk, Bruce N., 162, 164
Fitzgerald, John T., 4, 162
Fitzmyer, Joseph A., 81, 119
Fletcher-Louis, Crispin, 78
Ford, J. Massyngberde, 132
Foss, Clive, 268
Foster, Paul, 225–26, 246n4
Fotopolous, John, 162n58
Foulkes, Francis, 188n8
France, Richard T., 59, 78
Franklin, James L., 32
Freese, J. H., 235
Frey, Jörg, 246
Furnish, Victor Paul, 47, 49, 56, 181n62
Gadamer, Hans-Georgr, 169
Garani, Myrto, 28
García Serrano, Andrés, 92, 95, 100
Garland, David E., 126
Gaventa, Beverly Roberts, 27, 132, 139, 140n38
Gerber, Christine, 47, 132
Gheorghita, Radu, 65
Ghisalberti, Giosuè, 149, 151, 153, 155, 161
Gibson, Craig A., 213
Gill, Christopher, 235

Gillihan, Yonder Moynihan, 132, 136–38, 137n29, 141n44
Gillmayr-Bucher, Susanne, 23
Glad, Clarence E., 7, 162
Glasson, Thomas Francis, 222n39
Gockel, Christin, 244
González, Justo L., 97
Gooch, Peter D., 162
Goodacre, Mark, 99
Goodwin, Mark J., 55
Graham, Daniel W., 173
Grant, Frederick Clifton, 168
Grant, Michael, 40
Graverini, Luca, 32n11
Gregory, Andrew, 193
Green, Joel B., 93, 95–101, 104–106, 126
Griffith, Terry, 286
Guite, Malcolm, 99
Gulick, Charles Burton, 282
Gundry, Robert H., 78, 88n36
Gundry-Volf, Judith M., 12, 140
Gupta, Nijay K., 50
Guthrie, George H., 59, 72, 220
Hackworth Petersen, Lauren, 34
Hafemann, Scott J., 45–47, 52–54, 52n29, 52n30, 52n32,
Halliday, M. A. K., 264
Halliwell, Stephen, 226
Hanson, Anthony T., 67
Harmon, A. M., 148, 236
Harris, Murray J., 181
Harrison, James R., 144, 145n60, 283
Hartnett, Jeremy, 33
Harvey, A. E., 101
Hau, Lisa Irene, 199
Hayes, Christine E., 136, 139n33
Hays, Richard B., 11n16, 17n1, 23, 26, 43, 71–72, 80, 91–93, 95–96, 100, 102, 105, 105n75, 164, 178, 188, 198, 237, 252
Hays, Judith C., 91–93, 95–96, 100, 102, 105, 105n75
Hedrick, Charles, 31n9
Heilig, Christoph, 24
Hellholm, David, 49

Helyer, Larry R., 91, 106
Henderson, Jeffery, 237
Henning, Bruce, 11, 88, 90
Hicks, Robert D., 150
Hilhorst, Anthony, 247
Hills, Julian, 287
Hillyer, C. N., 78–79, 80n7
Hoag, Gary G., 278
Hofius, Otfried, 132, 146
Hollander, John, 242
Hoppin, Ruth, 60, 225
Horrell, David G., 132–35, 162, 164
Horsley, Greg H. R., 275
Hübner, Hans, 21
Hughes, Graham, 60–61
Huizenga, Leroy A., 256n51
Hurd, John C., Jr., 159
Huttunen, Niko, 169
Hylen, Susan E., 40n30
Ibita, Marilou, 100
Innes, Doreen C., 233
Inselmann, Anke, 103, 106
Iverson, Kelly R., 225–26
Jackson, Bernard S., 261, 278
Janko, Richard, 233, 237, 239
Jaquette, James L., 177
Jauhiainen, Marko, 22, 2
Jauss, Hans Robert, 225
Jeremias, Joachim, 84, 132n3
Jewett, Robert, 182
Jobes, Karen H., 63, 65
Johnson Hodge, Caroline, 143–45, 145n58, 145n59, 147n65
Joshel, Sandra R., 34, 41
Juel, Donald, 81
Just, Arthur A., 99
Karrer, Martin, 61, 65
Käsemann, Ernst, 134n12, 141n43, 142, 142n47
Kee, Alastair, 100
Keegan, Peter, 34
Keener, Craig S., 80, 105n72
Keesmaat, Sylvia C., 44
Kennedy, George A., 212–13, 226
Kerr, Norbert L., 244
Kersten, Holger, 232
Kilburn, K., 213
Kim, Seyoon, 6, 163–64, 164n67

King, Justin, 212–13
Kirk, J. R. Daniel, 39
Kistemaker, Simon, 61
Klauck, Hans-Josef, 54, 160n49, 196
Klein, Ralph W., 112–13
Knibbe, Dieter, 275
Knox, Peter E., 37, 42
Koch, Dietrich-Alex, 19
Koch Piettre, Renée, 149
Koenraad, Verboven, 176n42
Koester, Craig R., 7
Konstan, David, 235
Koskenniemi, Heikki, 54
Krentz, Edgar, 247n7
Krückemeier, Nils, 91, 100
Kruse, Colin G., 181, 286
Kujanpää, Katja, 19
Kuschnerus, Bernd, 53
Kwon, Oh-Young, 159
LaFosse, Mona Tokaret, 91
Lampe, Peter, 55
Land, Christopher D., 47
Lane, William L., 220
Laurence, Ray, 36n24
Lee, Max J., 4, 6–7, 16, 28, 164, 184–85, 213n14, 287–88
Lee, Michelle V., 168n8, 170, 173–74, 178
Lemke, Jay L., 247, 253–56, 254n42, 263, 265
Lenski, R. C. H., 86–88
Leonard, Jeffery M., 23
Lessing, Erich, 40
Levenson, Jon D., 250
Levin-Richardson, Sarah, 35n19
Levine, Amy-Jill, 121–23
Lieu, Judith, 126, 270, 273n24, 285n79
Lightstone, Jack N., 247n8, 265
Lim, Timothy H., 64
Linant de Bellefonds, Pascale, 273
Lindemann, Andreas, 132n3, 138
Linell, Per, 126n25
Litwa, M. David, 50
Lloyd, G. E. R., 189
Loader, William, 138
Löhr, Hermut, 240
Lohr, Joel N., 249–51, 253

Long, Anthony A., 172n24, 173, 176, 194
Longenecker, Bruce W., 8–9, 13, 31, 34, 198
Longenecker, Richard N., 6, 182–83
López Mauleón, Jesús María, 104
Lucas, Alec J., 23, 246
Lutz, Cora E., 146
Lyotard, Jean-François, 192
Macaskill, Grant, 81
MacDonald, Dennis R., 13
MacDonald, Margaret Y., 91, 132, 134–37
MacGillivray, Erlend D., 36
Maher, Michael, 260
Malherbe, Abraham J., 7, 143, 170, 170n22, 180, 197n38
Marcovich, Miroslav, 211
Marcus, Joel, 80, 107n84
Marguerat, Daniel, 213
Marshall, I. Howard, 101, 106, 126, 198, 269
Martin, Dale B., 185
Martin, Michael Wade, 239, 241–42, 243
Mason, Eric F., 246n2
Mason, Steve, 198, 201
Matthiessen, Christian M. I. M., 264n70
McAuley, David, 24n26
McCullough, J. Cecil, 61–62
McDonough, Sean M., 22, 219
McGhee, Paul, 244
McGowan, Andrew B., 143
McKelvey, R. J., 78, 85
McKeown, J. C., 37
McKnight, Scott, 7
McNamara, Martin, 261
McNeile, Alan Hugh, 86–87
McNutt, Paula M., 250
Meeks, Wayne A., 4
Meltzer, Gary S., 235
Méndez, Hugo, 119, 121
Merkle, Benjamin L., 101
Meyer, Ben F., 78–79
Mikalson, Jon D., 149, 151–52
Miller, Geoffrey D., 23,
Miller-McLemore, Bonnie, 91

Milnor, Kristina, 30–31, 34
Minear, Paul S., 93, 94n12, 98, 105n73, 106
Mitchell, Margaret M., 4, 135n14, 165, 185
Modica, Joseph B., 7
Moffitt, David M., 223n42
Momigliano, Arnaldo, 198
Moo, Douglas J., 6, 22
Moor, Johannes C. de, 85
Morales, Rodrigo J., 44
Morrison, James C., 202
Motyer, Stephen, 222
Moyise, Steve, 17n2, 19, 44, 192, 247
Müller, Peter, 132
Muraoka, Takamitsu, 272
Murphy, A. James, 91
Murphy-O'Connor, Jerome, 50, 132, 138–39, 163, 274n26, 275, 282
Naddaf, Gerard, 193
Nasrallah, Laura Salah, 40
Ndoga, Sampson S., 220
Newberry, Julie Nicole, 11, 95, 103
Neyrey, Jerome H., 120, 226
Nicklas, Tobias, 201
Nienhuis, David R., 270
Nolland, John, 78, 86
Norton, Jonathan D. H., 21
Nünlist, René, 214–15
Oakes, Peter, 33n15, 287n83
Oates, Whitney Jennings, 171, 174–77
Obbink, Dirk, 149, 152, 157–58
Öhler, Markus, 43
O'Keefe, Tim, 157
Oliver, H. H., 94, 105
O'Neil, J. C., 132
Ong, Hughson T., 257
Oropeza, B. J., 8–9, 17, 22, 25, 54, 163n63, 165, 225, 241, 244n58,
Osborne, Robin, 151
Oster, Richard E., 277–78
Oster, Richard E., Jr., 163
Otto, Konrad, 9, 47
Ounsworth, Richard, 73
Overland, Paul B., 111n1

Padilla, Osvaldo, 213
Painter, John, 269
Papousek, Ilona, 244
Parker, Julie Faith, 91
Peeler, Amy L. B., 214
Perrin, Nicholas, 81
Petterson, Anthony R., 81
Pfister, Manfred, 32n11
Phillips, Elaine A., 83
Pierce, Madison N., 14–15, 66, 216, 219
Piotrowski, Nicholas G., 79, 79n3
Pitts, Andrew W., 4
Plett, Heinrich F., 18
Pomeroy, Sarah B., 144, 146
Portefaix, Lilian, 275
Porter, James I., 215
Porter, Stanley E., 4, 18–19, 21, 21n13, 23–24, 43–44, 169, 252, 257
Price, Simon, 151
Punt, Jeremy, 91
Quarles, Charles L., 87
Rabbie, Edwin, 227
Rabens, Volker, 197
Rabinowitz, Peter J., 225
Rackham, Harris, 153, 231, 233–34, 238
Radner, Ephraim, 191, 193
Ramelli, Ilaria, 143, 145, 189
Rasco, Emilio, 94
Rathmayr, Elisabeth, 283
Rawson, Beryl, 132
Reinmuth, Eckart, 91
Robbins, Vernon K., 117n8, 225
Roberts, W. Rhys, 233
Robinson, John, 178
Robinson, Laura, 6, 99
Robson, James E., 53–54
Rodriguez, Rafael, 6
Rogers, Guy M., 268, 273–83
Rondeau, Marie-Josèphe, 210–11, 216, 221
Rosenberg, Gil, 35
Rosner, Brian S., 138, 141
Rouse, William H. D., 152, 154
Rowe, C. Kavin, 4, 173, 190, 196, 198

Runge, Steven E., 102, 105
Rüpke, Jörg, 151, 160
Russell, Donald A., 229–32, 234
Samely, Alexander, 67
Sanders, Kirk R., 156
Sandmel, Sam, 44, 169–70, 256
Sandnes, Karl Olav, 201
Saver, Jeffrey L., 199
Schafroth, Verena, 54
Schnabel, Eckhard J., 22
Schnackenburg, Rudolf, 269
Schnelle, Udo, 21
Schrage, Wolfgang, 138n31, 139
Schreiner, Patrick, 78n1
Schrenk, Gottlob, 54
Schutz, Charles E., 232–33
Schweitzer, Albert, 178
Schweizer, Eduard, 78, 83
Scott, Ian W., 197–98
Scott, James C., 41
Seddon, Keith, 169, 175–76
Sedley, David N., 194
Seim, Turid Karlsen, 95, 99, 105, 120
Seitz, Oscar J. F., 88n37
Sevenster, J. N., 168, 170
Sháfer, Peter, 78
Shakhnovich, Marianna, 153
Shaw, David A., 23
Shepherd, David, 82
Shum, Shiu-Lun, 24
Silva, Moisés, 20n10, 85
Simpson, Adelaide D., 149
Sloan, Robert B., 126
Slusser, Michael, 212n8, 221
Smillie, Gene, 248
Smith, C. F., 214
Smith, Dennis E., 160n49
Smith, Jonathan Z., 169
Smith, Martin Ferguson, 36, 152, 154, 158
Smith, Wesley D., 230
Snodgrass, Klyne, 80, 84n21
Solin, Heikki, 35
Spencer, F. Scott, 92–93, 93n9, 101–2, 102n56, 104, 107
Spicq, Celsas, 93, 101, 104
Spinelli, Emidio, 151, 153, 157, 159
Spivak, Gayatri Chakravorty, 117n7

Stafford, Emma, 237
Stamps, Dennis L., 246
Stanley, Christopher D., 9, 25, 25n29, 28n2, 43–44, 44n8, 50–51, 187
Stephens, William O., 175
Stewart-Sykes, Alistair, 226
Steyn, Gert J., 61, 64, 69
Still, E. Coye, 162–63
Stockhausen, Carol K., 45, 47, 49
Stott, John R. W., 269n7
Strecker, Georg, 269, 287
Striker, Gesila, 235
Summers, Kirk, 151, 153–55
Sutton, E. W., 233–34, 238
Swetnam-Burland, Molly, 42
Talbert, Charles H., 94, 107, 117, 126
Tannehill, Robert C., 117, 126
Tatum, W. Barnes, 94, 106n80
Thatcher, Tom, 251–53
Theobald, Michael, 52
Thielman, Frank, 183
Thiessen, Matthew, 6, 163
Thiselton, Anthony C., 132, 138n32, 142n45, 165, 178–79
Thom, Johan C., 7, 12
Thomas, Kenneth J., 60–62
Thompson, Michael, 24
Thorsteinsson, Runar, 6n8, 176
Thraede, Klaus, 54
Thrall, Margaret E., 47, 49, 56
Thür, Hilke, 283
Thurston, Bonnie Bowman, 95, 98, 100n42, 107n83
Tillich, Paul, 167–68
Tite, Philip L., 163
Tomlin, Graham, 161
Tomson, Peter, 132, 135–36
Tooman, William A., 72n38
Toussaint, Stanley D., 86
Trebilco, Paul R., 15–16, 133, 267, 280, 284n76, 286n80
Trinacty, Christopher, 28
Tsumura, David Toshio, 111n1, 112
Tuck, Steven L., 41n35
Turner, David, 86
Tyson, Joseph B., 94

Vaage, Leife E., 132, 134–37
van Maaren, John, 163
Vansina, Jan, 199
Varela, Alfredo Tepox, 95
Varone, Antonio, 40
Vegge, Tor, 44
Verde, Francesco, 151, 153, 157, 159
Veyne, Paul, 160
Viviano, Benedict T., 86
Vogt, Katja Maria, 56
von Campenhausen, Hans, 101
von Harnack, Adolf, 88
Waaler, Erik, 163–64
Wagner, J. Ross, 19, 22, 25, 44
Waltke, Bruce K., 248–50
Walvoord, John F., 86, 88
Watson, Duane F., 53
Watson, Edward W., 159
Watson, Francis, 186–187
Watson, Walter, 227
Watts, Rikk E., 11, 200–201
Weinstein, David, 190
Weissenrieder, Annette, 56
Wendt, H. H., 269
Wenkel, David, 103
Westphal, Merold, 192
White, Benjamin G., 4
White, Joel R., 23–24, 192, 198
White, L. Michael, 4
Whitlark, Jason A., 14, 233, 239, 241–43
Wilcox, Max, 86, 88n37
Wilder, Terry L., 22
Wilk, Florian, 43, 45–46, 58
Williams, Demetrius K., 104
Williams, H. H. Drake, 28
Willis, Wendell Lee, 162–63
Wilson, Brittany E., 96–97, 108
Wilson, John Francis, 83
Wilson, S. G., 94
Winn, Adam, 7
Wise, Michael O., 82n18
Wishart, Ryder A., 13, 261
Witherington, Ben, III, 78, 82–83, 83n19, 121–23, 162, 198
Wolter, Michael, 98
Wright, N. T., 44, 78, 81, 88, 192, 197–98

Wurster, Sonya, 156
Wynne, J. P. F., 151
Xue, Xiaxia E., 254
Yarbrough, O. Larry, 142
Yarbrough, Robert W., 271–72
York, John, 104

Young, Kay, 199
Zadorojnyi, Alexei V., 40
Zakai, Avihu, 190
Zanker, Paul, 41n35
Zeller, Dieter, 45

Index of Ancient Sources

OLD TESTAMENT

Genesis

1–4	270
1:1	35n21, 270
1:11–12	73
2:2	68
2:7	112
2:24	20
3	269–70
3:7–18	73
3:19	112
4	248, 251, 256–57, 261, 270
4:1–17	257
6:1—9:29	68
11–21	97
11:1–9	68, 70
11:30	97n26
11:31—12:5	70
15:5–6	97n26
15:8	97n27
15:15	96
16:1	97n26
17:1	97n26
17:12	99n41
17:17	97
18–19	221
18:1–15	70
18:10	97
18:11	96
18:12	97
18:14	97, 97n26
18:30–32	67
19:1–22	70
19:4	105
21:6	97n26
21:7	96, 97
21:8	99n41
21:12	67
21:17–21	189
22:16–17	73
25:33	73
26:34–35	240n45
28:10–22	79n6
28:11	84n21
28:15	70
42:38	96
44:29	96
44:31	96
47:29–31	69
47:31	69
48:12	69

Exodus

1	205
4	52
4:10	46–47, 52
4:10–11	9
4:11	52, 52n31
4:28	52n32
10:9	105
19:9–24	69
19:12–13	67
24:8	68
25:40	61, 69
28:30	79
29:37	141n44

31:14	194	29:17	73, 242
32:6	21n14	30:6	53
32:7	165	31:6	61, 69, 70
33:7–11	72	31:8	70
33:19	222 n40	32	221
34	49, 50	32:1–43	61
34:29–30	49	32:4	84
34:29–35	45, 57	32:36	70
		32:43	70

Leviticus

6:18	141n44	Joshua	
11:45	224	1:5	70
16:27	72	13:1	96
17:3	72	24:15	243n51
19:18	163	24:17	224

Numbers

10:31	96	Judges	
11:4	165	6:11–24	70
12:6–8	50	6:13	224
12:7	73	13	96
14:13	224	13:2–23	70
14:16	21n14		
15:20–21	141n41	1 Samuel	
15:37—16:3	70	1–2	96
16:2	70n32	1:24–28	98
16:5	20	2	11
21:4–9	165	2:1–10	109, 111
22:19	67	2:3	109
23:1–30	68	2:6	223
25:1–9	165	2:7–8	124
		2:22	98
Deuteronomy		2:22–25	96
4:11–12	69	2:35	73
4:24	70	3:1–18	68
6:4	163, 188	3:21	96
7:3	131n1, 143	4:18	96
9:3	70	17:49	84
9:19	67, 69	18:10–11	116
11:11	73	19:8–10	116
22:4	112	20:31	116
22:21	19	23	116
22:21–24	19	24	116
22:24	19	25	116
23:1	19	26	116
27–30	192	28	116

2 Samuel

1	116
4	116
7	81, 81n14
7:5–7	81
7:11	81
7:11–14	82, 82n18
7:13	81
7:14	68
7:14–15	81
7:23	72
11	116
11:4	116
12:17	112
22:3	70

1 Kings

1:1–4	96
1:1–37	96
2	116
5–6	81
17:4	67

2 Kings

4:14	96

1 Chronicles

17	81
17:14	73
28:20	70

Job

4:3	73
4:4	112
5:12–13	21
41:32	20
42:6	112

Psalms

2:7	68, 72, 216n26
2:8	72
7:18	222
18:31	84
22	188n7
22:1	211
22:22	69, 211n6
22:23	222
24:1	163
29:2	222
34:4	222
39:3	223
39:7–9	219
40:6	63, 65
40:6–8	63
40:7	67
43:3	67
50:12	163
50:14	72
62:2	84
89:11	163
90–106	219
95	73
95:7–11	64, 73
95:11	68
96:7	70
101	220–21, 224
101:1	220
101:1–12	220
101:2–4	220
101:5–12	220
101:13–23	220
101:14	220
101:16	220
101:19–23	221–22
101:21	220
101:22	222
101:24	220–21, 223
101:24–25	223
101:25	223–24
101:26	219
101:26–28	219, 223–24
101:26–29	220
102	219
104:4	61
106:19–27	22
107:22	72
110	221
110:1	67, 72
110:4	61, 67
113:4	112
116:17	72

118	85, 85n25		84–85, 85n25, 89
118:6	69	28:17	80n11
118:22–23	85	28:18	80n11
134:14	70	29:13	80
148:12	105	35:3	72, 73
		44:28—45:1	81
		45:17	72

Proverbs

4:26	73	45:23	21n13
16:31	96	49:1	201
25:14	20	53:12	72
30:17	96	54	80n7
		55:8	194
		57:20	20
		61:1–2	126n26, 217

Ecclesiastes (Qoh)

3:11	272n19	61:1–3	88n39
4:10	112	63:11	72
		66:22	72

Song of Solomon

17:30	272

Jeremiah

1:5	201
1:6	67

Nehemiah

11:1	141	15:1	194
13:25	131n1, 143	31:31–34	62, 69
		31:33	9, 53, 62
		38:18	53
		38:31	49

Isaiah

2:6	272n20	38:31–34	48, 218
5	78	38:32	53
8	80	38:33	9, 48, 53
8:14	80	38:34	54
8:17	70	39:40	54
8:17–18	69	50:32	112
11:9	141		
22:11	272n19	Lamentations	
22:13	19	2:21	105
22:22	88		
25:8	20		
26:11	72	Ezekiel	
27:13	80	9:6	105
26:13	20	11:19	9, 48, 53
26:20	71	16:55	272n20
28	80, 80n11	18:24	73
28:11–12	20	20:9–18	53
28:15	80n10, 80n11	20:36–44	53
28:16	80, 80n7, 80n12, 83,	34	72

Ezekiel (continued)

36:26	48, 53
36:26—37:14	54, 54n37
37	54
37:6	53
37:26	54
38–39	72
48:1	272n20

Daniel

1:20	194
2	78n1
9:4–19	72

Hosea

1–4	240
6:2	112
13:14	20
14:3	72

Joel

3	11
3:1	92, 101, 102, 104, 104n64, 105, 106, 107
3:1–5	102, 105
3:2	104–5

Amos

9:11	82n18

Jonah

3:9	194

Habakkuk

1:12	272n19
2:3–4	71
2:4	65n19
2:16	64

Haggai

2:6	67, 69, 72
2:11–14	138n32
2:21	72

Zechariah

4:7–9	79n6, 82
6:12	82n16
6:12–13	81–82
6:15	82n15

Malachi

1:2b–3a	204
3:23	101n51

JEWISH TEXTS

Apocrypha

Tobit (Tob)

3:10	96

Judith (Jdt)

16:22–23	98

Wisdom of Solomon (Wis)

7:26	72
10:3	260
10:3–4	258
12:11	272
14:13	272
18:20–25	22

Sirach/Ecclesiasticus (Sir)

16:26	272
24:9	272
25:23	73
36:13	272

36:16	272	35:6	67
51:20	272	48:1	67
		50:3	67
		53:1–13	68
		56:6	67

1 Maccabees (1 Macc)

14:9	105

4 Maccabees (4 Macc)

5:1–12	163
5:7	194
5:22–24	163
18:11a	258

Testament of Benjamin (T. Benj.)

7:3–5	258

Testament of Issachar (T. Iss.)

5:4	258

Pseudepigrapha

Apocalypse of Moses (Apoc. Mos.)

1:3—3:3	259
4:2	259
40:3–5	259

Testament of Abraham (T. Ab.)

[A]13:2	258
[B]11:2	258

Apocalypse of Sedrach (Apoc. Sedr.)

1:18	258

Testament of Solomon (T. Sol)

23:6–8	79

Dead Sea Scrolls

1QpHab (Pesher Habakkuk)

1 Enoch (1 En.)

14:8–25	72
22:7	258

XI, 9–13	64

1QS

8:4–8	80

Jubilees (Jub.)

4:1–2	258
4:11	258
4:31	259
25:1	240

4Q174	68, 82
4Q175	68
4Q176	68
4Q177	68
4QFlor	82n18

Targumic Texts

Pseudo-Philo (LAB)

Targum Isaiah (Tg. Isa.)

3:1–12	68
6:3–18	70
7:1–5	68
15:5–6	22
16:1	70
18:1–14	68
23:2	67

28:16	84
53:5	82

Targum Neofiti (Tg. Neof.)

Gen 4:8	261

Targum Pseudo-Jonathan (Tg. Ps.-J.) = Targum Yerusalmi (Tg. Yer. I)

Gen 4:1	260
Gen 5:3	260
Exod 28:30	79
Num 16:2	70n32
Zech 4:7	82n16
Zech 6:12	82n16

Rabbinic Texts

m. Qidd.

2.1	136n22

b. Sanh.

110a	70n32

m. Yoma

5:2	79, 79n6

b. Yoma

53b	79n6
54b	79n6

Pirqe Rabbi Eliezer (Pirqe R. El.)

21	260

Leviticus Rabbah (Lev. Rabb.)

1.14	50

Numbers Rabbah (Num. Rab.)

16:3	70n32

NEW TESTAMENT

Matthew

1:20	106
2:12	106
2:13	106
2:19	106
2:22	106
3:17	216n26
4:17	89
5:3–4	88n39
7:24–27	88n36
8:17	18
10:6	88n39
10:7	89
11:6	88n39
12:6	78
12:39–42	21
15:8–9	80
16	78
16:13–28	81
16:18	77–78, 78n1, 79–80, 80n7, 81, 83–85, 87, 89
16:18a	79
16:18b	79
16:19	88
19:3–12	131n1
19:4	268n5, 272n21
19:6	143n49
19:8	268n5
21	78
21:1–11	78
21:12–13	78
21:14–16	78
21:31–41	78
21:41	88n39
21:42	78, 84–85, 85n25, 88n36, 88n39
21:43	88n39
22:41–45	67
23:35	248, 263
23:38	79

24:21	268n5, 272n21	1:37	97n27
24:1–31	78	1:40–44	106
24:31	80	1:41	99, 105, 106
25:61	79	1:41–44	94
27:40	79	1:41–45	96
		1:42–45	105
Mark		1:44	99, 103n61
1:11	216n26	1:46–47	117
7	163n62	1:46–50	117
7:15–19	163, 163n62	1:46–51	126n26
9:35	101	1:46–55	109, 126
9:42–50	164n67	1:48–49a	117
10:2–12	131n1	1:49b–50	117
10:6	268n5, 272n21	1:50a	122
10:45	164n67	1:51	109, 117, 122
12:35–37	67, 187n5	1:51–53	124
13:9	272n21	1:51–54	121
13:19	268n5	1:51–55	117, 121
		1:52	122
Luke		1:52–53	104n68, 117, 122, 123
1	11, 94, 96n21, 98n34	1:54	99n39, 123
		1:54b	123
1–2	91n1, 92, 92n6, 93, 93n10, 94n12, 95, 95n20, 96, 97, 98, 103, 103n61, 104n62, 104n63, 105, 106, 106n80, 107, 107n83	1:54–55	117, 123
		1:55	98, 123
		1:58	97n26, 103n61
		1:59	99
		1:59–66	99
		1:66	99
1:2	268n5, 272n22	1:67	105, 106
1:5—2:40	92, 105	1:67–79	96
1:5–9	96	1:69	99n39
1:6	97n26	1:73	98
1:7	93, 95, 97, 97n26	1:76	99, 100n46, 106
		1:76–77	94
1:14	103n61	1:79	120
1:15	106	1:80	99
1:16–17	94	2	93, 100, 103
1:17	101, 103	2:10	103n61, 120
1:18	93, 95, 96, 97, 97n27	2:12	99
		2:14	120
		2:16	99
1:22	106	2:17	99
1:34	99n35	2:25	105
1:35	106, 106n80	2:25–26	93, 96
1:36	93, 95, 97, 97n26	2:25–38	96
		2:26	95, 105
		2:27	99, 106

Luke (continued)

2:29	93, 95
2:29–32	106, 120
2:34–35	106
2:36	95, 106
2:36–37	93, 95
2:37	96
2:40	99
2:41–52	100
3:3–6	94
3:6	120
3:15–18	94
3:22	106, 216
3:23	100n45
3:38	120
4	217
4:1	106
4:14	106
4:16–21	216
4:16–30	120, 126n26
4:18	106
4:24	106
4:38–44	217
5:39	100n47
7:2–9	120
7:11–17	100
7:14	100n46
7:24–28	106
7:31–35	100n47
8:40–56	100
8:42	100n46
8:51	99n39, 100n46
8:54	99n39, 100n46
9:42	99n39
9:46–48	100
9:48	93
10:21	106
10:30–37	120
11:29–32	21
11:51	248
12:16–20	234
15:25	101n50
16:16	94, 106
16:18	131n1
17:11–16	120
18:15	99
18:15–17	100
20:41–44	67
22:26	101, 104
24:44–47	18n5
24:47	120
24:49	106
24:53	107n83

John

1:1	35n21
1:1–3	284
8:44	268n5, 272n23
13:34	285n79
15:27	268n5, 272n22
19:24	18

Acts

1–2	104n63
1:1–8	106
1:8	106n80
2	92, 103, 106n80, 107
2:4	106
2:17	92, 93n9, 101–4, 104n64, 104n68, 105–7
2:17–21	102, 102n53
2:18	104–5
2:25	18
2:33	106
2:46	107n83
3:2	101
4:5	101
4:11	85
4:22	101
5:17	6n6
6:1–6	107n83
7	98n33
7:3	68
7:4–8	98
7:7	68
7:19	99n36
7:23	101
7:26–28	68
7:30	101
7:32–34	68
7:35	68

7:36	101	5:5	139n35
7:37	68	5:12–21	198
7:40	68	5:21	203
9:43	138n32	7:14–25	22
10:25–26	138n32	8:2–11	180
10:28	138n32	8:27	138n30
13:6–12	199	9	11, 186, 203
13:32–35	216n26	9–11	187, 191, 198, 203
15:2	101	9:1–5	203
15:5	6n6	9:1–26	203
16:16–40	199	9:4–5	192
16:7	203	9:4–6	191
17	191, 196	9:6	187, 201
17:18	190, 196	9:6–33	142n47
17:18b	196	9:33	80, 84
17:18–34	169n12	10:6–8	189n10
17:22	196	10:11	80
17:23	196	10:16	189n10
17:26–31	196	11	203
17:27b–28a	196n35	11:5–6	134
17:28b	196n35	11:9–10	189n10
17:31b–32a	196	11:16	132, 134, 140–41, 141n44, 142
18:1–18	199		
19	286		
19:21–41	286	11:16a	141n43, 142
20:12	99n39	11:16b	142
21:18	101	11:17	141
22:3	196	11:17–24	142
23:24–35	199	11:20	141
24:1–26	199	11:23–24	141
24:5	6n6	11:35	20
25:6–12	199	12	182
26:4	268n5	12:4	182
		12:4–5	181
Romans		12:4–21	177, 181
1:4	203	12:5	182
1:7	133n5, 138n30, 141n42, 203	12:5–8	182
		12:6–13	181
1:17	18, 65n19	12:9–21	182
2	6	12:10	182
2:17	6	12:13	138n30
2:17–29	6, 6n8	12:14	182
3	6n8	12:15	182
3:2	187	12:18	182
4:18–21	98, 107	12:20	182
4:24	203	12:21	182
5	190	14–15	163n62

Romans (continued)

14–21	181
14:14	138n32, 163n63
14:17	139n35
15:3	189n10
15:9	189n10
15:13	139n35
15:16	140n39, 141n42
15:25	138n30
15:31	138n30
16:2	138n30
16:5	132n2
16:10	132n2
16:15	138n30

1 Corinthians

1–3	159n44
1–4	159n44
1:2	133n5, 133n6, 134, 138n30, 140n39, 142
1:5	159n44
1:17	159n44
1:19–22	159n44
1:21	159n44
1:22	55
1:24–27	159n44
1:25	159n44
1:27	159n44
1:30	159n44
2:1	159n44
2:3	159n44
2:4–7	159n44
2:8	159n44
2:11	159n44
2:13	159n44
2:14	159n44
2:14–16	180
2:16	159n44
3:1–2	132n2
3:10	84, 159n44
3:18–20	159n44
3:19	21n13
3:20	159n44
4:10	159n44
4:14–21	132n2
4:19	159n44
5:13	19
6:2	138n30
6:11	50, 133n6
6:12–20	139n33
6:19	139n35
7	131
7:8	165
7:10–11	131
7:12	203
7:12–14	132
7:12–16	12, 131, 143, 143n51
7:14	12, 132n3, 132n4, 133–34, 136–37, 137n28, 138–40, 141n44, 142–43, 145, 147
7:14a	132
7:14b	132, 138n31
7:15–16	132
7:16	142n48
7:17–24	140n38
7:18–19	50
7:25–38	137
7:34	140n39
7:39	137–38
8	159n44
8–10	159, 159n44, 162, 162n58, 163n62, 164n67
8:1–3	159n44, 162
8:1–4	150
8:1–13	159, 162
8:3	166
8:4	10, 149, 162
8:4–6	163
8:4–13	147n65
8:6	187, 187n5, 188
8:7	50, 159n44, 164
8:8	163, 163n63
8:9	159n44
8:10	164
8:10–11	159n44
8:10–12	159n44
8:12	164
8:13	164

9:4	163n63
9:22	159n44
10	22, 58n46, 198
10:1–11	21
10:1–14	146
10:1–22	149, 159, 164
10:6	199
10:7	21n14, 164
10:10	22
10:14	165
10:14–33	146n63
10:15	159n44
10:21	165
10:21–22	146
10:22	159n44, 165
10:23–26	162
10:23–30	159, 162
10:23–33	147n65
10:25	164
10:25–27	164
10:27–29	164
10:27–30	162
10:28–29	147, 164
10:30–31	163n63
11:17–34	146n64
11:21—12:13	244n58
11:25	55
12	182
12:2	50
12:3	139n35
12:12–27	177
12:12	178
12:13	179
12:15–16	179
12:19	179
12:22	179
12:22–26	182
12:23–24	179
12:25	179
12:27	178
14	135
14:21	19
14:23	135
14:33	138n30
14:36	187
15	199
15:1	19
15:3	196n35
15:3–4	18n5
15:4–8	199
15:9	53
15:13	19
15:32	19
15:45	181
15:54–55	
16:1	138n30
16:15	138n30

2 Corinthians

1:1	133n5, 138n30
2:14—4:6	9, 45–46, 50–51, 57, 58
2:14—7:4	46
2:16c	47, 52
2:17	46, 52n32
3	45n9, 52, 53, 55–56, 58n46, 198
3–4	57
3:2–3	48
3:3	46
3:4–6	46
3:5	53
3:6	48, 54
3:7–18	57
3:11	54
3:12—4:6	52
4:1–6	46, 49
4:2	52n32
4:6	54
4:13	189n10
5:17	181
5:17–21	52
5:18–20	202
6:6	139n35
6:11–12	132n2
6:14—7:1	138n32
7:3	55
8:4	138n30
9:1	138n30
9:12	138n30
12:14b–15a	132n2

Galatians

1:15–16a	201
1:18	199
2	199
3	199
3:6–28	198
3:11	65n19
4:19	132n2
4:21–31	198
4:22	18n5
4:24	189

Ephesians

1:22	183
2:20	84, 89
4:15	183
5:18–33	145n60
5:23	183
5:31	20
6:1–4	132n2

Philippians

1:1	133n5, 138n30
1:19	203
2:6–11	285n78
2:10–11	21n13
2:22	132n2
3:8–12	202
4:1	55
4:21	138n30

Colossians

1:15–20	285n78
1:18	183
2:8	195
3:19–21	132n2

1 Thessalonians

1:1	187–88
1:5	139n35
2:7	132n2
2:11	132n2
2:13	187
2:17	55
3:13	138n30
4:8	139n35
5:23	133n6, 140n38

2 Thessalonians

1:10	138n30

1 Timothy

3:4	132n2
3:12	132n2
5:4	132n2
5:8	132n2

2 Timothy

1:5	132n2
2:19	20
3:15	99n36

Titus

1:6	132n2
1:12	196n35
2:4	132n2

Philemon

1:9	96

Hebrews

1	218, 219
1:1	66
1:1–4	72, 72n39
1:2	65, 218
1:5	68, 81, 216n26, 218
1:5–13	18, 66
1:6	70, 218
1:7	61
1:8–9	218
1:10–12	210, 218, 219, 224
1:13	218
2	219
2:1–18	241n47
2:4	65
2:5–9	243
2:6–8	217

2:11–13	59	8:8–12	62, 69, 218
2:12	219	8:9	62
2:12–13	69, 218–19	8:10	62
2:13a	70	9:11	62
2:14	219	9:20	68, 217
2:14–15	65	9:28	72
2:16	18, 219	10	219
2:17	62, 219	10:5	65
2:18	219	10:5–6	63
3–4	219	10:5–7	59, 63, 66, 218–19, 223
3:1	62		
3:1–6	73	10:5–10	65
3:2–6	73	10:7	67
3:6	244	10:9	67
3:7–11	66	10:15–18	219
3:7—4:11	216n26, 219	10:19	218
		10:19—12:13	241, 241n47
3:7—4:13	216n47		
3:10	64	10:21	62
3:12–14	241	10:25	241
3:16—4:3	73	10:26–31	241
3:17	64	10:27	72
4:3	65	10:30	70
4:4–5	68	10:35–36	241
4:9–10	65	10:37–38	71
4:14–15	62	10:38	65n19
5	218	11	21, 69, 241–42
5:1	62	11:1	244
5:5	62, 218	11:1—12:1	73
5:5–6	66	11:4	247, 248, 263
5:6	61, 67, 218	11:11	107
5:9	72	11:17–18	67
5:10	62	11:21	69
5:11—6:20	241, 241n47	11:35–39	70
		11:39–40	70
6:4–5	65	12:4–11	241
6:4–6	241	12:5–6	66
6:4–14	73	12:12	72
6:11–12	241	12:12–17	73
6:20	62	12:14–17	241, 241n46
7	218		
7:1–25	73	12:15–17	73
7:17	61, 67, 218	12:16	14, 227, 238, 241, 244
7:21	67, 218		
7:26–28	62	12:18–24	69
8:1	62	12:18–29	65
8:5	62, 69, 71n34	12:20	67
8:8	62	12:21	67, 69, 217

Hebrews (*continued*)

12:21–24	69
12:23	241
12:24	248, 263
12:25	241
12:25–29	241n47
12:26	67, 69
12:27	72
12:29	70
13:1–8	218n30
13:2	70, 73
13:5	61, 66, 70, 71n34, 218n30
13:5–6	69
13:10–20	72
13:15	72
13:20	72, 223
13:24	60n3

James

4:5	18n5

1 Peter

2:2	99n36
2:6	80
2:6–7	84–85
2:6–8	80
3	133

2 Peter

1:16	199
3:4	268, 272n21

1 John

1	199
1:1	268n5, 271–72
1:1–2	269
1:1–3	197n41
1:2	271
2:2	269n8
2:7	268n5, 270, 270n14
2:7–8	285, 285n79
2:8	285n79
2:12	269
2:13	268n5, 269
2:13–14	268–69, 272, 284
2:14	268n5, 269
2:19	271
2:24	268n5, 270n14
3:8	268n5, 269–70, 272
3:11	268n5, 270n14, 271
3:12	248, 263, 269–70
4:10	269n8
5:5	269
5:20–21	286
5:20b–21	288

2 John

5	270n14, 285, 285n79
5–6	268n5
6	270n14

Jude

11	248, 263
12	20
13	20

Revelation

2:14	163, 240
2:20	163, 240
3:7	88
21:14	86, 89

PHILO

De vita contemplativa (Conf.)

166	61

In Flaccum (Flacc.)

85–96	163

Legum allegoriae (Leg.)

3.99–101	50
3.155–57	163

De vita Mosis (Mos.)

2.115	195

De opificio mundi (Opif.)

12	195
136	61

De praemiis et poenis (Praem.)

53	195
68	270

Quaestiones et solutions in Genesin (QG)

2.59	195
3.21	195

De sacrificiis Abelis et Caini (Sacr.)

1:2	259

De specialibus legibus (Spec.)

1.65	200
4.149–50	50

JOSEPHUS

Jewish Antiquities (Ant.)

1:53–61	260

Against Apion (Apion)

1.78	195
1.225	195
1.237	195

J.W.

2.158	195
2.162–64	6

Life

1.10–12	6

NEW TESTAMENT APOCRYPHA

The Epistle of Barnabas (Barn.)

6:2	81
6:2–3	84

Protoevangelium of James (Prot. Jas.)

9	99

NAG HAMMADI LIBRARY

Apoc. John

22	260n60

Hyp. Arch.

19–31	260n60

GREEK AND ROMAN TEXTS

Apsines
Rhet.
10.55 — 241

Aristophanes
Aves
141–45 — 237n39

Aristotle
Ars rhetorica
3.187 — 227

Eth. nic.
4.8.3 — 230
4.8.9 — 231n17

Poetica
1149a1–5 — 227
1149b20–22 — 227

Rhet.
1.11.35 — 229
2.4.2 — 235n34
3.11.6 — 233
3.19.1 — 242

Athenaeus
Deipn.
8.361D — 282n67

CIL
4 — 34n18
4.1261 — 39
4.2213 — 34
4.3072 — 37
4.3118 — 37
4.3139 — 37
4.3275 — 33n14
4.3913 — 37
4.4373 — 37
4.5224 — 33n14
4.6707 — 34n18
4.6893 — 33n14
4.9116 — 34n16
4.9125–32 — 34n16
4.9131 — 32

Cicero
De or.
2.178–216 — 230
2.216–90 — 230
2.217 — 227–28
2.218–19 — 229
2.218–20 — 238n42
2.222 — 231
2.226–27 — 236
2.236 — 230–31
2.237–38 — 230
2.240 — 229
2.247 — 230
2.248 — 229
2.250–63 — 239
2.251 — 229
2.254–55 — 234n33
2.255 — 233n30
2.262 — 232
2.264 — 239
2.265 — 229
2.266 — 234
2.274 — 234n32
2.281–85 — 233
2.289 — 230–31

Fam.
7.32 — 228
207.2 — 238n41

Inv.
1.25 — 230n12
1.98–105 — 242

INDEX OF ANCIENT SOURCES 353

Nat. d.
1.45	153n15, 160n50
1.56	158n40
1.117	151n9

Part. or.
71	231n15

Second Philippic
42	236
44	236
50	236

Demetrius
Eloc.
152	233n27
243	241

Dio Cassius
Hist. rom.
42.23–25	232
73.21.1	231n18

Dio Chrysostom
Or.
76	56n43

Diogenes Laertius
Lives
10.9–10	156n28
10.76–78	153n16
10.120	158n40
10.123	158n38
10.123–24	150n8
10.139	150n7, 153n15, 160n50

Diogenes of Oinoanda
fr. 19.II.12–III.5	158n40

Dionysius of Halicarnassus
Antiq. rom.
4.25.4	278n44

Epictetus
Diss.
1.7.27	173n32
1.9.5	173
2.5.24–27	171–72, 174
2.6.25	176n44
2.8.11	173n32
2.9.15	175
2.10.3–6	174
2.10.5	184
2.19.13	175n37
3.3.18–22	177n45

Epicurus
Ep. Herod.
76–78	153n16

Ep. Men.
123–24	150n8
128	158n36

KD
1	150n7, 153n15, 160n50
29–30	157n35

VS
77	158n37, 160n45

Us. (Usener, *Epicurea*)
30	158n40
388	152n14
390	158n40

Euripides
Phoen.
392	41n34

Galen

De usu part.

1.22	228

Top.

3.2.1077	234

Hermogenes

Prog.

9	213

Hippocrates

Ep.

10.1	230n13
17.4–5	230n13

Homer

Il.

6.234–36	235n35
466–85	232n25

IEph

26	275n30
27.91	280n54
27.164–65	280n60
27.168	280n60
27.173	280n60
27.183	280n74
27.186–87	280n60
27.196	280n60
27.358–65	281n65
501A	283n72
557A	283n72
644.12	283n73
1606.15	278n44
1615.11	278n44
4114.4	278n44

Lucian of Samosata

Alex.

18	148n1
38	6n6, 148n2

How to Write History

58	213n15

Tox.

22	236n36

Lucretius

DRN

1.1	37
1.2	37
1.3–4	37
1.45	152n12
1.145	37n26
1.933–950	37n26
2.1	36n23
2.646	151
2.646–50	151
2.651	152
4.11–25	37n26
5.1198–1203	153, 154n19
5.1198–1240	151
5.1201–2	151
5.1223	151
5.1229	151
6.73–75	154n20

Musonius Rufus

Or.

14.20–32	146n61

P. Bodmer

XXIV	61, 64

P. Oxy.

XVII 2068	215
215, col. 2.8–11	152n14

Pausanias

Descr.

7.2.8	282n68

INDEX OF ANCIENT SOURCES   355

Philodemus
Piet., PHerc 229
col. 71.2022–43	160n51
col. 71.2031–50	158n39, 160n48

Piet., PHerc 452
col. 62B.1784–91	149n6

Piet., PHerc 1077
col. 29.1078	160n46
col. 30.843–84	160n46
col. 36.1036	160n50
col. 45.1282–92	152n13
col. 50.1430–31	157n35

Piet., PHerc 1077/1093
col. 45.1282–92	152n13

Piet., PHerc 1098
col. 28.792–97	157n33, 160n45
col. 31.879–84	149n5
col. 31.879–80	157
col. 31.885	157
col. 31.887–88	157
col. 31.879–95	157n32
col. 33.928–57	152n13
col. 33.929	152
col. 33.931–32	152
col. 33.933–37	152
col. 33.936–37	152
col. 33.950–52	152
col. 43.1231	157

Plato
Rep.
451A–452B	234
452D	230

Resp.
II.379A	194n32
II.380D–383C	193

Pliny the Elder
Naturalis historia
7.2	228
7.72	228
7.79–80	228
24.164	228

Plutarch
Adul. amic.
51b	235

Amic. multi.
94b	235

Cic.
26–27	228

Comp. Dem. Cic.
1	228

Conj. Praec.
140D	144

Quaest. conviv.
2.1.11–12	228

Suav. viv.
1102A–C	160n49
1102B	158n40

Pompeii Inscriptions
1.2.21	37
1.4.25	33n14
7.16.22	35
9.13.5	31n10, 32, 33

Porphyry
Homeric Questions on the Iliad
6.265	215n24

Prudentius

Peristephanon

2.313–29	232n25
2.409–12	232n25

Pseudo-Dionysius

Rhet.

8.9	231

Pseudo-Longinus

Subl.

34.2	233n29

Quintilian

Inst.

5.10.83	231n16
6.2.1–36	230
6.3.1	230
6.3.1–112	230
6.3.5	228
6.3.6	230
6.3.7	230n13
6.3.10	232n24
6.3.21	231
6.3.22	228
6.3.23	229, 231
6.3.23–24	233n27
6.3.25	232
6.3.27–28	231
6.3.31	230
6.3.33	230
6.3.37	229
6.3.37–38	229
6.3.44	236
6.3.63	234n33
6.3.64	233n27
6.3.65–70	229
6.3.66	229
6.3.68–69	229
6.3.71	230n13
6.3.74	236
6.3.84	233n27
6.3.96–98	239
6.3.98	239
6.3.89	229n11
6.3.99	233
6.3.101	229
6.3.102	228
10.1.107	230

Rhet. Her.

1.10	230n12, 233
2.47–49	242
3.15	231

Seneca

Ben.

4.4.1	152n14

Strabo

Geogr.

14.1.20	
14.1.3	282n68
14.1.20	274n27
	275n30
	278n44

Tacitus

Ann.

3.60–63	278
3.61	274n26, 278n41
3.61.1	274n27

Theon

109	229

Prog.

1	212

Thucydides

History of the Peloponnesian War

1.22.1	214
2.43.2	54n39

INDEX OF ANCIENT SOURCES

Tibullus
Poem
III.12.1–5   145n57
III.12.14–15   145n57

Tractatus Coislinianus
     227, 229, 233, 237, 239–40

Valerius Maximus
Memorable Doings and Sayings
6.1.1   40n30

Virgil
Aeneid
Book 1   30
Book 2   30, 34, 34n18

Xenophon of Athens
Anab.
5.3.9–13   160n49

Oec.
VII.8   144
XI.8–9   146

Xenophon of Ephesus
Anthia and Habrocomes
1.2.2–4   279n46

☙

EARLY CHRISTIAN TEXTS

Ambrose
Off.
1.29.142   81, 84

Augustine
Civ.
19.4   167

Didache
6:3   163

Eusebius
Hist. eccl.
6.19.4–8   189

Irenaeus
Haer.
3.21.7   84n22

Justin Martyr
1 Apol.
36.1–2   212

Dial.
36.38   212n8

Origen
Cels.
4.48   189
4.50   189
4.51   189
7.18   189
7.66   158

Tertullian
An.
43   190

Praescr.
7   167

Prax.
11   217

Ux.
2.5–7   147

www.ingramcontent.com/pod-product-compliance
Lightning Source LLC
Chambersburg PA
CBHW021338300426
44114CB00012B/1000